A NARRATIVE HISTORY OF THE AMERICAN PRESS

Beginning with the American Revolution and spanning over two hundred years of American journalism, *A Narrative History of the American Press* provides an overview of the events, institutions, and people who have shaped the press, from the creation of the First Amendment to today. Gregory A. Borchard's introductory text helps readers develop an understanding of the role of the press in both the U.S. and world history, and how American culture has shaped—and been shaped by—the role of journalism in everyday life. The text, along with a rich array of supplemental materials available online, provides students with the tools used by both reporters and historians to understand the present through the past, allowing readers to use the history of journalism as a lens for implementing their own storytelling, reporting, and critical analysis skills.

Gregory A. Borchard, a Professor at the University of Nevada, Las Vegas (UNLV), USA, teaches courses for the Hank Greenspun School of Journalism and Media Studies in journalism history, reporting, and research methods. Borchard's previous books include *Lincoln Mediated: The President and the Press through Nineteenth-Century Media* (Routledge, 2015), *Abraham Lincoln and Horace Greeley* (2011), and *Journalism in the Civil War Era* (2010).

A NARRATIVE HISTORY OF THE AMERICAN PRESS

Gregory A. Borchard

NEW YORK AND LONDON

First published 2019
by Routledge
711 Third Avenue, New York, NY 10017

and by Routledge
2 Park Square, Milton Park, Abingdon, Oxon OX14 4RN

Routledge is an imprint of the Taylor & Francis Group, an informa business

© 2019 Taylor & Francis

The right of Gregory A. Borchard to be identified as the author of this work has been asserted by him in accordance with sections 77 and 78 of the Copyright, Designs and Patents Act 1988.

All rights reserved. No part of this book may be reprinted or reproduced or utilised in any form or by any electronic, mechanical, or other means, now known or hereafter invented, including photocopying and recording, or in any information storage or retrieval system, without permission in writing from the publishers.

Trademark notice: Product or corporate names may be trademarks or registered trademarks, and are used only for identification and explanation without intent to infringe.

Library of Congress Cataloging-in-Publication Data
Names: Borchard, Gregory A. author.
Title: A narrative history of the American press / Gregory A. Borchard.
Description: New York : Routledge, 2018. | Includes bibliographical references and index.
Identifiers: LCCN 2018010015 | ISBN 9781138998452 (hardback) | ISBN 9781138998469 (pbk.)
Subjects: LCSH: Press—United States—History. | Journalism—United States—History.
Classification: LCC PN4855 .B67 2018 | DDC 071/.3—dc23
LC record available at https://lccn.loc.gov/2018010015

ISBN: 978-1-138-99845-2 (hbk)
ISBN: 978-1-138-99846-9 (pbk)
ISBN: 978-1-315-65866-7 (ebk)

Typeset in Times New Roman
by Apex CoVantage, LLC
Printed and bound by CPI Group (UK) Ltd, Croydon, CR0 4YY

Visit the eResources: www.routledge.com/9781138998469

Dedicated to Denitsa

Contents

List of Illustrations — xi
Preface — xiv
Acknowledgments — xvi

Introduction — 1
  Natural Law and the Press — 4
  The Trial of John Peter Zenger — 6
  The First Amendment — 8
  The First Rough Draft of History — 10
  Recapping the Introduction — 11
  Notes — 11

1 **Pre-Revolution Print: The Colonial Origins of the American Press** — 12
  The Culture of Colonial Printers — 14
  Benjamin Franklin and Elizabeth Timothy — 15
  Boston and the Radical Press — 19
  Fomenting Revolution in the Pages of the Press — 24
  Recapping This Chapter — 25
  Notes — 26

2 **Thomas Paine, the Partisan Press, and "The Dark Ages of American Journalism"** — 27
  Common Sense and *The American Crisis* — 28
  The Press, the Declaration, and the Constitution — 34
  The Partisan Press and the Alien and Sedition Acts — 36
  Leaving "The Dark Ages of American Journalism" — 43
  Recapping This Chapter — 43
  Notes — 44

3 **The Penny Press: Sensationalism, Populism, and Progress** — 45
  Selling News Like Hotcakes — 47
  The Commercialization of Content — 51
  Horace Greeley, Margaret Fuller, and Reform — 55
  Abolitionists Publish a New Revolution — 63
  Recapping This Chapter — 67
  Notes — 67

CONTENTS

4 Nineteenth-Century Publishing Innovations in Content and Technology — 69
  The Telegraph's Impact on Journalism — 70
  Henry Raymond, the *Times*, and News "Without Passion" — 73
  The Transatlantic Cable — 75
  Nellie Bly and Stunt Journalism — 77
  Recapping This Chapter — 83
  Notes — 83

5 The Press in the Civil War Era: Pioneers in Print and Photography — 84
  The Press and Antebellum Politics — 85
  The Evolution of Newspaper Conventions During the Civil War — 87
  Photojournalism Comes into Its Own — 89
  Realism and Reality in Photography — 94
  Recapping This Chapter — 100
  Notes — 100

6 The Press in Transition: From Reconstruction to the Gilded Age — 102
  The Political and Cultural Context of Reconstruction — 103
  Horace Greeley Campaigns for the Presidency — 105
  The American Dream in the Gilded Age — 107
  Ida B. Wells and *The Red Record* — 109
  Recapping This Chapter — 113
  Notes — 114

7 Muckraking: Reporters and Reform — 115
  The Making of a Movement — 116
  Lincoln Steffens and "The Shame of Cities" — 121
  Upton Sinclair's *The Jungle*, and the Pure Food and Drug Act — 124
  A Man with a Muck Rake: David Graham Phillips — 126
  Recapping This Chapter — 129
  Notes — 130

8 Yellow Journalism: Pulitzer and Hearst Battle for Readers — 131
  Joseph Pulitzer and the *New York World* — 134
  William Randolph Hearst and the *New York Journal* — 139
  Remembering the Maine — 141
  The Emergence of a Media Empire — 146
  Recapping This Chapter — 149
  Notes — 149

9 Public Relations: How the Press Launched an Agency of Its Own — 151
  Muckraking Targets the Standard Oil Company — 152
  Public Relations Christened by Parker and Lee — 155
  A New Purpose for the Press — 157

	Edward Bernays and *Propaganda*	160
	Recapping This Chapter	164
	Notes	164
10	**Early Infotainment in Broadcast and Film**	**166**
	Early Innovators in Broadcast Technology	167
	NBC, CBS, and the Making of Mass Communication	170
	Orson Welles and the Battle Over Media	172
	Mass Media at Mid-Century	175
	Recapping This Chapter	178
	Notes	179
11	**The Press at War: Propaganda in Print and Film**	**180**
	The Committee on Public Information and the Engineering of Consent	181
	A Powerful and Horrifying Piece of Propaganda	185
	Hemingway and "The Spanish Earth"	186
	The Warnings of Orwell and Eisenhower	189
	Recapping This Chapter	192
	Notes	192
12	**The Press in the Cold War: Murrow, McCarthy, and Shakespeare**	**194**
	Hersey's *Hiroshima*	195
	Bridging Media: Print, Radio, Television, and Film	198
	The Press Reacts to the Red Scare	201
	Fun over Fear	204
	Recapping This Chapter	206
	Notes	207
13	**New Journalism and the Counterculture: Watchdogs and Watergate**	**208**
	The Living Room War	210
	The Press and Judicial Change	213
	Going Gonzo	215
	Reporting the Watergate Scandal	218
	Recapping This Chapter	222
	Notes	222
14	**The Press and the Making of Modern Media**	**224**
	The New Media Landscape	225
	Making a Media Empire	230
	Global Corporations and Content	233
	A New Regulatory Environment	235
	Recapping This Chapter	238
	Notes	238

Conclusion	**241**
The World of the Web	242
Balancing Business and Ethics	245
User-Created Content	247
Millennials and the Next Generation of Media	250
Recapping the Conclusion	252
Notes	252
Afterword	255
Glossary	257
Index	267

Illustrations

All images listed and included in the text were accessed through the digital archives of Library of Congress <loc.gov> and require no reproduction permission.

Introduction
  1 Invention of Printing   3
  2 Andrew Hamilton Defending John Peter Zenger   7

1 Pre-Revolution Print: The Colonial Origins of the American Press
  1 The Bloody Massacre   21
  2 Four Coffins of Men Killed   23

2 Thomas Paine, the Partisan Press, and "The Dark Ages of American Journalism": *Common Sense* and *The American Crisis*
  1 *Common Sense*   31
  2 The End of Pain   33
  3 The Federal Pillars   35
  4 D—n, d—n, the Author & Publisher I Say!   37

3 The Penny Press: Sensationalism, Populism, and Progress
  1 Lunar Animals and Other Objects   49
  2 One of the News-B'hoys   52
  3 American Citizens!   56
  4 Editorial Staff of *The New York Tribune*   57
  5 Margaret Fuller   59
  6 Frederick Douglass   64

4 Nineteenth-Century Publishing Innovations in Content and Technology
  1 Mexican News   72
  2 Progress of the Century   76
  3 Representative Journals & Journalists of America   78
  4 Nellie Bly   79
  5 Round the World with Nellie Bly   81

5 The Press in the Civil War Era: Pioneers in Print and Photography
  1 Photo of Lincoln   91
  2 Hon. Abraham Lincoln   92
  3 Gettysburg, Pa., Alfred R. Waud   93
  4 Petersburg, VA, Dead Confederate Soldier with Gun   93
  5 An Incident of Gettysburg   94
  6 Major General A. E. Burnside   95
  7 Cold Harbor, Va. Gen   96

	8 A Burial Party on the Battle-field	97
	9 Washington, D.C. Hanging Hooded Bodies	98
	10 Execution of the Conspirators	99
6	**The Press in Transition: From Reconstruction to the Gilded Age**	
	1 The First Vote	104
	2 Discovery of the Sage of Chappaqua	106
	3 Ida B. Wells	110
7	**Muckraking: Reporters and Reform**	
	1 Jacob Riis	118
	2 "How the Other Half Lives"	119
	3 David Graham Phillips	127
8	**Yellow Journalism: Pulitzer and Hearst Battle for Readers**	
	1 The *New York Times*. Easter	133
	2 Joseph Pulitzer	135
	3 McFadden's Row of Flats	137
	4 The Big Type War of the Yellow Kids	138
	5 Hearst, William R.	140
	6 Yellow Press	145
9	**Public Relations: How the Press Launched an Agency of Its Own**	
	1 Ida Minerva Tarbell	153
	2 Lee, Ivy L.	156
	3 Freedom of the Press	159
10	**Early Infotainment in Broadcast and Film**	
	1 Woman with Radio	169
	2 A Television Receiver	171
	3 Portrait of Orson Welles	173
	4 Walter Cronkite	177
11	**The Press at War: Propaganda in Print and Film**	
	1 CPI Delegates to Europe	182
	2 I Want You for U.S. Army	183
	3 President Dwight Eisenhower Giving a Television Speech	191
12	**The Press in the Cold War: Murrow, McCarthy, and Shakespeare**	
	1 Nagasaki, Japan, under Atomic Bomb Attack	196
	2 Senator Joseph McCarthy	200
	3 Head-and-shoulders Photograph of Ed Sullivan	205
13	**New Journalism and the Counterculture: Watchdogs and Watergate**	
	1 John F. Kennedy Motorcade	210
	2 A Man and a Woman Watching Film Footage	211

		3 Anti-Vietnam War Protest and Demonstration	212
		4 Nixon	221
14		**The Press and the Making of Modern Media**	
		1 Media Position	226
		2 Clare Boothe Luce and Husband Publisher Henry Luce	231
		3 Set-up for Press and Convention Parties	233
		4 Remote Control, 2000	235
		5 Google Headquarters	236
	Conclusion		
		1 Marine Corps. H.Q. Computer Rooms	243
		2 City News, a Shop and Newsstand	247
		3 A Rare Sight in America late in 2012	248
	Afterword		
		1 The Future	255

Preface

A Narrative History of the American Press uses the tools of reporters and historians to re-create and interpret a compelling narrative of press, media, and communication history for today's students. While providing a new understanding of personalities and events by closely examining primary sources, this book also looks at the development of American press with the insight of scholars who have studied it.

The individual chapters you will read in this book stem from lectures I have delivered for more than a decade in the Hank Greenspun School of Journalism and Media Studies at the University of Nevada, Las Vegas (UNLV). As a media historian, I have headed dozens of semesters of classes for both undergraduate and graduate students that focus on the history of journalism. The people, events, developments, and concepts found in this book in most cases came straight from lecture materials and the written work of students, and they now compose a text for use by other instructors and students alike.

A Narrative History of the American Press will help develop an understanding of the role of the press in the United States, as well as in world history. Although the book does not focus on current events, readers will use the tools of both reporters and historians to help understand the present through the past. Using a historiographical approach to interpret texts, students will find ways to develop an intellectual framework for understanding the materials featured in this book. Instead of interpreting sources on a cursory level from a contemporary perspective, this book seeks to understand primary sources in the context in which writers produced them. Using the techniques of reporters and historians alike to ask the questions of "who," "what," "where," "when," "how," and "why," this book also seeks an answer to the question "so what?"

While focusing on American news, *A Narrative History of the American Press* also features material from media other than print newspapers alone. Texts about the history of journalism have tended to focus on only American newspapers, and when they do, they often use multiple authors to contribute to the text. A defining feature of this book is its integration of multimedia (public relations, advertising, broadcast, and the Internet), focusing on the story of the American press to build a singular narrative for a wide audience.

A review of recent scholarship on the subject of the history of the press will reveal both the strengths of this book and ways in which it contributes to an area of study with room for improved understanding. Among the many primary and secondary sources provided throughout this book, the following remarkable textbooks have also contributed to the development of journalism and media history as unique fields.

- Brennen, Bonnie, and Hanno Hardt. *The American Journalism History Reader.* New York: Routledge, 2010.
- Conboy, Martin. *Journalism: A Critical History.* London: Sage, 2006.

- Daly, Christopher B. *Covering America: A Narrative History of a Nation's Journalism*. Amherst, MA: University of Massachusetts Press, 2012.
- Emery, Michael, and Edwin Emery. *The Press and America: An Interpretive History of the Mass Media*. Boston: Allyn and Bacon, 2000.
- Fellow, Anthony. *American Media History*. Boston: Wadsworth, 2013.
- Nord, David Paul. *Communities of Journalism: A History of American Newspapers and Their Readers*. Urbana: University of Illinois Press, 2001.
- Pettegree, Andrew. *The Invention of News: How the World Came to Know about Itself*. New Haven, CT: Yale University Press, 2014.
- Sloan, Wm. David. *The Media in America*. Northport, AL: Vision Press, 2014.
- Stephens, Mitchell. *A History of News,* New York: Oxford University Press, 2007.

While the other textbooks on the subject provide useful individual accounts of the development of areas of the media, *A Narrative History of the American Press* incorporates brief biographies of important media figures, first-person accounts from professional press practitioners, and primary materials to keep students engrossed in the content. It also demonstrates the importance of the First Amendment as an integral aspect of press development. In packaging this book's host of sources and resources, I hope to provide both instructors and students with the tools to appreciate this fascinating subject. Please visit the publisher's online listing for this book at www.routledge.com/9781138998469 to find supplemental eResource material, including a wealth of primary and secondary multi-media sources, review questions, and interactive exercises.

Professor Gregory A. Borchard
December 2017

Acknowledgments

While a professor at the University of Nevada, Las Vegas, students in my journalism history classes over the years have helped on a number of levels in preparing this text, both in supplying bibliographic references and in transcribing spoken lectures into written notes and then converting those notes into usable text.

With appreciation, I thank administrators at the University of Nevada, Las Vegas, for facilitating my research with support both directly and indirectly. Provost Nancy Rapoport and the entire Nevada System of Higher Education system deserve credit for providing a sabbatical spring 2017, without which this manuscript would still be only class notes, and Dean Robert Ulmer has been very helpful with feedback and encouragement.

Professor William McKeen, my doctoral advisor at the University of Florida who has remained a good colleague and friend since then, has contributed to the following text ways that deserve more than acknowledgment alone. Thanks, also, to Dr. David Bulla, a co-author and collaborator on several publications over the years who has contributed both directly and indirectly to the research featured in several chapters of this book.

Credit, thanks, and respects are also due graduate students in the Journalism and Media Studies program at UNLV for helping put into written words material that began as PowerPoint notes. Dan Michalski, Kianoosh Mousavi, Tiffany Pelton, Alexandra White, and Amaya Worthem contributed to content by listening to lectures and converting them to Word documents. Thanks to Karintha Tervalon, who volunteered her research skills and found entirely valuable and appropriate sources to accompany chapters in this book. Other graduate students—Jocelyn Apodaca, Madeline Edgmon, Margaret George, and Margo Malik—also played an important role in finding citations.

Additional thanks go to countless undergraduate students in the History of Journalism (JOUR 413) class who both helped scour the Library of Congress for images you will see featured in this book and supplied profile information. Students also provided content of special importance for the contemporary issues featured in closing chapters. While I cannot thank you all by name, you will have left your mark on future students, contributing directly to their educational experience.

INTRODUCTION

The Introduction explains the importance of a free press in the history of American journalism:

- It begins with a description of Enlightenment ideas about natural law that argue all people are born with unalienable rights;
- and it cites the pre-Revolutionary trial of John Peter Zenger as an antecedent for the First Amendment, which guaranteed press freedoms in the United States, along with other civil liberties in the Bill of Rights.

Using materials from this chapter, students should be able to identify the five freedoms guaranteed by the First Amendment:

- They should also be able to identify language introduced by influential early Americans (i.e. James Madison) that frames subjects featured in subsequent chapters of the book;
- and they should be able to explain the conventional methods of studying history compared with journalism history, describing the way in which the press has had a remarkably unique role in telling stories, a function that an American publisher once called the first rough draft of history.

Key words, names, and phrases associated with the Introduction include:

- John Milton and natural law;
- the trial of John Peter Zenger;
- the First Amendment, freedom of the press, freedom of speech;
- and the first rough draft of history.

The press serves as a platform for expressing the ideas of journalists. The history of the press accordingly tells a story about journalism—most notably, in historic terms, newspapers—and in doing so describes the people who created news and the way the press affected readers. The history of the press therefore describes the way in which people have interacted with information, both creating change with it and experiencing change from it. Understanding these changes, especially when communicated in a story-like form, makes it possible for students of the press to empower their own professional goals while observing the changes media continue to make on the world in which they live.

On the first day of class in my journalism history lectures, I have often told students a simple-yet-important truth: Each of us can only understand ourselves by examining where we have been and what we have done; by knowing our past, we can succeed in our future. I also address a misconception about our past—that it is, according to an odd but familiar complaint, somehow only a collection of names and dates. This uncomfortableness with history comes mostly from those who have encountered it only as a textbook endeavor, but it loses seriousness when we discuss the fascinating stories of the people and events who have preceded us. After all, everyone, whether young or old, student or professional, likes a story. It has been my endeavor in the classroom—and now with this book—to tell an especially compelling story, the story of the American press.

The history of the American press specifically is a story about all the people, events, and institutions tied together by the American experience—their institutions and innovations, and of the unique protections found in the First Amendment of the U.S. Constitution. The following pages provide a narrative of this story.

While numerous authors have attempted to tell this story in various formats, few have succeeded in creating a unified account that features the personalities and creations of journalists who worked with identifiably shared characteristics. The people and events you will see featured in this book all reached audiences through the press—they used the press for entertainment and for profit, as well, but they did all of this because of abilities provided by an experiment rooted in the idea that news had an intrinsic social value.

Other books on this subject have treated the history of the American press either in only topical or period fashion, relying perhaps too much on the old "names and dates" formula for storytelling. Other accounts have focused almost entirely on the conceptual elements of the press' institutional qualities, sacrificing the human dimensions of our shared interests. Even more accounts have relied on a compilation of submissions from various authors, missing the unified narrative that only a single author can supply. While this book has evolved from my experiences in nearly two decades of instruction and studies, it outlines for students in an accessible way the flesh and bones on those names and dates, describing the vibrant role journalists of the past have given to our own endeavors today.

Why—you may ask if you are not a journalism student—study the history of the American press? First, given the highly complex, globalized and converged set of communication technologies in the contemporary media landscape, information consumers (all of us) can begin to understand the relative value of the news they receive on a daily basis given the context of the many movements and institutional developments that have preceded the twenty-first century. Second, for the same unique reasons the First Amendment became part of the American experience, it has shaped the world in which we—not just journalists—have lived, affording everyone rights to expression that we cannot take for granted. And, finally, history has revealed that open societies have thrived on the availability of information; accordingly, a study of the history of the American press can provide a gauge of our current ability to access news and in doing so determine what kind of steps we can take to maintain a healthy system of governance.

Newspapers have in fact been a primary source of daily information for several centuries, offering the public a way to find important information about events around the world. Newspapers have also changed dramatically over time, and although we live in an increasingly interactive world of news delivery, many—if not most—of the conventions used in developing our most popular forms of media evolved directly from newspaper publishing.

For starters, among the most dramatic changes in Western history occurred when German goldsmith Johannes Gutenberg developed around 1440 the first effective

Image 0.1: "Invention of Printing, Gutenberg taking the first proof," Gutenberg with three other people and the printing press, published 1869.[1]

printing system. The Gutenberg Press adapted existing technologies to make possible the precise and rapid creation of print in large quantities.

Use of Gutenberg's basic device spread quickly in the following decades, reaching more than 200 cities in a dozen European countries. By 1500, printing presses in operation throughout Western Europe had produced more than twenty million volumes of text, rising in output to an estimated 150 to 200 million copies over the century. The operation of a press became so synonymous with the enterprise of printing that it lent its name to an entire new social institution—the press.

By automating the production of the newspaper, the number of papers available to the public greatly increased, making it affordable for people to purchase one. Over time, newspaper costs rose and the number of newspaper subscribers fell, which led to a vast reduction in the number of newspapers and newspaper editions in every market. With the increase in the use of technology, the public no longer needed the newspaper for its sole source of information. Other media such as radio, television, and the Internet started to replace the paper as an information source. Even though the method of delivery has changed, the news industry still has a niche in the world, and consumers of it still desire information; however, this is only the beginning of our story.

NATURAL LAW AND THE PRESS

A conflict over control of the press quickly emerged after Gutenberg's device demonstrated the power available to those who accessed information. The Reformation, which visionary German priest Martin Luther tied directly to the rights of the individual to read and interpret scripture, turned social orders throughout Europe upside down. This notion that common people could determine their own destinies more effectively than could a king stemmed in no small part from access to printed words previously available only to the elite.

Newspapers played a large role in the long-term democratization of rights afforded by literacy, which first began to catch fire in the sixteenth century, beginning in Germany via the printing press and then spreading into Western Europe. While other publications that preceded the newspaper provided what we might consider news, newspapers began to take a particular definition at this time, one that has lasted for the most part through the present day. Newspapers—like books, broadsheets, and other hard-copy media—have had by definition a printed component to them, but they also meet four additional criteria: They have up-to-date information; they circulate at regular intervals; the public can access them with reasonable ease; and they cover a range of topics. Under this working definition, Strasburg, Germany publisher Johann Carolus (1575–1634) produced in 1605 what historians consider the first newspaper with *Relation aller Fürnemmen und gedenckwürdigen Historien* (or, an *Account of all distinguished and commemorable news*).[2]

The spread of the printing press to parts of Western Europe took several decades, and in many cases, its arrival stirred tensions between the ruling class and those with new access to information. In England, a remarkable development in this transformation took place during the English Civil War between Parliamentarians and Royalists in which poet John Milton published a call for freedoms expressed by Protestants that saw fruition in what Americans would later call the First Amendment. Milton's publication of *Areopagitica* on November 23, 1644, argued forcefully against the 1643 *Ordinance for the Regulating of Printing*, which allowed pre-publication censorship of material considered threatening to the Crown.

This ordinance, which would also directly affect the work of publishers in the American colonies, interfered with not only the ability of printers to publish freely but also the ability of citizens to speak openly and to follow religious beliefs—for Milton, those freedoms coexisted together. "Give me the liberty to know, to utter, and to argue freely according to conscience," he wrote, "above all liberties."[3]

The English press subsequently emerged at least in part from Milton's exhortations, and largely with the proliferation of pamphlets advocating on behalf of either Parliamentarian or Royalist sides. Pamphlets—small, printed articles that contained arguments or information about a particular subject—served as precursors to a newspaper-based press, and during the English Civil War, production of them skyrocketed as opposing sides attempted to convince the other of the righteousness of their cause, most often through propaganda.[4]

The *London Gazette*, which began circulation on November 7, 1665, (it first appeared as the *Oxford Gazette* and later changed its name) represented this change, appearing shortly after the conclusion of the war and Protestant ascendancy. Other English papers started publishing three times a week, and later the first daily papers emerged. They typically included short articles, ephemeral topics, some illustrations, and classified articles. Multiple authors often contributed articles without identification. The newspapers contained some advertisements, but at the time, they did not include sections.

The *Daily Courant*, the first successful English newspaper issued on a daily basis, was published between 1702 and 1735, with Elizabeth Mallet as its first editor for ten days in March 1702. In the English colonies on the eastern coast of North America, the governor of Massachusetts in 1704 allowed publication of the *Boston News-Letter*, a newspaper published on a weekly basis, as the first continuously published newspaper in the colonies. A different Boston newspaper that preceded the *News-Letter* set a different kind of precedent, one that would add fuel to uniquely American ideas of press freedom.

On September 25, 1690, Benjamin Harris had issued *Publick Occurrences Both Forreign and Domestick*, which represented the first true multi-page publication outside the British mainland. *Publick Occurrences* lasted only one issue, as the king suppressed it, finding the method of its publication and its content objectionable. At the time, a publisher needed the government's approval to print news. Harris and printer Richard Pierce had not obtained a correct printing license and had to close down their newspaper after only one issue. Perhaps even more telling, the British government found the newspaper had criticized the British military for mistreating French prisoners in conflicts over control of North America and that it contained spurious information, including rumors of incest and immorality in the French royal family.

The American press—far from silenced—had experienced only its first foray into challenging established institutions, providing a service that would reach an audience resistant to government control. This philosophy, as well as the theory of the social contract, had antecedents in Roman law and Greek philosophy but came to fruition during the age of Enlightenment. While John Milton had advocated specifically for a free press, free speech, and free religion, proponents of guaranteed rights in general included English philosophers Thomas Hobbes and John Locke, who suggested that natural law applied to each individual. This belief defied an order that preceded it, an organization of society under a system of authoritarian rule known as the Divine Right of Kings. Natural law proponents argued that human reason could understand this system as one in which certain natural rights or values are inherent by virtue of human nature, and in time, this system would deduce binding rules of moral behavior.

The theories of natural law at first exercised influence on the development of English common law, and later, the founding documents of the American republic made them manifest. The U.S. Declaration of Independence and the Constitution demonstrated the intersection between natural law and natural rights, with the Declaration, for example, emphasizing the "consent of the governed," who assumed their role in pursuing life under "the Laws of Nature and of Nature's God." Tied directly to the Constitution's expression of these ideals, the First Amendment addressed the importance placed on five freedoms among those championed by proponents of natural law—the freedoms of religion, speech, press, assembly, and to petition the government.

THE TRIAL OF JOHN PETER ZENGER

The most significant colonial challenge to British control of the press took place in 1733, still decades before ratification of the First Amendment. As commonly practiced at the time, printers published content determined by licensed patrons, who often had their own partisan allegiances. In the case of John Peter Zenger, the *New York Weekly Journal* included content supplied by publisher James Alexander, a partisan who had complaints against William Cosby, incumbent royal governor of New York.

Alexander's career in politics included appointments to the Governor's Council in New York and to the Council and Attorney General of New Jersey, and in these roles, he frequently opposed Cosby's policies. In 1732, Cosby succeeded in having Alexander removed from the New York Council. Soon thereafter, Alexander started the *New York Weekly Journal* to publish anti-Cosby material. While Alexander wrote many of the pieces most critical of Cosby, Zenger, a German immigrant, published it.

Among the contents of the newspaper that caught the attention of Cosby included the allegation that he had rigged the 1734 state elections. The printed attacks called Cosby a "Nero" and an "idiot," and in 1735, Cosby had Zenger arrested and jailed on sedition charges, with the governor issuing a proclamation that condemned the newspaper as "scandalous, virulent, false, and seditious." A public burning of the *Journal* intended to silence opposition.

Zenger's fate caught the attention of Andrew Hamilton, a prominent Philadelphia lawyer at the time, who agreed to defend the printer. Hamilton recognized that Zenger's situation went beyond the fate of a single printer. In fact, later in the history of journalism, an editor or publisher—not a printer—would have assumed liability for the contents of a newspaper, but Hamilton saw in Zenger an opportunity to make a case that would affect the rights of all printers.

Hamilton went voluntarily and without charge to New York on Zenger's behalf. Against what would have been an established norm at the time, he admitted Zenger had printed and published the offending article but insisted the facts published remained true. In making his defense of Zenger, Hamilton set a precedent for later definitions of libel law. His argument began with the simple observation that Zenger had not published false information, only information that the governor found offensive. His eloquence in making the argument ultimately secured a "not guilty" verdict, but on a much grander scale. Hamilton made a closing statement that would echo for decades, one that likely resonated in the minds of those who drafted the First Amendment.

"Power may justly be compared to a great river," Hamilton said. "While kept within its due bounds it is both beautiful and useful. But when it overflows its banks, it is then too impetuous to be stemmed; it bears down all before it, and brings destruction and desolation wherever it comes."

> The question before the Court and you, Gentlemen of the jury, is not of small or private concern. It is not the cause of one poor printer, nor of New York alone, which you are now trying. No! It may in its consequence affect every free man that lives under a British government on the main[land] of America. It is the best cause. It is the cause of liberty. And I make no doubt but your upright conduct this day will not only entitle you to the love and esteem of your fellow citizens, but every man who prefers freedom to a life of slavery will bless and honor you as men who have baffled the attempt of tyranny, and by an impartial and uncorrupt verdict have laid a noble foundation for securing to ourselves, our posterity, and our neighbors, that to which nature and the laws of our country have given us a right to liberty of both exposing and opposing arbitrary power (in these parts of the world at least) by speaking and writing truth.[6]

Image 0.2: "Andrew Hamilton Defending John Peter Zenger in Court, 1734–5," published in Martha Lamb, *History of the City of New York*, v. 1 (New York: A. S. Barnes, 1877–96), 552.[5]

Chief Judge James De Lancey had instructed jurors to decide only the question of whether Zenger had published the issues of the *New-York Weekly Journal* in question, but after a brief deliberation, they sided with Hamilton. The authorities released Zenger from prison, and he returned to his printing business and published an account of his trial, influencing how people thought about press freedoms and the protections later embodied in the First Amendment.

THE FIRST AMENDMENT

We will see in the following chapters other instances in which colonists realized the importance of a free press in securing a new form of government, but the Zenger trial often receives credit for laying the elementary notions expressed in the First Amendment. As adopted in 1791, the First Amendment protected five freedoms with language that reads, "Congress shall make no law respecting an establishment of religion, or prohibiting the free exercise thereof; or abridging the freedom of speech, or of the press; or the right of the people peaceably to assemble, and to petition the Government for a redress of grievances."

Aside from the philosophical abstractions expressed in the ideals of natural law, a primary reason for writing such protections into the fabric of the nation had both a practical question and answer attached to it: How would the founders have secured a republic without a well-informed people? Answer: This new government could not succeed without the free flow of information.

This rationale found perhaps its clearest expression in the words of James Madison, who played a major role in the drafting of the Constitution itself. Madison, in an August 4, 1822, letter to jurist W. T. Barry, wrote:

> A Popular government without information, or the means of acquiring it, is but a prologue to a farce or tragedy; or perhaps both. Knowledge will forever govern ignorance; and a people who mean to be their own governors must arm themselves with the power which knowledge gives.[7]

This rationale behind the First Amendment expresses clearly and decisively why an understanding of the history of the press can only contribute to a fuller appreciation of the uniqueness of journalism as practiced in the United States. The news can entertain us, but according to its original purpose in the founding of this nation, it must primarily inform us.

One of the first major tests to freedom of the press came, as we will see in Chapter 2, in the late 1790s with the Alien and Sedition Acts, legislation enacted in 1798 by President John Adams' Federalist Party to ban seditious libel. The lead author of the speech and press clauses, James Madison, argued against the narrowing of freedom to what had existed under English common law, arguing the legislation was unconstitutional. A free press in the United States, he argued, must be entitled to respect more than had been practiced in England.

However, it was well more than 100 years later until the Supreme Court ruled on the constitutionality of any federal law regarding the free speech clause of the First Amendment, having never ruled on the Alien and Sedition Acts. As other chapters in *A Narrative History of the American Press* will show, the First Amendment continues to play an essential role in the vitality of the press in ways the government continues to challenge.

For example, the first major challenge to the First Amendment in the twentieth century took place during the administration of Woodrow Wilson when the Supreme Court addressed free speech issues entailed by the Espionage Act of 1917. During World War I—much like legislation passed since then—the government imposed sentences for anyone who caused or attempted to cause "insubordination, disloyalty, mutiny, or refusal of duty in the military or naval forces of the United States." The legislation allowed for punishment of anyone who facilitated the entrance of enemies into or over the United States and who obtained information from a place connected with the national defense. Hundreds of prosecutions followed passage of this legislation (see *Schenck v. United States*; *Debs v. United States*; *Frohwerk v. United States*; and *Abrams v. United States*). The Supreme Court upheld the prosecutions, and from them emerged Justice Oliver Wendell Holmes' "clear and present danger" test. The question in every case, Holmes argued, was "whether the words used are used in such circumstances and are of such a nature as to create a clear and present danger that they will bring about the substantive evils that Congress has a right to prevent."[8]

Yet, in a decision that countered government interference with a free press, the Supreme Court issued a landmark decision in the 1931 *Near v. Minnesota* case, rejecting prior restraint, or pre-publication censorship. In this case, the Minnesota legislature had passed a statute allowing courts to shut down "malicious, scandalous, and defamatory newspapers," allowing a defense of truth only in cases where the truth had been told "with good motives and for justifiable ends." In a 5–4 decision, the Court applied the Free Press Clause to the states, rejecting the statute as unconstitutional. Hughes quoted Madison in the majority decision, writing, "The impairment of the fundamental security of life and property by criminal alliances and official neglect emphasizes the primary need of a vigilant and courageous press."[9]

We will examine prominent Supreme Court decisions about the First Amendment in prominent press-related issues that emerged in the twentieth century later in this book (among them, the *Times v. Sullivan* and the *New York Times Co. v. United States* cases). For a preliminary idea of how important press freedoms remain to the makeup of our rights as journalists, the following descriptions of just four of the many cases from the past 50 years describe issues of continuing importance for professional reporters.

A Few First Amendment Cases Since *Near v. Minnesota*

- 1971: *Branzburg v. Hayes*. Reporter Paul Branzburg interviewed several Kentucky drug users for an article in the *Louisville Courier-Journal*. State grand juries called him twice to testify about his confidential sources, and he refused to do so. The Supreme Court ruled that confidential information does not allow reporters to withhold their sources in a government investigation. Reporters have subsequently gone to jail rather than reveal confidential sources.
- 1976: *Nebraska Press Association v. Stuart*. A Nebraska judge prevented reporters from publishing accounts of confessions to the police made by the accused in a

widely publicized murder trial, holding prior restraint ensured a fair trial, but the Supreme Court found that implementing prior restraint would not affect the trial's outcome.
- 1981: *Chandler v. Florida*. A Miami Beach jury convicted two police officers of conspiracy to commit burglary and larceny at a restaurant. The officers objected to the media presence, claiming the attention would prevent them from receiving a fair trial. The Supreme Court upheld the trial court's position of allowing cameras in the courtroom, which set a precedent for live courtroom television shows.
- 1988: *Hazelwood School District v. Kuhlmeier*. The principal of Hazelwood East High found two articles inappropriate for the school newspaper and prohibited their publication. Students on the newspaper staff brought the case to court, saying the First Amendment protected their rights. The Supreme Court said the educators had a right to censor the material as long as their actions had legitimate concerns.

Such has been the ebb and flow of judicial interpretations of the First Amendment, which over the years has had a direct correlation with the vitality of the press in reporting news to the American public. We continue to see demonstrations of a free press in spite of attempts by the government to infringe on it in ways that even resemble authoritarian measures from our early history. While the overall quantity and quality of contemporary First Amendment legal cases goes beyond the scope of this particular book, the law itself plays an important role in the story of the press, as law, along with journalism and history, requires facts and precedent.

THE FIRST ROUGH DRAFT OF HISTORY

With this cursory overview of the legal protections provided by the First Amendment, it may help journalism students to understand the history of the press as a process that integrates the three interrelated fields of journalism, history, and law. These three areas of practice each rely on a few essential, shared components that include the use of sources, facts, and precedent. No journalist, historian, or lawyer can succeed without a mastery of these tools.

What we seek to do in studying the history of the press is create a reliable account of what has happened given a vast body of sources, beginning with eyewitnesses. The eyewitnesses in our case come from those who the press featured at the time events took place. While news as initially reported may not always contain the most accurate account, as sources sometimes provide conflicting versions of events, we can begin to sort through the evidence and compile a trustworthy version of history that measures up to tests of credibility. This process—writing about what went into the creation of news on a historical level—has been likened to re-creating the first rough draft of history.

In this sense, we can again describe the history of journalism as a story unto itself, explaining it in a way that *Washington Post* publisher Phillip Graham once called the first rough draft of history. In an April 1963 speech to the overseas correspondents of *Newsweek* in London, Graham called on the press to provide "a first rough draft of history" that would "never really be completed about a world we can never really understand."[10] With this perspective, we can begin to see how our drafts of history—with even this book as an example—will continue to change as long as readers seek to understand the past from the contexts in which they read.

Graham's perspective is also one that students in my history of journalism classes have seen and one that you will see integrated in the following chapters. Using a concept known as historiography, a broad concept relevant to a number of disciplines, we essentially produce a history of history, or a meta-history, to understand the basis of narratives. Because we will focus on the history of journalism, you will in effect read about writers who not only wrote about history, they provided an eyewitness account of it—one that subsequent historians (including ourselves) hope to reproduce as faithfully as possible.

RECAPPING THE INTRODUCTION

Looking back on this chapter, you should see a focus on the development of the press. Beginning with Enlightenment ideas about natural law that argue all people are born with unalienable rights, Americans in particular first articulated these ideas in the pre-Revolutionary trial of John Peter Zenger, which—as an antecedent for the First Amendment—helped ensure press freedoms in the United States, along with other civil liberties in the Bill of Rights.

Using content from the preceding pages, you should be able to identify the five freedoms guaranteed by the First Amendment and identify language introduced by influential early Americans (specifically James Madison) that frames subjects featured in subsequent chapters of the book. Finally, given Philip Graham's words on the "first rough draft of history," you should also be able to explain the conventional methods of studying history compared with journalism history, describing ways the press has had a remarkably unique role in telling stories that transcends those sometimes tedious "names and dates" alone.

The following chapter will explain how these ideas played into the American Revolution, focusing on the ways particular colonists used newspapers as a tool to call for a political separation from Britain.

NOTES

1 "Invention of Printing," Library of Congress, accessed December 9, 2017, <item2006690328>.
2 *World Association of Newspapers*, "Newspapers: 400 Years Young!" accessed August 20, 2017, <http://tinyurl.com/y7p3g6vn>.
3 John Milton, *Areopagitica: A Speech for the Liberty of Unlicensed Printing to the Parliament of England* (London, 1644), 35.
4 Joad Raymond, *Pamphlets and Pamphleteering in Early Modern Britain* (Cambridge, New York: Cambridge University Press, 2003), 165.
5 "Andrew Hamilton Defending John Peter Zenger," Library of Congress, accessed November 19, 2016, <item/2006687175>.
6 *The Tryal of John Peter Zenger* (London: Printed for J. Wilford, 1738), 29.
7 James Madison to W. T. Barry, August 4, 1822, *The Writings of James Madison*, Gaillard Hunt, ed., 9 vols. (New York: G. P. Putnam's Sons, 1900–1910), 9: 103–9.
8 *Schenck v. United States*, 249 U.S. 47 (1919).
9 *Near v. Minnesota*, 283 U.S. 697 (1931).
10 Katherine Graham, *Personal History* (New York: Knopf, 2002), 324.

1

PRE-REVOLUTION PRINT
THE COLONIAL ORIGINS OF THE AMERICAN PRESS

This chapter explains the role of the press in the American Revolution, focusing on the ways particular colonists used newspapers as a tool to call for a political separation from Britain.

- Among these printers, the chapter features Benjamin Franklin's work as illustrative of a publishing style that reached a wide audience, noting how diverse content and contributors fueled news literacy in the decades preceding the Revolution;
- and the chapter features the way Samuel Adams used his *Boston Gazette* to propagandize the colonists' move toward independence, as his print accounts of events swayed ambivalent readers to oppose British rule.

Using materials from this chapter, students should be able to explain why those in the press still practice Franklin's approach to publishing as a way to maximize profits.

- Conversely, they should also be able to describe how the press and popular publications—sometimes by publishing only one side of the story—persuaded readers at the time to increasingly support calls for independence from Britain;
- and they should differentiate between the notion of balanced reporting (or "objective reporting") with efforts to attract advertisers, or Franklin's approach to sustaining a profitable enterprise.

Key words, names, and phrases associated with Chapter 1 include:

- Postmasters, the postal exchange;
- Benjamin Franklin, *Apology for Printers*, Elizabeth Timothy;
- the radical press;
- and Samuel Adams, *Boston Gazette*, the Boston Massacre.

The transition from the press of America's colonial days to the one we find familiar today did not happen overnight. It evolved over centuries, growing from movements that set different standards for understanding the purpose and the utility of the printed press, first, and later of media we now commonly use. To grasp the roots of contemporary standards, we can begin by looking at the colonial era, keeping in mind—as the rest of this book illustrates—that both storytelling and history is a process, one that unfolds over time. And as each subsequent generation in American history has learned (and sometimes forgotten) lessons from the experiences of our past, the press of today has an indelible link to the contributions of the people and practices preceding it.

Although the development of the colonial press itself had antecedents in the contributions of previous generations, the years between the trial of John Peter Zenger and the outbreak of the American Revolution marks an extraordinary moment for study. Colonists had established a network of postmasters who received copies of foreign publications and distributed them to a wide range of readers. The postmaster accordingly assumed responsibility for not only delivering news but also establishing newspapers in towns emerging up and down the East Coast. Postmasters filled publications with news gleaned from journals across the Atlantic and from other postmasters and printers in the colonies. This network provided colonists with information that contributed to the formation of a unique social consciousness, creating an identity separate from their ancestral roots, which for many of them would entail a breaking of ties with the governing political system imposed by England.

Two major types of print—newspapers and pamphlets—addressed colonial politics in the years leading to the American Revolution. Often written by elites under pseudonyms and published by booksellers, newspapers served as messengers of these ideas, carrying commercial information for a wide range of readers. With roots in the popularization of contested ideas during the English Civil War, pamphlets also contributed in a large way to the dissemination of the revolutionary ideas in the colonies (see this book's Introduction).

By the 1770s, dozens of newspaper printers functioned in the American mainland, each producing a four-page issue every week. These weekly papers sometimes reached the public as one-sheet broadsides, a large sheet of paper printed on one side only as a poster for reading in town squares. Because of the structure of the newspaper business in the eighteenth century, the stories that appeared in each paper were "exchanged" from other papers in different cities, creating a uniform effect akin to a modern news wire. With no copyright fees, required permissions, or even rules for giving credit for the use of previously published material in newspapers, the exchange system allowed publishers to reproduce stories, providing Revolutionaries a way to develop a sense of unity among colonists.

THE CULTURE OF COLONIAL PRINTERS

The major source of income for publishers came from political contributors, which included subscriptions and advertisements bought by supporters and partisans who subsidized like-minded content. Partisans in the government rewarded publishers for their affiliations and loyalty by providing them with printing contracts.

At the same time, in the years preceding the American Revolution, newspapers matured as venues through which publishers could promote their own particular opinions. Historians have since recognized that the ability of printers to express themselves individually and as a group separate from English control played a role in the outbreak of the Revolution itself. Beginning in the 1760s and into the period in which the most vocal calls for independence would erupt, the number of newspapers in the colonies more than doubled, with major publishing centers emerging in Annapolis, Boston, Philadelphia, New York, and Williamsburg.

During this era preceding the Revolution, social class depended on a combination of appearance, demeanor, personal habits, education, and occupation, and while those who paid for newspapers often enjoyed an elevated class status, those who printed the materials tended to do worse. Printing demanded long hours and sleepless nights. Type was set by hand, a letter at a time, in a hand-held composing stick, locked into a frame and placed on a press. Before each impression, type had ink applied to it, and the press produced prints one sheet at a time. Even though the process of printing at the time required extensive labor, those who did it often received little pay. In public, a printer might have revealed himself with physical deformities that resulted from pulling on a hand press over time, which included an elongated right arm, a limp, or back injuries. Printing office culture also tended to revolve around on-the-job drinking as a way to relieve both boredom and pain, contributing to alcoholism and other health issues.

Yet, this culture—or subculture, as it were—built a community among colonists that began to act more independently by the mid-eighteenth century, with colonial printers exercising voices that spoke for particular audiences, increasingly without regard to the dictates of a British Crown thousands of miles away. In 1754, for example, during the French and Indian War, publishers included the first cartoon in American newspapers, which called for colonial unity. The picture showed a snake cut into sections with each part representing a colony, and accompanying it, the caption: "Join or Die." Symbolically, the cartoon not only represented the creator's ability to create new forms of imagery with the newspaper industry but also reflected the growing sense of loyalty among colonists to one another. The creator's name was Benjamin Franklin.

BENJAMIN FRANKLIN AND ELIZABETH TIMOTHY

Often heralded as an American renaissance man, Benjamin Franklin exercised many talents, perhaps none more effectively than as a printer, a skill he gleaned at an early age while apprenticing for his brother James. Even though subsequent generations later knew him for a host of achievements—as an author, political theorist, postmaster, scientist, inventor, civic activist, and diplomat—he identified himself in his *Autobiography* primarily as a printer, which in fact was among his most lucrative pursuits.

BENJAMIN FRANKLIN

Benjamin Franklin was born January 17, 1706, in Boston, Massachusetts. He contributed directly to the language in the Declaration of Independence and the U.S. Constitution, but he identified chiefly as a printer and a publisher, setting the course of journalism on a path still traveled today. As a boy, Franklin enjoyed reading books. He followed the career of his brother James Franklin, a printer, and when Benjamin turned 15, he joined James in printing the *New England Courant*, the first newspaper in Boston. Under the pseudonym "Silence DoGood," Benjamin started his career as a journalist and later left for Philadelphia to start on his own. During his time in Philadelphia, he established himself with enough money to run his own printer shop as well as a regular shop with his wife, Deborah Read. He then started a newspaper that set a business precedent for modern journalism. Buying the *Pennsylvania Gazette* in 1729, he funded and contributed to the paper as a journalist where his work gained financial support. In 1733, Franklin began producing *Poor Richard's Almanack* under the pseudonym Richard Saunders. In 1737, the British Crown Post appointed him postmaster of Philadelphia, a position that helped a publisher gather and distribute news. As postmaster, Franklin could decide what newspapers could travel inexpensively or at no cost in the mail—or in the mail at all. Franklin surveyed post roads and post offices. He introduced a simple accounting method for postmasters and had riders carry mail both night and day. Having a news background himself, Franklin mandated delivery of all newspapers for a small fee, a practice instrumental in later legislation that encouraged the circulation of information as essential to the republic.

Franklin's career—as was his approach to almost every facet of life—took an innovative approach to the industry. His model for publishing set a template for future generations, as he linked print shops and post offices in a coastal chain, spreading news throughout the colonies.

Franklin also had a knack for making money, and in doing so, he became a powerful voice for colonial interests. The *Pennsylvania Gazette* and *Poor Richard's Almanack*, likely his most famous publications, demonstrated his adeptness at the business of publishing, with the *Gazette* achieving a commercial success more than virtually any other colonial newspaper and the *Almanack* wielding wide cultural significance. As newspapers founded under Franklin's supervision generally prospered and as troubles with Great Britain mounted, Franklin himself emerged as among the leading voices that posed an increasing threat to English dominance over the internal affairs of its subjects.

Still in his twenties and only a few years after launching the *Pennsylvania Gazette*, a remarkable incident involving advertisers led him to write a classic series of articles still cited today on the necessity of running a newspaper both wisely and profitably, which in Franklin's estimation were one and the same. At the time, a group of the newspapers' readers—specifically, clergy—had taken offense to words used in an advertisement that they felt had discriminated against them. These particular readers were angry with the publisher and the newspaper itself for having referred to them as "Sea Hens" and "Black Gowns" and therefore decided to organize a boycott.

In addressing the complaints of the clergy and others offended by the contents of the ad, Franklin explained that he published a wide range of content, and even though derogatory phrases might from time to time appear in print, just as much content reflected positively on the same subjects. The newspaper, Franklin wrote, depended on publishing whatever content could create revenue. The publication of his "An Apology for Printers" appeared in the *Pennsylvania Gazette*, June 19, 1731, explaining his rationale. "Being frequently censur'd and condemn'd by different Persons for printing Things which they say ought not to be printed," Franklin wrote, "I have sometimes thought it might be necessary to make a standing Apology for my self, and publish it once a Year, to be read upon all Occasions of that Nature."

> Printers are educated in the belief, that when men differ in opinion, both sides ought equally to have the advantage of being heard by the publick; and that when truth and error have fair play, the former is always an overmatch for the latter: Hence they cheerfully serve all contending writers that pay them well, without regarding on which side they are of the question in dispute.[1]

"If all printers were determined not to print anything till they were sure it would offend nobody," Franklin concluded, "there would be very little printed."

While media professionals today describe this style of publishing as telling "both sides of a story" (or, in other respects, being fair and objective), Franklin had advanced the approach for slightly different reasons. While he recognized that there is indeed more than one side of any story, he looked to attract various voices because—from a business standpoint—it just made good economic sense to welcome all readers as potential subscribers and, even more importantly, to attract a diverse and voluminous range of advertisers. In other words, if publishers—or any other practitioners of news for that matter—want to survive, they should include as much content as possible from a diverse range of sources.

The talent for business Franklin displayed with the *Pennsylvania Gazette* shined in another famous publication, *Poor Richard's Almanack*, first published not long after his "Apology." Franklin, who adopted the pseudonym of "Poor Richard" or "Richard Saunders," published the *Almanack* annually from 1732 to 1758 and did so with remarkable success, printing 10,000 copies per year. The content published offered a mixture of seasonal weather forecasts, practical household hints, puzzles, and other amusements, with most or nearly all entries offering financial advice to readers.

To this day, we find sayings from the *Almanack* repeated as witty phrases, as readers took to heart, among many others, the following sayings.

- As Pride increases, Fortune declines.
- Drive thy Business, or it will drive thee.
- Great spenders are bad lenders.
- Haste makes waste.
- Having been poor is no shame, but being ashamed of it, is.
- If you know how to spend less than you get, you have the philosopher's stone.
- Keep thy shop, and thy shop will keep thee.
- No gains without pains.
- Nothing but money, is sweeter than honey.
- Patience in market, is worth pounds in a year.[2]

It should come as no surprise—with one of his most famous sayings being "a penny saved is a penny earned"—that his portrait was later selected top appear on the $100 bill.

The *Almanack* also featured an innovative approach to news, publishing in a serial format, so that readers would purchase it year after year to find out what happened to characters. In some respects, the *Almanack* set a precedent for the content we see in newspapers like the *Wall Street Journal* of today.

However, Franklin's approach produced more than just profit. In seeking as many voices to appear in print as possible, he also opened opportunities to contributors who might have ordinarily not participated in the news industry.

One of the more remarkable examples of this phenomenon first emerged with a newspaper in Charleston, South Carolina. Lewis Timothy, husband to Elizabeth Timothy and publisher of the *South Carolina Gazette*, had made a contract with Franklin to publish the newspaper in 1734. Four years later, Lewis died. Instead of closing, the newspaper continued without the public noticing a change in the publisher.

Readers were later surprised to discover that Lewis had died, as the news they received arrived uninterrupted because his wife Elizabeth had assumed responsibility for the paper, thus becoming the first female publisher in the United States. She performed these roles with distinction, especially considering her other responsibilities as a mother and homemaker.

The Timothy family had emigrated from France in 1731, arriving and settling in Philadelphia. With one of Lewis's first employment opportunities, Franklin hired him to become the first editor of the *Philadelphische Zeitung*, a German newspaper intended to reach a growing audience. Issues appeared on May 6, 1732, and on June 24, 1732, but none thereafter. Recognizing Timothy's talents regardless of the short-lived newspaper, Franklin then hired him to perform printing duties at the *Pennsylvania Gazette*.

Franklin had a practice of encouraging competent printers who worked for him at his *Pennsylvania Gazette* to publish and print in other colonies, and one of them, Thomas Whitmarsh, had moved to Charles Town (later Charleston) to establish the *South Carolina Gazette*. Not long after the paper began publication, Whitmarsh died of yellow fever, and Lewis Timothy stepped in to take his place.

Franklin and Timothy entered into a six-year business agreement whereby Franklin furnished the press and other equipment, paid one-third of the expenses, and was to receive a third of the profits from the enterprise. Timothy revived the *South Carolina Gazette* in 1733 but died five years later with one year remaining on his contract with Franklin. The contract provided for Timothy's eldest son, Peter, to carry on the business until the contract expired. Lewis had anticipated the likelihood of his own demise because three previous South Carolina printers had died of fever soon after arriving in the colony. He had put in a special clause in the Franklin partnership contract that his eldest son Peter could succeed him if he prematurely died, but Peter was just 13 years old when Lewis died. Peter was training as an apprentice with his father but was too inexperienced to take over the business.

Franklin agreed to take on Elizabeth Timothy as a partner until Peter was capable of running the shop. When Elizabeth became Franklin's partner, she had six children. She assumed control of the printing operation and published the next weekly issue of the *South Carolina Gazette* on January 4, 1739, which carried the announcement that she was editing the paper, although the listing of publisher had to remain under Peter Timothy's name.

At the bottom of the right corner of the third page of the January 4, 1739, issue of the *South Carolina Gazette*, Elizabeth included an obituary for her husband, who "hath been deprived of his life by an unhappy accident." She informed her readers that it was customary in a printer's family in the colonies and in Europe for a wife and sons to help with the printing operation.

> I take this Opportunity of informing the Public, that I shall contain the said paper as usual; and hope, by the Assistance of my Friends, to make it as entertaining and correct as may be reasonable expected. Wherefore I flatter myself, that all those Persons, who, by Subscription or otherwise, assisted my late Husband, on the prosecution of the Said Undertaking, will be kindly pleased to continue their Favours and good Offices to this poor afflicted Widow and six small children and another hourly expected.

Under Elizabeth's control, the *South Carolina Gazette* remained four pages, approximately 8 by 13 inches in size, and type was at first set in two columns, later in three. At first, it carried little local news, and the contents relied on foreign and domestic news exchanges. Elizabeth herself often wrote homilies—inspirational pieces—and carried essays that emulated those in English journals. She reprinted dramas, poetry, and literary classics and printed the first efforts of new Southern writers. The content did not delve into political issues and remained non-controversial with authorities. Years later, Franklin praised Elizabeth Timothy, attributing her ability in this field to her having been "born and bred in Holland, where, as I have been informed, the knowledge of accounts makes a part of female education."[3] Her success with the press personified how content without bylines could contribute to the building of a national identity, bringing together men and women of different backgrounds over a vast geographic area. This feature of the press would create consequences demonstrated in a revolutionary movement that began before the 1770s and continued well after the formation of the United States.

BOSTON AND THE RADICAL PRESS

Not long after the British Empire's victory in the Seven Years' War (1756–1763), hints of this Revolution began to emerge. Finding itself deep in debt and looking for new sources of revenue, the British Parliament for the first time sought to tax the British colonies in America directly. In 1765, Parliament passed the Stamp Act, which required colonists to pay a new tax on most printed materials. The British added a fee for admittance to the bar, and it taxed newspapers, business papers, and legal documents.

The Stamp Act met intense resistance in parts of the colonies, as those affected most directly saw them as part of a larger divergence between British and American interpretations of the British Constitution and the extent of Parliament's authority in the colonies. One of the most vociferous opponents to the measure was Boston publisher Samuel Adams, who argued it would also hurt the economy of the British Empire. His home, Boston, as a port city, had hosted visitors from around the world and become a crucible of eclectic and sometimes radical ideas, and Adams' *Boston Gazette* fomented one of the most radical ideas of them all—revolution.

In June 1765, colonials organized resistance to the Stamp Act, with efforts to pressure Parliament to repeal it. Adams supported calls for a boycott of British goods, supporting a protest group in Boston called the Loyal Nine. The Virginia House of Burgesses followed this line of argumentation by passing a widely circulated set of resolutions against it.

On August 14, 1765, the Loyal Nine organized a protest that hung an effigy likeness of tax collector Andrew Oliver and, later that night, ransacked his home and demolished his office. Soon thereafter, Oliver resigned his commission and promised to abandon efforts to tax the colonists. Then, on August 26, an angry crowd destroyed the home of Lieutenant Governor Thomas Hutchinson, an act that would earn Adams the moniker that Hutchinson gave him, "the Grand Incendiary of the Province."

In the years following, the *Boston Gazette*, edited and printed by Benjamin Edes and John Gill, emerged as one of the most vocal advocates of colonial resistance to the British. Contributors John Hancock and James Otis joined with Samuel Adams' second cousin John Adams, who provided legal counsel, advancing arguments against taxation without representation. In time, the newspaper reflected the industriousness of Samuel Adams, who maintained anonymity as well as possible while encouraging readers to entertain the cause of revolution.

The public recognized the office of the *Boston Gazette*, located on Court Street, as the headquarters of the Revolutionary leaders. Hancock, Otis, and other contributors known as the Caucus Club met at the Green Dragon Tavern, an auxiliary newsroom, watching the public sentiment of the country respond to their publications and proofing their contributions in a manner that today might compare with a budget meeting in an editorial boardroom.

The acts of resistance advocated by these radicals succeeded in forcing the British to rethink their strategy in the colonies. Although Parliament had intended the Stamp Act to go into effect on November 1, 1765, it had no way to enforce the law because colonial protestors had ousted the stamp distributors, driving them out of town, and in turn, British merchants eventually convinced Parliament to repeal the tax. When news of the repeal reached Boston in May 1766, Adams made a public statement, thanking the British merchants for helping their cause.

However, the success of the resistance movement was short lived, and the British, far from simply capitulating to the colonists, made clear their next efforts would impose direct control over them. At first, Adams used channels approved by the Crown to protest, writing the "Massachusetts Circular Letter" in 1768 that attacked Parliament's persistence in taxing the colonies without proper representation. In response, the British Governor of Massachusetts Francis Bernard dissolved the state's legislature and sent troops to suppress disobedience with orders to enforce unpopular Parliamentary legislation. The Sons of Liberty threatened armed resistance to arriving British troops, but none emerged immediately.

On February 27, 1769, Adams then published in the *Boston Gazette* a call to Bostonians and colonists alike to defend themselves against the British. More than expressing a need for self-defense alone, "Right of Revolution" included language that would resonate for years in a fight for independence. Arguing against the imposition of military power as "forever dangerous to civil rights," Adams wrote, "we have had recent instances of violences that have been offer'd to private subjects, and the last week, even to a magistrate in the execution of his office!"

> Such violences are no more than might have been expected from military troops: A power, which is apt enough at all times to take a wanton lead, even when in the midst of civil society; but more especially so, when they are led to believe that they are become necessary, to awe a spirit of rebellion, and preserve peace and good order. But there are some persons, who would, if possibly they could, perswade the people never to make use of their constitutional rights or terrify them from doing it. No wonder that a resolution of this town to keep arms for its own defence, should be represented as having at bottom a secret intention to oppose the landing of the King's troops: when those very persons, who gave it this colouring, had before represented the peoples petitioning their Sovereign, as proceeding from a factious and rebellious spirit; and would now insinuate that there is an impropriety in their addressing even a plantation Governor upon public business—Such are the times we are fallen into![4]

Tensions in Boston only worsened, and by March 1770, the military occupation contributed to a climate that reached a crisis level. A subsequent event, later known as the Boston Massacre, has taken a permanent spot in the annals of American history.

As with most controversial events, the truth of what happened often depends on who tells the story. The facts gleaned from the night of March 5, 1770, indicate a Boston mob formed around a British sentry and subjected him to verbal abuse and harassment. Eight soldiers joined to support him, but the mob also subjected them to verbal threats and thrown objects. During an ensuing melee, the British fired shots into the crowd, instantly killing three people and wounding others. Two more people died later of wounds sustained in the incident. The crowd eventually dispersed after Acting Governor Thomas Hutchinson promised an inquiry, but reformed the next day, prompting the withdrawal of the troops. Authorities arrested and charged eight soldiers, one officer, and four civilians with murder. Defended by the lawyer and future American president John Adams, six of the soldiers were acquitted, while two others received manslaughter convictions and reduced sentences, which included branding on their hand.

From a press standpoint, the most significant outcome of the Boston Massacre appears in the propagandized versions of events in both prints and newspapers. According to the American press, British soldiers unloaded their weapons on a group of teens playing with snowballs. Likely, the most famous account of the Boston Massacre to etch

Image 1.1: "The Bloody Massacre Perpetrated in King Street Boston on March 5th 1770 by a Party of the 29th Regt.," Paul Revere, engraver, created in Boston, Engrav'd Printed & Sold by Paul Revere, 1770, a sensationalized version of the Boston Massacre, March 5, 1770.[5]

itself in the American consciousness, Paul Revere's famous illustration *The Bloody Massacre*, circulated throughout the colonies and depicted the British slaughtering innocent civilians with machinelike precision.

Revere created a masterpiece of propaganda. On the right, he depicts a group of seven uniformed British soldiers, who on the signal of an officer, fire into a crowd of Bostonians at left, with three of the latter bleeding on the ground. The crowd lifts two other casualties with a dog in the foreground and a row of houses, the First Church, and the Town House in the background. Behind the British troops, another row of buildings includes the Royal Custom House, bearing the sign "Butcher's Hall." Beneath the print, 18 lines of verse list the "unhappy Sufferers."

SAMUEL ADAMS

Samuel Adams was born in Boston, Massachusetts, September 27, 1722. He was the second cousin to U.S. President John Adams, and he took part in the organization of the Boston Tea Party and the signing of the U.S. Declaration of Independence. He was an opponent of British taxation and led the resistance against the Stamp Act of 1765. In addition, Adams was a legislator and founded the Boston's Committee of Correspondence, which was useful in communicating and coordinating events during the American Revolutionary War. In 1765, he was elected to the Massachusetts Assembly where he served as clerk for many years. In 1774, he was chosen to serve as a member of the provincial council during the crisis in Boston. He then received an appointment as a representative to the Continental Congress, where he was most noted for his oratory skills and as a passionate advocate of independence from Britain. In 1776, as a delegate to the Continental Congress, he signed the Declaration of Independence. Adams retired from the Congress in 1781 and returned to Massachusetts to become a leading member of that state's convention to form a constitution. In 1789, he was appointed lieutenant governor of the state, and in 1794, he was elected governor until he retired in 1797. As a publisher, Adams favored investigative reporting and appropriate emotional appeal since he wanted readers to care about the attempts to take away their freedom. He died October 2, 1803, in his hometown of Boston.

What Revere illustrated, Samuel Adams put into words, dedicating his newspaper to coverage of the massacre. Remarkably, the Boston Massacre as reported in the *Boston Gazette* March 12, 1770, used accounts from only the perspective of Bostonians, not the British. Under a header that read, "On the evening of Monday, being the fifth current, several soldiers of the 29th Regiment were seen parading the streets with their drawn cutlasses and bayonets, abusing and wounding numbers of the inhabitants," Adams' account intended to enflame the passions of readers.

Thirty or forty persons, mostly lads, being by this means gathered in King Street, Capt. Preston with a party of men with charged bayonets, came from the main guard to the commissioner's house, the soldiers pushing their bayonets, crying, make way! They took place by the custom house and, continuing to push to drive the people off pricked some in several places, on which they were clamorous and, it is said, threw snow balls. On this, the Captain commanded them to fire; and more snow balls coming, he again said, damn you, fire, be the consequence what it will! One soldier then fired, and a townsman with a cudgel struck him over the hands with such force that he dropped his firelock; and, rushing forward, aimed a blow at the Captain's head which grazed his hat and fell pretty heavy upon his arm. However, the soldiers continued the fire successively till seven or eight or, as some say, eleven guns were discharged. By this fatal manoeuvre three men were laid dead on the spot and two more struggling for life; but what showed a degree of cruelty unknown to British troops, at least since the house of Hanover has directed their operation, was an attempt to fire upon or push with their bayonets the persons who undertook to remove the slain and wounded![6]

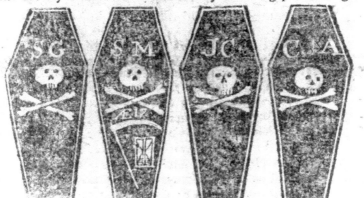

Image 1.2: "Four Coffins of Men Killed in the Boston Massacre," a print by Paul Revere, shows a section of a newspaper column published in the *Boston Gazette*, March 12, 1770, with illustrations of four coffins bearing skulls and crossbones with the initials of those killed.[7]

Combined with other media accounts of the event, the citizens of Boston and colonists in general received indications that occupying British forces put their lives danger. And to impress upon his readers the gravity of the situation, Adams included graphic representations of coffins produced by Paul Revere in the *Boston Gazette*, symbolizing the dead from the massacre.

The four coffins, representing the four who had died at the time of printing, included their initials with text explaining their fates and identifying them by name: Samuel Gray (S. G.), Samuel Maverick (S. M.), James Coldwell (J. C.), and Crispus Attucks (C. A.). Symbols on Samuel Maverick's tombstone include the Grim Reaper's scythe and an hourglass, indicating he died before his time, at the age of 17. Crispus Attucks, the first to die in the massacre, meanwhile earned martyr status as the first casualty of the Revolutionary War—with an ancestry that included Native American and African American ancestry, the first to die for a nation that has long had ethnic and racial issues in its heritage.

FOMENTING REVOLUTION IN THE PAGES OF THE PRESS

The language in Adams' *Boston Gazette* and the imagery of Revere's prints circulated widely throughout the colonies. What media consumers of the day would have understood as the official account revealed that a group of teenagers had just been playing in the streets when one threw a snowball, and then all mayhem broke loose.

However, the truth was something else. As John Adams discovered in defending the troops, the mob, which he described as "a motley rabble of saucy boys," endangered the soldiers who then defended themselves. In the end, the jury agreed with Adams, who had insisted all along that while he found the incident appalling, the troops deserved representation as any other subjects under law. While Bostonians generally found the "not guilty" verdict repugnant, memories of the event festered and contributed to the eventual outbreak of revolutionary fervor.

In fact, John Adams himself later suggested that the Boston Massacre quite literally incited the American Revolution. "Not the battle of Lexington or Bunker Hill," he wrote, ranked as significantly as the events of the Boston Massacre. "The death of four or five persons, the most obscure and inconsiderable that could have been found upon the continent, has never yet been forgiven in any part of America."[8]

The press—and no doubt the *Boston Gazette*—had helped advance the tenets of the American Revolution, as colonial publishers began to demonstrate that news should circulate freely, without government interference, and in defiance of attempts to silence it. The printers needed only an independent nation in which to operate, and, as we will see in the following chapter, John Adams—even more than his rabblerousing cousin did—would play a direct role in the way the American press evolved after the Revolution.

And while the *Boston Gazette* had played a role in triggering the American drive to independence, several other colonial publications would play an important role in transmitting stories about the American Revolution, helping to transform the newspaper into a foundational form of media for the American experience. The list below features a sample of newspapers that fit this description.

Prominent Newspapers Published During the Revolution[9]

- *Connecticut Courant*. Published in Hartford, the *Courant*'s importance grew from its ability to continue publishing while the British occupied neighboring cities. The circulation of the paper greatly increased throughout the states from New York northward because it was the only major newspaper continually published at this time.
- *Massachusetts Spy*. Produced in Boston by Isaiah Thomas, the *Spy* supplemented stories published in the *Boston Gazette*. The *Spy*'s most famous piece was Thomas' report on the Battle of Lexington in which he cast the British as wanton murderers.
- *New Hampshire Gazette*. The *Gazette* shied away from taking a strong political stand against the British government, but its tone generally favored colonial interests. Because the publication site was far from battles, *Gazette* editors provided news of events regularly to readers, and other printers across the country reprinted extracts from its accounts.
- *New York Journal*. The *Journal* advocated independence on a number of occasions, and given its proximity to the fighting during the Revolution, it served as a source for newspapers throughout the country.
- *Pennsylvania Evening Post*. The *Post* produced its contribution to the Revolution when its July 6, 1776, issue contained the recently adopted Declaration of Independence. Other newspapers followed and published the Declaration widely.
- *Pennsylvania Journal*. The *Journal* published news about the Continental Congress' meetings, which other newspapers then reprinted. The *Journal* traditionally received credit for first popularizing Thomas Paine's "American Crisis."
- *Providence Gazette*. The *Gazette* took a strong stand in favor of the rights of the colonies and supported independence. It became an important source of news about events in Boston and New York when the newspapers there no longer functioned.
- *Rivington's New York Gazetteer*. James Rivington, one of the best printers in America at the time, published the *Gazetteer* to lend support to the British. It provides important historical information about the Loyalist perspective.
- *South Carolina Gazette*. The *Gazette* supported American interests and had to suspend publication from time to time because of the tensions with Britain, but a group of advertisers helped keep the newspaper in circulation. It serves as an important source for information about the Southern colonies at the time.

Beginning in the 1770s and into the 1780s, these papers combined accounts of the news with both revolutionary ideas and battles for an audience that eventually grew interested in separating from Britain.

RECAPPING THIS CHAPTER

Looking back on this chapter, you should see a focus on how the press in these years played a significant part in motivating political figures and citizens alike to separate from Britain. The chapter showed how Benjamin Franklin and his newspapers illustrated a publishing style that reached a wide audience by including diverse content and contributors, which fueled news literacy in the decades preceding the Revolution. It also showed how Samuel Adams' *Boston Gazette* propagandized the colonists' move toward independence, as he swayed readers otherwise ambivalent to oppose British rule.

Using content from the preceding pages, you should be able to explain why those in the press still practice Franklin's approach to publishing as a way to maximize profits. Conversely, you should also be able to describe how the press and popular publications—sometimes by publishing only one side of the story—influenced readers into supporting the cause of independence from Britain, and they should differentiate between the notion of balanced reporting (i.e. "objective reporting") with efforts to attract advertisers.

The following chapter explains the role of the press in popularizing ideas articulated in the founding documents of the nation. It begins with a profile of Thomas Paine, a description of his famous works *Common Sense* and *The American Crisis*, and the context in which he wrote. It then delves into the partisan arrangements following the Revolution, which historians have called "the Dark Ages of American Journalism," and describes how partisanship had a stifling effect on expression, especially under the Alien and Sedition Acts.

NOTES

1 "An Apology for Printers," *Pennsylvania Gazette*, June 3–19, 1731.
2 Benjamin Franklin, *Poor Richard's Almanack for 1850* (New York: John Doggett, Jr. 1849), 24–46.
3 Benjamin Franklin, *The Autobiography of Benjamin Franklin* (New York: P. F. Collier & Son Company, 1909), 97.
4 *Boston Gazette*, February 27, 1769.
5 "The Bloody Massacre," Library of Congress, accessed November 19, 2016, <item/2008680173>.
6 *Boston Gazette*, March 12, 1770.
7 "Four Coffins of Men Killed," Library of Congress, accessed November 19, 2016, <item/2004672647>.
8 John Adams to Jedidiah Morse, January 5, 1816, in Jedidiah Morse, *Annals of the American Revolution* (Hartford, CT: Oliver D. Cooke, 1824), 209.
9 Carol Sue Humphrey, "Top 10 Revolutionary War Newspapers," *Journal of the American Revolution*, February 26, 2015, accessed August 21, 2017, <allthingsliberty.com/2015/02/top-10-revolutionary-war-newspapers>.

2

THOMAS PAINE, THE PARTISAN PRESS, AND "THE DARK AGES OF AMERICAN JOURNALISM"

This chapter explains the role of the press in popularizing ideas articulated in the founding documents of the nation:

- It begins with a profile of Thomas Paine, a description of his famous works *Common Sense* and *The American Crisis*, and the context in which he wrote;
- and it then delves into the political fighting through press content that followed the Revolution, an era dubbed "the Dark Ages of American Journalism," describing how partisanship stifled expression, especially under the Alien and Sedition Acts.

Using materials from this chapter, students should be able to describe how the rights to life, liberty, and the pursuit of happiness came to be cornerstones of the American experience, citing Paine's work:

- They should also see how enduring political tensions and press partisanship had their antecedents in the debates that raged following the Revolution;
- and they should be able to analyze the implementation of the Alien and Sedition Acts as a problematic moment in press history.

Key words, names, and phrases associated with Chapter 2 include:

- Thomas Paine, *Common Sense*, *The American Crisis*;
- Federalists (Alexander Hamilton), John Fenno, the *Gazette of the United States*;

- Republicans (Anti-Federalists), Thomas Jefferson, Philip Freneau, the *National Gazette*;
- and The Alien and Sedition Acts, John Adams, "The Dark Ages of American Journalism."

Journalism played both a direct and indirect role in the course of the American Revolution. At just a cursory glance, a comparison of the nation's founding documents reflects the language popularized in some of the most widely read journalistic pieces of the day. Even the famous description of fighting in 1775 at Lexington and Concord—the "shot heard round the world"—had its inspiration from the press, with Boston publisher Isaiah Thomas' *Worcester Spy*, on May 3, 1775, first reporting a revolution with global repercussions had begun. Not until well after the Revolution, however, did even those who had initially called for independence from Britain know where their words would take them.

At the beginning of the War for Independence, more than three dozen weekly newspapers operated throughout the colonies. When the British imposed a blockade on the colonies that curtailed the importation of paper, ink, and new equipment, newspapers decreased in size and took longer to produce, but when the war ended in 1782, two-thirds of the colonial newspapers had survived, and thirty or more began to start publishing. Readership in the new nation reached an audience in the hundreds of thousands, with newspapers circulating combined copies of about 40,000 per week.

This flourishing industry that published news had helped launch the Revolution and would become an essential part of sustaining the government inspired by it. While initial attempts to organize former colonies into a nation faltered under the Articles of Confederation, the founders recognized that the establishment of a new republic depended in part on a flourishing publishing industry. At the time when the founders recognized the nation needed a new Constitution to bind together states, well more than 200 newspapers circulated information.

While this arrangement had in part anticipated a later split between partisan interests by guaranteeing the freedoms of expression found in the First Amendment, the political parties that emerged after the Revolution used and, in some cases, abused newspapers in ways that ran counter to the revolutionary spirit. In the 1790s, Federalists and Republicans (Anti-Federalists) sponsored national networks of weekly newspapers, which attacked each other vehemently. The partisan newspapers of the era traded vicious barbs against their enemies, with the most heated rhetoric coming in debates over what measures the executive administration might take at home to avoid the terror of the French Revolution.

COMMON SENSE AND *THE AMERICAN CRISIS*

Had printers in particular not first called for independence from Britain and sustained these calls, the American Revolution likely would have failed. At first, the majority of colonials did not support the Revolution, having ethnic ties to England and cultural loyalties to the Crown. Moreover, the British Empire provided protection for its subjects; it built roads linking the colonies, and it facilitated trade, so many saw no reason to separate. Those that did support the Revolution were a minority, and even a smaller number of them actually joined the fight.

Faced with overwhelming odds, having to fight against one of the most professional and heavily armed militaries in the world, they turned to the leadership of George Washington, a respected Virginian who had extensive military experience under British command. Washington had agreed to head the Continental Army in its efforts to turn back British occupation after the battles of Lexington and Concord near Boston in April 1775. Nominated by John Adams of Massachusetts, he received an appointment as Commander in Chief. Washington recognized that the first year of fighting had gone poorly for the rebels. He faced a reality that his troops, demoralized and unsupported, might abandon their cause, and turned instead to the words of Thomas Paine for help.

Born in Thetford, England, in the county of Norfolk, Thomas Paine immigrated to the British American colonies with the help of Benjamin Franklin in November 1774, arriving just in time to participate in the American Revolution. In England, he had engaged in civic affairs and business matters, but followed Franklin's suggestion that successful opportunities awaited him in the colonies. In January 1775, he began editing the *Pennsylvania Magazine*, performing the role with considerable talent and ability, writing most of its contents. He advanced several causes that in many respects were ahead of his time, helping put into the minds of his readers the necessity for reforms. Among other causes, he advocated for the end of slavery, the emancipation of women, the abolition of dueling, and the prevention of animal cruelty. Paine saw the American Revolution as a catalyst for these endeavors and joined the rebels at first as a soldier and then as one of the most important journalists of the age.

THOMAS PAINE

Despite a lack of a formal education, Thomas Paine immersed himself in reading and writing. He married Mary Lambert in 1759, but shortly thereafter, both she and her child died in childbirth. Paine suffered other setbacks and decided to make a new life in America. By the end of 1774, he had moved to Philadelphia where he took up writing for the *Pennsylvania Magazine*. While this did not represent his first time publishing works that criticized the government, the magazine gave Paine the opportunity to discuss grievances with the public. Just as Shakespeare's plays were for a common audience, Paine aimed his words at a large number of readers. Using simple language, Paine sought to persuade colonists that the English Crown threatened their well-being. Prior to the publication of *Common Sense*, military measures were already underway between colonists and British soldiers, creating a climate ripe for Paine's content. *Common Sense* and *The American Crisis*, two of his most widely read pieces of anti-monarchist propaganda, earned him accolades throughout the Revolution. In 1777, Congress appointed Paine to serve as Secretary of Foreign Affairs. He published sensitive

> information about American negotiations with France in his pamphlets, which led to his expulsion from the committee but also to a mission to France. From this point forward, controversies shadowed his legacy, as his role and direct participation in the French Revolution alarmed Americans—although the United States was founded on an uprising similar in its contempt for monarchy, the French mob at the time demonstrated a frightening appetite for violence. Paine later published several pieces, including *Age of Reason* and *The Crisis Papers*. He eventually returned to America around 1802 to discover his role in the American Revolution had become a distant memory.

Upon the outbreak of fighting in the Revolutionary War, Paine enlisted as a private in the militia, and he was with Washington at Valley Forge; however, his services, it was agreed, would be more valuable with a pen than with a rifle. In Philadelphia, on January 9, 1776, he published his first in a series of anonymous pamphlets with arguments for separation from England. Signed only as "an Englishman," he advocated independence as the only logical line to pursue, as it would come eventually anyway and only be more difficult if delayed. (Paine wrote anonymously at first, as the punishment for such treason would undoubtedly entail death). Written in a style of English used every day by ordinary people, it was easy to read and accessible to a wide audience. Under the running title *Common Sense*, the series in name and text addressed what Paine described as arguments that all readers could and should understand.

The content spread quickly, with more than 100,000 copies read among the thirteen colonies' two million residents. Over the course of the Revolution, *Common Sense* sold more than 500,000 copies. Including unauthorized editions, the readers often passed copies around and read them aloud in taverns, contributing significantly to spreading the idea of republicanism. The text also encouraged recruitment for the Continental Army, and because of the outcome of what it recommended, Paine later took the title of "Father of the American Revolution."

Paine not only provided new and convincing arguments for independence in *Common Sense* by orienting readers to a future that compelled them to make an immediate choice, he offered a solution for Americans alarmed at the threat of tyranny. His attack on monarchy aimed precisely at King George III. Whereas colonials initially directed their resentments against the king's ministers and Parliament, Paine laid the responsibility firmly at the king's door.

Common Sense was the most widely read pamphlet of the American Revolution, as virtually every rebel either read or heard a reading of it, making it the all-time best-selling piece of its time. Written in a direct and lively style, it denounced European governments as decrepit and mocked monarchies as absurd, calling for opposition to the corrupt British legal system and for Americans to embrace their role as providers of liberty for refugees from around the world.

Regardless of the zeal and effectiveness of *Common Sense*, the rebels had suffered a disastrous first year of fighting, with hundreds of volunteers in the American forces having already deserted and another winter approaching. Paine, who was then serving

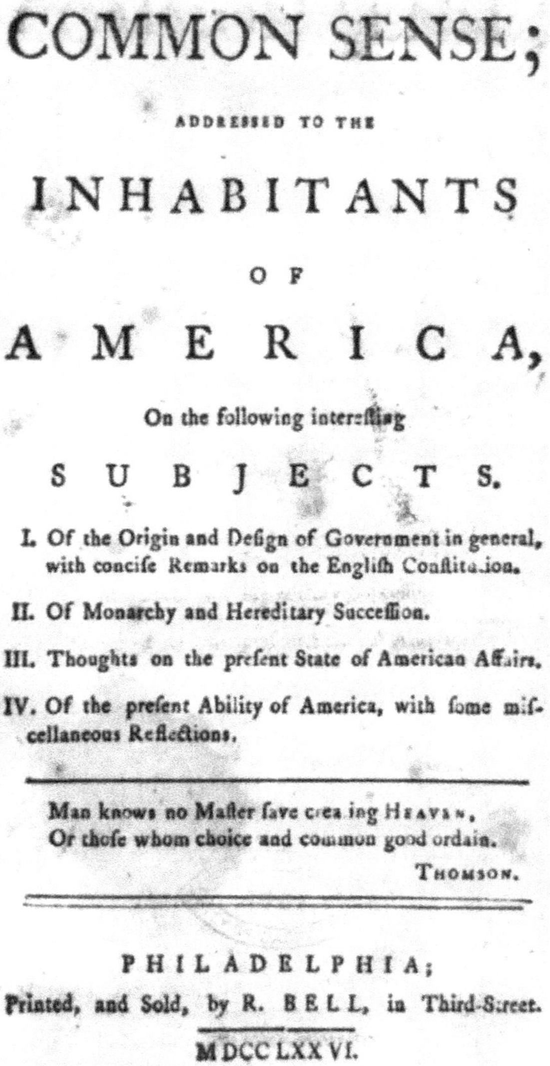

COMMON SENSE;

ADDRESSED TO THE

INHABITANTS

OF

AMERICA,

On the following intereſting

SUBJECTS.

I. Of the Origin and Deſign of Government in general, with conciſe Remarks on the Engliſh Conſtitution.

II. Of Monarchy and Hereditary Succeſſion.

III. Thoughts on the preſent State of American Affairs.

IV. Of the preſent Ability of America, with ſome miſcellaneous Reflections.

Man knows no Maſter ſave creating HEAVEN,
Or thoſe whom choice and common good ordain.

THOMSON.

PHILADELPHIA;
Printed, and Sold, by R. BELL, in Third-Street.
MDCCLXXVI.

Image 2.1: *"Common Sense; Addressed to the Inhabitants of America, on the Following Interesting Subjects,"* the title page from Thomas Paine's work, published in Philadelphia, printed and sold by R. Bell in 1776. The cover page identifies four parts of the subsequent text, which include, "the origin and design of government" . . . "monarchy and hereditary succession" . . . "thoughts on the present state of American affairs" . . . and "the present ability of America."[1]

with General Nathanael Greene as volunteer aide-de-camp, then embarked on the first installment in a series of influential tracts called *The American Crisis*.

In its first issue, December 23, 1776, Paine wrote famous words, which in contemporary terms we might call a "lead"—a lead, in this case, for the ages. "These are the times that try men's souls," Paine wrote. "The summer soldier and the sunshine patriot will, in this crisis, shrink from the service of their country; but he that stands by it now, deserves the love and thanks of man and woman." In this lead, Paine refers directly to the dire conditions facing the troops at Valley Forge, where brutal weather and a lack of material support had taken its toll. "Tyranny, like hell, is not easily conquered," Paine wrote, "yet we have this consolation with us, that the harder the conflict, the more glorious the triumph."

> What we obtain too cheap, we esteem too lightly: it is dearness only that gives every thing its value. Heaven knows how to put a proper price upon its goods; and it would be strange indeed if so celestial an article as FREEDOM should not be highly rated. Britain, with an army to enforce her tyranny, has declared that she has a right (not only to TAX) but "to BIND us in ALL CASES WHATSOEVER" and if being bound in that manner, is not slavery, then is there not such a thing as slavery upon earth. Even the expression is impious; for so unlimited a power can belong only to God.[2]

As demonstrated in this passage, one of Paine's greatest attributes was his ability to write in a style that everyday people, including soldiers, could appreciate. In this famous passage, along with many others, he rendered complex ideas intelligibly, with clear, concise writing unlike the formal style favored by many of his contemporaries, a contribution that initiated a public debate about independence previously muted by authorities.

AN ELEMENT OF STYLE

Thomas Paine's "lead" in *The American Crisis* reached such a wide audience that over the years, editors have deconstructed it to see if there might be any other ways to rewrite it, using grammar that follows conventional rules. Reading the first sentence, you will see that Paine uses a passive verb with no clear subject, an anathema to copy editors. However, in *The Elements of Style*, editors William Strunk and E. B. White concede that even basic rules sometimes have exceptions, as revising "These are the times that try men's souls" leads to unfortunate if not (ridiculous) results, such as:

- "Times like these try men's souls."
- "How trying it is to live in these times!"
- "These are trying times for men's souls."
- "Soulwise, these are trying times."[3]

The words "These are the times that try men's souls" and those that followed indeed had a dramatic effect on Paine's audience, and according to traditional accounts, the most tangible results emerged from the campfires of Valley Forge. Upon publication, George Washington gathered his troops on December 25, 1776, so that he could read to them the installment of *The American Crisis* published just days before. At first cold and demoralized, the troops found courage in Paine's words. They then launched boats in the middle of the night. Crossing the Delaware River, they surprised Hessian forces the next morning in Trenton, New Jersey. With subsequent rebel victories over the course of the next week, news of the initiative of Washington and his soldiers reached the colonists and in turn raised their spirits. Paine's work, it was said, provided the fuel necessary for demonstrating the Continental Army could defeat the British.

Image 2.2: "The End of Pain. The Last Speech, Dying Words, and Confession of TP/TO [Ovenden] Fecit," this 1793 print satirizes Thomas Paine's career, ending it ingloriously well before his actual death with an execution for treason.[4]

Eventually, the successes of the American rebels influenced the course of revolution in France. Thomas Paine moved to France and lived there for most of the 1790s, becoming deeply involved in the French Revolution. The French would adopt language in their Declaration of the Rights of Man that had similarities with the U.S. Declaration of Independence, drawing in many ways from the ideas popularized by Paine himself. Even though Americans initially lauded Paine for his help in securing independence from Britain, by the end of the bloody French Revolution, he lost favor with the American public for his ties to the tumultuous events, as well as his opposition to organized religion. In 1802, Paine returned to the United States, where he died on June 8, 1809. Only six people attended his funeral.

THE PRESS, THE DECLARATION, AND THE CONSTITUTION

The introductory paragraphs of the Declaration of Independence restate the principles of natural law to which many of the founders subscribed, establishing first the reasons for announcing a separation from England.

> When in the Course of human events it becomes necessary for one people to dissolve the political bands which have connected them with another and to assume among the powers of the earth, the separate and equal station to which the Laws of Nature and of Nature's God entitle them, a decent respect to the opinions of mankind requires that they should declare the causes which impel them to the separation.[5]

The language that follows uses sentiments popularized by Thomas Paine, and in some cases, even the same language he championed.

> We hold these truths to be self-evident, that all men are created equal, that they are endowed by their Creator with certain unalienable Rights, that among these are Life, Liberty, and the pursuit of Happiness. That to secure these rights, Governments are instituted among Men, deriving their just powers from the consent of the governed, That whenever any Form of Government becomes destructive of these ends, it is the Right of the People to alter or to abolish it, and to institute new Government, laying its foundation on such principles and organizing its powers in such form, as to them shall seem most likely to effect their Safety and Happiness.[6]

Prior to the ratification of the U.S. Constitution, the newly independent states attempted to hold together a loose form of nationalism under the Articles of Confederation. The form of government provided by the Articles had found inspiration in part from the writings of Thomas Paine, who in a 1776 issue of *Common Sense* had argued that "custom of nations" demanded a formal declaration of American independence if any European power were to mediate a peace between the Americans and Great Britain. The Articles, to which the colonies subscribed, agreed to a "perpetual Union," but they provided no form of central administration for the new government, leaving the ability of the new government to function at the hands of individual and sometimes conflicting interests.

As a remedy for the weaknesses of this new confederacy, advocates of a stronger central government advanced arguments for a federal system, which combined national, regional, and local units. The process of recruiting state-by-state support for this new Constitution required the efforts of advocates who used the press to make the case for a stronger Union. Chief proponents of Federalism, namely Alexander Hamilton, James Madison, and John Jay, published a series of seventy-seven articles in New York's the *Independent Journal* and the *New York Packet* between October 1787 and August 1788, explaining the benefits of the system.

Subsequent generations of political thinkers have consulted with these articles, later packaged under the title *The Federalist Papers*. The newspaper articles and essays, eighty-five of them originally, promoted ratification of the Constitution. Although not legal documents in and of themselves, scholars have compared the persuasiveness in which the authors make their arguments to Thomas Paine's writings as masterpieces of propaganda.

Ultimately, the arguments for a Union carried the day, but not without compromises made between states both large and small. After significant deliberation, the U.S. Constitution, which described how the different branches of this system would work, replaced the Articles as the document that proscribed subsequent functions of the federal system. The executive, legislative, and judicial branches of the new system would check the powers of each other to ensure liberty among the governed, and, of no small detail, a free press protected from government overreach would ensure a

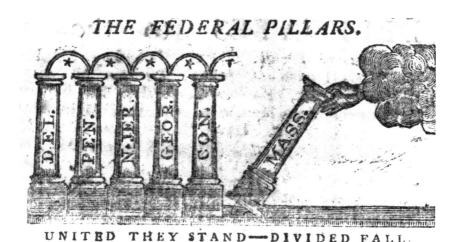

Image 2.3: A series of images under the title "The Federal Pillars" from the *Massachusetts Centinel*, January 16, June 11, and August 2, 1788, depicted adjacent columns, each labeled after a state and placed upright by a hand extending from a cloud. In this, the first print (January 16, 1788), titled "United they stand—divided fall," the Massachusetts column joins those of Delaware, Pennsylvania, New Jersey, Georgia, and Connecticut. A later version of this illustration, "Redeunt Saturnia Regna," or "the Kingdom of Saturn Returns," (June 11) shows the Maryland and South Carolina columns in place and the Virginia column raised into position, with the New Hampshire column reclining on the right. The final print (August 2) shows New Hampshire ahead of Virginia, New York in place, and the hand placing the North Carolina column into position.[8]

well-informed electorate would choose only the strongest representatives to serve the people as a whole.

A story about the formation of this system has passed down through the years. According to the anecdote, a woman saw printer extraordinaire Benjamin Franklin exiting the Constitutional Convention on September 17, 1787. She asked him, "What kind of government have you given us, Dr. Franklin?" He replied, "A republic, if you can keep it."[7]

Having gained support from larger states such as New York and Pennsylvania—in no small part from the publication of *The Federalist Papers*—the task of those developing the new federal system next needed to enlist the support of smaller states, especially those in the South. To this end, the Bill of Rights provided a list of freedoms that the government would ensure, with the freedom of the press among those most prominent.

With a rationale for the First Amendment (as well as the other amendments in the Bill of Rights) rooted deep in the concepts of natural law, James Madison's words explained how the founders thought of a free press as vital to the integrity of the republic. "A Popular government without information, or the means of acquiring it, is but a prologue to a farce or tragedy; or perhaps both," Madison wrote. "Knowledge will forever govern ignorance; and a people who mean to be their own governors must arm themselves with the power which knowledge gives."[9]

It can—and should—be noted that the First Amendment contains language directly protecting the professional activities of a certain group of individuals, and nowhere else in the founding documents will you find such a guarantee for a particular occupation. With this perspective, both contemporary practitioners of journalism, as well as press historians, can appreciate the unique role the press has had in maintaining the American political system. Reading the First Amendment again—and in context—should give both students of press history and members of the Fourth Estate an understanding of the unique and vital qualities of their endeavors. "Congress shall make no law respecting an establishment of religion, or prohibiting the free exercise thereof; or abridging the freedom of speech, or of the press; or the right of the people peaceably to assemble, and to petition the Government for a redress of grievances."[10]

THE PARTISAN PRESS AND THE ALIEN AND SEDITION ACTS

George Washington, the first president to serve under this newly formed federal system, has received credit for (among his other remarkable accomplishments) maintaining a non-partisan style of administration, opposing political parties even before he voluntarily stepped down from office. However, with the election of his vice president, John Adams, to the presidency, a coinciding era known as "The Dark Ages of American Journalism"—or, the era of the partisan press—emerged and, at the very least, complicated the role of the press in subsequent American history.

Two members of Washington's cabinet—Alexander Hamilton, Treasury Secretary, and Thomas Jefferson, Secretary of State—provided competing—if not oppositional—models for organizing the government, and both of them (and their followers) understood that the stakes in this competition entailed none other than the future of the country. Hamilton and Jefferson both financed newspapers as a way to persuade new followers to support each respective party: Hamiltonians allied with the Federalists, while Jeffersonians allied with Republicans. In very broad and general terms, the Federalists advocated a system of government that revolved around a strong, central administration, while the Republicans advocated decentralization and the maximization of individual liberties.

Accordingly, each faction had their own mouthpiece, which at the time consisted of a dominant newspaper—for Hamilton and the Federalists, this newspaper was the *National Gazette*, and for Jefferson and the Republicans, it was the *Gazette of the United States*. While contributing writers and those with financial interests influenced the content of each newspaper, two editors played major roles in the material published: for the Federalists, John Fenno; and for the Republicans, Philip Freneau.

The "dark" part of the era (as historian Frank Luther Mott first dubbed it "The Dark Ages of American Journalism") emerged from the intense competition between the two opposing political newspapers.[11] Readers could find content from either the Federalist perspective or the Republican perspective, with little else in-between, as many newspapers in the middle (or what we might call "moderate") just closed, either because they had no audience or because they were destroyed by the larger competing partisan newspapers, which were generally more well-funded via government contracts.

The partisan newspapers often contained vitriolic attacks on members of the opposition, as the way to win public support at the time (in a way that likely sounds familiar to audiences of our own era) was to destroy the reputation of the one and only other option available for those interested in participating in the electoral system.

Image 2.4: "D—n, d—n, the Author & Publisher I Say!" an engraving in *The Echo with other Poems*, published in New York, 1807, shows a man (likely a political figure) rising from a barber's chair and cursing after he reads an inflammatory article in the newspaper. Such a reaction might have accompanied the typical content of newspapers during the era, which often resorted to personal attacks as a way of silencing partisans who opposed one another. The victims of these attacks sometimes even resorted to violence as a way of finding satisfaction for injured reputations.[12]

Another reason for the name "dark ages" stemmed from the fact that we simply know very little about the attitudes and values of the common audience at the time, as the news depicted in the partisan newspapers rarely reflected the interests of anyone outside the ruling class. From a partisan standpoint, the stakes were indeed very high during this period, and in the minds of Hamilton and Jefferson, the press would help determine what kind of system the American people of subsequent generations would live under. Would the United States function with a strong central government determining the role of intrastate commerce? Or would individuals more closely determine the rights afforded to participating members of this new republic?

At least for the moment, both sides agreed that the new government should facilitate a robust press. Since Washington, partisans had thrived with the understanding that news was crucial for an informed electorate and helped to pass the Post Office Act of 1792, which distributed newspapers to subscribers for 1 penny up to 100 miles and 1.5 cents over 100 miles. Under this legislation, printers could send their newspapers to other newspaper publishers at no cost, while postage for letters, by contrast, cost between 6 and 25 cents depending on distance. The postmaster, an important and powerful federal position, could decide how much postage would apply to printed news circulated throughout the nation. (The growth in the number of post offices alone demonstrates the importance of this legislation: In 1788, less than 100 post offices connected the national mail routing system, but by 1800, this number grew to almost 1,000, and twenty years later to 4,500).

Of special note, The Post Office Act of 1792 marked an important moment in the way citizens thought about the government's relationship to the press, where subsidies for the delivery of magazines helped a free press flourish. It also colored contemporary debates about the relationship between the government and the press, where citizens' freedom for a free and diverse press legitimated the subsidy. In subsequent years, this perspective changed, as citizens tended to see a free press as necessarily free from government ties; while today, we often think of the First Amendment as restricting government control over speech, the Post Office Act showed the government has power to shape the arenas in which speech happens.

At the same time, competition between partisan forces via the free circulation of information helped to form the system of two-party competition under which the United States still operates today. Other men, most notably James Madison and John Adams, also contributed to the formation of political parties, but Hamilton and Jefferson came to represent the divisions that shaped the early national political landscape. Although both men had been active in the Revolutionary effort and in the founding of the United States, Hamilton and Jefferson did not work together until Washington appointed Hamilton the first Secretary of the Treasury and Jefferson the first Secretary of State. From the beginning, the two men harbored opposing visions of the nation's path. While Jefferson believed that America's success lay in its agrarian tradition, Hamilton promoted industry and commerce. While Jefferson placed his trust in the people as governors, Hamilton believed that the federal government should wield considerable power in order to steer a successful course for the nation. Perhaps because of their differences of opinion, Washington made these men his closest advisors.

In time, these different political visions transformed under the names of different political parties (in the 1830s, the Federalists reorganized as Whigs and the Republicans took the title of Democrats, and shortly before the Civil War, the Whigs took the name Republicans). By 1804, despite President Washington's early efforts to develop national unity, political differences proved too deep to promote consensus, and the advent of political parties necessitated a constitutional amendment that changed the electoral process to allow presidential and cice presidential tickets on ballots.

As opposing factions began aligning with either Alexander Hamilton or Thomas Jefferson during their service as cabinet members in President Washington's administration, political newspapers took on new levels of importance. The three-column folio printed by Fenno had a role as the mouthpiece for the government, and it in turn received contributions and assistance from prominent Federalists such as John Adams. Hamilton used the *Gazette of the United States* in a variety of manners, publishing content under various pseudonyms and rescuing the editor from bankruptcy in 1793 by raising thousands of dollars to pay off creditors.

Hamilton advocated expansion in both the physical size of the United States and in the power of the federal government. To popularize these ideals, he had Fenno publish content that supported the administration of John Adams. The *Gazette of the United States* had a relatively more sophisticated tone than the average of its contemporaries, and Fenno served the Federalists well through its columns, although the circulation never exceeded 1,400. Copies circulated to major cities where other Federalist newspapers freely copied the news and editorials.

JOHN FENNO

John Fenno was born on August 12, 1751, in Boston, Massachusetts, and became known as the creator of the first national political newspaper. His career started at the *Massachusetts Centinel* with Benjamin Russell as his editor. Fenno's work impressed many leaders, and he approached other Federalist leaders about starting a paper in the nation's capital. On April 15, 1789, shortly before George Washington took the presidential oath of office, the first issue of the *Gazette of the United States* came off the press in New York. Fenno opened the newspaper to contributions from influential partisans, including John Adams and Alexander Hamilton, allowing them to write political essays. In turn, Alexander Hamilton, both a Federalist and the Treasury Secretary, made sure Fenno received printing jobs with the government. The *Gazette of the United States* began printing from Philadelphia in 1790 when the federal government made its capital there. Newspapers such as the *Gazette of the United States* became increasingly important, and Fenno's paper became associated with official government news. As the paper grew in reputation, Fenno battled with adversaries such as Philip Freneau, editor of the *National Gazette* and Benjamin Franklin Bache's *Philadelphia Aurora* for influence on political agendas. Fenno had an impact even after his death on September 14, 1798, as his 19-year-old son took over the paper in 1800 until it closed operations in 1818.

On April 11, 1789, in the same month George Washington began his presidency, Fenno founded the *Gazette of the United States* in New York City. The following year, the paper moved operations to the capital in Philadelphia and soon became a focal point of contestation from Jefferson's Republicans. In the long and often bitter debates that ensued, the *Gazette of the United States* assumed the role of the mouthpiece for Federalism, and Fenno became an important printer of political works. Alexander Hamilton was a frequent contributor, and in 1793, he personally helped keep the newspaper financially solvent.

Thomas Jefferson, meanwhile, used the *National Gazette*, edited by Philip Freneau, to promote the more limited scope of powers advocated by the Republican (or Anti-Federalist) partisans. In 1790, Freneau assisted in editing the *New York Daily Advertiser*, and soon after, James Madison and Secretary of State Thomas Jefferson worked to get Freneau to move to Philadelphia in order to edit a partisan newspaper that would counter the Federalists' *Gazette of the United States*.

Jefferson and Freneau, in trying to limit the power of Adams' administration, enlisted the support of firebrand publisher Benjamin F. Bache and his *Philadelphia Aurora*, which often took great pains to challenge President John Adams directly with some of the most scathing language of the partisan press era. Freneau, for his part, advocated against what he saw as the monarchist tendencies of the Adams presidency, and for his efforts, Freneau received praise as "the poet of the Revolution" for vitalizing ideas advanced first by none other than Adams himself.

PHILIP FRENEAU

Philip Freneau was born on January 2, 1752, in New York, New York. His father, a wine merchant, died in 1767, leaving an enormous financial debt to his family. However, through several connections he maintained through his father, Philip managed to pay for his education. In 1768, he attended Princeton University, a decision that would end up being pivotal to his poetic and Revolutionary success. His roommate at Princeton was none other than James Madison, who later went on to become the fourth president of the United States. The two became very close, forming a bond over politics and literature alike. Freneau took a deep interest in public writing but went through a phase where he questioned the direction of his future. He received his degree in 1771. With distaste for teaching and a lack of desire to continue studying, he began to divulge in what he felt was public service through patriotism. The Revolutionary War was approaching in 1775, and Freneau wrote unabashedly anti-British sentiments, composing pieces that blended serious content with satire and poetry. In 1778, he dabbled in the militia and became a sea captain, sailing the Atlantic. On a seafaring trip, the British captured him and held him on a prison ship for six weeks. After almost dying, he escaped and used his frustrations to write a piece of literature titled *The British Prison Ship*. Freneau inspired and prompted many others to write political satires and patriotic literature that fueled anti-British feelings through

America. He married Eleanor Forman in 1790 and held a brief role as an assistant editor at the *New York Daily Advisor*. Soon after taking the job, James Madison called on his former roommate for a favor. Along with Thomas Jefferson, Madison wanted Freneau to move to Philadelphia and start the *National Gazette*, which would express the partisan positions of the Republicans that had formed after the founding of the new nation.

Jefferson's critics jumped at the chance to criticize him for hiring Freneau to translate for the State Department, even though Freneau spoke no foreign languages except French, which Jefferson already spoke fluently. Freneau accepted this undemanding position, which left free time to head the Democratic-Republican newspaper Jefferson and Madison envisioned. This partisan newspaper, the *National Gazette*, provided a vehicle for Jefferson, Madison, and others to promote criticism of the rival Federalists. the *National Gazette* took particular aim at the policies promoted by Alexander Hamilton and, like other papers of the day, would not hesitate to shade into personal attacks.

Indicative of the intensity at the time, these editors (as did others) often spared no attacks, whether in ink or with physical blows. As a highly visible Federalist representative, Fenno at one point in the 1790s engaged in verbal disputes that led to fisticuffs with Benjamin Bache, who as editor of the *Philadelphia Aurora* and in alliance with Freneau had suggested the Federalists had grown to represent the interests of the elite. Fenno charged Bache with being in the pay of France, and Bache retorted that Fenno had sold out to the British. The next day the two editors met on Fourth Street. Fenno attacked Bache, and Bache in turn hit Fenno over the head with a cane. True to the volatile and sometimes hostile nature of the era, Hamilton in a separate incident met an infamous end when in July 1804 he died from a gunshot wound in a duel over partisan differences.

Beyond the personal rivalries of individual members of the press, a problematic part of the political climate of the time affected the freedom of the press as a whole. The Alien and Sedition Acts, a package of legislation enacted in 1798, remains the most controversial aspect of Adams' presidency and indeed a problematic part of his legacy to this day. Adams sought to quell insurrectionary violence in the United States that representatives in the new republic feared might erupt in the mayhem of the French Revolution—the Acts passed by Congress sought to stabilize the political climate at home, but through measures that silenced criticism of the administration.

With the French Revolution in full throes, colonists from all over Europe and especially France had fled to the newly established United States as a safe haven. Congress at the time intensely deliberated on how to control the influx of French immigrants in particular, who were perceived as a potential threat. Over the span of a decade, the French Revolution had descended into mob-led executions, and in the eyes of Americans, refugees seeking safety could easily be confused with purveyors of terror. While the Federalists argued the legislation was to quell the possible outbreak of violence in the United States, Republicans saw the measures as just as much of an attempt to quell opposition to the Federalist Party.

As part of the attempts to control immigration, the Naturalization Act, which Adams signed June 18, 1798, made it harder to gain citizenship, extending the period of residency necessary for becoming a citizen from five to fourteen years. The Alien Act allowed for the deportation of people over the age of 14 who threatened United States territory. For publishers, the most pressing part of the legislation—the Sedition Act—allowed the government to prosecute publishers who printed "false, scandalous and malicious writing" against officials, punishing editors who encouraged "insurrection, riot, unlawful assembly, or combination" with jail sentences of five years or fines of $5,000.

President Adams argued that the measures would keep the United States out of a war with France. He succeeded in maintaining peace, but at the same time, the measures contradicted the freedoms he had advocated just prior to the establishment of the Constitution.

While Jefferson acknowledged the dangers of the press in spreading falsehoods, he also believed, like Madison, that without the free flow of ideas, the citizenry would be doomed to despotism, having written Virginia soldier and jurist Edward Carrington shortly before the adoption of the First Amendment on the subject.

> The people are the only censors of their governors: and even their errors will tend to keep these to the true principles of their institution. To punish these errors too severely would be to suppress the only safeguard of the public liberty. The way to prevent these irregular interpositions of the people is to give them full information of their affairs thro' the channel of the public papers, and to contrive that those papers should penetrate the whole mass of the people. The basis of our governments being the opinion of the people, the very first object should be to keep that right; and were it left to me to decide whether we should have a government without newspapers, or newspapers without a government, I should not hesitate a moment to prefer the latter.[13]

In another one of his many statements on the issue of press freedom, Jefferson also said quite simply, "Where the press is free, and every man able to read," he wrote, "all is safe."[14]

The press at the time was in fact not free, with an estimated twenty-five arrests under the Sedition Act and ten eventual convictions. Among those charged, Benjamin Franklin Bache, editor of the *Philadelphia Aurora* and grandson of Benjamin Franklin, was found to have libeled the executive government. He had, according to the trial, excited sedition and opposition to the law by referring to the president in April 1798, for instance, as "old, querulous, Bald, blind, crippled, Toothless Adams." John Adams' wife Abigail, who essentially assumed the role of the nation's first press secretary, made a ritual of reading to the president the attacks from the press upon him. While the partisanship that had emerged since Adams' days in the Continental Congress alarmed him, Abigail's protestations likely motivated at least in a small part the president's attempts to control what was seen as seditious libel in the press at the time.

The arrest of Bache, among others, brought a public outcry against the Alien and Sedition Acts and contributed to the election in 1800 of Republican Thomas Jefferson. Jefferson pardoned all those convicted under the Sedition Act and Congress restored all fines paid with interest. Jefferson understood that even if Adams had intended to hear the voice of the people through their elected officials—and even if the Alien and Sedition Acts had passed Congress following protocol—freedom suffered. When Jefferson assumed the presidency immediately after Adams, he pardoned several of those convicted in the previous administration.

The Supreme Court would later describe the result of federal measures to curtail free speech as imposing a "chilling effect" on the exercise of the free press and of free speech. Publishers, editors, and individual citizens living under the Alien and Sedition Acts often feared speaking their minds, contrary to what the founders had intended in ratifying the First Amendment.

LEAVING "THE DARK AGES OF AMERICAN JOURNALISM"

Despite their bitter rivalries during their respective presidencies, Adams and Jefferson shared the same fundamental beliefs in the purpose of the American Revolution, which began an experiment in government that long outlived both men. The circumstances surrounding their deaths reveal a testament to their shared beliefs. After mending differences and corresponding as friends for the following decades, they both passed away on the same day, July 4, 1826, exactly fifty years after the issuing of the Declaration of Independence.

During the ensuing era, under what political scientists and historians call the nation's Second Party System (also known as "The Age of Jackson" after President Andrew Jackson), politicians coopted the press to reach the "common man." Likewise, the press expanded content to reach a wider audience, whether for commercial purposes, political, or both. This Second Party System, which dated roughly from the 1830s to the 1850s, consisted of Whigs (former Federalists) and Democrats (former Republicans and Anti-Federalists).

The press of this time transformed commensurately, using new reporting styles and new technologies that in many cases reached beyond the abilities of the old political order to control. An anecdote from the journal of Alexander Boloni Farkas sets the scene: While traveling through the United States in the 1830s, the Transylvanian reformer marveled as the stagecoach driver hurled out settlers' newspapers right and left as they passed remote cabins along the road through the whole day's travel. "No matter how poor a settler may be, nor how far in the wilderness he may be from the civilized world," Farkas concluded, "he will read a newspaper."[15]

RECAPPING THIS CHAPTER

Looking back on this chapter, you should see a focus on the role of the press in popularizing ideas articulated in the founding documents of the nation. The chapter showed how the work of Thomas Paine affected the new nation and how the press slipped into an era sometimes called "The Dark Ages of American Journalism" in which the Alien and Sedition Acts played a role in stifling First Amendment rights.

Using content from the preceding pages, you should be able to describe how the rights to life, liberty, and the pursuit of happiness came to be cornerstones of the American experience. You should also see how enduring political tensions and press partisanship had their antecedents in the debates that raged following the Revolution.

The following chapter describes the penny newspapers of New York in the 1830s as a democratizing agent, explaining how sensational content contributed to sales and expanded readership. It profiles leading editors of the penny press era as instrumental in building long-standing notions about citizen involvement in government and the developing economy. It also describes how the new sales model of low-priced newspapers, combined with high circulation and a reliance on advertising to help produce mass movements and political formations during the era.

NOTES

1. *"Common Sense,"* Library of Congress, accessed November 19, 2016, <item/2006681076>.
2. Thomas Paine, *The Crisis*, No. 1, December 23, 1776; Paine, *Collected Writings* (New York: Library of America, 1955), 91.
3. William Strunk, Jr., and E. B. White, *The Elements of Style* (New York: MacMillan, 1972), 60.
4. "The End of Pain," Library of Congress, accessed November 19, 2016, <item/93502766>.
5. *U.S. Declaration of Independence* (1776), paragraph 1.
6. *U.S. Declaration of Independence* (1776), paragraph 2.
7. "Papers of Dr. James McHenry on the Federal Convention of 1787," in Charles C. Tansill, comp. *Documents Illustrative of the Formation of the Union of the American States* (Washington, DC: U.S. Printing Office, 1927), 952.
8. "The Federal Pillars," Library of Congress, accessed November 19, 2016, <item/2004676796>.
9. James Madison to W. T. Barry, August 4, 1822, *The Writings of James Madison*, Gaillard Hunt (ed.), 9 vols. (New York: G. P. Putnam's Sons, 1900–1910), 9: 103–9.
10. U.S. Constitution, Amendment 1.
11. Frank Luther Mott, *American Journalism: A History of Newspapers* (New York: Macmillan, 1941), 167–80.
12. "D—n, d—n, the Author & Publisher I Say!" Library of Congress, accessed November 19, 2016, <item/2002705940>.
13. Jefferson to Edward Carrington, January 16, 1787, *The Jefferson Papers*, 11: 48–9.
14. Jefferson to Charles Yancey, January 6, 1816, *The Writings of Thomas Jefferson* (Washington, DC: Memorial Edition, 1903–04), 14: 384.
15. Sándor Bölöni Farkas, *Journey in North America* (Philadelphia: American Philosophical Society, 1977), in Jeffrey L. Pasley, *The Tyranny of Printers: Newspaper Politics in the Early American Republic* (Virginia: The University Press of Virginia, 2001), 8.

3

THE PENNY PRESS

SENSATIONALISM, POPULISM, AND PROGRESS

This chapter describes the penny newspapers of New York in the 1830s as a democratizing agent, explaining how sensational content contributed to sales and expanded readership:

- It profiles leading editors of the penny press era as instrumental in building long-standing notions about citizen involvement in government and the developing economy;
- and it also describes how the new sales model of low-priced newspapers combined with high circulation and a reliance on advertising would in addition combine with mass movements and political formations during the era.

Using materials from this chapter, students should be able to interpret how individual personalities helped contribute to the development of what became the modern press:

- They should also be able to identify the particular publishing strategies of the major penny press newspapers;
- and they should be able to explain how sensationalism to this day plays a role (for better or worse) in raising the interest levels of news audiences.

Key words, names, and phrases associated with Chapter 3 include:

- Horatio David Shepard and hotcakes;
- The *New York Sun* (Benjamin Day), the *New York Herald* (James Gordon Bennett), the *New York Tribune* (Horace Greeley);

- Margaret Fuller and the Seneca Falls Convention;
- and *The Liberator* (William Lloyd Garrison) and Frederick Douglass' *Narrative of the Life of Frederick Douglass, an American Slave.*

Having emerged from the partisan press era and restrictions under the Alien and Sedition Acts, the press in the United States maintained a check on the power of the federal government. A new system of publishing and a new political order took hold, ones that would more closely represent popular interests over political ones. While the American Revolution and the press had not only shared roles in the direction of the United States, their dual roles had an effect that reached Europe and eventually wide-ranging areas of the world. Likewise, the French Revolution that erupted in the final decade of the eighteenth century in turn would have a reflexive effect on the development of the American press, sending reverberations globally.

French society had before the revolution organized along an understanding of three Estates—the Clergy, Nobility, and People. With the emerging ideals of a republic, the new governments of both the United States and the French Republic developed an appreciation for the press as an independent agent. French in concept, the phrase still associated with the press in this context—the Fourth Estate—represents both in the United States and abroad the function of an agent that seeks to represent the interests of the public. In this model, members of the press alert the public (akin to a watchdog) to excesses or abuses by the government.

As part of this transatlantic development, American efforts to vitalize a free press gained the attention of Europe. When French writer and politician Alexis de Tocqueville traveled to the United States in 1831 to write *Democracy in America*, he described an abundance of newspapers circulating throughout the United States and told readers that at least part of the reason for the success of the young American government came from a well-read electorate. If Europeans were to secure republican forms of government, de Tocqueville believed they should follow the words of James Madison and "arm themselves with the power which knowledge gives."[1]

"When once the Americans have taken up an idea, whether it be well or ill founded, nothing is more difficult than to eradicate it from their minds," de Tocqueville wrote.

> I attribute this to a cause that may at first sight appear to have an opposite tendency: namely, to the liberty of the press. The nations among whom this liberty exists cling to their opinions as much from pride as from conviction. They cherish them because they hold them to be just and because they chose them of their own free will; and they adhere to them, not only because they are true, but because they are their own.[2]

SELLING NEWS LIKE HOTCAKES

The sales and business model that most clearly defined the press during the Age of Jackson has been called the penny press for the simple reason that newspapers increasingly lowered their prices, oftentimes selling for as little as one cent. While this trend was a national one, for the purposes of this chapter three New York newspapers in particular—the *Sun*, the *Herald*, and the *Tribune*—illustrate the contents and marketing strategies of publishers at the time. While each of these newspapers and other penny press newspapers throughout the nation had their own unique approach to targeting particular audiences, they all shared a motivation to reach as many readers as possible, regardless of political affiliations, putting them in contrast with the partisan newspapers of the preceding era. While the content of each newspaper sometimes enlightened and educated these large groups of readers, they more commonly entertained them, grabbing the attention of subscribers and advertisers with sensational stories of scandal, sex, and crime.

In a number of ways, the ingredients of the penny press newspapers set the template for subsequent waves of sensationalism that we still see today—a strategy that indeed entertains but, perhaps more importantly from a business standpoint, attracts the advertising dollars necessary to sustain operations. In the early 1830s, Horatio David Sheppard launched this new model of newspaper content and sales. We do not often hear Sheppard's name in association with the history of the press, as he was not a journalist at the time, but a medical student in New York City. He made observations of other New Yorkers on their way to work who, in a hurry, would buy hotcakes and other small, morning food items from street vendors. The items were generally inexpensive, only a penny, and usually in high demand.

Sheppard realized that the street vendors, often very young, could turn a profit on these items because of the large volumes sold. The demand for the items came from the spicy ingredients they included, which tantalized the senses (hence the saying "sell like hotcakes"). In deducing that other items might sell with comparable ingredients, Sheppard decided to propose to publishers a similar arrangement with newspapers—each copy would be priced low with sensational (or "spicy") content, a formula more attractive to mass readership than the well-established expensive partisan papers at the time.

While no publisher could turn a profit on low prices and spicy ingredients alone, the driving force behind penny press sales came from advertising. The increased circulation attracted advertisers on an unprecedented scale, as more readers would encounter and subsequently buy commercial products. In turn, publishers could lower their advertising rates, increase the volume of ads, and make more money than ever before. The scheme was ingenious, but the transformation in the publishing industry took time, and, as the following penny press experiments reveal, quite a bit of trial and error went into the formative years of the penny press.

Horatio David Sheppard approached publishers with his idea at first with little success, but in 1833, his luck changed after convincing Benjamin Day to launch a penny paper. Day was a publisher who soon thereafter grew in reputation as one of the most influential innovators in press history. Along with the penny press model proposed by

Sheppard, Day introduced in the *New York Sun* several reorganizational techniques that have endured into the twenty-first century. He developed a hierarchy for his staff. In the partisan press era, a publisher and a printer more or less controlled the majority of content. However, Day understood the need for specialization if readers were to engage in content that went beyond the ordinary political machinations of the partisan press. Now a common practice, Day was the first to institute a workflow system that consisted of a managing editor and beat reporters. He hired one such reporter, George Wisner, to write a column of brief "Police Office" items, making Wisner the first American police reporter.

BENJAMIN DAY

Benjamin Henry Day was born in Springfield, Massachusetts, April 10, 1810. He started his news career in 1824 as a printer's apprentice of the *Springfield Republican* and later moved to New York City. He saved enough money to start his own printing business, which nearly failed when the cholera epidemic of 1832 sent a panic through the city. In efforts to salvage his business, he decided to start the *New York Sun*. To build circulation, Day emphasized the human side of the news, stressing crime and sensation but including elements of pathos and humor all at an affordable rate so that all New Yorkers, including immigrants, could afford the news. Having sold the *Sun* in 1838 for $40,000, Day launched in 1840 the *True Sun*, another penny paper. In 1842, Day created the *Brother Jonathan*, the first illustrated weekly in the United States. He also imported to the United States a system known as the London Plan, a method of newspaper distribution in which paper carriers bought newspapers in bulk from the publisher and sold them to the reading public for a profit. By the 1860s, Day had retired and lived on his investments. Despite his relatively short tenure in the American newspaper business, he triggered a revolution in the newspaper industry by marketing to a mass audience. He died in New York City on December 21, 1889, at the age of 79.

Regardless of these innovations and the efforts at the *Sun* to make it a sustainable newspaper, it at first struggled for reasons Day had not anticipated. In a common practice that dated back to the exchange papers of colonial times, newspapers often cannibalized each other, using content from other publishers without attribution. While the *Sun* had labored to develop original content, it lacked an audience, as potential readers usually found the *Sun*'s content in well-established newspapers and simply stayed with the familiar and trusted names in the industry.

In order to combat the larger and more expensive newspapers that were essentially stealing the work of his writers, readers, and advertisers, Day resorted to an extreme tactic that paid dividends, printing what would become known as the most spectacular hoax in news history. In August 1835, the *Sun* featured a series of articles detailing the alleged discovery of life on the moon. The first installment of the moon hoax appeared

Image 3.1: "Lunar Animals and Other Objects Discovered by Sir John Herschel in His Observatory at the Cape of Good Hope and Copied from Sketches in the *Edinburgh Journal of Science*," published August 29, 1835, a print showing an illustration for the *New York Sun* relating to the Great Moon Hoax with human-bat creatures, unicorns, and other imaginary figures on the moon.[3]

in the August 25, 1835, edition of the *Sun* on page two, under the heading "Celestial Discoveries." A brief initial passage read:

> We have just learnt (sic) from an eminent publisher in this city that Sir John Herschel at the Cape of Good Hope has made some astronomical discoveries of the most wonderful description, by means of an immense telescope of an entirely new principle.

In fact, Herschel had set up an observatory in Cape Town, South Africa, in January 1834. Three columns of the first page of the *Sun* contained a story credited to the *Edinburgh Journal of Science*. (The *Sun* withheld the fact that the *Journal* had already suspended publication well before the pseudo-story broke). "We counted three parties of these creatures, of twelve, nine, and fifteen in each, walking erect towards a small wood," the account continued. "Certainly, they were like human beings, for their wings had now disappeared and their attitude in walking was both erect and dignified."

> About half of the first party had passed beyond our canvas; but of all the others, we had perfectly distinct and deliberate view. They averaged four feet in height, were covered, except on the face, with short and glossy copper-colored hair, and had wings composed of a thin membrane, without hair, lying snugly upon their backs from the top of the shoulders to the calves of their legs. The face, which was of a yellowish color, was an improvement upon that of the large orangutan, so much so that but for their long wings they would look as well on a parade ground as some of the old cockney militia.[4]

So fascinating were the descriptions of trees and vegetation, oceans and beaches, bison and goats, cranes and pelicans that people on the streets of New York buzzed with the news even before the fourth installment appeared on August 28, 1835, with the discovery of furry, winged men resembling bats. The accounts continued in "Great Astronomical Discoveries."

> The hair of the head was a darker color than that of the body, closely curled but apparently not woolly, and arranged in two circles over the temples of the forehead. Their feet could only be seen as they were alternately lifted in walking; but from what we could see of them in so transient a view, they appeared thin and very protuberant at the heel. Whilst passing across the canvas, and whenever we afterwards saw them, these creatures were evidently engaged in conversation; their gesticulation, more particularly the varied action of their hands and arms, appeared impassioned and emphatic. We hence inferred that they were rational beings, and, although not perhaps of so high an order as others which we discovered the next month on the shores of the Bay of Rainbows, that they were capable of producing works of art and contrivance. . . .
>
> We could perceive that their wings possessed great expansion and were similar in structure of those of the bat, being a semitransparent membrane expanded in curvilinear divisions by means of straight radii, united at the back by dorsal integuments. But what astonished us most was the circumstance of this membrane being continued from the shoulders to the legs, united all the way down, though gradually decreasing in width. The wings seemed completely under the command of volition, for those of the creatures whom we saw bathing in the water spread them instantly to their full width, waved them as ducks do theirs to shake off the water, and then as instantly closed them again in a compact form.[5]

As was anticipated in the *Sun*'s office, the public reacted enthusiastically to the news, which at the time was plausible. Even more remarkably, while sales of the *Sun* began to soar, larger newspapers took notice, and as Day had likely anticipated, they began to republish the information, as they had in countless instances before, without attribution and without verifying the basic truthfulness of the story.

Eventually word spread that the story was a hoax; however, the most compelling subsequent story that ensued made the well-established papers lose credibility for stealing the *Sun*'s material without checking—the more expensive papers lost readers, while advertisers grew increasingly drawn to the idea of reaching readers through the penny press. Even though Day never directly confessed to actively deceiving his readers, they vindicated him with appreciation for providing entertainment in its own right. Rather than taking offense or seeing scandal in the story, readers accepted Day's approach to diverting the public's attention from the economic hardships of the day. Showman P. T. Barnum even called it "the most stupendous scientific imposition upon the public that the generation with which we are numbered has known."[6]

As sensationalism surrounding the moon hoax ended, the *Sun* in the end possessed the largest circulation of any newspaper in the world at nearly 20,000 copies. In subsequent years, other innovations advanced the distribution of penny press papers, including the use of steamships, trains, horses, and carrier pigeons to deliver information more quickly. Day had to fight, using tactics that no responsible publisher should practice, but in the end, he paved the way for successful newspapers for decades to come.

THE COMMERCIALIZATION OF CONTENT

Following the example set by Benjamin Day's *New York Sun*, Scottish immigrant James Gordon Bennett launched an even more financially successful penny press newspaper in 1835. Bennett modeled the *New York Herald* after the pricing and advertising scheme established by Day, taking content to the next level by providing extensive coverage of sensational and entertaining news, as contrasted with the typically political and national news of the larger papers that still dominated the news industry.

Bennett introduced several lasting innovations in journalism, such as publishing the closing prices of stocks traded each day on the New York Stock Exchange, hiring reporters to cover stories ahead of his competitors, and utilizing a wide range of available communication and technological resources to meet deadlines. He used small boats in the Atlantic to intercept the steamships crossing with news and used the telegraph extensively for news coverage. He established correspondents in Europe, introduced a society column, and insisted on changing advertisements frequently to boost consumer sales that in turn profited the newspaper sales. Bennett's newspaper succeeded in part also because it maintained a measure of political independence, allowing him to target political figures of all persuasions.

JAMES GORDON BENNETT

James Gordon Bennett, Sr., publisher and founder of the *New York Herald*, was born in Scotland, September 1, 1795. In 1823, he made his way to New York City, initially working as a freelance writer and assistant editor for the *New York Courier and Enquirer*. In May 1835, he launched the *Herald*, which became a prominent newspaper after publication of sensational stories, including the noteworthy coverage of a murder in New York City involving prostitute Helen Jewett. Adapting the successes of the *New York Sun*, a predecessor in the penny press industry, the *Herald* contributed to the development of the press by establishing correspondents in Europe and also initiated a cash-in-advance policy for advertisers, which became the industry standard. From mid-century into the 1880s, the *Herald* maintained the highest circulation in America. Bennett knew members of the public might purchase only one newspaper a day, and that they would naturally choose the paper that was the first with the news, so he took efforts to break news stories before rivals, a practice that became a standard goal in the industry. After Bennett's death, on June 1, 1872, his son James Gordon Bennett, Jr., ran the *Herald*, which continued as a successful operation into the twentieth century.

Bennett used shrewd tactics in reaching readers who by the 1830s had taken more interest in local stories than the politics of Washington, D.C. These readers, mostly working class or of low economic means, took a measure of delight in seeing the wealthy endure misfortune.

To meet this demand for scandal, Bennett had no qualms about publishing bankruptcy reports—the rich at the time would have considered it shameful for the public to know about economic failures, but Bennett's audience was not wealthy. Likewise, his

Image 3.2: "One of the News-B'hoys," *Sketches of N. York*, No. 18 (New York: T. W. Strong, 1847), a lithograph by Sarony & Major showing a newsboy in tattered clothing selling newspapers as two men fight in front of the offices of the *New York Herald*.[7]

readers gobbled up details about the upper class' private lives, which Bennett exposed with outlandish reporting techniques. He had a history of attending parties uninvited in New York's wealthier areas, disguised as a distinguished guest to eavesdrop on the conversations of partygoers. With exclusive stories that appeared in the *Herald* on following days, the primary audience of course relished in the juicy scoops while the elites of the city read in shock the details of private lives—both of their associates and their own.

Bennett's consistent attacks on the rich, combined with the *Herald*'s use of street vernacular in its text, eventually attracted attention in the form of backlash. New York City's rich refused to support the *Herald* with advertising or purchases, and Bennett himself became the target of physical attacks—at one point, he even received a bomb at his newspaper office with the markings, "For Mr. Bennett only."[8]

The content of newspapers in the penny press era differed radically from the partisan approaches of previous publishers. The *Sun*, *Herald*, *Tribune*, and many other new newspapers included information about the stock market, entertainers, politics, sports, and weather, all of which became standard features of news. Reporters strove to deliver news in a timely manner and sometimes relied on the electric telegraph to gather and share information. Penny press journalists were the first people to report on crises and crime news, and penny press papers introduced continuing reports on the same story read by thousands of people on the same day.

Sensational reporting of local crime news had become a particular staple of nineteenth-century journalism as noted in stories such as those of a crooked mayor who embezzled money or a well-known doctor who went insane and murdered his entire family. Homicide in particular seemed to resonate with readers, with an example being the coverage of the April 10, 1836, murder of Ellen Jewett (also known as Helen Jewett), a prostitute in New York City whose death brought attention to a number of her customers who were among Manhattan's elite.

The press coverage of the murder and trial was highly polarized, with reporters either sympathizing with Jewett and vilifying Richard P. Robinson, her alleged killer, or attacking Jewett as a seductress who, according to nineteenth-century standards, deserved her fate. James Gordon Bennett's *New York Herald* provided the most complete coverage of the event. The newspaper was among the few to question Robinson's guilt and attempt to describe Jewett's personal history and her character; however, at the same time, Bennett emphasized the sensational nature of the story and worked to exploit the sexual, violent details of Jewett's death for the newspaper's gain. In an unprecedented move for an editor—or anyone affiliated with the news industry for that matter—Bennett even visited the scene of the crime and described in detail the sight of the dead body, a shocking account for readers of the era, or for any era for that matter. Among the countless lines of text devoted to the murder between April 11 and 16, 1836, the *Herald* published the following lurid observations.

> Slowly I began to discover the lineaments of the corpse, as one would the beauties of a statue of marble. It was the most remarkable sight I ever beheld—I never have, and never expect to see such another. "My God," exclaimed I, "how like a statue! I can scarcely conceive that form to be a corpse." Not a vein was to be seen. The body looked as

> white—as full—as polished as the purest Parisian marble. The perfect figure—the exquisite limbs—the fine face—the full arms—the beautiful bust—all—all surpassed in every respect the Venus de Medicis, according to the casts generally given of her. . . . For a few moments, I was lost in admiration at this extraordinary sight—a beautiful female corpse—that surpassed the finest statue of antiquity. I was recalled to her horrid destiny by seeing the dreadful gashes on the right temple, which must have caused instantaneous dissolution. . . . This extraordinary murder has caused a sensation in this city never before felt or known. It was Saturday night. The murdered girl was most beautiful—a perfect Milwood. She was a remarkable character and has come to a remarkable end. The house is in danger from the mob; let the authorities see to it. A morbid excitement pervades the city.[9]

Bennett's newspaper prospered because of not only his flair for sometimes publishing the morbid details of crime but also his ability to commercialize it into an attractive product for consumers. He blended news with advertising and information with entertainment, often blurring the line between what readers needed and what they wanted.

A notorious example of this style can be found in a July 10, 1844, ad that appeared in the same columns of news detailing the outbreak of violence in Philadelphia during the summer of 1844, riots attributed to tensions between native-born Americans ("Protestants") and immigrants ("Catholics") over public resources. The ad's headline, "Bloody and Brutal Murders of Protestants and Catholics—Shame on Philadelphia City," in itself contained a mix of news and editorial. The text, as follows, blended sardonic humor with news, which Bennett apparently condoned as an exhortation for Philadelphians to clean up themselves, so to speak.

> Are ye men or devils, that you thus murder, deface, disfigure and maim God's handy work—rendering them more disgusting to behold than if they were covered with eruptions, freckles, sunburn, pimples blotches or by disease of the skin, which can be cured by Jones' Italian Chemical Soap to clear the complexion, cure eruptions, chapped and tender flesh, &c. &c. The most remarkable discovery in medical science for disease of the skin was that made by M. Vesprini, the celebrated Italian physician. He shaped discovery in the form of a beautiful piece of soap called the Italian Chemical Soap. Many physicians will hardly believe till they have seen the astounding effect of this. The proprietor himself has had for two years and a half a dreadful scrofulous head disease: he has had three practical surgeons in that; has taken several grains of calomel a day for weeks; had the head shaved twice a week, had taken sarsaparilla without the slightest effect; had his head washed two weeks with it, and it is curing it fast. This much for eruptions. For ladies or children, for clearing the skin of tan pimples, freckles or roughness, nothing can equal this. It makes dark and yellow skin white and clear—one trial will astonish all who try it for chapped flesh, bits of mosquitoes, &c. Price 50 cents per cake. This is sold (mind only the places in the city where you can get the genuine) at the sign of the American Eagle. 2 Chatham Street, or 223 Broadway, N.Y., or 130 Fulton Street, Brooklyn. Beware of counterfeits.[10]

The ad's blend of contemporary tensions featured in the news with a commercialized appeal to buy products no doubt pleased the *Herald*'s advertisers, but it also blurred the underlying facts with appeals to a market independent of them. While the sensational approach to news in the penny press era generally targeted particular demographics often neglected by what we might call mainstream newspapers, the approach at times exploited tensions between groups that eventually ruptured in the years before the Civil War. Publishers merged anti-immigrant sentiments with entire news agendas—similar approaches, as we will see, can be found in the treatment of suffrage and abolitionist movements of the time.

> **AMERICAN PATRIOT**
>
> Image 3.3 depicts a temple of Liberty standing at left on a mound labeled "Constitution and Laws." Native-born Americans (including sailors, farmers, soldiers, and a Revolutionary War veteran) gather at the foot of the hill. They hold banners emblazoned with such mottoes as "The Bible the Cornerstone of Liberty," "Beware of Foreign Influence," "None but Americans Shall Rule America," and "Education, Morality, and Religion." Other banners bear the names of sites of great revolutionary battles. In the background: A harbor with ships and the skyline of a city contrasted with an unruly contingent of foreigners, mostly Irish, alight from a newly landed ship at right. The ship, "from Cork," bears the papal coat of arms. The foreigners (clerics, a drunken mother with several children, and a few unkempt ruffians) carry banners reading, "We Are Bound to Carry out the Pious Intentions of His Holiness the Pope," "Americans Shan't Rule Us!" and "Fradom of Spache and Action!" [sic]. One of the newcomers (lower right) beats a man with a club. In the distance, across the ocean, the basilica of St. Peter's in Rome is visible. From it issues a giant basilisk wearing the pope's crown, seized by a large hand from above. A commentary provided in the lengthy continuation of the title reads, "Already the enemies of our dearest institutions, like the foreign spies in the Trojan horse of old, are within our gates."

HORACE GREELEY, MARGARET FULLER, AND REFORM

As might be expected, the *New York Herald* attracted critics. Among the most outspoken of them—indeed, Bennett's most outspoken critic until his death—was likely the most widely known publisher of the era, Horace Greeley. Under Greeley's leadership, the *New York Tribune* became the most widely read newspaper to advocate an anti-slavery platform for Whig and Republican political candidates. Greeley himself even later ran for president as both a Democrat and Liberal Republican, making him, in the words of *Harper's Weekly*, "the most perfect Yankee the country has ever produced."[12]

Horace Greeley was born in Amherst, New Hampshire, on February 3, 1811, to a poor family. His father Zaccheus Greeley suffered economic hardship during the Panic of 1819, and although Horace received irregular schooling until age 15, he nonetheless developed a voracious appetite for reading. In 1826, he sought work as a young

Image 3.3: "American Citizens! We Appeal to You in all Calmness!" published in Boston by J. E. Farwell & Co., 1852, an advertisement announcing publication of the *American Citizen*, a short-lived nativist newspaper, illustrated with an anti-Catholic scene.[11]

apprentice at the *Northern Spectator*, a weekly newspaper in rural East Poultney, Vermont. When the paper failed, he moved briefly to Erie County, Pennsylvania, and in August 1831, at the age of 20, he gathered his possessions and traveled to New York City. Arriving with only $10 in his pocket, he worked as a newspaper compositor and found refuge in the meetings of Workingmen, a group organized to advocate the rights of laborers.

Greeley's first successes in the publishing industry began with a weekly literary and news journal he founded, the *New-Yorker*, which featured politics, social issues, and the arts and sciences. The lively content attracted the attention of Whig partisans, who approached him to assist in local, state, and national campaigns. With the success (albeit short-lived) of the 1840 campaign for President William Henry Harrison, Greeley subsequently began issuing his most successful newspaper, the *New York Tribune*, which first appeared on April 10, 1841 (coincidentally the same day of Harrison's funeral).[13]

In response to the success of his daily issues, Greeley began publishing in 1842 a Saturday edition, the *New York Weekly Tribune*, which sold for $2/year or $1/year to clubs of twenty or more readers. The *Weekly Tribune* featured highly intelligent content from writers of a wide range of backgrounds and included content useful to just about any reader. The content appealed to readers who read it seriously, so much so it was said to be read "next to the Bible" in certain portions of the country.[15]

Image 3.4: "Editorial Staff of *The New York Tribune*," a photograph by Mathew Brady, published between 1844 and 1860, captures left to right seated: George M. Snow, financial editor, Bayard Taylor, literary critic, Horace Greeley, publisher, and George Ripley, literary editor; and left to right standing: William Henry Fry, music editor, Charles A. Dana, managing editor, and Henry J. Raymond, who left the *Tribune* in 1841 and ten years later founded the *New York Times*.[14]

> **HORACE GREELEY**
>
> Horace Greeley, founder of the *New York Tribune*, was a publisher, social reformer, and political figure that left an indelible mark on the history of journalism. Born into humble beginnings, he created the *Tribune* in 1841 as a way to reach working class-readers with Whig doctrine while packaging local and national news of use to them. He popularized the notion that the urban poor could find relief in the nation's unsettled regions, advancing the slogan "Go West." He opposed slavery and capital punishment, and he supported organized labor and planned communities. During the Civil War, he vacillated in support of the Lincoln administration, and in 1862, published in the *Tribune* a letter titled *The Prayer of Twenty Millions*. In it, he called on President Lincoln to change the course of the war from an effort to restore the Union to one that would end slavery. When Lincoln issued the Emancipation Proclamation, the public recognized the *Tribune* as influential in ending slavery. Greeley ran for president in 1872 and earned endorsements from both the Democratic Party and the Liberal Republican Party, but during the campaign, he suffered misfortune when his control of the *Tribune* faltered, his wife Mary ("Molly") died, and he became sick. After losing the election to incumbent President Ulysses S. Grant, hopeless and ill, Horace Greeley died November 29, 1872.

The working class of New York City and other urban areas considered Greeley a representative and a hero. Although particular reforms Greeley advocated in the *Tribune* did not always rest on sound premises, readers recognized and appreciated his efforts to make their conditions—often harsh and insufferable—more tolerable and humane. Greeley advanced, for example, a doctrine known as associationism, which suggested individual efforts in a group setting could produce utopian conditions if labor produced harmony.[16] This ideal linked Greeley to a radical philosophy later popularized by Karl Marx, which saw social organization in economic terms.

Indeed, unlike many reformers calling for the end to slavery in the United States, Greeley advanced a way of thinking that had less to do with racial inequalities as with economic ones. He said he saw slavery as an institution that affected white laborers and the homeless of urban areas as dramatically as the African Americans in bondage in the South.

> I understand by Slavery, that condition in which one human being exists mainly as a convenience for other human beings—in which the time, the exertions, the faculties of a part of the Human Family are made to subserve, not their own development, physical, intellectual, and moral, but the comfort, advantage, or caprices of others. In short, wherever service is rendered from one human being to another, on a footing of one-sided and not of mutual obligation—where the relation between the servant and the served is one not of affection and reciprocal good offices, but of authority, social ascendency and power over subsistence on the one hand, and of necessity, servility, and degradation on the other—there, in my view, is Slavery. You will readily understand, therefore, that, if I regard your enterprise with less absorbing interest than you do, it is not that I deem

Slavery a less but a greater evil. If I am less troubled concerning the Slavery prevalent in Charleston or New-Orleans, it is because I see so much Slavery in New-York, which appears to claim my first efforts.[17]

In regards to publishing, the underlying approach Greeley implemented more effectively than anyone at the time—and perhaps since—practiced an open-minded philosophy toward content. Greeley wanted as many voices represented in his newspaper as possible.[18] While James Gordon Bennett regularly printed anything that would sell newspapers, Greeley in a more nuanced way published as much content as possible that would benefit society, an experiment heralded as championing constructive democracy.

Greeley also experimented personally with a political career. In 1848, after campaigning on behalf of Whig presidential candidate Zachary Taylor, Greeley earned a seat in the U.S. House. He took advantage of the opportunity by repeating calls he had made in the *Tribune* for federally recognized homestead settlements in the West and promoted a bill that discouraged speculation on public lands and that would allow any citizen to own 160 acres of the new territories in the West. Congress did not address the bill until February 27, 1849, with a fellow House member wanting to know why a New Yorker should busy himself with the disposition of the public domain. Greeley replied that he represented "more landless men than any other member."[19] In 1862, President Abraham Lincoln, who had served in the House at the same time as Greeley, signed the Homestead Act, which had direct ties to the *Tribune*.

Image 3.5: "Margaret Fuller," pioneering feminist, published between 1840 and 1880.[20]

Among the reformers attracted to the *New York Tribune*'s liberal editorial policies, Margaret Fuller, a pioneering feminist, contributed directly both to Horace Greeley's newspaper and in a much broader sense to the advancement of women in the United States.

Fuller began her career as a journalist with the well-known transcendentalist philosopher and writer Ralph Waldo Emerson. Greeley, who also promoted the transcendentalist movement, took an interest in both the work of Emerson and Fuller, promoting both writers and participating in a utopian community sponsored by Emerson. While co-editing with Emerson *The Dial*, a quarterly literary journal of the transcendentalist movement, Fuller did her part to advance the equality of women, who at the time enjoyed few of the legal and political rights as men. "The Great Lawsuit," the most famous piece she wrote for *The Dial*, caught Greeley's attention, arguing on behalf of not only women but also others disenfranchised at the signing of the Declaration of Independence. In a sign of respect for Fuller's work, Greeley hired her at the *Tribune* and made her among the most widely read female writers of the time.

"The Great Lawsuit," as its title suggested, indicated that the political and social system envisioned by the founders needed correction, and appropriately, she turned to the press to settle the dispute. "It should be remarked that, as the principle of liberty is better understood, and more nobly interpreted," Fuller wrote, "a broader protest is made in behalf of Woman."

> Though the national independence be blurred by the servility of individuals; though freedom and equality have been proclaimed only to leave room for a monstrous display of slave dealing and slave keeping; though the free American so often feels himself free, like the Roman, only to pamper his appetites and his indolence through the misery of his fellow beings, still it is not in vain, that the verbal statement has been made, "All men are born free and equal." There it stands, a golden certainty, wherewith to encourage the good, to shame the bad. The new world may be called clearly to perceive that it incurs the utmost penalty, if it rejects the sorrowful brother. And if men are deaf, the angels hear. But men cannot be deaf. It is inevitable that an external freedom, such as has been achieved for the nation, should be so also for every member of it.[21]

Fuller's reference to the phrase "all men are created equal" came directly from the Declaration of Independence, but with no hint of irony, she noted that this phrase excluded a great portion of society that had a direct interest in the well-being of the nation.

MARGARET FULLER

Sarah Margaret Fuller, born May 23, 1810, in Cambridgeport, Massachusetts, preferred the name Margaret and dropped "Sarah" at a young age. As the eldest child of Timothy Fuller and Margaret Crane Fuller, Margaret had five siblings, two of whom died shortly after birth. Timothy Fuller, a respected lawyer who also served in the U.S. Congress, made sure his daughter received an education on par with her male cohort, an extraordinary endeavor given the era. She attended prestigious schools, including the Cambridge Port Private Grammar School. Fuller learned how to speak and write Latin, German, and French, opening opportunities for her to translate and teach. Her publishing career began in 1835 when she was invited to write as a contributor for the *Western Messenger*, a magazine with contents that promoted liberal religious ideals that included appeals to national duty and calls for the abolition of slavery. She then met writer and thinker Ralph Waldo Emerson, who invited her to join the growing circle of transcendentalists at the time. She co-edited with Emerson *The Dial* and, in 1840, became the first female editor of a major intellectual journal. In 1843, she embarked on a book project, becoming the first woman to access the Harvard Library at Gore Hall for research. Her work would eventually produce *Woman in the Nineteenth Century*, a groundbreaking document that promoted the interests of women. In the meantime, her work at *The Dial* attracted the attention of *New York Tribune* publisher Horace Greeley, who asked her to join the newspaper staff. Greeley eventually sent her to Italy to cover the unrest that swept Europe in the late 1840s, an assignment that made her the first female foreign correspondent for a leading newspaper. In Italy, she met her husband Giovanni Angelo Ossoli, with whom she started a family. Ossoli, Fuller, and their newborn child, Angelo Eugene Philip Ossoli, died tragically when the ship bringing them to the United States crashed and sank July 19, 1850. Fuller left an imprint on the women's suffrage movement that had formally begun at the Seneca Falls Convention in 1848, using language inspired by her work earlier in the decade.

According to Fuller, America had not reached equality (as it professed) because it inherited depraved institutions from Europe, as made manifest in its treatment of Native Americans, African Americans, and women. She advocated transcendental love, as demonstrated by abolitionists (those who called for an immediate end to slavery) who, in acting on their universal respect for universal humanity, included women as part of their group.

In time, her observation caught the attention of an increasingly vocal movement that advocated on behalf of women and others disenfranchised from the vote. Horace Greeley took notice, and in 1844, he hired Fuller as a literary critic for the *Tribune*, its first female staff member. In 1845, Greeley published Fuller's *Woman in the Nineteenth Century*, which made the claim, among others, that the quality of a soul knows no gender, and there is "no wholly masculine man, no purely feminine woman."[22] Fuller's growing body of work, along with calls for reform from feminists Susan B. Anthony and Elizabeth Cady Stanton, appeared thereafter in language adopted by those who met in 1848 for the Seneca Falls Convention, a gathering of reformers who called for the broadening of suffrage rights beyond the limits proscribed in the Constitution.

This movement, tucked in the heart of the Age of Jackson, attracted both support and resistance from the status quo. Those who supported the sentiments Fuller expressed in "The Great Lawsuit" included both women and African Americans, a majority of whom could not participate in the functions of government because of their status as slaves. The ruling class generally opposed this movement, as did the audiences targeted by the penny press newspapers, such as working class white males who had little interest in compromising their social status.

A typical reaction to the mid-nineteenth century suffrage movement can be found in none other than the *New York Herald*, which had appealed most often to the instincts of the "common man" (and not the common woman, as it were). An editorial published in September 1852 expressed not only James Gordon Bennett's editorial opinion about calls for expanded suffrage at the time but also the attitudes of a majority of voters. "The Woman's Rights Convention—The Last Act of the Drama" began with the questions "Who are these women? What do they want? What are the motives that impel them to this course of action?" In condescending language, no doubt offensive to subsequent generations, the *Herald* dismissed participants in degrading terms.

> The *dramatis persona* of the farce enacted at Syracuse, present a curious conglomeration of both sexes; some of them are old maids, whose personal charms were never very attractive, and who have been sadly slighted by the masculine gender in general; some of them women who have been badly mated, whose own temper, or their husbands', has made life anything but agreeable to them, and they are therefore down upon the whole of the opposite sex; some having so much of the virago in their disposition, that nature appears to have made a mistake; some of boundless vanity and egotism, who believe that they are superior in intellectual strength to "all the world and the rest of mankind," and delight to see their speeches and addresses in print; some silly little girls, of from fifteen to twenty, who are tickled to death with the idea of being one day a great orator, a lawyer, a doctor, a member of Congress, perhaps President of the United States.

The editorial closed by casting the movement as only "the natural offspring of the silly socialist and abolition doctrines that have agitated their country for a number of years."[23] Indeed, readers of the *Herald* and other newspapers targeted for the masses likely saw the calls for reform as a threat to the newly acquired sense of social standing they had received in the new era, and they would have resisted relinquishing this sense of improvement to include others. Regardless of this resistance, Fuller helped launch what became the longest civil rights struggle in American history, culminating first with the Reconstruction Amendments after the Civil War and the eventual passage of the Nineteenth Amendment in 1920, granting women the right to vote.

While women and men had gathered at the Seneca Falls Convention to adopt statements that demanded changes to the Constitution, Fuller had taken an assignment in Europe to cover a series of revolutions that had broken out in the late 1840s. Greeley sent her to Italy, a site of unrest, and her job was to file correspondences about the revolutionary events for the *Tribune*. While in Italy, Fuller met a nobleman, with whom she had a child. When the revolutions calmed down, she returned to the United States, but died tragically with her family when the ship on which she traveled sank. Her death rattled contemporaries, and at the urging of Ralph Waldo Emerson, fellow transcendentalist Henry David Thoreau traveled to New York to search the shore for her body. Both Fuller's body and her husband's body were not recovered, but their son was buried under an inscription in Cambridge, Massachusetts, to her that reads, "By birth a child of New England; By adoption a citizen of Rome; By genius belonging to the world."

ABOLITIONISTS PUBLISH A NEW REVOLUTION

While both the penny press and the political parties of the Age of Jackson celebrated the "common man" (usually at the expense of women and anyone else who did not fit this definition), both institutions failed to address an issue unresolved since the founding of the nation. The Constitution had codified slavery, allowing it as part of a compromise between states under the federal system. While John Adams and Thomas Jefferson both anticipated the severe moral problems of slavery while drafting the Declaration of Independence, they believed, albeit wrongly, the institution might die under its own weight.

Among the most outspoken critics of the American political and economic system, Frederick Douglass championed one of the most remarkable stories from the era. He was born into slavery, and could not read or write, as the law prohibited literacy for slaves. Through a series of remarkable personal developments, Douglass taught himself how to read and write and to become a free human being, an achievement he later understood as both a blessing and a curse, as the freer he became, the more he realized the degradation of slavery. At the age of 8, he was sent to Baltimore, Maryland, to live as a houseboy servant for Hugh and Sophia Auld. His new mistress made the mistake, according to her husband, of teaching young Frederick a few letters of the alphabet, which allowed him to begin the process of self-education. After learning to form words and sentences, Douglass could forge a plan to escape slavery, and at the age of 20, he fled the United States for freedom.

Anti-slavery advocates in England helped Douglass pay for his freedom, and upon receiving it, he returned to the United States, where he met William Lloyd Garrison. Garrison, as the flamboyant and controversial publisher of *The Liberator*, had gained an audience—though not an entirely sympathetic one—by appealing to the moral sensibilities of readers at the time. As editor of *The Liberator*, Garrison had written "To the Public" in a January 1, 1831, article, "I am in earnest will not equivocate I will not excuse I will not retreat in a single inch and I will be heard."[24] In response to his calls, a mob once nearly killed him, dragging him through the streets of Boston. Unwavering, he later publicly burned a copy of the Constitution, calling it a "covenant with death" and "an agreement with Hell" because it permitted slavery.[25]

WILLIAM LLOYD GARRISON

William Lloyd Garrison was born in Newburyport, Massachusetts, on December 10, 1805. As a child, Garrison received only a basic education, but he used journalism as a means for advancement. In 1828, he moved to Boston, where he secured a job as a journeyman printer and editor for the *National Philanthropist*, and at the age of 25, he joined the American Colonization Society. Garrison at first believed that this society's mission was to promote freedom, but he soon realized that the intention of the group was to minimize the number of freed slaves in the United States. Thus, in 1830, he set out to start *The Liberator*, a newspaper with the motto, "Our country is the world—our countrymen are mankind." In 1832, he helped form the New England Antislavery Society and shortly after founded the American Antislavery Society. After decades of publishing that was often met with severe resistance—and after the nation's bloody Civil War—Garrison's endeavors were finally rewarded in 1865 with passage of the Thirteenth Amendment in 1865, which ended slavery in both the North and the South. In December of 1865, he published the final issue of *The Liberator*, announcing his vocation as an abolitionist had ended. He died in New York City on May 24, 1879.

While Garrison stood out as a radical among contemporaries, he heard Douglass' story and found it beyond anything he could imagine—so much so that he recruited Douglass to provide lectures for audiences at meetings of the Massachusetts

Image 3.6: "Head-and-Shoulders Portrait of Frederick Douglass," John White Hurn, photographer, published in Philadelphia, January 14, 1862.[26]

Anti-Slavery Society. Douglass complied and traveled throughout the Northeast with Garrison, explaining to incredulous listeners the details of his escape from slavery. In fact, those who heard Douglass' tale were often so mystified at his eloquence that some received it with skepticism and doubt, while others simply rejected it as too spectacular to believe. In response, Douglass wrote his *Autobiography*, a testimony in his own words of the life that he had lived.

Douglass wrote *Narrative of the Life of Frederick Douglass, an American Slave* in 1845. "I was born in Tuckahoe, near Hillsborough, and about twelve miles from Easton, in Talbot County, Maryland," Douglass wrote, and with these words, put himself on equal footing with every human, dead, alive, or yet to live—we all have the same quality of being born. As he continues, however, he confesses a dislocation from those who surround him:

> I have no accurate knowledge of my age, never having seen any authentic record containing it. By far the larger part of the slaves know as little of their ages as horses know of theirs, and it is the wish of most masters within my knowledge to keep their slaves thus ignorant . . . I do not remember to have ever met a slave who could tell of his birthday. They seldom come nearer to it than planting-time, harvesttime, cherry-time, spring-time, or fall-time. A want of information concerning my own was a source of unhappiness to me even during childhood. The white children could tell their ages. I could not tell why I ought to be deprived of the same privilege. I was not allowed to make any inquiries of my master concerning it. He deemed all such inquiries on the part of a slave improper and impertinent, and evidence of a restless spirit. The nearest estimate I can give makes me now between twenty-seven and twenty-eight years of age. I come to this, from hearing my master say, some time during 1835, I was about seventeen years old.[27]

Since 1845, publishers have reissued several editions and revisions of his text, as the original autobiography did not include how he escaped from slavery because—practicing the protection of confidential sources—he did not want to jeopardize the safety of any other slaves trying to escape. Douglass' autobiography would come to represent a stunning piece of journalism, a true classic in the stories of American history and an even more remarkable story about a journalist by a journalist.

FREDERICK DOUGLASS

Frederick Douglass was a former slave who escaped and became a powerful anti-slavery activist. His mother was a slave who was unable to care for him; therefore, his grandmother raised him until he was sent to Baltimore as a house slave for the family of Thomas and Lucretia Auld. In Baltimore, he taught himself how to read and write in secret. While running errands for his master, he would stop and talk with other young boys who would help him spell, write, or read. When he was home alone, he would take his master's schoolbook and trace the words to learn how to write, which contributed directly to his ability to escape from slavery. Leaving for England and then returning to the United

> States, Douglass used literacy as a tool for empowering those still in bondage. He began writing for two New York-based weeklies, the *National Anti-Slavery Standard* and the *Ram's Horn*. In 1845, Douglass wrote his autobiography, *Narrative of the Life of Frederick Douglass, an American Slave*, and in 1847 established a weekly abolitionist paper, the *North Star*. Douglass' *Narrative* describes the savagery of slavery in matter-of-fact detail, giving a first-person perspective unequal in its credulity at the time. Douglass was a prominent character in the province of sociopolitical theater. His attendance at the first women's suffrage convention at Seneca Falls in 1848 solidified his role as a purveyor of democracy and a champion for individual rights.

While both Garrison and Douglass spoke vehemently against slavery, they also maintained consistent editorial arguments that favored suffrage for women. As Margaret Fuller had noted in her writings, the U.S. Constitution at the time had disenfranchised just about anyone who was not a white, male, landowner of a certain age who paid taxes. It should come as no surprise then that, in line with this political reasoning, Garrison and Douglass joined feminists at the 1848 Seneca Falls Convention, agreeing that a new understanding of the Constitution should afford equal rights to everyone.

Douglass' reaction to the events at Seneca Falls in particular described the event much more respectfully than other newspapers of the era. On July 28, 1848, he published in the *North Star* the observation that "One of the most interesting events of the past week was the holding of what is technically styled a Woman's Rights Convention at Seneca Falls."

> Several interesting documents setting forth the rights as well as the grievances of women were read. Among these was "The Declaration of Sentiments," to be regarded as the basis of a grand movement for attaining the civil, social, political, and religious rights of women. We should not do justice to our own convictions, or to the excellent persons connected with this infant movement, if we did not in this connection offer a few remarks on the general subject which the Convention met to consider and the objects they seek to attain. In doing so, we are not insensible that the bare mention of this truly important subject in any other than terms of contemptuous ridicule and scornful disfavor, is likely to excite against us the fury of bigotry and the folly of prejudice. . . .
>
> While it is impossible for us to go into this subject at length, and dispose of the various objections which are often urged against such a doctrine as that of female equality, we are free to say that in respect to political rights, we hold woman to be justly entitled to all we claim for man. We go farther, and express our conviction that all political rights that it is expedient for man to exercise, it is equally so for woman. All that distinguishes man as an intelligent and accountable being, is equally true of woman; and if that government only is just which governs by the free consent of the governed, there can be no reason in the world for denying to woman the exercise of the elective franchise, or a hand in making and administering the laws of the land. Our doctrine is that "right is of no sex." We therefore bid the women engaged in this movement our humble Godspeed.[28]

The changes made to the content and marketing of newspapers during the penny press era set a precedent for the way newspapers operate today. Newspapers still rely heavily on advertising as a main source of revenue, and to this day, newspapers still pay more attention to their surrounding communities. The formula of high circulation with "spicy" content changed coverage so that publishers relied on ads instead of subscriptions or daily sales to make a profit.

At the same time, the penny press newspapers succeeded because contributing writers undertook efforts to make their stories understandable to wide audience, using language that translated to various demographics outside the traditionally educated audiences of the partisan presses. News items and stories were also shorter than the contents of elite papers, as writers endeavored to capture the attention of as many readers as quickly as possible.

New York's penny papers in particular published stories about remarkable personalities, covering compelling aspects of the human condition. To connect with the urban, mostly working-class readership, New York reporters wrote about ordinary people and their experiences. This, in combination with the speed of news delivery and thoroughness in the coverage of local news, not only changed the direction of American journalism, it paved the way for social changes unprecedented in the history of the United States.

RECAPPING THIS CHAPTER

Looking back on this chapter, you should see attention to the contents of penny newspapers in the 1830s, and you should see how this content provided a democratizing agent and expanded readership. The chapter also described how the new sales model of low-priced newspapers, combined with high circulation and a reliance on advertising, combined with mass movements and political formations during the era.

Using content from the preceding pages, you should be able to interpret how individual personalities helped contribute to the development of what became the modern press. You should also be able to identify the publishing strategies of the major penny press newspapers, and you should be able to explain how sensationalism to this day plays a role (for better or worse) in raising the interest levels of news audiences.

The following chapter focuses on changes to content brought by technological advances, as well as the famous "stunt journalism" practiced by Nellie Bly in her historic travels around the world. It begins by noting the changes brought to the penny press industry by the *New York Times*, which relied on a "facts only" approach. It also shows how the immediate transmission of news changed the very nature, content, and construction of information, eventually leading to news global in scope.

NOTES

1 James Madison to W. T. Barry, August 4, 1822, *The Writings of James Madison*, Gaillard Hunt, ed., 9 vols. (New York: G. P. Putnam's Sons, 1900–1910), 9: 103–9.
2 Alexis de Tocqueville, *Democracy in America* (New York: Barnes and Noble, 2003), 166.
3 "Lunar Animals and Other Objects," Library of Congress, accessed November 19, 2016, <item/2003665049>.

4. "Great Astronomical Discoveries Lately Made by Sir John Herschel at the Cape of Good Hope," *New York Sun*, August 25–31, 1835.
5. Ibid.
6. P. T. Barnum, *The Humbugs of the World* (New York: Carleton, 1866), 259.
7. "One of the News-B'hoys," Library of Congress, accessed November 2, 2016, <item/2003664125>.
8. Frederick Hudson, *Journalism in the United States* (New York: Harper Brothers, 1873), 466.
9. "Visit to the Scene," *New York Herald*, April 11, 1836.
10. "Bloody and Brutal Murders of Protestants and Catholics—Shame on Philadelphia City," *New York Herald*, July 10, 1844.
11. "American Citizens!" Library of Congress, accessed November 19, 2016, <item/2008661538>.
12. "Hon. Horace Greeley," *Harper's Weekly*, 4, 194 (September 15, 1860): 581, 582.
13. "Funeral of the Late President," *New York Tribune*, April 10, 1841, 4.
14. "Editorial Staff of *The New York Tribune*," Library of Congress, accessed November 19, 2016, <item/2004663939>.
15. Bayard Taylor, *Life and Letters of Bayard Taylor* (Boston: Houghton, Mifflin and Company, 1885), 1: 263.
16. Charles Fourier, *Theory of Social Organization* (New York: C. P. Somerby, 1876), 10.
17. Horace Greeley, *Hints Toward Reform* (New York: Harper and Brothers, 1850), 353, 354.
18. Greeley, *Recollections of a Busy Life* (New York: J. B. Ford, 1868), 136.
19. Greeley, *Recollections of a Busy Life*, 217.
20. "Margaret Fuller," published between 1840 and 1880, Library of Congress, accessed November 19, 2016, <item/2002712183>.
21. Margaret Fuller, "The Great Lawsuit: Man versus Men, Woman versus Women," *The Dial*, 4, 1 (July 1843): 8.
22. Margaret Fuller Ossoli, *Woman in the Nineteenth Century: And, Kindred Papers Relating to the Sphere, Condition and Duties of Woman*, Arthur B. Fuller, ed. (New York: Greeley and McElrath, 1845), 103.
23. "The Woman's Rights Convention—The Last Act of the Drama," editorial, *New York Herald*, September 12, 1852.
24. "To the Public," *The Liberator*, January 1, 1831.
25. Garrison to Rev. Samuel J. May, July 17, 1845, in Walter M. Merrill, ed., *The Letters of William Lloyd Garrison*, 3 (1973), 303.
26. "Frederick Douglass," Library of Congress, accessed November 19, 2016, <item/2013645427>.
27. Frederick Douglass, *Narrative of the Life of Frederick Douglass, an American Slave* (Boston: Anti-Slavery Office, 1845), 1–2.
28. Frederick Douglass, "The Rights of Women," *The North Star* (Rochester, NY): July 28, 1848.

4

NINETEENTH-CENTURY PUBLISHING INNOVATIONS IN CONTENT AND TECHNOLOGY

This chapter focuses on changes to content brought by technological advances, as well as the famous "stunt journalism" practiced by Nellie Bly in her historic travels around the world:

- It shows how the immediate transmission of news changed the very nature, content, and construction of information, eventually leading to global news, and how it affected socially constructed ideas of time, space, and place;
- and it describes the changes brought to the penny press industry by the Associated Press and the *New York Times*, which both relied on "facts only" approaches to news, a historical development in news style that coincided with the introduction of the telegraph to the reporting industry.

Using materials from this chapter, students should be able to see how technological developments in communication affected news delivery speed and content itself:

- They should also be able to compare and contrast the kinds of news content that were popular both before and after the introduction of the telegraph, seeing a correlation between technology and timeliness;
- and they should explain how traveling the world at record speed contributed directly to the development of the international scope of the news delivery,

describing Nellie Bly's stunt journalism as both sensational news content and pioneering journalism.

Key words, names, and phrases associated with Chapter 4 include:

- the telegraph and transatlantic cable;
- the inverted pyramid and the Associated Press;
- the *New York Times* (Henry Raymond);
- and Nellie Bly and stunt journalism.

Journalism changed dramatically in the mid-nineteenth century, with several technological innovations affecting the press dramatically. Major developments included improvements in the steam press, the diffusion of a telegraphic network, and (as we will see in the following chapters) the advent of documentary photojournalism. This chapter shows how the telegraph affected news by quickly transmitting information over long distances, and it looks at how improvements in the ability to produce newspapers at greater speeds allowed publishers to expand audiences.

Readers of the period demanded information on the daily events that affected their friends and family members. The concurrent expansion of the railroads at a rate of more than 1,000 new miles each year in the 1850s allowed publishers means for selling newspapers over vast distances, with the amount of track jumping from 8,589 miles in 1850 to 30,591 in 1861. Along with the railroads, the postal service was another major channel for delivering newspapers and magazines. In the 1850s, the post office would typically deliver more than 100 million journals in a single year, with the bulk of those being newspapers. In 1860, of the nation's 3,300 newspapers in the United States, 373 were published Monday through Saturday.[1]

This explosion of printed material, which had its roots in the penny press era, allowed publishers to reach unprecedented audiences. The introduction of new technologies into the printing industry at mid-century increased the production speed of printers and the delivery rate of information, transforming news from an endeavor focused on local issues to an industry that had international dimensions.

THE TELEGRAPH'S IMPACT ON JOURNALISM

Centuries after Johannes Gutenberg first revolutionized the rapid and mass creation of information with his printing press, Friedrich Koenig, another German, in 1814 developed a two-cylinder steam press capable of printing on both sides of paper by using a movable bed that carried the type back and forth for inking after each impression to produce 1,100 newspapers per hour. By 1830, David Napier in England tuned Koenig's press so that it could produce more than 3,000 papers per hour. By 1843, Richard M. Hoe of New York invented a rotary press, known as the "lightning press," which

American publishers began using in 1846. The Hoe press at first produced 12,000 newspapers per hour, and by the 1860s nearly doubled that number.

Yet, with the exception of the printing press itself, no single invention in human history has had a more profound effect on mass communication than the electronic telegraph. Coinciding with the introduction of the steam press in the middle of the nineteenth century, the telegraph made speed the key trait of information transmission and reception.

Danish physicist Hans Christian Oersted in 1819 first discovered that a wire carrying an electronic current had an effect on a magnetized needle compass. From Oersted's observation grew the development of the modern electronic telegraph when, first, an electromagnet replaced the needle, and later, American Joseph Henry developed in 1830 a device that could ring a bell on a wire more than a mile in length. In 1838, Samuel F. B. Morse and Alfred Vail improved on Henry's invention with the development of a telegraphic key that imprinted a code of dots and dashes on a roll of paper. Morse constructed a code that corresponded to the alphabet and the numbers zero to nine, creating the basis for transmitting messages almost instantaneously over long distances, a revolution in communication that has had effects through today, with modern telecommunications networks owing their adoption to the innovation.

Morse lived in a time of enormous technological change in which he directly participated. Born April 17, 1791, in Charlestown, Massachusetts, he was the son of Reverend Jedidiah Morse. Although he struggled through life to find buyers of his patent on the telegraph, he died April 2, 1872, with the success he had sought.

Morse's career initially took him to New York University, where he taught in the school of Literature of Arts and Design. At NYU, Morse assembled equipment to form a telegraph, and in 1838, he demonstrated the invention to President Martin Van Buren, asking for $30,000 in government support, a request denied. After years of trial and error, adapting the innovations of other experimenters, Morse transmitted the first reported telegraphic message using his device on May 24, 1844, in a test for former President James Madison and his wife Dolly Madison. He sent the enigmatic message from the Bible "What Hath God Wrought" from the Capitol building in Washington, D.C., to Baltimore, Maryland. With additional development, the telegraph was able to type ten words per minute at the time Morse premiered it in New York City. In 1858, Morse's tireless work earned money, as ten governments recognized him with an award of $80,000 as thanks for the invention that had brought countries together.

In terms of journalism, electronic telegraphy had the greatest impact on reporting news. Only fifty years before its introduction, a story published by a Charleston, South Carolina, newspaper about an event in New York might require twenty days before it reached its audience in the Southern port city. Now the telegraph enabled journalists to transmit and receive information instantly over long distances. Newspapers would subsequently have telegraphic editions, and between ordinary news-cycle publications, there might be several telegraphic editions in a single day about extraordinary events.

By the mid-nineteenth century, the telegraph was king of the communications industry. Newspaper editors in New York were among the first to realize the potential of the new invention. Along with a daily newspaper in Philadelphia, they formed the

Associated Press (AP) wire service to share information over long distances. Before the Associated Press (originally the New York Associated Press), the newspapers had competed for time on the wire, and this was too costly. Furthermore, managing all of the information was a task beyond the abilities of even the best-managed metropolitan dailies. The AP originally had bureaus in New York, Albany, and Washington, and it established favorable relationships with Western Union and the American Telegraph Company. These newspapers cooperated with each other originally, as they wanted to share news from the war in Mexico (1846–48) and then the California Gold Rush shortly thereafter. Editors competing with the AP worried that these few urban newspapers would come to dominate the shape of news in the country and began forming their own wire services. By 1860, more than 50,000 miles of telegraph wire stretched across the country, much of it along railroad routes, with a line from New York to San Francisco opening in 1861.

Image 4.1: "Mexican News," Woodville, Richard Caton, artist, circa 1851, a group of people on the porch of the American Hotel read news of the war with Mexico.[2]

Because telegraphic transmissions, equipment, and the labor associated with it cost money, reporters learned to create stories with concise style and minimal use of words, as shorter messages correlated to less expense for the publisher. The result of this trend in content led to the omission of certain rhetorical devices, the elimination of gratuitous description—including the use of adjectives and adverbs—as well as less opinion and more emphasis on fact. Fearing the disruption of their stories during transmission might lead to the loss of critical information, editors increasingly insisted on the use of an inverted pyramid construction with news stories, which emphasized essential information first and secondary information later. The sooner they could transmit the story the better, so it made sense to put the most important information at the top of the story. In other cases, editors expected delivery of news in the inverted pyramid model, which emphasized essential information first and secondary information later. While writers today still use this storytelling approach for its effectiveness in capturing the attention of readers, editors in the 1850s expected writers to use the inverted pyramid as another way to minimize cost, as the prioritization of facts correlated with less wordy telegraphic transmissions and therefore less expense.

With this rationale, the Associated Press formed initially as a not-for-profit news cooperative in May 1846 when daily newspapers in New York City agreed to share the cost of transmitting news about the Mexican-American War in a combination of communications networks that included boats, horses, and the telegraph. The original members realized that the expenses associated with transmitting news over a long distance would prohibit one individual newspaper alone from being able to cover the war. As demonstrated in coverage of the California Gold Rush, pooling correspondents would allow each member of the AP to provide news from one reporter, who still sent it from a distance, but at a fraction of the cost compared to the price of several transmissions of the same report.

Moses Yale Beach, who spearheaded the idea after he had assumed control of the *New York Sun* in 1838 gained support from editors of New York newspapers that included the *Herald*, *Courier and Enquirer*, *Journal of Commerce*, *Evening Express*, and the *Tribune*. A seventh member, the *Times*, joined shortly after its founding in September 1851 and added an editorial philosophy that complemented the demands of the new technology in both style and cost efficiency. Initially known as the New York Associated Press (NYAP), the organization later faced competition from the Western Associated Press (1862), which criticized its monopolistic newsgathering and price-setting practices.

HENRY RAYMOND, THE *TIMES*, AND NEWS "WITHOUT PASSION"

One of the leaders of the news industry at this time took full advantage of the styles and techniques associated with the "facts only" style of reporting that the telegraph encouraged. During the 1840s, Henry J. Raymond's primary source of income was as the managing editor of the *New York Courier and Enquirer*, a decidedly Whig publication and one of the original members of the Associated Press. Raymond had graduated from the University of Vermont in 1840 at the age of 18 and was at first a contributing writer for two of Horace Greeley's papers, first *The New-Yorker* and then for a short time as chief assistant for the *New York Tribune*. Raymond's conservative upbringing led him to split with Greeley and venture into a publishing career of his own, one that left a legacy that has survived into the twenty-first century.

Raymond was born January 24, 1820, on a family farm near Lima, New York. He believed in basic news qualities of objective and accurate reporting, which also influenced his editorial philosophy, later seen in his leadership of the *New York Times*. Throughout his career as a writer and editor, even before launching the *Times*, Raymond held beliefs in the strength of both the individual and the free market. In this respect, he differed from his first boss, Greeley, who advocated collective approaches to social problems. A classic exchange between the two minds in a publication titled *Association Discussed* illustrated the differences in their understanding of the purpose of newspapers, as well as their ideas about the way a proper society should function.

The exchange began with a letter published by Greeley in the *Tribune* on September 7, 1846, that invited the editor of the *Courier and Enquirer* to present to the public his opinions about social reform. Raymond responded, and for the following eight months, Greeley and he wrote dueling editorials about the subject in their respective newspapers. On one week, Raymond would respond to the *Tribune*'s arguments from the previous week and then advance an argument beyond what had been already written. The next week, Greeley would do likewise—respond to the *Courier and Enquirer*'s previous column and at the same time advance a new line of discussion. Repeatedly, for these eight months, columns published in the *Tribune* pressed steadily for labor rights, government-subsidized agrarian reforms, and homestead legislation to guarantee security in the West, while the *Courier and Enquirer* argued for the extension of the free market, capitalism, and a laissez-faire policy toward property in newly acquired territories.[3]

Although the public generally sided more with Raymond's ideas, Greeley earned respect and enough recognition from political leaders in New York to fill a term in the Thirtieth Congress. In late 1848 through the first few months of 1849, Greeley served as a Whig representative in the U.S. House, where he met Abraham Lincoln, also a Whig representative at the time. The two began a relationship that lasted well into the Civil War and helped to pass the Homestead Act of 1862 as well as the eventual end of slavery.

Raymond, meanwhile, had proved his ability to publish articulate arguments on behalf of business interests, leading to his rise as a publisher of the "facts only" *New York Times*. On September 18, 1851, he issued the inaugural edition of the newspaper, which included "A Word about Ourselves," explaining the objective of the newspaper. "There are very few things in this world which is worth-while to get angry about," Raymond wrote, "and they are just the things that anger will not improve."

> Upon all topics,—Political, Social, Moral, and Religious,—we intend that the paper shall speak for itself; and we only ask that it may be judged accordingly. . . . We do not believe that everything in society is either exactly right, or exactly wrong; what is good we desire to preserve and improve; what is evil, to exterminate, or reform.
>
> We shall endeavor so to conduct all our discussions of public affairs, as to leave no one in doubt as to the principles we espouse, or the measures we advocate. And while we design to be decided and explicit in all our positions, we shall at the same time seek

to be temperate and measured in all our language. We do not mean to write as if we were in a passion, unless that shall really be the case; and we shall make it a point to get into a passion as rarely as possible.... In controversies with other journals, with individuals, or with parties, we shall engage only when, in our opinion, some important public interest can be promoted thereby:—and even then, we shall endeavor to rely more upon fair argument than upon misrepresentation or abusive language.[4]

As the only newspaper from this era to have survived through today, Raymond had established a clearly sound philosophy to news, and even though the newspaper did not bring to a close the practice of sensationalism widespread at the time, it did temper some of the attacks between penny press editors. Raymond remained active in politics, directly contributing to the development of the Republican Party, until his sudden death of a heart attack on June 18, 1869. He was 49 years old.

Among the great journalistic achievements of the *Times* in the years following Raymond's death included its exposé of the corruption surrounding the infamous extortionist William ("Boss") Tweed. Along with *Harper's Weekly* and through both publications' use of Thomas Nast's satirical cartoons, the *Times*, in July 1871, ran a series of news stories exposing massive corruption by members of Tammany Hall, the Democratic political machine in New York City run by Tweed. In a precursor to muckraking (see Chapter 7), the *Times* published evidence that the Tweed Ring had siphoned money—nearly $200 million in today's amounts—from the public in the form of inflated payments to government contractors, kickbacks to government officials, extortion, and other malfeasance.

Nast, an illustrator of considerable talent, had made the Tweed Ring the subject of his satires for years already, and in the summer and fall of 1871 joined the *Times* in depicting the Tweed Ring as vultures and thieves. With a readership that consisted increasingly of immigrants, some of whom could not read English, Nast's contributions to the *Times* and *Harper's Weekly* were a hit, with Boss Tweed reportedly exclaiming distress about the press, "I don't care a straw for your newspaper articles; my constituents don't know how to read, but they can't help seeing them damned pictures!"[5]

Eventually, rivals in the Democratic Party, who sought the spoils of office for themselves, turned on Tweed. They provided evidence of his corruption to local newspapers, which eventually gave prosecutors the proof needed for a conviction. Tweed attempted to evade charges by fleeing to Europe, but authorities captured him and returned him to the United States, where he died in prison on April 12, 1878, marking an episode in press development in which a combination of hard news reporting and illustrations combined to serve the public interest in weeding out corruption.

THE TRANSATLANTIC CABLE

At mid-century—and on top of the launching of the *New York Times*—another development in technological and journalistic innovation began to emerge. The transatlantic cable transformed not only journalism but also the way people around the world began to see themselves—not just as members of individual states but also as participants in a global society.

Before the first transatlantic cable, communications between Europe and the Americas took place only by ship. Sometimes, however, severe winter storms delayed ships for weeks. As envisioned by its creators, the transatlantic cable would reduce communication time considerably, allowing a message and a response in the same day.

Initial work on the project began in 1854 when Cyrus West Field, an American financier, secured a charter to lay a well-insulated line across the floor of the Atlantic Ocean. Beginning in 1857, he obtained the aid of British and American naval ships that fed the connective lines to the ocean floor. After four unsuccessful attempts to make a connection, by August 5, 1857, engineers finally made a successful connection with the cable after stretching it nearly 2,000 miles across the Atlantic at a depth often of more than two miles.

The first official telegram to pass between two continents was a letter from Queen Victoria of the United Kingdom to the U.S. president James Buchanan on August 16, 1858. "Europe and America are united by telegraphy," the Queen wrote in a message that took sixteen hours to send, and she closed, "Glory to God in the highest; on earth, peace, and good will toward men." The Queen expressed hope that the connection would prove "an additional link between the nations whose friendship is founded on their common interest and reciprocal esteem." Buchanan responded exuberantly, "May the Atlantic telegraph under the blessing of Heaven, prove to be a bond of perpetual peace and friendship between the kindred nations, and an instrument destined by Divine Providence to diffuse religion, civilization, liberty, and law throughout the world."

Image 4.2: "The Progress of the Century—The Lightning Steam Press, the Electric Telegraph, the Locomotive, [and] the Steamboat," a lithograph by Currier & Ives in New York, 1876, depicts a man using a telegraph in the foreground, and in the background, others who use a steam press.[6]

However, the first transatlantic cable connection produced signal quality that declined rapidly, and it slowed transmission to an almost unusable speed, functioning for only three weeks. Other efforts followed and led to steadier connections between the United States and Europe. Another attempt in 1865—completed July 28—with much-improved material produced a better connection, and by the 1870s, transatlantic communication became a regular part of news.

The resulting effect of the telegraph on social attitudes both at the time and since the nineteenth century cannot be understated. Thanks to Morse's invention, communication for the first time in history no longer had limits to the speed at which a physical message could pass between locations. So long as telegraphic wires linked them, humans had no limits in reaching one another relative to distance.

Prior to the telegraph, members of nations saw themselves as parts of isolated geographic regions, having little knowledge of news elsewhere other than dated reports at best. The telegraph, however—much like its descendant the Internet—permitted a message to travel faster than the deliverer, a development that communications scholar James Carey described as a watershed moment in human history inasmuch as communication for the first time controlled physical processes. "The simplest and most important point about the telegraph is that it marked the decisive separation of 'transportation' and 'communication,'" Carey wrote. "Until the telegraph, these words were synonymous. The telegraph ended that identity and allowed symbols to move independently of geography and independently and faster than transport."[7]

On journalistic levels, as the telegraph began to put the country and eventually the world on one mass communication channel, it tended to create a level of objectivity in stories, as literary description with adjectives, adverbs, and extended characterization simply cost too much money given the limits of the new technological form of delivery.

This development, however, led to another change, a new style of reporting that competed for readers with a return to sensational content comparable to the press before the introduction of the telegraph. While the *New York Times* had slowly begun to establish itself as the newspaper of record for readers interested in hard news, other readers became increasingly hungry for the kind of entertainment that the penny press had popularized before the Civil War. While a number of leading newspapers dabbled increasingly with more features-based stories, as well as with color illustrations and simply fun content, the career of one journalist in particular epitomized this transformation at the end of the nineteenth century. Combining a form of reporting known as muckraking with a style of publishing known as yellow journalism, Nellie Bly created a new style of storytelling, unique in its own right.

NELLIE BLY AND STUNT JOURNALISM

Adventurous, courageous, and curious are just a few words someone might use to describe the *New York World*'s Nellie Bly. Nellie Bly made a name for herself in the male-dominated journalism world of the late nineteenth century by launching a new and daring kind of investigative reporting in the 1880s that made an impact on the history of the press both in America and around the world. Because men dominated the news industry in the nineteenth century, and women were still in the beginning stages

Image 4.3: "Representative Journals & Journalists of America," published October 6, 1882, includes portraits, entirely of men, surrounding New York publisher Thurlow Weed. The featured leading editors of the day include Whitelaw Reid (*New York Tribune*), Henry Watterson (*Louisville Courier-Journal*), Edwin Haskell (*Boston Herald*), Charles Dana (*New York Sun*), Joseph Medill (*Chicago Tribune*), George Childs (*Philadelphia Public Ledger*), James Gordon Bennett (*New York Herald*), Royal Pulsifer (*Boston Herald*), Murat Halstead (*Cincinnati Commercial*), Oswald Ottendorfer (*New York Staats-Zeitung*), and Joseph Hawley (*Hartford Courant*).[8]

NINETEENTH-CENTURY PUBLISHING INNOVATIONS   79

of exploring careers outside of being a homemaker, it was rare for a woman to break into the world of journalism.

Bly not only succeeded in her career as a reporter, she developed an entirely new and innovative kind of storytelling known as stunt journalism. Blending hard news with features style, Bly covered difficult or unpleasant topics and reported them through first-person experience. While members of the press still produced stories using these techniques, Bly injected into her stories both reform and sensationalism, creating a precedent for both women and reporters in general that has had no comparison.

Image 4.4: "Nellie Bly," stunt journalist extraordinaire, published February 21, 1890.[9]

Born Elizabeth Cochran on May 5, 1864, in Cochran's Mills, Nellie wanted to make a name for herself by standing out from her fifteen brothers and sisters. In the early 1880s, she picked up an edition of the *Pittsburgh Dispatch* and read an editorial written by "The Quiet Observer" that suggested women were at their best when doing domestic duties, such as raising children and looking after the house. Offended by the chauvinism, Bly wrote a three-page response to the editorial with the name "Lonely Orphan Girl." Her passionate writing caught the attention of the paper's managing editor and he responded back offering her a job. Now a reporter, Bly could write about all the women's issues she felt needed attention, but in time, she sought adventure and headed to New York City.

The publishing culture of New York—indeed of virtually everywhere in the United States at the time—was dominated by men, but in 1887, Bly approached John A. Cockerill, managing editor at the *New York World*, seeking a job. Cockerill agreed to let Bly take an assignment, one of the most difficult he could imagine at the time, as a way of seeing if she would pass the test.

Bly would take an undercover assignment for which she agreed to feign insanity to investigate reports of brutality and neglect at the Women's Lunatic Asylum on Blackwell's Island. After a night of practicing deranged expressions in front of a mirror, she checked into a working-class boardinghouse. She refused to go to bed, telling the boarders that she was afraid of them and that they looked crazy. They soon decided that she was insane and, the next morning, summoned the police. Taken to a courtroom, she feigned amnesia. The judge concluded someone had drugged the young woman, and doctors ordered her taken to Blackwell's Island.

Bly wrote of her experience through a series of articles for the *World* that was later published in a book titled, *Ten Days in a Madhouse*. In this, she described of the horrific treatment that the patients faced on a daily basis.

> I was never so tired as I grew sitting on those benches. Several of the patients would sit on one foot or sideways to make a change, but they were always reproved and told to sit up straight. If they talked they were scolded and told to shut up; if they wanted to walk around in order to take the stiffness out of them, they were told to sit down and be still. What, excepting torture, would produce insanity quicker than this treatment? Here is a class of women sent to be cured. I would like the expert physicians who are condemning me for my action, which has proven their ability, to take a perfectly sane and healthy woman, shut her up and make her sit from 6 a.m. until 8 p.m. on straight-back benches, do not allow her to talk or move during these hours, give her no reading and let her know nothing of the world or its doings, give her bad food and harsh treatment, and see how long it will take to make her insane. Two months would make her a mental and physical wreck.[10]

Bly's report caused a sensation and brought her lasting fame. While embarrassed physicians and staff struggled to explain how Bly had fooled so many professionals, a grand jury launched its own investigation into conditions at the asylum, inviting Bly to assist. The jury recommended the changes she had proposed, and its call for increased funds for care of the insane prompted an $850,000 increase in the budget of the Department of Public Charities and Corrections.

Riding the fame from her reform of Blackwell's Island story—along with numerous other adventures as a stunt reporter for Joseph Pulitzer—Bly's next big story brought sensationalism to a new level (one explored in more detail in Chapter 8 of this book). In 1888, Pulitzer designed a masterpiece of self-promotion by suggesting Bly travel around the world as a reporter for his *New York World*. The feat would mimic what only a fictional character until that time had accomplished in Jules Verne's book *Around the World in Eighty Days*. It would also test the limits of human endurance and the communications networks that over time had established the possibility of rapid message delivery on a global scale.

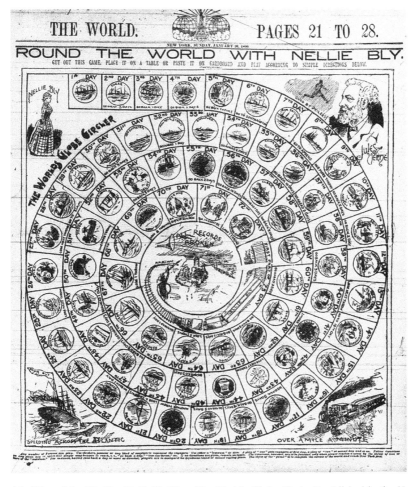

Image 4.5: "Round the World with Nellie Bly—The *World*'s Globe Circler," published in the *New York World*, January 26, 1890, a board game about journalist Bly's around the world trip shows squares for each of the seventy-three days of her journey arranged in a circular pattern, flanked with images of Bly, Jules Verne, a steamship, and a train.[11]

Bly agreed to the challenge, and on November 14, 1889, she left New York for a journey of almost 25,000 miles, which at the time would have taken several months for an ordinary traveler to complete. She brought with her the dress she wore, an overcoat, several changes of underwear, and a small travel bag carrying her toiletry essentials, carrying most of her money in a bag tied around her neck. Bly traveled through England and then to France, where she met Jules Verne. She then went to Southern Italy, the Suez Canal, Colombo (Ceylon), the Straits Settlements of Penang and Singapore, Hong Kong, and Japan. The development of efficient submarine cable networks and the electric telegraph allowed Bly to send short progress reports, though longer dispatches had to travel by regular post and took several weeks to reach print.

To sustain interest in the story, the *World* organized a "Nellie Bly Guessing Match" in which readers were asked to estimate Bly's arrival time to the second, with the grand prize consisting at first of a free trip to Europe and, later, spending money for the trip.

Because of rough weather on her Pacific crossing, she arrived in San Francisco on the White Star Liner Oceanic two days behind schedule. To make up for the time, Pulitzer chartered a private train to bring her home, and she arrived in New Jersey on January 25, 1890, completing the trip in only 72 days, 6 hours, 11 minutes, and 14 seconds.

Her reports for the *World* had included details on exotic places for readers who followed her descriptions with genuine intrigue and fascination. As the first woman to travel around the world unaccompanied at all times by a man, she became a role model for women everywhere, having accomplished the inconceivable at that point, opening travel possibilities in a way that the telegraph had opened communication connections. Bly personified changes in the newspaper industry in other ways, both in the content she produced and in the era in which she lived. Leading editors in the era before the steam press and telegraph had made sporadic attempts at cooperation in obtaining national news, but the 1848 formation of the New York Associated Press marked the first successful collaboration. Out of this idea grew other local, then state, and finally national associations. The telegraph, on yet another revolutionary level, made possible the delivery of information on a global scale. With the establishment of the transatlantic cable that in the 1860s connected the East Coast of the United States with Europe, information from thousands of miles away was available almost immediately for the first time in human history.

Prior to the introduction of the technological advances in the mid-nineteenth century, newspaper content had been locally oriented and directed toward the individual. Afterwards, it came to meet the demands of the emerging business ethos of the country. The changes in the economic basis of the newspaper contributed directly to the transition, as advertising became more and more general with the increase in circulation and appealed to a less specific local audience. The revenues of newspapers consequently tended to depend more on the favor of the advertiser than upon subscribers, giving the former a powerful although indirect influence on editorial policies.

While city news associations continued to collect local items of interest, national press associations, composed of newspapers across the country, collected and distributed news of national importance to cater to the new publishing model. As a result, the scope of news naturally broadened, and stylistically, it included innovations such as interviews that featured dialogue and direct quotation, allowing reports on business, markets, and finance to take on a new professionalism. Another increasingly favorite feature was the series of letters from the editor or another member of the staff who traveled abroad and wrote of what he heard or saw. The growth of these features also meant the unprecedented growth of staffs—writers and manual laborers—that exceeded the size and professional organization of anything developed by publishers of preceding eras. It also brought an added emphasis on the talents of individual writers over the style of a particular editor.

RECAPPING THIS CHAPTER

Looking back on this chapter, you should see how it focused on changes to content brought by technological advances, as well as the famous "stunt journalism" practiced by Nellie Bly in her historic travels around the world. The chapter began by noting the changes brought to the penny press industry by the *New York Times*, which relied on a "facts only" approach. It also showed how the immediate transmission of news changed the content and construction of information, eventually leading to global news.

Using materials from this chapter, you should be able to see how communication technologies affected the speed of news delivery and content itself. You should also be able to compare and contrast the kinds of news content that were popular both before and after the introduction of the telegraph, seeing a correlation between technology and mass production, and you should explain how traveling the world at record speed contributed directly to the development of the newspaper industry.

The following chapter describes the role the press had in reporting the Civil War, focusing on the way in which the war transformed the press into a more visually based form of communication. It provides an overview of the print and photographic materials published in the mid-to-late nineteenth century press to demonstrate how images gradually became part of the mainstream press, and it profiles Mathew Brady as a pioneer in a form of media much more common today than it was in the 1860s.

NOTES

1. David W. Bulla and Gregory A. Borchard, *Journalism in the Civil War Era* (New York: Peter Lang, 2010), 106.
2. "Mexican News," Library of Congress, accessed June 6, 2016, <item/90715229>.
3. *Association Discussed; or, The Socialism of the Tribune Examined, Being a Controversy Between the New York Tribune and the Courier and Enquirer, by H. Greeley and H.J. Raymond* (New York: Harper, 1847), Preface, 9, 10, 34.
4. "A Word about Ourselves," *The New York Times*, September 18, 1851, p. 21.
5. "Political Boss William March 'Boss' Tweed, in *The New York Times*, 1871," in Charles F. Wingate, *Harper's Weekly* (July 1875): 150.
6. "The Progress of the Century," Library of Congress, accessed May 25, 2016, <item/90716345>.
7. James Carey, *Communication as Culture* (New York, London: Routledge, 1989), 213.
8. "Representative Journals & Journalists of America," Library of Congress, accessed June 6, 2016, <item/2003680823>.
9. "Nellie Bly," Library of Congress, accessed June 5, 2016, <item/2004671937>.
10. Nellie Bly, *Ten Days in a Mad-House* (New York: Ian L. Munro) "Promenading with Lunatics," para. 16.
11. "Round the World with Nellie Bly," Library of Congress, accessed June 4, 2016, <item/2002716792>.

5

THE PRESS IN THE CIVIL WAR ERA
PIONEERS IN PRINT AND PHOTOGRAPHY

This chapter describes the role the press had in reporting the Civil War, focusing on the way in which the war transformed the press into a more visually based form of communication:

- It provides an overview of the print and photographic materials published in the mid-to-late nineteenth century press to demonstrate how images gradually became part of the mainstream press;
- and it profiles Mathew Brady as a pioneer in a form of media much more common today than it was in the 1860s.

Using materials from this chapter, students should appreciate the press of the Civil War era relative to innovations in technologies that have demonstrated a recurring reliance on pre-existing forms of communication, including artistic expression:

- They should be able to identify similar and different features in the storytelling techniques of print and visual media;
- and they should explain the role of the Civil War in helping to popularize new media.

Key words, names, and phrases associated with Chapter 5 include:

- Antebellum print (Elijah Lovejoy and Harriet Beecher Stowe);
- Mathew Brady and his photographers;

- daguerreotypes and visual technologies;
- and *Harper's Weekly* and *Frank Leslie's Illustrated*.

The press during the mid-nineteenth century underwent a gradual but dramatic change, moving from text-based content to more visually oriented content at the end of the century. While readers of the news before the Civil War would find mostly words communicating information, innovations in technology allowed publishers to include to a greater extent illustrated and photographic work, offering new forms of enlightenment and entertainment.

Throughout the course of the Civil War itself, images—whether illustrated or photographic—captured a sense of humanity that the written word alone could not communicate. At the same time, illustrations provided the opportunity for an artist to include a certain level of humanity that photos alone could not convey. The interplay between the two mediums—whether drawn manually or produced technologically—created in some cases a singular form of communication that both complemented and transcended the written word alone, providing an additional dimension for the language of text.

The transition from woodcut technologies to photography was not immediate; in fact, drawings and sketches continue to exist in editorial cartoons and other forms of hand-created artwork for journalistic purposes. Regardless, photography continued to evolve into new technologies such as the halftone, color imagery, and on to the digital imagery of today. These changes continue to play an instrumental role in the way media depict events and shape our understanding of them.

THE PRESS AND ANTEBELLUM POLITICS

The context for these developments included political, social, and cultural issues that extended well beyond the publishing world. The Whig Party, active in the penny press era, collapsed in 1852, leading to a new party configuration that affected social institutions and the press itself. The Republican Party filled the absence of the Whigs and first nominated a candidate for president in 1856, John C. Frémont, who represented the pioneer spirit in the settlement of the West. Although Frémont received support from those who advocated an end to the spread of slavery, the Democrats won the 1856 election with candidate James Buchanan, who subsequently did nothing to quell the growing national crisis about the role slavery would play (or not play) in the West. Republicans then set their sights on the 1860 election and had better success with Abraham Lincoln, a media-savvy candidate who more decisively represented Northern interests.

An abolitionist publisher from Illinois had well before Lincoln's nomination captured the attention of the press and the electorate alike in the way he had described slavery as the most pressing moral issue of the day. Reverend Elijah Parish Lovejoy, born in Albion, Maine, November 9, 1802, began his career in newspapers as editor of the *St. Louis Observer*, which opposed Jacksonian politics. He studied at the Princeton

Theological Seminary in New Jersey and become an ordained Presbyterian minister. When he returned to St. Louis, he set up a church and resumed work as editor of the *Observer*, running condemnations of slavery and advocating a strictly denominational approach to religion. Angry mobs responded to the content of his editorials by destroying his printing presses on three separate occasions. He then moved to Alton, Illinois, where he established his fourth and final printing press. On November 7, 1837, a pro-slavery mob shot Lovejoy dead while he attempted to protect the press that would have printed the *Alton Observer*.[1]

Awareness and concern about the abolitionist cause spread throughout the North, as a citizen practicing under protection of the First Amendment had died defending his beliefs. The Northern public revered Lovejoy with the moniker "Martyr on the Altar of American Liberty." In a ceremony that honored Lovejoy, attendee John Brown, an intensely zealous figure who would appear recurrently in national news in the years before the Civil War, grew so incensed he vowed he would dedicate his life to ending slavery.[2]

The abolitionist movement for the most part in the years following Lovejoy's martyrdom remained a small-but-vocal collection of reformers, but one publication in particular helped turn anti-slavery sentiment into a mainstream cause. And although the piece had a literary audience (not a journalistic one) in mind when its author, Harriet Beecher Stowe, wrote it, it had its greatest impact through the press, as copies of it were published and republished countless times in newspapers throughout the United States and into Europe. It might even be said that *Uncle Tom's Cabin*—first published in 1851 and again and again ever since—has become one of the most widely read pieces of American writing ever.

Harriet Beecher Stowe was born on June 14, 1811, in Litchfield, Connecticut, to Reverend Lyman Beecher and Roxanna Foote Beecher. In 1851, Gamaliel Bailey of the *National Era* asked her to compose a story that would illustrate the lives of those affected by slavery. Originally released in serial form, its publisher released *Uncle Tom's Cabin* as installments from June 5, 1851, to April 1, 1852. The storyline focuses on a slave, Uncle Tom, who escapes bondage to find freedom in the North and suggests that Christian love can overcome the destructive impact of the enslavement of fellow human beings.

Many of the book's readers, whether they found it in hard copy or newspapers, or saw it depicted as a play, found the graphic horrors of slavery depicted in dramatic and realistic form for the first time. *Uncle Tom's Cabin* became such a sensation that it was the best-selling novel of the nineteenth century, second to only the Bible in overall sales of any book. In the first year after its publication, readers bought more than 300,000 in the United States alone, with one million more copies sold in Great Britain. It became a best-seller in European and Asian countries with translations in more than 65 languages.

Combined with the dramatic and sensational elements of the book, part of the reason for its success had to do with the publication practices of the era. Publishers paid no attention to copyright issues, as most of the conventions about asking for permission to reproduce did not evolve until the next century. The mass reproduction of *Uncle Tom's Cabin*, both in the United States and throughout Europe, had become so remarkable that at one point during the Civil War, according to legend, President Lincoln met the author and said, "So you're the little woman who wrote the book that started this Great War?"[3]

The effect of *Uncle Tom's Cabin* when combined with the political and economic developments of the 1850s galvanized moral sentiment in the North against the institution of slavery to the point it was no longer politically sustainable in the existing configuration of the Union. Americans who lived in Southern states increasingly saw the anti-slavery and abolitionist movements as direct threats to their way of life, as both Congress and the presidency appeared unable to maintain a balance between competing economies in the new western states, ultimately throwing into chaos questions of representation, taxation, and power in Washington, D.C.

In a stunning example of this polarization, John Brown, who in 1859 acted on his vow to end slavery, organized a haphazard raid on Harpers Ferry, he said, to initiate a slave insurrection. When Brown died in an execution for treason and murder, formerly pacifist editors praised the militant. While Ralph Waldo Emerson compared Brown to Jesus in their mutual self-sacrifice, Frederick Douglass, after initially rejecting Brown's plans to start an insurrection, later said simply and profoundly, "I could live for the slave, but he could die for him."[4] William Lloyd Garrison suggested—in the following excerpt from a speech he delivered, as published in *The Liberator*—that the time for armed conflict had arrived.

> The raid of Brown and his subsequent execution, and their reception at the North revealed how vast was the revolution in public sentiment on the slavery question which had taken place there, since the murder of Lovejoy, eighteen years before. Lovejoy died defending the right of free speech and the liberty of the press, yet the Attorney-General of Massachusetts declared that "he died as the fool dieth." Brown died in an invasion of a slave State, and in an effort to emancipate the slaves with a band of eighteen followers, and he was acclaimed, from one end of the free States to the other, hero, and martyr.... The sympathy and admiration now so widely felt for him, prove how marvelous has been the change affected in public opinion during the thirty years of moral agitation—a change so great indeed, that whereas, ten years since, there were thousands who could not endure my lightest word of rebuke of the South, they can now easily swallow John Brown whole and his rifle into the bargain. In firing his gun, he has merely told us what time of day it is. It is high noon, thank God![5]

While the nation's problem with slavery was not a new one—present since well before the ratification of the Constitution—it clearly played a role in triggering the events that led to conflict. The press, in this respect, both reflected the nation's antagonisms at the time, and despite efforts to reach compromise, it actually helped to fuel the nation's greatest crisis.

THE EVOLUTION OF NEWSPAPER CONVENTIONS DURING THE CIVIL WAR

Eyewitnesses have covered no event in American history as thoroughly as the Civil War, as it occurred in the literal and metaphorical backyards of millions of people.

For four years, nearly everyone affected participated in coverage either as a reader or sometimes as a supplier of news, with citizens often providing the most direct accounts of events in written form for newspapers. While publishers turned over almost all of the space reserved for editorials to war coverage, technology aided in reporting, allowing for increases in quantity, quality, and speed of transmission of news.

As a result, no less than two features of news that we still consider common today—the inverted pyramid and the byline—actually first became standardized practice at this time. Although certain publishers for particular reasons used both the inverted pyramid and the byline before the Civil War, these practices became more and more widely used as standard journalistic protocol, with the rationale stemming from war strategy.

- With the risk of enemy combatants intercepting sensitive information by tapping the wires of telegraphs for messages, the inverted pyramid style of news delivery ensured that the most important information would at least reach the intended receiver before any additional information was lost to an interfering party.
- Likewise, with the widespread publication of sensitive information in popular newspapers—much to the dismay of Union military leaders—Abraham Lincoln's Secretary of War Edwin Stanton required writers to include bylines as a way for the government and potential prosecutors to determine if the author inadvertently or intentionally disclosed to Southern intelligence news that jeopardized the lives of troops.

For example, the *New York Tribune* at one point in the war had revealed General William Tecumseh Sherman's plans of attack. Southern commanders adjusted their strategy accordingly and cost the Union lives. While Stanton attempted to quell reckless publication, Sherman called for nothing less than censorship. After the incident, the general said, "If I could have caught Mr. Greeley . . . I would have hung him."[6]

In terms of journalistic content itself, likely the most dramatic of singular press developments during the war came in the form of an editorial that in a number of ways changed the course of the war itself. Historians have described Horace Greeley's "Prayer of Twenty Millions" as one of the most famous (if not the single-most famous) columns written in American history, as it called upon President Lincoln to change his strategy for prosecuting the war. Until its publication, the Union had lost decisively in most battles under the premise that Northern armies were fighting to bring seceded states back into the Union. Greeley made a plea to Lincoln on behalf of the laborers of the North (the twenty million represented in the title) to give workers a cause in which they could believe, one that liberated millions of others in bondage. He wrote:

> I do not intrude to tell you—for you must know already—that a great proportion of those who triumphed in your election, and of all who desire the unqualified suppression of the Rebellion now desolating our country, are sorely disappointed and deeply pained by the policy you seem to be pursuing with regard to the slaves of the Rebels. I write only to set succinctly and unmistakably before you what we require, what we think we have a right to expect, and of what we complain.

Greeley in subsequent paragraphs advocated a number of corrective steps for Lincoln to take in boosting morale, and among his most salient points, Greeley writes, "We complain that the Union cause has suffered, and is now suffering immensely, from mistaken deference to Rebel Slavery." [7] In this passage, along with others referencing slavery, the *New York Tribune* editor called on Lincoln to change the strategy of the war from one designed to restore the Union to one that would end slavery as a cause of higher moral value.

The editorial received wide exposure, and when Lincoln did in fact issue the Emancipation Proclamation, the news-reading public assumed that Greeley had inspired the edict with his bold publishing maneuver. What the public did not know at the time was that Lincoln had already drafted the Emancipation Proclamation, and a complex series of events had preceded Greeley's publication. Publicly, Lincoln could not indicate he had already decided on essentially the same strategy that Greeley proposed, as changing the course of the war at a point in which the Union had not won a battle or series of battles would look weak and desperate, counteracting any benefit that might be derived. By necessity, Lincoln published a response to Greeley in a Washington, D.C., newspaper on August 22, 1862, saying the Union first—and not the liberation of slaves—was his top priority.[8]

Within a month of this exchange, however, the Union won a highly contested tactical victory at Antietam. On September 17—what is still on record as the bloodiest day in American history—more than 23,000 Union and Confederate soldiers suffered casualties. Yet Lincoln received the victory for which he had waited, and five days later, he issued preliminary details of the Emancipation Proclamation to the public, which would take effect January 1, 1863.[9]

After the fact, Greeley claimed he had understood that the president was deliberating emancipation before Antietam, but publicly, Greeley's readers and detractors alike recognized him as having helped to make abolition a goal of the war. His own editorials proclaimed the edict would usher in a new era of freedom, a recurring phrase in both the lexicons of Lincoln and the *Tribune*, and that it would lead to the end of the war.

PHOTOJOURNALISM COMES INTO ITS OWN

In the years leading up to the Civil War, photography enjoyed its most popular individual use in the form of personal mementoes, not for the news. Images in circulation included vignettes, or headshots with surrounding detail and a blurred torso. The major photographic studios sold photographs of famous persons, which owners valued as precious collectibles.

With the increasing popularity of photographs among the public, leading magazines at mid-century sought to capitalize on the phenomenon and began publishing illustrations, woodcuts, and other representations of pictures on the same pages that carried the news. *Harper's Weekly* and *Frank Leslie's Illustrated* led the trend and, as early as the 1850s, published large illustrations sometimes based on woodcut versions of photographs. The center pages of these publications contained large pictorials, known a century later as "double-truck" artwork, which during the war often depicted panoramic prints of battle.

Both of these publications first began publishing after the Mexican War, so they became the first American journals to cover warfare with extensive graphical art. James, John, Wesley, and Fletcher Harper had christened Harper and Brothers publishing in 1825, and Fletcher began publishing *Harper's Monthly* in 1850. He originally intended the publication as a vehicle to promote authors such as Dickens and Thackeray, but it was so successful he began *Harper's Weekly* in 1857. His primary competitor, Frank Leslie, was born Henry Carter in Suffolk, England. Leslie was an illustrator who had begun his journalistic drawing career with the *Illustrated News*. Leslie developed a publishing empire based on graphic journalism, and his strengths as a publisher came from the in-house engraving department and presses he designed for pictorial work, giving him an advantage with both price and in the quality of his illustrations.

The interplay between the illustrated work and photographic work that appeared in publication involved a complex process that evolved over time. Actual photographs of the Civil War at first appeared only in exhibitions, with the first formal presentation—pictures of soldiers' corpses on battlefields—appearing in the studio of Mathew Brady, a pioneering producer of photography, shortly after the 1862 Battle of Antietam. The visual record of the conflict captured the horrors of war in a way never before seen, as illustrated magazines had only sometimes converted photographs into wood engravings for use in the mass production of images. Most often, the illustrated magazines dispatched their own sketch artists to the scenes of battle.

As part of this process, enterprising photographers had opened studios throughout the country, exhibiting their pictures and promoting this innovation. The public became increasingly familiar with this new medium, and as it grew in popularity, soldiers and politicians routinely visited these photographers to have their pictures taken, and common people adopted daguerreotypes as family heirlooms and household decorations. Taking its name from Louis-Jacques-Mandé Daguerre, a French chemist who first produced the photographic medium, the daguerreotype eventually faded as a form of photography, as new technologies developed likenesses of people and events with realistic precision.

While Brady hired employees to take the actual photographs he would circulate and display, taking fewer photos of his own as his career progressed, an extraordinary photo he took of Abraham Lincoln in 1860 provides a sample of the power this new media had in capturing the attention of the news-reading public.

On February 27, 1860, the day Brady took this photo, Lincoln gave a speech at the Cooper Union Institute in Manhattan. Before the speech, he visited Brady's New York studio and had his portrait taken. In the photograph, Lincoln, who was not yet sporting a beard, stands next to a table, resting his hand on some books. The photograph, known as the "Cooper Union Portrait," became iconic as a model for distributed engravings, and the image would be the basis for campaign posters in the 1860 election. Lincoln himself reportedly credited the photo to helping him win in November, as it familiarized the public with his appearance.

The November 10 issue of *Harper's Weekly* later that year published the woodcut version of the photo on its cover, celebrating Lincoln's election.

With the mirrored reversal of Lincoln's image reflecting the stenciled version of the photograph when transposed to a woodcut impression, Winslow Homer, a premier American painter and printmaker, prepared the sketch for *Harper's Weekly* even before

Election Day. The outcome of the vote would not be certain for another week or two, but *Harper's Weekly* issued the cover anyway.

Throughout the war, both *Harper's* and *Leslie's* used woodcuts—manually etched stencils of photographs—that were impressed upon paper to create images that closely resembled photographs. These engravings came from illustrations made by sketch artists in the field. Use of a multiple-block system increased speed by dividing a drawing into four or five segments—after different engravers completed working on each segment, they locked each block into a frame for a more efficient form of production. A master

Image 5.1: "Photo of Lincoln (Cooper Union photo, 1860)," Mathew Brady, photographer, 1860.[10]

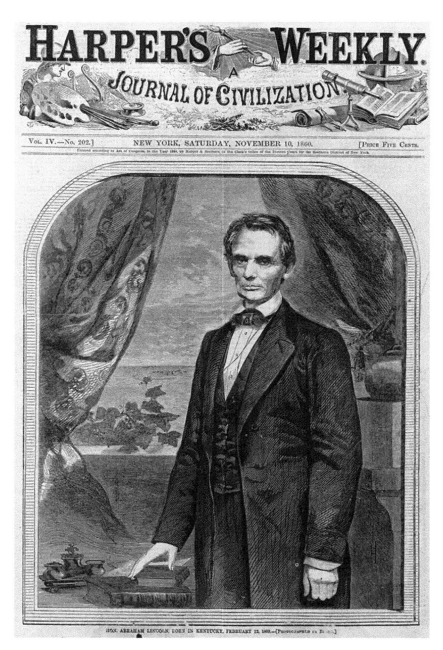

Image 5.2: "Hon. Abraham Lincoln, born in Kentucky, February 12, 1809," Mathew Brady, photographer, illustration in *Harper's Weekly*, 4 (November 10, 1860): 705.[11]

Image 5.3: "Gettysburg, Pa., Alfred R. Waud, Artist of *Harper's Weekly*, Sketching on Battlefield," Timothy H. O'Sullivan, photographer, Gettysburg, July 1863.[12]

Image 5.4: "Petersburg, VA, Dead Confederate Soldier with Gun," published April 3, 1865, a photograph from the main eastern theater of war during the siege of Petersburg.[13]

Image 5.5: "An Incident of Gettysburg—the Last Thought of a Dying Father," published in *Frank Leslie's Illustrated* (January 2, 1864): 236, a dead New York volunteer holds a picture of his children.[14]

engraver cut the lines that crossed the various blocks. The center pages of these publications contained a large pictorial, known a century later as "double-truck" artwork, which during the war often depicted panoramic prints of battle and gave a sense of a battle's scope. They featured action, which made the prints far less static than portraits and maps.

While professional photographers with the luxury of hindsight have since taken the opportunity to criticize Mathew Brady's photographers for manipulating their subjects into more dramatic poses, the practice, at a time of unprecedented journalistic innovation, would have withstood at least the immediate scrutiny of his peers, as Brady had none. Moreover, as these two images demonstrate, Brady's photographers in many ways simply mimicked, as might be expected, a common practice among newspaper illustrators.

The body of the subject featured in the photo, similar to the illustrated soldier at Gettysburg (below), was also manipulated (in this case, propped into a visually compelling position), demonstrating how photography often worked to meet the expectations of audiences more accustomed to artistically rendered stories.

It is unlikely, for example, that the artist of "An Incident of Gettysburg" portrayed the subject in a wholly realistic manner; however, it is also unlikely that readers expected him to do so.

REALISM AND REALITY IN PHOTOGRAPHY

A photo by Brady of General Ambrose Burnside and his staff at Cold Harbor, which publishers also printed in woodcut version, typifies the approach of using a photo and then a woodcut for mass production. It also captures the interplay between available technologies, with the woodcut version—based on a combination of photography and the liberties of an illustrator—in some ways improving on the detail of the photograph, while the photograph itself captured a realism that escaped the most observant of illustrators.[15]

As a portrait, the picture compares well with the portraiture paintings of the era; yet, much of the background fades into invisibility due to overexposure and the technological limitations of photography at the time. Much of the detail in the foreground is also overexposed. The lighter foreground and background contrasts with the linear group in their dark uniforms, framed by trees on either side.

The illustrated version of this image at least somewhat corrects the imperfections of the photo. The illustrator reinserted objects not even visible in the photograph, such as the building in the background and the detail of tree branches.

Another image from the Brady collection that left a lasting impression on viewers, this photo, among the most harrowing from a member of a burial site, sits a member of a burial party with a stretcher full of skulls and partial corpses as he and other men reinter the dead months after the battles of Gaines' Mill and Cold Harbor.

Unlike popular notions before the war of the United States as a place where American culture would civilize the world through advances in technology and wealth, the burial party at Cold Harbor exposed death as wild and wreaking havoc on the idea that humans were humane.

The following excerpt from a caption for the picture originally published in Alexander Gardner's *Photographic Sketch Book of the War* describes a "sad scene" in language that would have resonated with contemporary readers.

Image 5.6: "Major General A. E. Burnside and Staff," illustrated in *Harper's Weekly* (July 23, 1864): 469, a photograph credited to Mathew Brady taken at Cold Harbor June 11 or 12, 1864.[16]

Image 5.7: "Cold Harbor, Va. Gen. Burnside and His Staff at 9th Corps Headquarters," published in *Harper's Weekly* (July 23, 1864): 469, illustrated from a photograph by Mathew Brady.[17]

Image 5.8: "A Burial Party on the Battle-field of Cold Harbor," photographed by John Reekie, April 1, 1865, in *Gardner's Photographic Sketch Book of the War*, Vol. 1, plate 94, 1866, showing a member of the group tasked with re-burying the remains of fallen soldiers. He sits next to a stretcher containing remains from the battles of Gaines' Mill and Cold Harbor.[18]

> It speaks ill of the residents of that part of Virginia, that they allowed even the remains of those they considered enemies, to decay unnoticed where they fell. The soldiers, to whom commonly falls the task of burying the dead, may possibly have been called away before the task was completed. At such times the native dwellers of the neighborhood would usually come forward and provide sepulture for such as had been left uncovered.[19]

Photography from near the war's end provides a sample of the realism—or in a sense, the over realism—gleaned from this new form of media in the pictures of survivors from the infamous Andersonville prison camp in central Georgia. Confederates held thousands of Union soldiers at Andersonville, and because of scarce resources and gross mismanagement, the troops suffered from exposure and unfathomable conditions. The photos of survivors from the camp reveal images of people who appear barely alive, emaciated, and in horrific corpse-like condition.

Doctors did not leave exhaustive accounts about the condition of every single Andersonville survivor, but in one particular analysis, they pointed to similar features between an observed survivor and those captured in photographs. The photographic evidence was so compelling that the defense at the trial of the overseers of the camp was reduced to claiming that the photographs had been faked and that they were nothing more than "fancy sketches."[20]

Not surprisingly, the assassination of President Lincoln prompted a wealth of imagery, although accurate eyewitness accounts were rare. At first, the public relied on news accounts and editorials to piece together the events. When, on the night of April 14, John Wilkes Booth fired a bullet into the president's head and killed him, the nation grieved with a sorrow as profound as that which had afflicted families who lost loved ones during the war. America never before had experienced a presidential assassination. According to the *New York Times*, "news of the assassination of Abraham Lincoln carried with it a sensation of horror and of agony which no other event in our history has ever excited."[21] The newspaper that effectively had become Lincoln's hometown journal, the *Chicago Tribune*, reinforced the sentiment, with editorials describing the assassination as the worst crime since Jesus' crucifixion. "The nation mourns. Its agony is great," the *Tribune* wrote. "Its grief is dumb. Never before have the American people been so stricken. The ball that pierced the President has pierced the hearts of all of us."[22]

The public did not begin to gather a more unfiltered depiction of his events until after the trial and execution of the conspirators who arranged his assassination. The hanging of his co-conspirators was especially a public spectacle.

Along with photographer Alexander Gardner's gothic photography, Frank Leslie's "special artists" portrayed the event in sketches, and the two sets of depictions form the basis for understanding how the scene appeared.

The spectacle of the executions, along with other condemnations from the Northern press of the role of the South in the war, brought former Confederate president Jefferson Davis to condemn the press of the Civil War era. In 1865, he reportedly said:

Image 5.9: "Washington, D.C., Hanging Hooded Bodies of the Four Conspirators; Crowd Departing," Alexander Gardner, photographer, July 7, 1865.[23]

Image 5.10: "Execution of the Conspirators, Mrs. Mary E. Surratt, Lewis Powell (Alias Payne), George Ahzerodt and David E. Harold," published in *Frank Leslie's Illustrated Newspaper*, 20, 512 (July 22, 1865): 280, 281, an illustration based on photographs depicting the Prison Yard of the Old Penitentiary, Washington, D.C., July 7.[24]

> The Northern press had been working with treble power and at fever-heat for some years, and would require another year to calm back into ordinary journalism. Sensationalism was the necessity at present, and offenses which would have been dismissed with a paragraph in the police reports four or five years ago, were now magnified into columns or a page of startling capitals.[25]

However, events after the war and the press' coverage of them revealed Davis might have actually underestimated the public's appetite for sensational content, as violence from the Civil War spilled into the new era of Reconstruction.

The Civil War also cemented a role for photography among the public by first introducing them to the power of visual images and then creating an interest in creating generations of photographers to follow. Within decades, amateur photographers soon blossomed and made the new medium a mainstay in American culture. Several innovators helped popularize this transformation, but George Eastman (July 12, 1854– March 14, 1932) succeeded in doing so most dramatically. Founding the Eastman Kodak Company, he helped make photography a mainstream endeavor by producing film rolls at an affordable price. Photographs continue to provide essential sources of information to audiences intrigued by both news and entertainment.

RECAPPING THIS CHAPTER

Looking back on this chapter, you should see how it described the role the press had in reporting the Civil War, focusing on the way in which the war transformed the press into a more visually based form of communication. The chapter provided an overview of the print and photographic materials published in the mid-to-late nineteenth century press to demonstrate how images gradually became part of the mainstream press, and it profiled Mathew Brady as a pioneer in a form of media much more common today than it was in the 1860s.

Using materials from this chapter, you should appreciate the press of the Civil War era relative to innovations in technologies that have demonstrated a recurring reliance on pre-existing forms of communication, including artistic expression. You should be able to identify similar and different features in the storytelling techniques of print and visual media and should be able to explain the role of the Civil War in helping popularize the new form of media.

The following chapter describes the triumphs and failures of the press in the second half of the nineteenth century. It opens with Horace Greeley's failed campaign for president in 1872, juxtaposed with Ida B. Wells' crusade against lynching, and it shows how Reconstruction journalism bridged traditional models of publishing popularized before the Civil War into a new wave of sensational content fueled by technological development.

NOTES

1 "A Martyr on the Altar of American Liberty," *Alton Observer*, November 7, 1837.
2 F. B. Sanborn, *The Life and Letters of John Brown, Liberator of Kansas, and Martyr of Virginia* (Boston: Roberts Brothers, 1891), 620.

3 Charles Edward Stowe, *Harriet Beecher Stowe: The Story of Her Life* (Boston and New York: Houghton Mifflin), 203.
4 Frederick Douglass, *John Brown, An Address by Frederick Douglass, at the Fourteenth Anniversary of Storer College, Harper's Ferry, West Virginia, May 30, 1881* (Dover, NH: Morning Star Job Printing House, 1881), West Virginia Archives & History, accessed April 28, 2016, <wvculture.org>.
5 William Lloyd Garrison, "Annual Meeting of the Massachusetts Anti-Slavery Society, January 27, 1860," as quoted in *The Liberator*, February 3, 1860.
6 Gregory A. Borchard, *Lincoln and Greeley* (Carbondale: Southern Illinois University Press, 2011), 76.
7 "The Prayer of the Twenty Millions," *New York Tribune*, August 20, 1862.
8 Lincoln to Greeley, August 22, 1862, in Roy Basler, *Collected Works* (New Brunswick, NJ: Rutgers, 1953–55): 5:388–89.
9 Lincoln, "Emancipation Proclamation," September 22, 1862, Library of Congress, accessed May 2, 2016, <memory.loc.gov>.
10 "Photo of Lincoln," Library of Congress, accessed May 25, 2016, <item/npc2008008818>.
11 "Hon. Abraham Lincoln," Library of Congress, accessed June 8, 2016, <item/98518286>.
12 "Gettysburg, Pa., Alfred R. Waud," Library of Congress, accessed June 8, 2016, <item/cwp2003000198/PP/>.
13 "Petersburg, VA, Dead Confederate Soldier with Gun," Library of Congress, accessed May 23, 2016, <item/cwp2003000604/PP>.
14 "An Incident of Gettysburg," Library of Congress, accessed May 23, 2016, <item/2002709419>.
15 Gregory A. Borchard, Lawrence J. Mullen, and Stephen Bates, "From Realism to Reality: The Advent of War Photography," *Journalism & Communication Monographs*, 15, 2 (Summer 2013): 66–107.
16 "Major General A. E. Burnside," Library of Congress, accessed May 23, 2016, <item/2013647582>.
17 "Cold Harbor, Va.," Library of Congress, accessed May 23, 2016, <item/cwp2003001113/PP>.
18 "A Burial Party on the Battle-field," Library of Congress, accessed May 23, 2016, <item/2002713100>.
19 Alexander Gardner, *Gardner's Photographic Sketch Book of the War*, Vol. 2 (Washington: Philp & Solomons, 1865–66), Plate 94.
20 General N. P. Chipman, *The Horrors of Andersonville Rebel Prison* (San Francisco: Bancroft Company, 1891), 66.
21 "The Murder of President Lincoln," *New York Times*, April 16, 1865.
22 "Our Great Affliction," *Chicago Tribune*, April 17, 1865.
23 "Washington, D.C. Hanging Hooded Bodies," Library of Congress, accessed May 24, 2016, <item/cwp2003001014/PP>.
24 "Execution of the Conspirators," Library of Congress, accessed May 24, 2016, <item/99614003>.
25 John J. Craven, *Prison Life of Jefferson Davis* (New York: Carleton, 1866), 276–77.

6

THE PRESS IN TRANSITION
FROM RECONSTRUCTION TO THE GILDED AGE

This chapter describes the triumphs and failures of the press during Reconstruction, focusing on Ida B. Wells' *The Red Record* as a landmark piece of journalism:

- It opens with a narration of Horace Greeley's failed campaign for president in 1872, juxtaposed with Wells' crusade against lynching;
- and it shows how Reconstruction journalism bridged traditional models of publishing popularized before the Civil War into a new wave of sensational content fueled by technological development at the end of the nineteenth century.

Using materials from this chapter, students should know why Reconstruction introduced precedents in the role of the press as an agent for social change:

- They should identify key problems both highlighted and ignored by the press leaders and politicians of the era;
- and they should be able to explain why Ida B. Wells deserves credit for taking a particularly brave stance as a writer in exposing the abhorrent practice of lynching.

Key words, names, and phrases associated with Chapter 6 include:

- Horace Greeley, the Liberal Republicans, and the 1872 election;
- Ida B. Wells, lynching, *The Red Record*;

- Mark Twain and the Gilded Age;
- and Horatio Alger and the American Dream.

When an assassin killed Abraham Lincoln in 1865, the Civil War ended, but a new struggle in an era known as Reconstruction began. The process of rebuilding the nation economically, politically, and culturally required enormous efforts, and in some ways, it was never completed.

The Reconstruction era technically lasted until 1877 when a controversial election reset the direction of the nation. Although Republican candidate Rutherford B. Hayes lost both the popular vote and initially the electoral vote to Democrat Samuel Tilden, electors agreed to put Hayes in the presidency with a guarantee that Northern troops would leave the South and restore a measure of sovereignty to the former Confederate States. Accordingly, the press of the era reflected the nation's internal contradictions as editors featured stories of terrific triumph and spectacular failure, looking for ways to find common ideals among their readers.

Among Lincoln's final victories before his death, Congress approved ratification of the Thirteenth Amendment, which he advocated to abolish slavery beginning January 31, 1865. Under the presidency of victorious Union General Ulysses S. Grant, the federal government took measures to guarantee equal protection under law for former slaves and assure their right to vote, which the Fourteenth Amendment and the Fifteenth Amendment protected respectively.

These modifications to the Constitution, known as the Reconstruction Amendments, helped define the era. The amendments alone, however, did not assure the goals of Republicans in Congress were met, and because of violence in the South aimed at discouraging newly emancipated voters from participating in the electoral system, Grant called on the military to intervene again, creating a climate in which the Civil War had not yet met closure.

THE POLITICAL AND CULTURAL CONTEXT OF RECONSTRUCTION

From 1869–1877, President Grant's administration set the template for the nation's best and worst experiences. To this day, Grant's legacy has mixed reviews from historians, with most finding fault with him for appointing corrupt subordinates. However, Grant also stabilized the nation during a turbulent time and prosecuted the Ku Klux Klan, a newly formed organization that terrorized newly emancipated voters, so although his presidency was problematic, its legacy has enjoyed a resurgence among those concerned with the advancement of civil rights.

Although the physical battles of the Civil War had ceased years before Grant's 1868 election, many of the most intense issues addressed by the press in the years leading up to the war continued to influence the course of the nation. From a northern perspective, editors sought to legitimize the battles in which thousands of Yankee soldiers

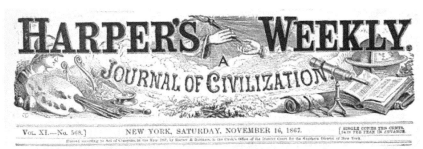

Image 6.1: "The First Vote," A. R. Waud, illustrator, published in *Harper's Weekly*, 11, 568 (November 16, 1867): 721, an illustration showing a queue of African American men: the first, dressed as a laborer, casts his vote; the second, dressed as a businessman; the third wears a Union army uniform; and the fourth appears dressed as a farmer.[1]

had died, and from a southern one, editors in major cities saw the efforts of the federal government, as exercised under the administration of the former Union general, as a continuation of the impositions by Washington before the war.

Horace Greeley's editorial content in the *New York Tribune* had supported President Grant during his first term. By 1871, Greeley and members of the liberal wing of the Republican Party had come to resent what they considered Grant's subservience to hardline Republicans who wanted to keep former Confederates from rejoining the political system at large. Opposing both Grant's military-based Reconstruction efforts and his foreign policy that called for expansion into the Caribbean, the *Tribune*, along with Senators Carl Schurz of Missouri, Lyman Trumbull of Illinois, and Charles Sumner of Massachusetts, began encouraging in the later part of the president's first term a dissident movement of Republicans. In May 1872, the group formed the Liberal Republican Party and, at their convention in Cincinnati, Ohio, picked Greeley as the party's presidential nominee, calling for the restoration of the nation more closely in line, they believed, with the ideals that Lincoln had advocated.

HORACE GREELEY CAMPAIGNS FOR THE PRESIDENCY

Weak and demoralized Democrats in the South saw in Greeley a way for their voices to register nationally. Greeley did indeed receive the Democrats' endorsement, the only time in U.S. history when a major party adopted through a separate endorsement a third-party candidate.

The endorsements initially flattered Greeley, but with an onslaught of negative campaigning and smears against his record, he would later regret the honor, saying, "I have been assailed so bitterly that I hardly knew whether I was running for the Presidency or the penitentiary."[2] Greeley's bid for the presidency began hopefully enough, promoting "Universal Amnesty," which made it possible for southern Democrats to support him because he promised to restore rights to former Confederate officers; however, voters in the South were at the same time alienated by the call, as it entailed the enforcement of rights for freed slaves.

In the North, Greeley's competitors in the newspaper industry exploited his candidacy as an opportunity to build their own circulations with sensational attacks on his character. His critics had little trouble finding controversial editorials published in the *Tribune* during the previous forty years, pointing to them (in many cases out of context) as indicative of Greeley's radicalism. By the end of the summer of 1872, the press campaign against Greeley degenerated into a mudslinging melee, epitomized by the anti-Greeley cartoons of Thomas Nast in *Harper's Weekly*. In one such attack, Nast took Greeley to task in the July 13, 1872, issue that featured a cartoon titled "Red Hot." It showed Greeley, who had published controversial material for decades, forced under much stress to eat his own words hunched over a steaming bowl of "My Own Words and Deeds," doing his best to choke them down.[3]

In what today's operatives of campaigns might describe as a "dirty trick," Nast had likely availed himself of the Republican Congressional Campaign Committee's file of Greeley's speeches and writings. Organized by Senators James Edmunds and Zachariah

Chandler, nearly 300 staff members allocated funds of $30,000 toward searching through decades of Greeley's publications to find material that cast the editor as a radical or fool. The Edmunds-Chandler task force adopted the technique of the modern press agent, publishing a monthly magazine and a pamphlet called "The Greeley Record," as well as distributing a "clip sheet" of damning information to newspapers across the country. While many of the quotes resurfaced in 1872 with little or none of the original context in which they were published, readers at the time could only see Greeley as a radical or a fool based on what he had said or written in the 1840s, 50s, and 60s.

Greeley did receive a measure of support from the anti-Grant cartoons of Matt Morgan in *Frank Leslie's Illustrated Newspaper*, which branded Grant a dictator and a drunk, and of course from his own *Tribune*, but more powerful were condemnations from Grant's supporters that depicted Greeley as a traitor. Greeley had, after all—true to his word—acted on his belief in amnesty for former Confederates and signed the bail bond that allowed former Confederate States of America president Jefferson Davis to leave prison. The move cost the *Tribune* thousands of upset readers, but if anything, Greeley's commitment to being open-minded and forgiving was his downfall.

Still a candidate, Greeley attempted to return to work at his *Tribune* office during the final weeks of the campaign, but managing editor Whitelaw Reid, who worried about Greeley's deteriorating health and the negative effect it might have on the newspaper's

Image 6.2: "Discovery of the Sage of Chappaqua by H. M. Stanley. The Sage Disappears Mysteriously Nov. 5th 1872," published in New York as a lithograph by Ferd. Mayer & Sons, 96 & 98 Fulton Street, 1872, a caricature of Horace Greeley and his disappearance from public life after his defeat in the presidential election. Journalist Henry Morton Stanley, famous for finding David Livingstone in East Africa in 1871, discovers Horace Greeley in a jungle. Greeley embraces a pig with a copy of the *Tribune* at his side. A monkey plays with Greeley's trademark white hat while another reaches for a coconut. The U.S. Capitol shines brightly in the distance.[4]

circulation, forced him to relinquish the post. In October, Greeley's health worsened after his wife, Mary, died, and this was compounded with the election returns—Grant won in a landslide. Greeley fell mortally ill, suffering the stress of an exhausting campaign, the loss of his wife, and the devastating election results. He was interned in an asylum in Pleasantville, New York. Hopeless and ill, Horace Greeley died November 29, 1872.

After his death, even Greeley's harshest detractors realized the loyal Yankee did not deserve the treatment he had received in previous months. After all, the poor man had died only doing only what he thought was best for the country. In turn, and in a change of heart, the same detractors combined with Greeley's supporters to give him a large funeral ceremony, complete with a parade of commemorators and speeches. Greeley's body lay in state for a day in the City Hall, and more than 50,000 visitors came to bid respects. Attendants at the funeral included President Grant and Vice President Schuyler Colfax, Chief Justice Chase, and leading United States senators. Henry Ward Beecher delivered a eulogy, capturing the tale of a man who lived righteously. Among other words spoken, Theodore H. Cuyler, a Presbyterian minister from Brooklyn, said Greeley had died of a broken heart. The *New York Times* and other newspapers published the speeches December 2, 1872, giving Greeley's legacy the wide circulation it deserved. He was buried in Greenwood Cemetery, Brooklyn.

THE AMERICAN DREAM IN THE GILDED AGE

While the Reconstruction Amendments afforded constitutional rights to a segment of society newly enfranchised after centuries of indentured servitude—namely African American men—the language in the Thirteenth, Fourteenth, and Fifteenth Amendments said nothing about women, which to the dismay of women suffragists, created a schism in a movement that had begun well before the Civil War. In 1869, it became clear to reformers who had stood together at Seneca Falls Convention that women would have to continue the fight for suffrage rights.

The new wave of activism that called for the empowerment of women coincided with the popularization of an increasingly sought-after myth known as "The American Dream." Although not directly related, a belief at the heart of this ideal that hard work would lead to success did emerge at the same time women in particular—as well as a new wave of immigrants—began activism toward another constitutional amendment.

Even before the Civil War, Americans had subscribed in some part to a nineteenth-century philosophical perspective on life held that humans could generally work together on benevolent terms, and as each new generation progressed in ways that improved upon practices of the previous generation, individuals could improve the conditions of their lives. These ideas contributed largely to a vision of upward mobility and general optimism. The notion itself had antecedents in the Declaration of Independence's promotion of the right to pursue happiness but became a more fully ingrained part of the American psyche through its popularization in the publications of writer Horatio Alger (January 13, 1832–July 18, 1899), who wrote voluminously about the rags-to-riches myth. While the experiences of millions of sweatshop workers, including immigrants, children, and modern wage slaves, showed the fallacy of Alger's ideas, other examples from the late-nineteenth century show that the individual spirit and its ability to triumph in the face of adversity was in fact a story to follow.

The Gilded Age, a period of industrialization and immigration immediately following Reconstruction, captured the dichotomies of what the United States afforded in a time of tremendous opportunity, and, at the same time, one in which only the rich and powerful enjoyed its rewards. Ironically, this period received its moniker from a satirical observation from Mark Twain, who had coined the phrase "Gilded Age" to describe the elusiveness of material success in inherently corrupt surroundings, as the opulence of the United States covered social decay like a thin gold foil.[5]

The most powerful group of the Gilded Age consisted not of laborers, but a group of industrialists known as the "robber barons." And at the same time, a new generation of reporters, who composed a movement known as muckraking, took the responsibility of exposing the excesses of the elite by using investigative methods and a sense of reform for their purpose.. Among the wealthiest of this class of barons included financial giants J. Pierpont Morgan, Andrew Carnegie, William Vanderbilt, Jay Gould, and John D. Rockefeller—their families ascended during Reconstruction and built industrial empires.

> ### A CLASS OF LEISURE
>
> While there is no hard number to associate with those who composed the robber barons, at least a handful of them developed legacies that have lived through today as representative of the personalities and fortunes of the era. Several of the following industrialists became targets of the muckraker press (Chapter 7).
>
> - Philip Danforth Armour (May 16, 1832–January 6, 1901) made his fortune on food and innovations in the transportation of it with refrigerated rail cars. He founded the Chicago-based firm of Armour & Company and made millions selling meat to the United States Army during the Civil War. In 1875, he moved his base to Chicago and developed an assembly line system for the canning of his product.
> - Andrew Carnegie (November 25, 1835–August 11, 1919) lived the archetypical American Dream, beginning life in poverty and immigrating to the United States with his family from Scotland. He built his empire primarily on steel, an essential component of the Industrial Revolution. During the last eighteen years of his life, he gave away hundreds of millions from his fortune to charities, foundations, and universities.
> - Jason "Jay" Gould (May 27, 1836–December 2, 1892), a leading American railroad developer and speculator, served as an early example of corruption and graft in high finance. In the 1870s, he faced justice, along with William Marcy Tweed, a corrupt politician and labor organizer, for partaking in a large New York embezzlement ring. Tweed and Gould became the subjects of political cartoons by Thomas Nast in 1869, and in October 1871, with Tweed held on $1 million bail, Gould served as chief bondsman.

- John Pierpont (JP) Morgan (April 17, 1837–March 31, 1913) dominated American financing, and during the early 1900s, he and his partners had financial investments in many large corporations and had significant influence over both the nation's banking industries and Congress. He was the leading financier of the Progressive Era and described as America's greatest banker.
- John Davison Rockefeller (July 8, 1839–May 23, 1937) took advantage of conditions in the Reconstruction era to turn Standard Oil into a monopoly. He became the target of a famous muckraking piece (see Chapter 9), and the federal government used antitrust legislation to break Standard Oil into subsidiaries. He is widely considered the wealthiest American of all time and the richest person in modern history.
- Cornelius Vanderbilt (May 27, 1794–January 4, 1877) made his fortunes from the railroads. Known as "Commodore" Vanderbilt, he built his reputation on construction of the New York Central Railroad. As one of the richest Americans in history and wealthiest figures overall, Vanderbilt was the patriarch of a wealthy, influential family.

The Robber Barons engaged in what sociologist Thorstein Veblen (July 30, 1857–August 3, 1929) called "conspicuous consumption" in his book *The Theory of the Leisure Class: An Economic Study in the Evolution of Institutions* (New York: Macmillan), 1899. This phrase described what he observed as behavioral characteristics in the upper social class that emerged from the accumulation of capital in the Gilded Age. He applied it to the men, women, and families who used their great wealth as a public demonstration of their power and prestige by acquiring lavish material objects that would both intimidate and awe those with less money.

IDA B. WELLS AND *THE RED RECORD*

Likely one of the most iconic success stories from this era occurred in spite of the popular ideas at the time. Ida B. Wells transcended nearly every expectation of reformers and dreamers of the day, living the American Dream beyond the confines of race, class, and gender alone. She did so primarily as a journalist, setting a model for reporters and writers through today.

Wells (July 16, 1862–March 25, 1931) once said, "One had better die fighting against injustice than die like a dog or a rat in a trap," which explained her brave approach to reporting stories that other journalists would not touch.[6] She was born a slave in Holly Springs, Mississippi. When the Civil War ended, her freed parents moved to Tennessee. She went to college and became a teacher before cementing her legacy as a writer and publisher.

In 1883, Wells took a job in Tennessee's Shelby County school system. On May 4, 1884, a train conductor with the Memphis and Charleston Railroad ordered Wells to

Image 6.3: "Ida B. Wells, Head-and-Shoulders Portrait, Facing Slightly Right," published 1891, depicts the crusading feminist and anti-lynching advocate.[7]

give up her seat in the first-class car for women and move to the smoking car, which was already crowded with other passengers. When Wells refused to give up her seat, the conductor and two men dragged Wells out of the car. She returned to Memphis and hired an African American attorney to sue the railroad. Wells gained publicity in Memphis when she wrote an article about her treatment on the train for the *Living Way*, a weekly newspaper. In December 1884, Wells won her case when the local circuit court granted her a $500 award; however, the railroad company appealed to the Tennessee Supreme Court, which reversed the lower court's ruling.

Wells embarked on a career in journalism, writing weekly articles about race issues under the pen name "Iola." In 1889, she became co-owner and editor of *Free Speech and Headlight*, an anti-segregation newspaper started by the Reverend Taylor Nightingale and based at the Beale Street Baptist Church in Memphis. The position she had created for herself was in itself remarkable, as in a previous decade, part ownership of a newspaper by an African American woman in the South—or anywhere for that matter—would have been unimaginable, but during Reconstruction and given Wells' determination, she succeeded.

Wells had written about her experiences as a teacher and criticized the conditions created by segregation. She pointed out to readers that segregated schools had unequal distribution of resources, and students in poor, almost exclusively black areas, received few of the necessities for an education. In 1891, the Memphis Board of Education dismissed her from her teaching post, and although she was devastated, she concentrated her energies instead on articles for the *Living Way* and *Free Speech and Headlight* on the most troubling issues of the day.

She began an investigation into lynching, an endeavor that proved her bravery on a number of levels. The practice put victims to death without legal authority and often involved mob-led hangings. It was used most often to send a message of terror that would control minority populations, which usually (but not always) was targeted toward the black population of the South. To this day, historians have had a difficult time estimating the total number of victims, but have estimated that between 1882 and 1930, approximately 3,400 of the 4,800 lynchings involved African Americans.[8] The reason for the difficulty in arriving at hard numbers both then and now stems from the fact that few if any reporters alive at the time dared address the subject, as a reporter who published details about the activities would likely find themselves lynched as well.

Knowing this, it was no small matter for Wells to begin her reports. Her comprehensive analysis initially found 728 black men and women lynched by white mobs in Tennessee and surrounding areas—and on the rare occasion when people got arrested, two-thirds of the time they would walk out of jail, facing only convictions for small offenses such as drunkenness or shoplifting. Over time, lynching in the United States escalated.

In 1892, three friends of Wells became lynching victims, and when she published a story about it, a mob showed up at her newspaper intending to kill her. When the mob seeking her could not find her—she had fled to Philadelphia, escaping with her life—they instead destroyed the printing press she had used to produces her exposés. Wells then relocated to New York and began writing a weekly column for *New York Age*, where she published for Northerners the harsh realities she came to know in the South, and she soon became something of a celebrity journalist to a national audience captivated by her cold realism from a land so close, yet so far.

THE PRESS AND THE KKK

In the Reconstruction era, the press transformed from political agency to a reflection of contemporary society. Newspaper content just before the war had been locally oriented and directed toward the individual. Afterwards, it in part met the demands of the nation's businesses.

In the 1870s, the *Atlanta Constitution* had established one of the largest readerships in the nation. Among the leading causes addressed by the newspaper at the time included the Reconstruction Amendments, which editors suggested would not affect Georgians in any direct or dramatic way.[9] Opinion pieces from time to time asserted Atlanta's role as the capital of the New South, a cultural construct that emerged from the industrialization of an agriculturally based economy that existed before the Civil War. The *Atlanta Constitution* and other newspapers in the New South generally attempted to assure readers that white supremacy would maintain social order throughout in the region.[10]

A sample of the content about race relations from the *Atlanta Constitution* reflects similar news from other cities in the South at the time. In regards to the Ku Klux Klan, a new organization designed to re-assert the rule of the Democratic Party in the South, newspapers generally only published allegations that the Klan existed while at the same time stories either downplayed or simply ignored the organization's actual activities. As an example, the following letter published in the *Constitution* contained at least indirect threats of violence, but it also included a disclaimer from the editor who claimed its attribution to the head of the Klan in neighboring Tennessee was designed to embarrass citizens of the South and that the content was sensational beyond belief.

"Shame! Shame!! Shame!!!," *Atlanta Constitution*, December 18, 1870.[11]

To the Ghouls of every Den from the Tennessee to the Chattahoochee

Bones of the mighty arise! Again, by the light of a blood-red moon carrion crown whet their beaks upon the skulls of your fallen foes! Villainy stalks. Strike him! Ride in the smoke of every engine from Chattanooga to Atlanta, and wash the rust from your swords in the blood of every one who intends to vote illegally! With your bony fingers, clutch them when asleep upon the train, and drag them to your own pale realm! This done, then rest until the awful summons of your dread commander bids you again come forth. By command of the Grand Cyclops: X.Q.Z. Wizard of Chickamauga.

While the *Charleston Daily Courier* at one point claimed that the Klan existed "only on paper," other newspapers portrayed the threat of Klan violence as an imagined conspiracy by Northern politicians intent on continued disruption of the Southern political, economic, and cultural systems.[12]

The terroristic efforts of the Klan in particular stemmed from attempts to re-establish white supremacy in the South after the Civil War, she wrote. Former Confederates and Democrats in general feared "Negro Domination" through the new suffrage rights afforded under the Reconstruction Amendments. Wells urged black people in high-risk areas to move away to protect their families. She provided fourteen pages of statistics related to lynching cases committed from 1892 to 1895 and included pages of graphic accounts detailing specific acts of terrorism, noting that she found her data in articles by white correspondents, white press bureaus, and white newspapers. She extended her efforts to gain support of such powerful white nations as Britain to shame and sanction the racist practices of America.

In 1893, she brought her story of American lynching culture to Europe, where she traveled the lecture circuit. Upon returning to the United States, she published a pamphlet with Ferdinand Lee Barnett and Frederick Douglass titled *The Reason Why the Colored American Is Not in the World's Columbian Exposition*.

Wells published *The Red Record* in 1895 as a 100-page pamphlet describing lynching in the United States since the Emancipation Proclamation of 1863. During Reconstruction, most Americans outside the South did not realize the growing rate of violence against black people, and Wells suggested that before emancipation, such incidents were lower because slaves had economic value. According to Wells, mobs had killed thousands with no due process in illegal and horrifying executions.

In 1909, a forty-person committee helped found the National Association for the Advancement of Colored People (NAACP). By 1919, the group's magazine, *The Crisis*, edited by W. E. B. DuBois, was selling 100,000 copies a month at 10 cents a copy or $1 dollar a year. With the national organization and a publication to spread its word, Wells and others affiliated with the group continued to raise consciousness of issues that affected the African American community directly.

Although lynching did not cease, it did decline. Her efforts, which included addresses to an international audience, did influence a growing anti-lynching movement in the United States, and historians have since credited Wells for shining a light on this dark chapter of American history.

Wells had more work to do, however. The struggle women initiated in 1848 at the Seneca Falls Convention, which called for the right to vote on terms equal with men, had continued in what became—and still is—the longest civil rights struggle in American history. In the first and second decade of the twentieth century, Wells joined other women suffragists, this time as a correspondent for the *Chicago Tribune*, in marches on Washington, calling for ratification of the Nineteenth Amendment, which, unlike the Reconstruction Amendments, would include women specifically as part of the elective franchise.

Wells had blossomed into an editor, journalist, and activist who combined the best techniques of hard news reporting and the moral tone of muckraking, a movement for which she helped set a precedent. Among her final works, the autobiographical *Crusade for Justice* has become an essential contribution to the history of the press. She died of kidney failure in 1931 at the age of 69 before completing her autobiography, but not before running for Illinois state legislature the previous year. She lost the race, but set an important example and inspiring a slew of female candidates to follow her.

RECAPPING THIS CHAPTER

Looking back on this chapter, you should see how it described the triumphs and failures of the press during Reconstruction, focusing on Ida B. Wells' *The Red Record* as a landmark piece of journalism. The chapter opened with Horace Greeley's failed campaign for president in 1872, juxtaposed with Wells' crusade against lynching, and it showed how Reconstruction journalism bridged traditional models of publishing popularized before the Civil War into a new wave of sensational content fueled by technological development.

Using materials from this chapter, you should know why the Reconstruction era introduced important precedents in the role of the press as an agent for social change. You should identify key problems both highlighted and ignored by the press leaders and politicians of the era, and you should be able to explain why Ida B. Wells deserves credit for taking a particularly brave stance as a writer in exposing social problems.

The following chapter looks at the successes and shortcomings of a crusading form of journalism that emerged at the turn of the twentieth century by reporters who practiced storytelling with reform efforts in mind. It profiles a group of writers who flourished at a time in which yellow journalism, a famous style of publishing, also thrived, and the chapter reveals the dynamics between this group of writers and the administration of Theodore Roosevelt, who at first supported them but then had to distance himself for political reasons.

NOTES

1. "The First Vote," Library of Congress, accessed June 12, 2016, <item/2011648984>.
2. Greeley to Samuel Tappan, in Ovando James Hollister, *Life of Schuyler Colfax* (New York: Funk & Wagnalls, 1886), 387.
3. Thomas Nast, "Red Hot!" *Harper's Weekly*, July 13, 1872: 560.
4. "Discovery of the Sage of Chappaqua," Library of Congress, accessed May 16, 2016, <item/2003690770>.
5. Mark Twain, *The Gilded Age, a Tale of Today* (Hartford, CT: American Publishing, 1873).
6. Ida B. Wells, *Crusade for Justice* (Chicago: University of Chicago Press, 2013), 62.
7. "Ida B. Wells," Library of Congress, accessed May 16, 2016, <item/93505758>.
8. "Time Line of African American History, 1881–1900," Library of Congress, accessed February 26, 2017, <https://memory.loc.gov/ammem/aap/timelin2.html>; Lerone Bennett, *Before the Mayflower* (Chicago: Johnson, 1982); W. Augustus Low and Virgil A. Clift, *Encyclopedia of Black America* (New York: Da Capo Press, 1984), and Harry A. Ploski and Warren Marr, *The Negro Almanac* (New York: Bellwether Co., 1976).
9. *Atlanta Constitution*, "Negro Equality," March 15, 1870; "The Fifteenth Amendment," April 3, 1870.
10. *Atlanta Constitution*, "The 15th Amendment Celebration in Macon, Brilliant Proceedings," April 22, 1870.
11. "Shame! Shame!! Shame!!!" *Atlanta Constitution*, December 18, 1870.
12. *Charleston Daily Courier*, March 25, 1870.

7

MUCKRAKING
REPORTERS AND REFORM

This chapter looks at the successes and shortcomings of a crusading form of journalism that emerged at the turn of the twentieth century by reporters who practiced storytelling with reform measures in mind:

- It profiles a group of writers who flourished at a time in which yellow journalism, a famous style of publishing, also thrived;
- and it reveals the dynamics between this group and President Theodore Roosevelt, who at first supported them but then had to distance himself for political reasons.

Using materials from this chapter, students should understand how the writers and publishers of this particular era left a mark in history as reformers who at times directly affected social conditions:

- They should also be able to identify other waves of muckraking and how following the money trail generated many of the most famous episodes of reporting in press history;
- and they should be able to identify contemporary journalists who might qualify for the title of "muckraker."

Key words, names, and phrases associated with Chapter 7 include:

- Jacob Riis, "How the Other Half Lives";
- Josiah Flynt, "The World of Graft";

- Lincoln Steffens, "The Shame of the Cities," *McClure's*;
- Upton Sinclair, *The Jungle*;
- and David Graham Phillips, "The Treason of the Senate," and *Cosmopolitan*.

When President Theodore Roosevelt gave a speech titled "The Man with the Muckrake" in 1906, he compared radical members of the era's progressive press to a character from literature. "In [John] Bunyan's *Pilgrim's Progress* you may recall the description of the man with the muck rake, the man who could look no way but downward, with the muck rake in his hand," Roosevelt said. He said that certain investigative reporters at the time had within their reach "a celestial crown," but like this literary character, they would "neither look up nor regard the crown he was offered, but continued to rake to himself the filth of the floor."[1]

Although the president had long seen himself as an ally of the muckrakers, he gave the speech to distance himself from the movement out of political necessity. Had he not tried to criticize the most radical elements of the muckraker movement at the time, many of the reforms both he and the muckrakers advocated may have fallen victim to the political machinery that opposed them. Regardless, the style of reporting Roosevelt described, which exposed corruption and was thenceforth dubbed "muckraking," changed the United States forever.

For this reason and in a relatively short period of time (approximately the first decade of the twentieth century), a certain faction of the press helped to engineer social changes on local, state, and national levels, setting a model for subsequent reporters who still—as they did—follow the money trail. The period occupies a unique place in both the history of the press and American history in general, as muckraking also coincided with a publishing movement, yellow journalism, which, as we will see in Chapter 8, contributed to a unique era of change. (While muckraking can be understood as a reporting technique, yellow journalism, which essentially placed style over substance, can be seen as a publishing technique to increase sales.)

And while the definition of muckraking would evolve into a somewhat fluid description of investigative reporting in general, a few representative writers and reporters who fit the description established by Roosevelt can illustrate, for the purposes of this chapter, what muckraking did. While the journalists featured in this chapter do not encompass the entire muckraking movement, they do supply a sample that supplies a snapshot of their work.

THE MAKING OF A MOVEMENT

To remedy society's ills, the muckrakers advocated in their writings the redistribution of wealth. Muckraking had its golden years in the first decade of the twentieth century, but writers practiced this style of reporting well before then. For example, Ida B. Wells, in at least a few respects, had practiced muckraking, although she did so on different terms than the most prominent writers associated with the movement—while Wells focused on racial justice, more commonly the muckrakers focused on economic issues.

Another defining element of the movement included its reliance on popular magazines (not newspapers alone) to advance the agenda of social reform. These magazines set the trend for prominent issues by featuring extensive reports accompanied by elaborate color graphics and entertaining articles on a wide range of topics, with *McClure's*, as a leading muckraker magazine, leading the way, and *Cosmopolitan*—still in circulation today but more focused on news features at the time—providing innovation for the movement.

In the second half of the nineteenth century, magazines had grown to prominence, as publishers who had previously specialized in daily newspapers developed new media based on their successes in attracting advertisers and readers. Production methods that had formerly prohibited wide-scale distribution of magazine materials to audiences increased cost efficiency, allowing publishers to target readers with finely packaged magazines that featured long-form journalism and illustrations—by the end of the century, certain publishers could even afford to include color with their copy. Magazines became increasingly popular venues for writers, as well, attracting reporters who sought to escape the pressures of the daily deadlines that defined newspapers. Moreover, in making a solid case about the subject of their reporting, muckrakers in particular needed the extended space available in magazines to cover issues of national importance.

In determining the origin of muckraking, historians often point to Jacob Riis, whose photographs influenced both journalism and the world in which he lived. Sometimes called the grandfather (or "godfather") of muckraking, Riis put into visual perspective many of the most pressing problems facing the U.S.'s urban centers, specifically an infamous slum in New York City.

Riis was born on May 3, 1849, in Denmark. When he was 21, he took a steamship to the United States, where he started out homeless and unemployed. He worked numerous jobs, including ironworker, farmer, bricklayer, and sales clerk. Like many other immigrants, who in the 1880s and 1890s had arrived from various parts of Europe, he roamed the streets, which presented him with an unlimited supply of stories to tell.

He first made a connection sometime in the 1880s with Theodore Roosevelt, who at the time served as New York City police commissioner. The two formed a professional alliance and personal friendship. Roosevelt called on Riis to photograph the parts of the city that police would otherwise have a hard time patrolling. Riis, in time, would assist in Roosevelt's various political campaigns.

Riis' photography provided access to the dark alleyways impenetrable to both the police and newspapers, and soon New York editors wanted to publish his work, too—first the *Tribune* and then the *Sun*. His work, while sensational, revealed a hidden reality and educated the citizens of New York by exposing them to a reality they previously ignored or simply did not know existed.

Riis focused his attention on the lower east side of New York in an area known as the Five Points, where streets in the Bowery slum meet to form a five-pointed intersection. For decades, the area had awful living conditions inhabited primarily by newly arrived immigrants. Many had no jobs or income for basic housing.

Image 7.1: "Jacob Riis," half-length portrait, seated, facing right, Frances Benjamin Johnston, photographer, ca. 1900.[2]

Riis began his investigative work by taking photographs of the harshest environments and most weathered individuals. He used an innovative technique called "flash and dash" photography—comparable in some respects to the methods of modern paparazzi—to capture the raw emotion and feeling of a situation rather than a staged picture. To do this, he found subjects spontaneously and without announcement, surprising them sometimes with the flash from his camera. He would then exit quickly with a dash. The faces of the subjects in his pictures reveal the speed with which Riis operated, as their eyes sometimes closed from the blinding flash that accompanied his camera.

From his work in the Five Points, Riis published several photographic works, including *The Children of the Tenements*, *The Battle with the Slums*, and *The Making*

Image 7.2: "'How the Other Half Lives' in a Crowded Hebrew District, Lower East Side, N.Y. City," published 1907.[3]

of an American, but his archetypical piece *How the Other Half Lives* depicts the harsh conditions in New York that most people (at least "half") had never seen.

Riis' pictures grabbed the attention of an audience accustomed to finding news only in the printed section of the newspaper.

Riis found—and those who saw his pictures agreed—that pictures of children in particular proved much more effective than words alone in his efforts to enlighten the public about a problem. His pictures were in some cases so poignant and even graphic that he received inevitable criticism from detractors who claimed he sought simply to exploit the poor for his own fame. However, Riis simply pointed to the fact that he himself had lived amongst "the other half," and as someone who knew the life of those who had nothing, his efforts represented a genuine concern for their conditions.

Riis recognized the overcrowded tenement neighborhoods were unhealthy and helped breed crime, and to remedy the situation, he advocated effectively for the city to invest in parks and open spaces. Public officials in New York, who upon receiving an outcry from the wealthier "half," invested millions into the renovation of the Five Points area. Riis' efforts also led to the demolition of Mulberry Bend, which city planners turned into a park.

Riis' legacy includes his role in inspiring the passage of laws designed to create better housing and education, as well as to create better conditions for children in the workplace and for playgrounds. He died in Massachusetts at his farm on May 26, 1914, with subsequent generations of journalists finding in him a role model for preparing documentaries and instigating social reform.

Before Riis's approach to social reform would turn into a national trend, however, another personality in the muckraking movement, Josiah Frank Willard, helped fuel the transition from an audience focused in New York to a general one. Under the pen name Josiah Flynt, Willard described the corruption in other cities and found that New York certainly had no monopoly on urban problems. Many of Flynt's stories focused on the corruption tying law enforcement and organized crime. With Chicago often serving as the backdrop for his tales of criminality, Flynt published in *McClure's* and later compiled his reporting in books, such as *Tramping with Tramps*, *The World of Graft*, *True Stories of the Underworld*, and *My Life*.

At the very least, Flynt loosened up American English, not only providing his readers with remarkable stories but also giving them an entire new language, familiarizing audiences with the vernacular of the underground.

> Among words used in a typical piece by Josiah Flynt, the following may sound familiar from usage in later movies about organized crime; however, they would have struck readers at the time as tantalizing or just foreign.

- The Gun: Someone who played the role of "the Gun" carried out orders, even violent or murderous ones;
- Pinch: If someone was in a "pinch," the police had put the suspect in a tight spot, possibly under arrest or in a position where they had to divulge information;
- Squeal: A "squeal" referred to someone who gave up protected information;
- Speakeasies: Places known as "speakeasies" were private places, like clubhouses, for members only;
- Mugged Grafter: A "mugged grafter" was someone who had a criminal record, meaning they had a mug shot on file with the police;
- Unmugged Grafter: Police had yet to catch the "unmugged grafter."

This passage from *The World of Graft* (first published in an April 1901 issue of *McClure's*), for example, reveals how Flynt put this style to work by his use of phrases that he helped popularize.

> No one smiles more broadly than the Gun when one of the Powers that Rule goes before a grand jury or an assembly investigating committee and says that he has no knowledge of certain 'joints,' and no one is better informed than the Gun of how much the front office would tell if it wanted to. He believes, as his profession proves, in putting on a bold

front and taking chances; men who are afraid to do this and yet graft, be they policemen or politicians, become for him "unmugged thieves."[4]

With this narrative frame of reference, Flynt provided a framework for assessing any city that would prove useful for subsequent muckrakers. He described the criminality of the "Under World" and an "Upper World" as sometimes indistinguishable in consequence. When someone from the "Under World" got lucky and "made his 'pile,'" he went "uptown" to "put on the Ritz," pretending to be "high class," Flynt wrote. When aristocrats who lived in the "Upper World" needed money, they would venture "downtown" to scrounge up their own "pile."[5] This arrangement clearly posed problems for the functioning of a healthy society, and it provided fodder for further investigation.

At the time, Flynt's series attracted a tremendous number of readers. While his work does not have the same prominence in the popular legacies of other muckrakers, Flynt indeed earned an important role in helping the movement go mainstream. "In essence," wrote Edd Applegate, a press historian, Flynt

> laid the groundwork and, to a certain extent, established the tone for other muckraking journalists. He also used literary devices found in fiction to describe scenes and characters. Thus, his articles were examples of literary journalism.[6]

LINCOLN STEFFENS AND "THE SHAME OF CITIES"

Lincoln Steffens, you might say, was "in like Flynt." Quite possibly the most celebrated—as well as frustrated—of the muckrakers, Steffens followed Flynt's lead, having also found inspiration from Riis' photo documentaries. Steffens would give the burgeoning muckraker movement legitimacy, as he added a well-known voice and his methodical and lucid profiles of the crime in major American cities.

S. S. McClure's flagship publication *McClure's* provided Steffens the platform to reach a wide audience—although other magazines at the time had helped popularize muckraking content, *McClure's* had grown the most dramatically from a general interest publication to one that specialized in advancing the muckraker's reform agenda. As historian Doris Kearns Goodwin writes in *The Bully Pulpit: Theodore Roosevelt, William Howard Taft, and the Golden Age of Journalism*, a Pulitzer Prize–winning account of politics and the press of the era, McClure had both an eccentric and profound sense of what stories could change the course of history, and he encouraged his writers to pursue them.[7]

McClure's benefitted when it brought Steffens into its lineup of writers. As a well-known intellectual who wrote with both professionalism and passion, Steffens articulated clearly the scale of corruption beyond anything Riis or Flynt had been able to do. His most famous piece for *McClure's*, a series titled "The Shame of the Cities," challenged not only the political class but also the entire premise upon which the United States had built its economy.

Steffens went to the root of American society, looking much deeper into the origins of corruption than Riis could do with images alone. He studied the crime rampant in major U.S. cities as illustrations of endemic political and economic structures that had taken shape during the earliest days of the American experiment. "Political corruption is a process," he wrote.

> It is not a temporary evil, not an accidental wickedness, not the passing symptom of the youth of people. If this progress goes on, then this American republic of ours will be a government that represents the organized evils of a privileged class.[8]

LINCOLN STEFFENS

Lincoln Steffens exposed the true emotions from real Americans living through the back alleys and political corruption with investigative reporting. Aside from being a journalist, he published *The Shame of Cities* and *The Struggle for Self-Government*. Steffens covered international affairs like the Mexican Revolution and the revolutionary government change in the Soviet Union.

He was born April 6, 1866, in a lavish home in Sacramento, California, that later became the Governor's Mansion. His first job as a reporter came from the *New York Evening Post*, where he created his investigative reporting on economic conditions, politics, and culture. Jacob Riis, who was a veteran police reporter at the *Post*, mentored Steffens. Crime reporting introduced Steffens to a world of corruption, reform, and urban policies, and in 1901, he began working for *McClure's*, which had begun building a reputation for investigating subjects of interest to Steffens. "The Shame of the Cities," the epitome of this period of his work, reported on the workings of corrupt political machines in several major U.S. cities, along with a few efforts to combat them. As one of several early major pieces of muckraking journalism, Steffens later claimed this particular work made him "the first muckraker." Though Steffens' subject was municipal corruption, he did not present his work as an exposé of corruption; rather, he wanted to draw attention to the public's complicity in allowing corruption to continue.

Later in life, he witnessed the outcome of the revolution in Russia that created the Soviet Union. He visited the Soviet Union for three weeks accompanying low-level state department officials. His enthusiasm for communism soured by the time his memoirs appeared in 1931. The autobiography became a bestseller, leading to a short return to prominence for the writer, but Steffens would not be able to capitalize on it as illness cut his lecture tour of America short by 1933. Despite his success, Steffens died August 9, 1936, a disillusioned man at the age of 70, believing he had failed as a journalist because corruption still ran rampant.

Steffens tried to advance a theory of city corruption that he claimed was the result of "big business men" who corrupted city government for their own ends, and "the typical business man"—average Americans—who ignored politics and allowed such corruption to continue.

The first article in "The Shame of the Cities" series to advance this argument focused on the city of St. Louis, re-introducing the public to a character known to personify this kind of corruption. "Tweed Days in St. Louis," published in October 1902, described Circuit Attorney Folk's efforts to clean up the city's corruption (it was no coincidence that the name "Tweed" referred to the deceased Boss Tweed whose corruption ruled the Five Points in previous decades). Bribery, Steffens noted, had become commonplace in city government by the turn of the century, and St. Louis, while by no means extraordinary, provided far too many examples. Steffens suggested in the end "the better classes" of all cities were the sources of corruption, and based on what he could report from St. Louis, its business leaders were "the sources of evil."[9]

Steffens made more or less the same conclusions based on his experiences in Minneapolis, as featured in his January 1903 piece titled "The Shame of Minneapolis." The new addition to his series told the story of Mayor "Doc" Ames. Steffens claimed after Ames' election to mayor in 1900, he set out deliberately to engage in a career of unequalled corruption. Ames and the complicit police force, in exchange for bribes, chose to ignore illegal gambling and prostitution. This arrangement attracted criminals to the city, as many of them agreed with the police not to interfere with the business of one another. According to Steffens, "the government of a city asked criminals to rob the people."[10]

His conclusions were again reiterated in his next article, "Pittsburg: A City Ashamed," published in May 1903. He also re-introduced the corruption of Boss Tweed, writing that Pittsburgh made the organization of the Five Points in comparison "a plaything." Among other cities, Steffens also exposed Philadelphia, Chicago, and New York itself, driving home the point that the corruption in these cities was not unique; rather, the American economic system had a flaw in its ties to organized business.

The remedy he envisioned would come as the result of a revolution in public sentiment with a socialized economy at its end. Although he never formally linked his beliefs in socialism with communism and shied from directly joining the communist party, Steffens wrote and spoke unambiguously about his belief that a revolution based in communist ideals might save the United States. On several occasions, he stated unrestricted capitalism did not work well for all people because the wealthy accumulated riches at the expense of victims through uncontrolled exploitation. And when he received news of a revolution that had rocked Russia in 1917, he traveled to Moscow with excitement to investigate.

When Steffens arrived in what would become the newly formed Soviet Union in 1919, a new order, at least in theory, had replaced an elite governing body with the rule of workers, a revolution that at first impressed reformers, including Steffens, who saw signs that the United States might also change its ways. When he returned from his trip, an American financier reportedly asked Steffens to provide an account of what he had witnessed, and, as popularly told, Steffens said, "I have seen the future, and it works." Steffens later wrote in his *Autobiography* that what he said was "I have been over to the future, and it works."[11]

Steffens' optimism was short-lived. A global economic collapse brought on by the Great Depression followed by the rise of dictatorships throughout Europe contributed to Steffens loss of idealism. He in fact grew cynical about the role socialism and reform in general might play in improving the conditions of workers and lives in general. He died August 9, 1936, without seeing—similar to a number of other muckrakers—the reform he had hoped to achieve.

UPTON SINCLAIR'S *THE JUNGLE*, AND THE PURE FOOD AND DRUG ACT

Upton Sinclair, born in Baltimore, September 20, 1878, both shared the socialist philosophy of Steffens and took an understanding of corruption to a new level. Sinclair concerned himself primarily with the inequalities brought about by capitalism in a system he described as "wage slavery" in which workers received only enough money to survive. His most famous piece, *The Jungle*, examined the sickening realities of this system through the experiences of laborers in Chicago's meatpacking industry.

He had prepared his report as a form of documentary fiction by first acting as a reporter who visited the stockyards, taking notes, and then writing in a third-person form of fiction that too closely resembled reality. While his goal in the piece was to awaken the American public to the inherent problems of economic oppression at the time, he instead awoke their awareness of the filthiness involved in creating the meat and food products they ate on a daily basis. Reform did ensue from *The Jungle*, but it came in the way of hygiene, not money. Sinclair later recollected, "I aimed for the public's heart, and by accident I hit it in the stomach."[12]

A particularly gruesome excerpt from *The Jungle* demonstrates the descriptions of meat packing that horrified Sinclair's readers.

> There was never the least attention paid to what was cut up for sausage; there would come all the way back from Europe old sausage that had been rejected, and that was moldy and white—it would be dosed with borax and glycerin, and dumped into the hoppers, and made over again for home consumption. There would be meat that had tumbled out on the floor, in the dirt and sawdust, where the workers had tramped and spit uncounted billions of consumption germs. There would be meat stored in great piles in rooms; and the water from leaky roofs would drip over it, and thousands of rats would race about on it. It was too dark in these storage places to see well, but a man could run his hand over these piles of meat and sweep off handfuls of the dried dung of rats. These rats were nuisances, and the packers would put poisoned bread out for them; they would die, and then rats, bread, and meat would go into the hoppers together. This is no fairy story and no joke; the meat would be shoveled into carts, and the man who did the shoveling would not trouble to lift out a rat even when he saw one—there were things that went into the sausage in comparison with which a poisoned rat was a tidbit.[13]

Sinclair's work unsettled many at their morning breakfast tables, as a family read the newspapers that published installments of his accounts. Cries for reform came during the time of Roosevelt's presidency, and in 1906, Congress passed the Pure Food and Drug Act, which would begin to establish controls on food production. Sinclair's exposé led to reforms in not only meatpacking but also the patent-drug and food industries in general, with Congress approving a meat inspection law that required the U.S. Drug Administration to inspect animals destined for human consumption with carcasses subject to post-mortem inspections.[14]

MUCKRAKING AND PROGRESSIVE LEGISLATION

Historians commonly cite the Pure Food and Drug Act as the clearest example of legislation passed in response to muckraker activities; however, several other reforms emerged from Washington, D.C., because of the activities of progressive journalists during the era. Muckrakers had a role in pushing for the following remarkable pieces of legislation, among others.

- June 1906: At President Roosevelt's behest, Congress also passes the Hepburn Act, expanding the powers of the ICC beyond railroads to express companies and other forms of transportation, such as ferries and sleeping-car companies. The ICC can now reduce rates that it finds unreasonable.
- February 24, 1908: In *Muller v. Oregon*, the Supreme Court holds that Oregon can constitutionally pass a law limiting women's work in factories and laundries to ten hours a day. The Court had allowed states to regulate child labor within their borders, but until now, it has taken a more restrictive approach to laws concerning the conditions of adult female workers because it used to consider such regulations to be violations of adult employees' freedom of contract. The *Muller* decision reverses this trend.
- 1910: Congress passes The Mann-Elkins Act, strengthening the Interstate Commerce Commission.
- 1911: The Taft administration creates the Department of Labor, and it uses the Sherman Antitrust Act to regulate Standard Oil.
- 1913: February 3, the Sixteenth Amendment is ratified, empowering Congress to levy income taxes; April 8, the Seventeenth Amendment is ratified, allowing for the direct election of U.S. senators instead of through state legislators; October 3, President Wilson calls a special session of Congress to pass the Underwood-Simmons Tariff, which reduces the nation's protective tariff rates substantially for the first time since the Civil War. Progressives hope that this reform will encourage competition in the marketplace and undermine monopolization. To recoup the lost revenue, the government also passes the first income tax, levied on individuals and corporations earning over $4,000 a year.
- September 1914: Wilson signs the Federal Trade Commission Act, creating the five-person Federal Trade Commission (FTC) to regulate businesses and investigate possible violations of antitrust laws. Like the ICC (its predecessor), the FTC gradually succumbs to the influence of the very businesses it is supposed to regulate.

Upton Sinclair maintained a steady agenda of reform efforts. And while other muckrakers, including Steffens, Flynt, and Phillips (whom we will see next), often had difficulty staying consistent with the muckrakers' ideals, Sinclair fought—even if not always successfully—until his death in November 25, 1968. He moved in the 1920s with his wife to Monrovia, California, near Los Angeles, where he founded the state's chapter of the American Civil Liberties Union (ACLU). On several occasions, he sought political office on the socialist ticket, in 1920 for the U.S. House, in 1922 for the Senate, and in 1930 for governor. In 1934, Sinclair ran again for governor of California, this time as a Democrat. Hollywood studio bosses unanimously opposed him, and they pressured their employees to assist and vote for the Republican candidate Frank Merriam with propaganda films that attacked Sinclair. The multimedia assault on Sinclair marked a dramatic turn of the press on one of its own, and Sinclair detailed the events in a book he published the next year, "I, Candidate for Governor: And How I Got Licked." Among the most memorable line from the book, Sinclair wrote, "It is difficult to get a man to understand something, when his salary depends upon his not understanding it."[15]

A MAN WITH A MUCK RAKE: DAVID GRAHAM PHILLIPS

The muckrakers had for much of their existence written about the problems ailing major cities except for one, arguably the nexus of all major problems—Washington, D.C. The challenge of tackling government corruption at the federal level had struck many reformers as a task simply beyond the scope of any one writer or any single publication. However, Indiana journalist David Graham Phillips, at the behest of writers who knew his reputation as a fearless journalist, began a series on the subject that in ways surpassed expectations, even if only for a short period.

David Graham Phillips, the pen name for John Phillips, published "The Treason of the Senate" in 1906, after having begun his career as a newspaper reporter and then becoming a celebrated novelist with *The Great God Success*, a story about the joys and follies of material gain from labor.

Phillips was born to a politically active family in Madison, Indiana, October 31, 1867. He later changed his birth name from John Phillips to a pen name, David Graham Phillips, but first attended Indiana Asbury College and graduated from the College of New Jersey, now Princeton, in 1887. He started a career as a reporter with the *Cincinnati Times-Star*, and by 1890, he earned a job with the *New York Sun*. In 1893, he put his talents to work with the *New York World*, writing columns until 1902. He freelanced as an investigative journalist for a period while he wrote novels, enjoying commercial success with the novel *The Great God Success* (1901).

Charles Edward Russell sold the idea of exposing congressional corruption to newspaper magnate William Randolph Hearst, recent purchaser of *Cosmopolitan*, who looked constantly for ways to attract readership. Editor Bailey Millard invented the catchy name "The Treason of the Senate" before electing Phillips to write the article to go along with it.

At the time and according to the original language of the Constitution, state legislatures—not voters—selected members of the Senate, as the founders envisioned the legislative body to represent a well-seasoned class of deliberative members from the best and most informed strata of society. The intent, at least originally, was to have a

Image 7.3: "David Graham Phillips, Full-Length Portrait, Standing at Writing Table, Facing Slightly Right," published between 1890 and 1911.[16]

select legislative group to balance the more populist-oriented members of the House of Representatives.

The decades following Reconstruction produced results the founders had not anticipated, however, with this elite body, the Senate, having grown more and more intertwined with the increasingly powerful business interests of the nation. Not only did the general population have less control of the business matters of the nation, it also, as the muckrakers observed, exercised less influence over the decisions of the government. The Senate epitomized this trend, and Phillips, in turn, took action, exposing the unseemly ties between wealthy industrialists and officials, who he argued represented only their own interests.

"The Treason of the Senate" represented Phillips' efforts to expose in a methodical and lethal fashion the corruption of each senator, who he linked to business interests alone, not the will of the American people. Phillips began his attack by detailing the alleged crimes of New York senator Chauncey Mitchell Depew, someone with whom fellow New Yorker Theodore Roosevelt recognized the need for friendly political relations. Depew, Phillips claimed, had a direct interest in the success of railroad baron Cornelius Vanderbilt, and together, according to "The Treason of the Senate," the two colluded on behalf of the interests of the rich. "Their job was two-fold—to rob the people and to rob the capitalists whom they had induced to invest in the stolen railways," he wrote, claiming Depew had cost the American taxpayer more than $1 billion in monies that belonged to the public.[17]

Phillips initial diatribe on political privilege and injustice shook the Senate and exposed exploitation, and the success of the article led to a series of articles that investigated every state represented in the Senate. "The apportionment of legislators is such that one-eleventh of the population, and they the most ignorant and most venal, elect a majority of the legislature," wrote Phillips in his installment on Senator Nelson W. Aldrich of Rhode Island.[18] The attack on Aldrich linked the senator to John D. Rockefeller in establishing his oil monopoly, using particularly blunt and even flamboyant language.

> During the past winter, he has been concentrating on the "defense of the railways"—which means not the railways nor yet the railway corporations, but simply the Rockefeller-Morgan looting of the people by means of their control of the corporations that own the railways.
>
> Has Aldrich intellect? Perhaps. But he does not show it. He has never in his 25 years of service in the Senate introduced or advocated a measure that shows any conception of life above what might be expected in a Hungry Joe. No, intellect is not the characteristic of Aldrich—or of any of these traitors, or of the men they serve. A scurvy lot they are, are they not, with their smirking and cringing and voluble palaver about God and patriotism and their eager offerings of endowments for hospitals and colleges whenever the American people so much as looks hard in their direction!
>
> Aldrich is rich and powerful. Treachery has brought him wealth and rank, if not honor, of a certain sort. He must laugh at us, grown-up fools, permitting a handful to bind the might of our 80 million and to set us all to work for them.[19]

Using language comparable to the literary twists found in Josiah Flynt's exposé of the underworld, Phillips went on to unmask the duplicity of Senator Arthur P. Gorman of Maryland and Senator John C. Spooner of Wisconsin as well in equally graphic terms, indicting an entire portion of government as hopelessly corrupt.

While the American people lauded Phillips as a ferocious member of the Fourth Estate, he made plenty of enemies along the way to fame and acclaim. President Theodore Roosevelt referred to Phillips, although not by name, and others in the press with whom he associated in his address as "The Man with the Muck-Rake," criticizing them for focusing on the all the wrongs with the world without recognizing societal good. Pressures from outraged Republicans and Democrats and their constituents had combined to compel Roosevelt to deliver the famous speech in which he denounced and derided the "muckrakers," a metaphor he used to describe the dirty work that employed Phillips and his collaborators, namely Lincoln Steffens.

The presidential assault was the signal for a general attack on Phillips. He received threats against his life. "The reactionary press," as Russell had called it, rang with Phillips' name as chief among a seditious movement. Roosevelt, meanwhile, received praise for blasting the libel of the senators, who the public presumed were innocent and good.[20] Roosevelt also corresponded with Upton Sinclair and Phillips from the White House in the attempt to assure them that he had not betrayed the progressive cause.[21]

"The Treason of the Senate" in the end inspired legislation reforming the appointment of senators across the country, and in 1913, the U.S. Constitution henceforth called for the direct election of senators by the people.

> Constitution Amendment 17, ratified April 8, 1913
>
> The Senate of the United States shall be composed of two Senators from each State, elected by the people thereof, for six years; and each Senator shall have one vote. The electors in each State shall have the qualifications requisite for electors of the most numerous branch of the State legislatures.[22]

Phillips had undoubtedly formed political enemies, but his end came tragically from an entirely unanticipated kind of revenge. A musician named Fitzhugh Coyle Goldsborough had fostered animosity for Phillips because of a delusion that Phillips had modeled a character in the novel *The Fashionable Adventures of Joshua Craig* after Goldsborough. On January 23, 1911, Goldsborough shot and mortally wounded Phillips outside the Princeton Club. Phillips passed away the next day at the age of 44.

In the following years, as the United States edged closer to involvement in World War I in 1917, public sentiment would turn against the muckrakers, as the conflict redirected national interests. The news-reading public also grew tired of the constant shock associated with stories of corruption and instead consumed news following the war, which was dominated by the carefree and jazzy style of the Roaring '20s. Muckraking itself did not disappear, but rather went into a sort of hibernation and reemerged in a different kind of climate, one we will examine closer to the end of the twentieth century. (We will also see how Phillips and the muckrakers in general inspired at least in spirit the later exploits of reporters who "followed the money trail," such as Bob Woodward and Carl Bernstein in their famous exposé of the presidency of Richard Nixon.)

RECAPPING THIS CHAPTER

Looking back on this chapter, you should see how it described the successes and shortcomings of muckraking, a crusading form of journalism that emerged at the turn of the twentieth century. The chapter profiled this group of writers who flourished at a time in which yellow journalism, a famous style of publishing, also thrived, and it revealed the dynamics between this group and President Theodore Roosevelt, who at first supported the movement but then had to distance himself for political reasons.

Using materials from this chapter, you should understand how the writers and publishers of this particular era left a mark in history as reformers who at times directly affected social conditions. You should also be able to identify other waves of muckraking and how following the money trail generated many of the most famous episodes of reporting in press history, and you should be able to identify contemporary journalists who might qualify for the title of "muckraker."

The following chapter looks at the circulation war between publishing giants Joseph Pulitzer and William Randolph Hearst. It provides examples of the sensational content of the era and shows how the competitive nature of the rivals affected subsequent media development, and it describes a style that had roots in the penny press, flourished at the turn of the twentieth century, and has made recurring appearances since then, all the way through today.

NOTES

1. Theodore Roosevelt, "Address of President Roosevelt at the Laying of the Corner Stone of the Office Building of the House of Representatives (The Man with the Muck-rake)," April 14, 1906.
2. "Jacob Riis," Library of Congress, accessed May 16, 2016, <item/2001704010>.
3. "'How the Other Half Lives,'" Library of Congress, accessed May 16, 2016, <item/2005689085>.
4. Josiah Flynt, *The World of Graft* (New York: McClure, Phillips & Company, 1901), 38.
5. Josiah Flynt, *The World of Graft* (New York: McClure, Phillips & Company, 1901), 2.
6. Edd Applegate, "Josiah Flynt Willard (1869–1907)," in *Literary Journalism: A Biographical Dictionary of Writers and Editors* (Westport, CT: Greenwood, 1996), 287–290.
7. Doris Kearns Goodwin, *The Bully Pulpit: Theodore Roosevelt, William Howard Taft, and the Golden Age of Journalism* (New York: Simon and Schuster, 2013), 331, 332.
8. Lincoln Steffens, *The Autobiography of Lincoln Steffens* (New York: Harcourt, Brace, 1931), 413.
9. Lincoln Steffens, "Tweed Days in St. Louis," in *The Shame of the Cities* (Mineola, NY: Dover, 2012), 40.
10. Lincoln Steffens, "The Shame of Minneapolis," in *The Shame of the Cities* (Mineola, NY: Dover, 2012), 51.
11. Lincoln Steffens, *The Autobiography of Lincoln Steffens*, Vol. 2 (New York: Harcourt, Brace, 1931), 799.
12. Upton Sinclair, *The Autobiography of Upton Sinclair* (New York: Harcourt, Brace, 1962), 126.
13. Upton Sinclair, *The Jungle* (New York: Doubleday, 1906), 161, 162.
14. Pure Food and Drug Act of 1906, Public Law, 59–384.
15. Upton Sinclair, *I, Candidate for Governor: And How I Got Licked* (Berkeley, CA: University of California Press, 1994), 109.
16. "David Graham Phillips," Library of Congress, accessed June 5, 2016, <item/2002695538>.
17. David Graham Phillips, "The Treason of the Senate," *Cosmopolitan* 40, 5 (March 1906): 487.
18. David Graham Phillips, "Aldrich, the Head of It All," *Cosmopolitan* 40, 6 (April 1906): 628.
19. David Graham Phillips, "The Man Who Laughs," *Cosmopolitan* 40, 6 (April 1906): 638.
20. *New York Tribune*, April 15, 1906.
21. David Graham Phillips, *The Treason of the Senate* (Chicago: Quadrangle Books, 1964), 218, 223.
22. "The Constitution of the United States," Amendment 17, ratified April 18, 1913.

8

YELLOW JOURNALISM
PULITZER AND HEARST BATTLE FOR READERS

This chapter looks at the circulation war between publishing giants Joseph Pulitzer and William Randolph Hearst:

- It provides examples of the sensational content of the era and shows how the competitive nature of the rivals affected subsequent media development;
- and it describes a style that had roots in the penny press, flourished at the turn of the twentieth century, and has made recurring appearances since then.

Using materials from this chapter, students should understand how Pulitzer and Hearst took sensationalism to new levels, affecting more than a century of media development to follow:

- They should also be able to explain why the phrase "Remember the Maine" has special significance in the history of the press;
- and they should be able to identify particular stories published in the contemporary press that might qualify as yellow journalism.

Key words, names, and phrases associated with Chapter 8 include:

- Joseph Pulitzer, the *New York World*;
- William Randolph Hearst, the *New York Journal*, and *Cosmopolitan*;
- yellow journalism and the Yellow Kid;
- and chain ownership.

The increased use of photography and illustrations in newspapers, along with the investigative reporting of muckrakers who uncovered relatively sensational (or mucky) content, correlated with other developments in the press, namely, the rise of a publishing technique known as yellow journalism. The latter, defined by its attention to sensational topics with stylized packaging, created an extraordinary precedent for modern journalism by creating a transformation that changed the way publishers sold content and structured media ownership.

The lasting effects of this transformation can be seen through today, at the very least symbolically, with the highest honors in journalism recognize the two most influential personalities from this era. The Pulitzer Prize, named after *New York World* publisher Joseph Pulitzer, awards outstanding work in reporting, and the Hearst Award, named after *New York Journal* publisher William Randolph Hearst, celebrates the best collegiate journalism in the United States. While Pulitzer's *World* made a name for itself with daring reporters, edgy cartoons and illustrations, and a flair for self-promotion, Hearst's *Journal* contributed to the creation of chain of press outlets, a model more common than not these days.

Students of history should also remember that although muckraking and yellow journalism both exploded at the turn of the twentieth century, they were not one in the same. Muckraking as a reporting style entailed the following of a money trail to uncover corruption—while this kind of reporting sometimes appeared in the yellow press, yellow journalism more generally featured publishing tricks used to sell the news. In essence, yellow journalism placed an emphasis on style over substance. And if it helps to conceptualize the era even more clearly, yellow journalism had roots even farther back than the 1890s, with content comparable in some respects to the first wave of penny press sensationalism that preceded it in the 1830s and 40s. This second wave of sensationalism, as it was, approximately fifty years after the penny press, featured some of the same ingredients of scandal, such as violence and sex, but the largest publishers, in addition, included spectacular color illustrations (hence the connection to "yellow"), as well as a measure of pure fun and entertainment to sell newspapers.

Although Pulitzer and Hearst fueled sensationalism and did so very successfully, they remained extraordinary in their ability to profit from yellow journalism. In fact, most newspapers of the era maintained relatively standard news practices, with time-honored newspapers, such as the *New York Times*, celebrating the fact that they did not resort to yellow tactics.

While some newspapers around the country dabbled in what we today might call "fake news," just as many (if not more) at the time maintained traditional styles of reporting. Recent historians have argued that although New York's *World* and *Journal* made a spectacular show of news in Manhattan, the publishing capital of the world, smaller newspapers west of the Atlantic Coast tended to shy away from both the controversy and big budgets of these giant competitors. The story of Pulitzer and Hearst, regardless, remains one of the most compelling examples of media innovation that set a precedent for content—sometimes unfortunately—replicated still through today.

YELLOW JOURNALISM   133

Image 8.1: "The *New York Times.* Easter," published in New York by Lieber & Maass Lith., 1896, the artist depicts the *Times* as a civilized alternative to the yellow press, Library of Congress, accessed June 7, 2016, <item/93513098>.

At the same time, while historians typically point to the competition between these two men as the epitome of the era, others, of course, contributed to the development of the content that typified the era. The peak of competition between Pulitzer and Hearst took place in the 1890s, but comparable content from publisher Edward Willis (E. W.) Scripps (June 18, 1854–March 12, 1926) actually preceded their dominance. Scripps used yellow journalism, but he also avoided direct competition with New York newspapers, instead focusing on developing his own brand of news featured in the E. W. Scripps Company, a diversified media conglomerate, and United Press news service (which in 1958 became United Press International (UPI) when International News Service (INS) merged with United Press in 1958).

Scripps started work in the newspaper industry at the *Detroit News* in 1873, founded the *Penny Press* (later, the *Cleveland Press*), and in time built the media empire now named the E. W. Scripps Company. Scripps' papers commonly contained editorials from local activists who wrote about economic and social causes. These writers and the Scripps newspapers with which they were associated featured content that championed ordinary people. Pulitzer's *World* and Hearst's *Journal* later adopted and perfected this style of crusading journalism for the urban interests of readers in New York City.

JOSEPH PULITZER AND THE *NEW YORK WORLD*

Joseph Pulitzer, Hungarian-born editor and publisher, set standards for both editors and reporters that remain among those most recognized by contemporary journalists. He was born on April 10, 1847, in Mako, Hungary, to a wealthy grain-merchant father and a devout Roman Catholic mother, and although he came from a family that had just about everything, Pulitzer had to work hard to create a comfortable living for himself. His persistence in creating news that both informed and entertained contributed to his legacy and to this day has given him a name synonymous with quality news. When Pulitzer died October 29, 1911, his will designated $2 million for the establishment of a school of journalism at Columbia University in New York City, one of the several lasting contributions the visionary publisher made to the history of the American press.

As a young man growing up under the rule of the Austro-Hungarian Empire, private tutors, from whom he learned to speak German and French, educated Pulitzer. He tried to enlist in the army in Europe but could not because of poor vision and weak lungs.

Pulitzer immigrated to the United States in 1864 with an interest in joining the Union. His health again interfered with his ability to serve, so after the war, he turned to the newspaper business. Moving to St. Louis, Missouri, he found a large population of Germans who had emigrated after the failed revolutions of 1848 (the same uprisings that had received extraordinary coverage in the United States from *New York Tribune* correspondent Margaret Fuller). When he took a job as a reporter for a newspaper written in German named the *Westliche Post*, memories of the revolutions that had swept Europe in the 1840s inspired his belief that readers should find content that interested them, a populist ideal that met the demands of consumers. These beliefs also contributed to his political affiliations. He joined the Republican Party in the early 1870s, along with a group dubbed the Red Republicans, Germans with an affinity for liberal reform.

In 1872, Pulitzer sided with members of the offshoot Liberal Republican Party to serve as a delegate during the failed presidential election of Horace Greeley, editor of the *New York Tribune*. His efforts with the press paid off when later in the year he was able to sell his interest in the German newspaper and use the profits to buy the *St. Louis Post* for about $3,000. He also bought a different German paper and sold it at a $20,000 profit, which paid for his political activities and for law school. He started

Image 8.2: "Joseph Pulitzer, 1847–1911," publisher of the *New York World*.[1]

a law practice in Missouri, but he gave it up in 1878 after purchasing the troubled *St. Louis Dispatch*, then combining it with another St. Louis newspaper, the *Post*. Aided by John A. Cockerill, a brilliant editor in chief, Pulitzer launched crusades against lotteries, gambling, and tax dodging, and *The Post-Dispatch* in general sought to make St. Louis a more civic-minded community.

His successes in St. Louis made Pulitzer a wealthy man, and in 1883, he purchased the *New York World* from robber baron Jay Gould for $346,000. Pulitzer promised readers of the *World* that he would "expose all fraud and sham, fight all public evils and abuses" and "battle for the people with earnest sincerity."[2] To do so, he concentrated on human-interest stories and sensational material that included scandals.

Even as Pulitzer's eyes began to fail in the 1880s (he went blind in 1889), he carried on a battle for readers with William Randolph Hearst, publisher of the *New York Journal*. At first, Pulitzer opposed the sensationalism of large headlines and art, but in competing with Hearst, he resorted to the questionable journalistic practices. In doing so, he maintained an uncanny knack for appealing to interests of common readers, including immigrants who in some cases did not even need English to understand the contents of the paper. In 1887, he recruited the famous investigative journalist Nellie Bly, who tantalized the *World*'s audience with both her exposé of the Blackwell's Island asylum and her speedy travels around the world (see Chapter 4 of this book, "Nineteenth-Century Publishing Innovations in Content and Technology").

Then, in 1895, the *World* introduced Richard F. Outcault's fantastically popular The Yellow Kid comic series, one of the first strips featured in the newly launched Sunday color supplement. Under Pulitzer's leadership, circulation grew from 15,000 to 600,000, making it the largest newspaper in the country. His *World* featured illustrations, advertising, and a culture of consumption for working men who, Pulitzer believed, saved money to enjoy life with their families when they could. Even his publication's name, *New York World*, testified to Pulitzer's grandiose visions of self and self-promotion. Before Pulitzer, few papers included illustrations for wide circulation simply because they cost more to produce than the resulting revenue gathered by them. By the turn of the twentieth century, however, the *World*'s circulation reached an astronomical one million, and when combined with correlating advertising dollars, color illustrations emerged as a new norm in publishing.

THE YELLOW KID STARTS A WAR

Mickey Dugan, a comic character dubbed "the Yellow Kid," made one of his first appearances in the *New York World* in 1895 wearing white pajamas in a tough urban neighborhood known as Hogan's Alley. He spoke via text often written on his pajamas. As the comic developed a following, its creator, Richard Felton Outcault, experimented with color. To add vibrancy to his most popular character, Mickey Dugan's white pajama instead appeared yellow. William Randolph Hearst recognized the cartoon as contributing to Pulitzer's success, and instead of creating new techniques of his own, and as he had done on other occasions, Hearst simply bought the *World*'s most prized assets. In 1896, Hearst hired Outcault by offering him a salary higher than Pulitzer could pay. As a character in the *Journal*'s color illustrations, the Yellow Kid appeared in a new full-page color strip, growing increasingly more violent and even more vulgar than his earliest incarnations in an attempt to maintain audience interest.

This cartoon, one of the first Outcault drew for the *Journal* after he left the *World*, shows the Yellow Kid holding a football and charging through a group of players. Since the *World* owned the rights to "Hogan's Alley," Outcault transferred the Kid and his gang to the new location of McFadden's Row. The Kid's pet goat Plato and a biting dog add to the melee while his girlfriend Liz wears knickers and runs beside him and spectators cheer for him. The Kid's football sweater reads, "Talk about interference. Dis aint de first duck wot tried it wit me—He don't like de way I has me hair cut." A piece of paper reads, "When

Image 8.3: "McFadden's Row of Flats Inauguration of the Football Season in McFadden's Row," Richard Felton Outcault, 1896.[3]

he goes to bed at night, he is de undressed Yellow Kid—so he has hired out to a glove house fer undressed kid wich is to be all de style." Outcault, meanwhile, had failed to copyright his creation, allowing Pulitzer to hire illustrator George Luks, who continued drawing the original version of the Hogan's Alley for the

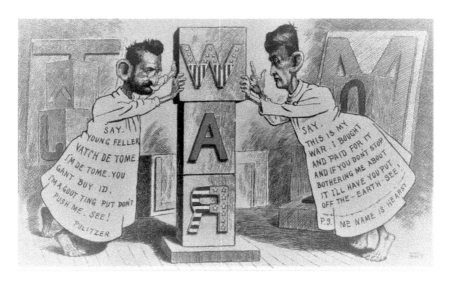

Image 8.4: "The Big Type War of the Yellow Kids," Leon Barritt, artist, published June 29, 1898, depicts Joseph Pulitzer and William Randolph Hearst each dressed as the Yellow Kid and pushing against opposite sides of a pillar of wooden blocks that spells "WAR."[4]

World. Although the new version of Hogan's Alley enjoyed less popularity, the Yellow Kid, in an unprecedented moment of publishing history, appeared simultaneously in two competing papers for about a year.

Another illustration from the era depicts the competition between Pulitzer and Hearst in the ways they utilized publishing tricks to maximize sales and influence readers.

The rise in the popularity of the Yellow Kid and sensational illustrations in general had coincided with troubles in Cuba over Spain's territorial interests in the nation. In time, the Yellow Kid represented a valuable asset between competing newspapers, comparable in some respects to the role Cuba played between the rivaling interests of the United States and Spain. To his credit, William Randolph Hearst understood ahead of those who followed him that the press could determine—and sometimes manipulate—public perception of international events. Seeking to develop a career in politics for himself, Hearst used his competition with Pulitzer as a platform for influencing political and public affairs. Although the "WAR" in this cartoon referred directly to the circulation war between Pulitzer and Hearst, as epitomized in their fight over rights to the Yellow Kid, it also alluded to the role the newspapers played in fueling tensions between the United States and Spain during the Spanish-American War.

Of all the developments in Pulitzer's growing empire, the Yellow Kid at least symbolically epitomized the era. The entertainment value of the cartoon character alone led otherwise disengaged readers to pick up the *World* simply to follow the exploits of this character and his cohorts who resided in the semi-fictional neighborhood of Hogan's Alley. The comic strip provided an escape from the otherwise drab business of daily news, featuring mischievous children in settings that contrasted brilliantly with the kind of material depicted in other, traditional newspapers, such as Jacob Riis' accounts of urban blight in "How the Other Half Lives" (see Chapter 7 of this book, "Muckraking: Reporters and Reform"). The public's fascination with the Yellow Kid, along with the new contents used to promote newspapers, helped coin the phrase "yellow journalism," which described the press and the strategy of publishers as a whole at the time.

In his later years, Pulitzer rethought his role in the news industry and considered ways he might develop a legacy that had much more to contribute to press history than the sensationalism in his war with Hearst. Recognizing the need for a more thoughtful approach to news, Pulitzer contributed an article to the May 1904 issue of the *North American Review* in support of founding of a school of journalism. His rationale for the proposal had principles tied to the founding of the nation and the role of the Fourth Estate in mind. "Our Republic and its press will rise or fall together," he wrote.

> An able, disinterested, public-spirited press, with trained intelligence to know the right and courage to do it, can preserve that public virtue without which popular government is a sham and a mockery. A cynical, mercenary, demagogic press will produce in time a people as base as itself. The power to mould the future of the Republic will be in the hands of the journalists of future generations.[5]

In the last years of his life (his health failed in 1911), Pulitzer sought to establish his envisioned journalism school by approaching Columbia University in New York with $2 million. The trustees initially resisted, believing journalism studies would not suit their high-minded students, but Pulitzer persisted, and Columbia opened the new school in 1912, shortly after he died.

WILLIAM RANDOLPH HEARST AND THE *NEW YORK JOURNAL*

American publisher William Randolph Hearst created in his time the most extensive empire of print media ever assembled by one man. His greatest professional influences came from none other than Joseph Pulitzer, who inspired him to both match and supersede the *World*'s success in reaching audiences. Hearst foresaw the role the press would have in determining the success of political campaigns, and, seeking to advance a role in politics for himself, he embarked on a career in publishing when in fact he could have done whatever it was he wanted to do in life.

Hearst succeeded as a publisher, editor, business owner, realtor, artist, and politician. According to a 1935 *Fortune* magazine article, Hearst at the time was one of the twentieth century's greatest spenders and a real estate mogul in a league of his own. Hearst's art collections were worth at least $20 million (a quarter billion in today's currency), and his ranches, mines, orchards, and packing plants another $30 million. His real estate holdings in New York City alone were assessed at $41 million, and his

Image 8.5: "Hearst, William R.," photography by Harris & Ewing, created between 1905 and 1945.[6]

newspapers, magazines, radio stations, motion-picture companies, real estate, and gold and other mining operations combined made him, according to *Forbes*, one of the wealthiest men alive at the time.[7]

On April 29, 1863, in San Francisco, California, William Randolph Hearst was born the only child of George and Phoebe Hearst. George Hearst had developed an enormous fortune through mining in northern Nevada and California. The wealth of the family allowed young William extraordinary opportunities, including the ability to travel the world at a young age with his mother and to see the great creations of artists and visionaries. He received the best education possible, landing at Harvard for his collegiate studies. His experience as an undergrad was hardly remarkable, other than for the fact that he developed a love for journalism as a writer and business manager for the *Harvard Lampoon*, an undergraduate humor publication. After a stunt in which he sent engraved silver chamber pots to his professor, Hearst returned to California, expelled from school but with a newfound purpose.

Among his countless assets, Hearst's father had acquired the *San Francisco Examiner* as repayment for a gambling debt. Although young William essentially could have done whatever he wanted upon returning from the east, he surprised everyone by indicating his first desire was to run the newspaper. The suggestion at first startled those close to him, as they initially thought he had no idea what he could do with his wealth. However, Hearst understood that the newspaper had become in its own right the primary source of both success and failure for those interested in a larger political or public career. He was determined to succeed, and he knew he would need the press to help him do so.

The *Examiner* itself had fallen into disrepair, but Hearst hired the best writers that money could buy and improved operations by investing more than $8 million of the family's riches. He focused specifically on implementing the techniques Pulitzer had used in building the *New York World*, engaging in crusades and sensationalism. Unlike Pulitzer, Hearst did not oppose the idea of "making" news—with reporters undertaking stunts that bordered on renegade social science experiments. In one incident, a reporter feigned fainting on the streets of San Francisco. The reaction of bystanders—whether or not someone would help—determined the type of story readers would get. Either someone would help the reporter, and if they did, the next day the paper would praise the compassion of San Francisco's good Samaritans; or if no one helped, which at the time was more likely, the paper would blast the awfulness of the people and call for social reform. In another stunt, for example, Hearst had a reporter jump off a ferry to see how long it would take people to rescue him. The stakes of such stunts were at first low, and although they provided entertainment, the purpose and results were in the end buffoonish. Hearst was just beginning his exploits as a publisher, however, and as his career progressed, the stunts became more serious and entailed much greater stakes.

His next step, a big one, took operations to New York City, where he challenged Pulitzer head on. Hearst bought the aging *New York Journal* from Pulitzer's brother Albert, marking the start of an intense battle with his previous mentor. Hearst also simply bought Pulitzer's best writers by offering them a higher salary and giving them license to write anything that sold newspapers.

REMEMBERING THE MAINE

To this day, controversy swirls over the role the yellow press played in pushing—or not pushing—the United States into war with Spain in 1898. The conflict began with the aftermath of an explosion on the USS Maine in Havana Harbor in Cuba, which led the United States to intervene on behalf of Cuba's push for independence from Spain. The United States subsequently acquired Spanish possessions in the Pacific, leading to its involvement in another war involving the Philippines.

The reason for the press' indelible tie to the outbreak of this war stem from the publishing strategy Hearst used at the time. Searching for a scoop that would boost his role as an influencer of foreign policy, Hearst grasped onto details about a possible Cuban revolt against Spain, a significant highlight in his professional journalism career. He persistently tried to spark U.S. intervention in Cuba and sent many high-profile writers and illustrators to Cuba in an effort to capture great stories. A famous legend—a myth that has no actual evidence to support it—typifies the controversy that had surrounded

Hearst's tactics. In stoking flames between the United States and Spain with inflammatory content and the intent of sparking a war, Hearst had sent famed illustrator Frederic Remington to Cuba to provide sketches of the rumored rumblings between natives and the Spanish. Remington found no conflict and sent a telegram back to his *Journal* boss that supposedly read, "Everything quiet. There is no trouble here. There will be no war. Wish to return." Although the alleged telegrams have never actually been discovered (and in all likelihood never existed), Hearst is alleged to have replied to Remington's message, "Please remain. You furnish the pictures and I'll furnish the war."

Even though historians have debunked the myth, the story persists as one that says more about the way Hearst's contemporaries perceived him than it does about Hearst himself.[8] Clearly, his readers, supporters, competitors, and detractors alike saw him as a ruthless and manipulative publisher who exercised his power over both his press and external affairs. And even though this particular story—like much of the happenings covered in the yellow press—was false, it represents the kind of content Hearst popularized, perhaps unintentionally, whether it be about him or from him.

In an all too appropriate and ironic twist, the war Hearst sought found him when, a few weeks later, the American ship USS Maine mysteriously exploded in Havana Harbor, killing 274 people. Although the cause of the explosion was unknown, the *Journal* ran page after page claiming Spain had committed treachery and in fact blew up the ship. The recurring mantra "Remember the Maine, to Hell with Spain!" entered the public's consciousness as a rallying cry for war primarily because the *Journal* led the charge while other newspapers followed, as Hearst's rivals could only hope to attract a portion of his audience, with the *Journal*'s readership now exceeding one million readers each day.

Hearst used the occasion to exercise his power over the content consumed by readers and in doing so built his influence on political figures as well. On February 17, 1898, the *Journal* ran a series of headlines that set the tone for subsequent issues in the days that preceded the formal outbreak of war between the United States and Spain. The following excerpt provides a sample of the countless lines—generally in giant, bold font, accompanied by sensational illustrations and photography—that were devoted to convincing both readers and competing newspapers that the Spanish should be destroyed.

"Destruction of the War Ship Maine was the Work of an Enemy."

"Assistant Secretary Roosevelt Convinced the Explosion of the War Ship Was Not an Accident."

"The *Journal* Offers $50,000 Reward for the Conviction of the Criminals Who Sent 258 American Sailors to Their Death. Naval Officers Unanimous That the Ship Was Destroyed on Purpose."

"Naval Officers Think the Maine was Destroyed by a Spanish Mine."

George Eugene Bryson, the *Journal*'s special correspondent at Havana, cables that it is the secret opinion of many Spaniards in the Cuban capital, that the Maine was destroyed and 258 men killed by means of marine mine or fixed torpeda. This is the opinion of several American naval authorities. The Spaniards, it is believed, arranged to have the

Maine anchored over one of the harbor mines. . . . Assistant Secretary of the Navy Theodore Roosevelt says he is convinced that the destruction of the Maine in Havana Harbor was not an accident. . . . The suspicion that the Maine was deliberately blown up grows stronger every hour. Not a single fact to the contrary has been produced.

Hearst wanted war, in part, because he believed that when the country was at war, his papers would have a constant supply of sensational articles to publish. In addition, a war would demonstrate his power to manipulate not only the public's perception of events but also his role in determining the course of international affairs—a steppingstone, as it was, in his plans to run for higher office, even the presidency itself.

It should come as no surprise then that the role of yellow journalism has filled academic histories for more than a century. It continues to trigger debate. Depending on how much blame a historical mind may wish to place on Hearst primarily and Pulitzer secondarily, newspapers had at least an influence on the attitudes of readers towards U.S. involvement in Cuba. And at the same time, much like the legendary legacies of both publishers, their exact contributions to foreign policy at the time has often been muddled in the hyperbole that they helped create.

For nearly a half-century or more, popular accounts virtually assigned responsibility for the U.S. invasion of Cuba to sensationalized accounts of rebel activity first spread by the *New York Journal* and then later by the *World*. Media theorists have more recently described this role as part of an agenda-setting process, which suggests media does not do a very good job at telling consumers how to think, but media can effectively tell consumers about which issues to think. Among scholars who have more recently given the traditional record assigned to Hearst a skeptical eye, W. Joseph Campbell notes that researchers would have found unambiguous references to Hearst's influence in the personal papers and the reminiscences of policymakers of the time, but none exist. "The yellow press is not to blame for the Spanish-American-War," writes W. Joseph Campbell, a scholar of the era. "The conflict was, rather, the result of a convergence of forces far beyond the control or direct influence of even the most aggressive of the yellow newspapers, William Randolph Hearst's *New York Journal*."[9] The reason Hearst's name to this day has an association with the event, according to Campbell, is because it provides a convenient way to excoriate yellow journalism.

Regarding Pulitzer's role, the *World* could have acted responsibly and depicted the clash accurately for its readers. The rising circulation rates of both the *World* and the *Journal* during this period indicates that publishers made money from inflated nationalism and that the competition between the two was so intense that Pulitzer could not afford the risk of falling behind Hearst's lead. In a race to the bottom, so to speak, both papers lowered their standards so much that they routinely reproduced their rivals' news, sometimes to their own peril.

Using an old journalistic trick, for example, Hearst at one point caught the *World* in the act of cannibalizing news. An article appeared in the *Journal* in 1898 describing the death of Colonel Reflipe W. Thenuz, whose name was a refashioning of the phrase, "We pilfer the news." The next day, Pulitzer's paper carried the item, even adding specific details to make the story appear authentic. The *Journal* celebrated the gaffe for over a month while the *World* maintained a "pained silence" on its blunder. To add insult to injury, the *Journal* sarcastically announced that it would solicit designs from artists for a Thenuz monument, and for days, the *Journal* printed letters from "readers" denouncing Pulitzer's staff as plagiarists.

Even Richard Harding Davis, the most respected foreign correspondent of his day, could not escape the lure of sensational content. At first, he resisted by leaving Cuba without asking for permission from his editors at the *Journal*. On his return home, he met a young Cuban woman named Clemencia Arango, a suspected guerrilla collaborator who told Davis that Spanish detectives had ordered her to disrobe while they searched her for messages to Cuban exiles in Tampa. Davis buried an account of her ordeal in a longer piece he submitted for the *Journal*, but when his editors found the salacious details, which were later understood as not entirely true, they featured them with an illustration of a naked young woman under a headline that read, "Does Our Flag Shield Women?"[10]

In Campbell's analysis, Pulitzer and Hearst influenced the debate about entering into a war with Spain, but it is much less clear if President McKinley paid any attention to the press' reports on events in Cuba. Campbell also found that no record of Hearst or Pulitzer exists relative to an influence they might have had on the vote of Congress to go to war with Spain. At the time, Hearst at least publicly bragged about the *Journal*'s ability to capitalize on events, asking readers on the front pages of May 1898 issues, "How do you like the *Journal*'s war?"[11] However, evidence suggests he succeeded more in increasing circulation than in actually directing the fight.

Depending on how much blame a historical mind may wish to place on Hearst primarily and Pulitzer secondarily, newspapers had at least an influence on the attitudes of readers towards U.S. involvement in Cuba. And at the same time, much like the legendary legacies of both publishers, their exact contributions to foreign policy at the time have often been muddled in the hyperbole that they helped create.

Despite the enormous potential at Hearst's disposal, including his wealth, his talents as a publisher, and his access to an unprecedented level of self-promotion in the press, his goals never quite matched reality. (This part of Hearst's life was later satirized in the famous movie *Citizen Kane* by Orson Welles, which is in part described in this book's Chapter 10, "Radio and Television: The Advent of Broadcast News and Entertainment.")

A series of unfortunate events combined with Hearst's lavish spending habits created consistent problems in his quest to succeed. An infamous incident that first steered Hearst's career from public service stemmed from a column written by famed editor Arthur Brisbane (and published by Hearst) that ran in the April 10, 1901, issue of the *Journal*. "Institutions, like men, will last until they die," Brisbane wrote, "and if bad institutions and bad men can be got rid of only by killing, then the killing must be done!"[12] Later that year, Leon Czolgosz, a deranged anarchist who had read the *Journal*, either took these words literally or simply acted on pre-existing delusions and shot President William McKinley dead. The event, not surprisingly, shook the nation and led to a tremendous public backlash against Hearst when it was discovered that he might have had at least an indirect if not wholly accidental link to the death of the president. In some locations, public libraries banned Hearst's newspapers, and elsewhere, clergy denounced Hearst from the pulpit. For contextual purposes, students should remember that the reaction to Hearst and his papers came at the behest of competing newspapers that said nothing at the time the *Journal* first

Image 8.6: "The Yellow Press," Louis M. Glackens, artist, published in New York by Keppler & Schwarzmann, Puck Building, October 12, 1910, an illustration showing William Randolph Hearst as a jester tossing newspapers with headlines such as "Appeals to Passion, Venom, Sensationalism, Attacks on Honest Officials, Strife, Distorted News, Personal Grievance, [and] Misrepresentation" to a crowd of eager readers, among them an anarchist assassinating a politician speaking from a platform draped with American flags. On the left, men labeled "Man who buys the comic supplement for the kids, Businessman, Gullible Reformer, Advertiser, [and] Decent Citizen" carry bags of money that they dump into Hearst's printing press. The text includes language from a letter published in the *New York Evening Post* by Mayor Gaynor, who wrote, "The time is at hand when these journalistic scoundrels have got to stop or get out, and I am ready now to do my share to that end. They are absolutely without souls. If decent people would refuse to look at such newspapers, the whole thing would right itself at once. The journalism of New York City has been dragged to the lowest depths of degradation. The grossest railleries and libels, instead of honest statements and fair discussion, have gone unchecked," Library of Congress, accessed May 16, 2016, <item/2011647630>.

published the inflammatory language, taking the opportunity of McKinley's death to heap criticism on their chief rival.

The incident no doubt affected Hearst's long-term plans to campaign for president. Voters did put him into the U.S. House as a representative from New York from 1903 to 1907, but he rarely attended committee meetings or even stepped foot in Congress. He failed in his attempts to win elections for mayor of New York City and governor of New York State. He also failed in attempts to become a U.S. senator from New York, as well as, eventually, the presidency in a third party he helped organize.

Meanwhile the presidency itself had taken dramatic turns not only with the assassination of McKinley but also with the unlikely rise of his successor who had enjoyed a direct link to the press in previous decades. Theodore Roosevelt, who contemporaries recognized as a force of nature, had made his way from the police commissioner of New York City (and ally of muckraker Jacob Riis) to the upper levels of government. From 1898 to 1900, Roosevelt served as governor of New York. He won celebrity status in the Spanish-American War as the head of a contingent known as the Rough Riders, and afterwards, McKinley appointed him vice president. With McKinley dead, Roosevelt assumed the presidency and engineered one of the most consequential administrations in U.S. history, both in terms of the political reforms he achieved and relative to the press' role in its relations with the executive branch through subsequent generations.

THE EMERGENCE OF A MEDIA EMPIRE

We would not have the media conglomerates or chains that we have today were it not for Hearst. The papers he published reached well beyond the readership of one particular city and led to the development of a modern dynasty. Hearst owned and published a number of newspapers and magazines around the country, a chain ownership model that set the template for modern media organizations to come.

Among his many publications used to advance personal interests, Hearst purchased and used *The Cosmopolitan* (now *Cosmopolitan* magazine) in 1905 to advocate for eight-hour workdays and support labor interests, a move that included supporting the concept of a federal income tax. Hearst saw the magazine as a vehicle to advance his plans to win elected office. He hired David Graham Phillips, a well-known and widely read writer and reporter, to prepare a series of attacks on the U.S. Senate as a sensational way to build sales, as well as to attract support from populists who saw the need for reform in the nation's capital. Hearst paid Phillips generously, he hired talented researchers, and he relentlessly advertised the series. *Cosmopolitan* would feature full-color artwork on its covers, important cartoonists produced frontispieces, and from February to November 1906, each monthly installment would include shocking details about the unseemly ties between politicians and moneyed industrialists. The strategy would appeal to Hearst's target audience, a demographic of populist voters who would turn to him, he thought, in his capacity as a would-be elected representative.

> ### "THE TREASON OF THE SENATE" AS YELLOW JOURNALISM
>
> "The Treason of the Senate," a classic piece of both muckraking (see Chapter 7, "Muckraking: Reporters and Reform") and yellow journalism, made claims that non-elected officials in the Senate had close ties to the heads of industry, who often used their connections to politicians to circumvent regulation. In building this case not only for reform but also for his publisher's political goals, David Graham Phillips relied on metaphorical descriptions of the actual wrongdoings of senators. One of his chief targets, New York senator Chauncey Mitchell Depew, he described as the "railroad" senator, a "sly tongued courtier-agent, with the greasy conscience and the greasy tongue and the greasy backbone and the greasy hinges of the knees."[13] In the opening issue of Phillips' series, a picture of Depew captured him with his head tilted back, mouth open, and laughing. Under the picture, a caption read, "Depew's joviality and popularity, according to Mr. Phillips, have cost the American people at least one billion dollars."[14]

Throughout "The Treason of the Senate," Phillips used terms he coined—"the Interests" and their victims "the People"—to describe the true constituency of the Senate, terms destined to endure.[15] "The Interests" could name their own handpicked agents to sit in the powerful Senate, where they would serve on important committees and where they work to either help pass or kill legislation based on the interests of "the Interests." He alleged the Senate passed measures that lined private pockets with literally millions of dollars extorted from the people.[16] The Senate had "so legislated and so refrained from legislating," Phillips maintained, "that more than half of all the wealth created by the American people belongs to less than one percent of them."[17]

The public, in spite of an outcry from Congress, quickly gave Phillips celebrity status with the publications. For months, the circulation of *Cosmopolitan* soared. By May 1906, it reached 450,000, double its 1905 average, and the presses could not produce enough copies. City newsstands sold out two months in a row. By the third issue in the series, subscriptions for *Cosmopolitan* were up by 50 percent, no doubt satisfying Hearst.

Phillips' articles had most directly attacked the system of appointment that the Constitution had originally designated for the selection of senators. Less than a decade after publication of "The Treason of the Senate," Congress ratified an amendment providing for the direct election of senators. In the same year, at least in part with the help of Hearst's work in Congress as a representative from New York, Congress also ratified the Sixteenth Amendment, which allowed for a federal income tax as a way to redistribute wealth.

Constitution Amendment 16, ratified February 3, 1913

The Congress shall have power to lay and collect taxes on incomes, from whatever source derived, without apportionment among the several States, and without regard to any census or enumeration.[18]

The Sixteenth, Seventeenth, Eighteenth, and Nineteenth Amendments, also known as the Progressive Amendments, represented the manifestation of work by the press and those elsewhere who had aimed for a variety of reforms, among which included the redistribution of wealth from the ultra-rich to a populist base eager for change. (Whether or not the Sixteenth or Seventeenth Amendments have accomplished their goals has been the subject of debate for more than a century.)

Hearst continued to experiment with every aspect of newspaper publishing, from page layouts to editorial crusades. Other newspapers bought stories by Hearst correspondents from around the world, giving rise to the Hearst International News Service and the Universal wire service. In the following decades, Hearst established the largest media conglomeration of any kind until that time. While other moguls in the later part of the twentieth century would transform companies into transnational operations beyond the control of any single corporate head, Hearst set the model and template for empires by exercising influence over vast geographic space.

Apart from having highly circulated magazines and owning dozens of newspapers in eighteen major cities from coast to coast (many of them under either the *American* or *Examiner* banners), read by one out of four Americans each day, Hearst also acquired radio stations and film companies to complement the content of his papers. (To this day, the Hearst media empire continues to hold investments in media that range from newspapers to the Internet.) As a sample of William Randolph Hearst's propensity to acquire media across the country, the following timeline provides a snapshot of just some of the newspapers (not including magazines) under his control during his heyday of influence.

Two Decades of Hearst Newspapers Acquired, Purchased, or Sold

1912:	*Atlanta Georgian* and *San Francisco Call*
1913:	*San Francisco Post*
1917:	*Boston Advertiser* and *Washington Times*
1918:	*Chicago Herald*
1921:	*Boston Record, Detroit Times, Milwaukee Telegram* and *Wisconsin News*, and *Seattle Post-Intelligencer*
1922:	*Albany Times-Union, Los Angeles Herald, Rochester Journal and American, Syracuse Telegram and American,* and *Washington Herald*
1923:	*Baltimore News and American* and *Rochester Post-Express*
1924:	*New York Mirror* and *San Antonio Light*
1925:	Hearst sells *Syracuse Telegram* to the owners of *Syracuse Journal*, while selling *New York Mirror* in 1928; however, he oversees the operations of both papers, and eventually buys back *Daily Mirror* in 1932.
1927:	Hearst acquires *Pittsburgh Post-Gazette*, and later in the year, he acquires *Omaha Bee and News*.
1931:	Hearst buys *Los Angeles Evening Express*, forming *Herald-Express*.

During the 1920s, nearly one in four Americans got their news from a Hearst paper. Historian Ian Mugridge estimates that, by 1930, Hearst owned newspapers in almost every major city and controlled a circulation of more than five million daily papers and nearly seven million Sunday papers—approximately thirty million people read a Hearst newspaper every day.[19] At Hearst's publishing pinnacle, he owned six magazines and more than two dozen newspapers nationwide with twenty daily and eleven Sunday papers in thirteen cities.

Hearst lost the majority of his capital during the Great Depression. In 1937, the two corporations that controlled the empire reached $126 million in debt. Hearst had to turn them over to a seven-member committee, and the committee's decisions helped him avoid economic failure by selling off much of his private fortune and all of his public powers as a newspaper owner. By 1940, his newspaper empire had shrunk by more than half, dwindling from its peak of forty-two names to seventeen.

Hearst died in 1951 at the age of 88 years old, leaving a legacy for the history of the press. Although his funds and empire diminished dramatically by the time of his death, he still led the largest news company of its kind. He established the William Randolph Hearst Foundation as a charity to contribute in the fields of education, healthcare, social services and arts throughout the United States, and, most importantly, he set the model for modern media dynasties.

RECAPPING THIS CHAPTER

Looking back on this chapter, you should see how it profiled an important moment in the history of the press, which consisted of the competition between publishing giants Joseph Pulitzer and William Randolph Hearst. The chapter provided examples of the sensational content of the era, and it showed how the competitive nature of the rivals affected subsequent media development. It described a style that had roots in the penny press, flourished at the turn of the twentieth century, and has made recurring appearances since then, all the way through today.

Using materials from this chapter, you should understand how Pulitzer and Hearst took sensationalism to new levels, affecting a century of media development that followed. You should also be able to explain why the phrase "Remember the Maine" has special significance in the history of the press, and you should be able to identify particular stories published in the contemporary press that might qualify as yellow journalism.

The following chapter profiles the work of Ida Tarbell as influential in causing the growth of public relations industries. It shows how Tarbell's expose of The Standard Oil Company inspired public relations pioneers, including Ivy Ledbetter Lee and Edward Bernays, to help repair the image of industrialists, and it shows how, as major parts of modern media, public relations has influenced content in ways sometimes unexpected for consumers.

NOTES

1 "Joseph Pulitzer," Library of Congress, accessed June 5, 2016, <item/2004672793>.
2 *New York World*, May 11, 1883.
3 "McFadden's Row of Flats: Inauguration of the Football Season in McFadden's Row," Richard Felton Outcault, 1896, Library of Congress, accessed April 8, 2017, <item/2003674039>.
4 "The Big Type War of the Yellow Kids," Library of Congress, accessed May 16, 2016, <item/95508199>.
5 Joseph Pulitzer, "The College of Journalism," *North American Review*, 178 (January 1904): 680.
6 "Hearst, William R.," Library of Congress, accessed May 16, 2016, <item/hec2009008137>.
7 "Hearst," *Fortune*, 12, 4 (October 1935): 43–54.
8 W. Joseph Campbell, "I'll Furnish the War: The Making of a Media Myth," in *Getting It Wrong: Debunking the Greatest Myths in American Journalism* (Oakland: University of California Press, 2017), 9–25.
9 W. Joseph Campbell, "Not to Blame: The Yellow Press and the Spanish-American War," in *Yellow Journalism: Puncturing the Myths, Defining the Legacies* (Westport, CT: Praeger, 2001), 97.
10 "Does Our Flag Shield Women?" *New York Journal*, February 12, 1897.
11 David Nasaw, *The Chief: The Life of William Randolph Hearst* (Boston, New York: Houghton Mifflin, 2000), 132.
12 Arthur Brisbane, editorial, *New York Journal*, April 10, 1901.
13 David Graham Phillips, "The Treason of the Senate," *Cosmopolitan*, 11, 6 (April 1906): 632.

14 David Graham Phillips, "The Treason of the Senate," *Cosmopolitan*, 15, 5 (March 1906): 487.
15 David Graham Phillips, "The Treason of the Senate," *Cosmopolitan*, 15, 5 (March 1906): 488.
16 David Graham Phillips, "The Treason of the Senate," *Cosmopolitan*, 15, 6 (April 1906): 643.
17 David Graham Phillips, "The Treason of the Senate," *Cosmopolitan*, 15, 6 (April 1906): 623.
18 "The Constitution of the United States," Amendment 16, ratified February 3, 1913.
19 Ian Mugridge, *The View from Xanadu: William Randolph Hearst and United States Foreign Policy* (Montreal: Queen's University Press, 1995), 19.

9

PUBLIC RELATIONS

HOW THE PRESS LAUNCHED AN AGENCY OF ITS OWN

This chapter profiles the work of influential muckraker Ida Tarbell as contributing to the growth of public relations industries:

- It shows how Tarbell's exposé "The History of the Standard Oil Company" for *McClure's* inadvertently motivated public relations pioneers, including Ivy Ledbetter Lee and Edward Bernays, to develop a branch of the press that worked on behalf of business interests;
- and it shows how, as major parts of modern media, public relations affects content in ways sometimes unexpected for consumers.

Using materials from this chapter, students should know the role of Tarbell's work in what would become public relations and why journalists and historians hold it in such high esteem today:

- They should know how Parker and Lee's "Declaration of Principles" contained language that both initiated public relations as we know it and set the practice apart from the traditional purpose of reporting by members of the Fourth Estate;
- and they should be able to explain how the public relations industry does a service to both corporations and consumers.

> Key words, names, and phrases associated with Chapter 9 include:
>
> - Ida Tarbell, "The History of the Standard Oil Company";
> - Ivy Ledbetter Lee; "Declaration of Principles" (Parker and Lee);
> - John D. Rockefeller and the Ludlow Massacre;
> - and Edward Bernays, "Torches of Freedom," and Simon and Schuster.

During the heyday of muckraking, S. S. McClure published *McClure's Magazine*, which demonstrated an ability to produce societal change through the content of its writers. One of the magazine's contributors in particular, Ida Minerva Tarbell, stood out in her ability to produce change through extensive and methodical research. Tarbell, who many historians tie directly to the development of the public relations industry, made her name writing biographies, backing her observations with facts and remaining neutral while consequential to the point of earning respect from subsequent generations as one of the great reporters of any time.

Oil baron John D. Rockefeller had forced Tarbell's father out of business, and having seen how predatory practices ruined her family's livelihood, Tarbell took it on herself to expose Rockefeller's Standard Oil Company specifically. "They had never played fair," she wrote of the corporate giant, "and that ruined their greatness for me."[1] In 1904, *McClure's* ran Tarbell's classic series "The History of the Standard Oil Company," which she later published as a book that took to task the predatory tactics of Rockefeller and likeminded moguls. In a turn of events, Rockefeller thereafter realized he had to employ new methods to keep the trust of consumers and employed the press to help publicize his product. From this back and forth between the press and business, a new kind of journalism emerged, with the newly developed public relations industry transforming the press into a mouthpiece for both public interests and—for the first time—business interests.

MUCKRAKING TARGETS THE STANDARD OIL COMPANY

The major accomplishment of investigative reporter Ida Tarbell's career provided a precedent for federal regulation of the Standard Oil Company. Tarbell's work from her earliest days as a writer indicated she would leave an impact, and to this day, her classic piece on John D. Rockefeller's empire ranks among journalism's masterpieces.

Tarbell was born November 5, 1857, in Erie County, Pennsylvania, to a family that depended on the oil industry for a livelihood. She was one of the most educated and smartest members of her class, and she began her career in journalism as an editor at the *Chautauquan*, producing a series of controversial articles that featured the accomplishments of women. She developed skills as both a journalist and historian, and in 1890, she moved to Paris and studied historiography. While in France, she wrote short features on prominent French women and Parisian life for a paper affiliated with *McClure's*. Publisher Samuel McClure in the United States took notice and offered her a position as editor for his namesake flagship magazine.

Tarbell began her work as an editor and contributor for *McClure's* writing biographical materials on Napoleon Bonaparte. Her twenty-part series on Abraham Lincoln that followed represented an achievement in in-depth research and a sharp sense of marketing. Her topic selection attracted an audience double the size of the magazine's original circulation and gave Tarbell a reputation as a leading scholar and authority on the president.

Enjoying momentum from this newfound recognition, Tarbell embarked on a series of a different kind, a biography steeped in what critics had called the literature of exposure (and what Theodore Roosevelt would later describe as muckraking). Her

Image 9.1: "Ida Minerva Tarbell, 1857–1944," Frances Benjamin Johnston, photographer, between 1890 and 1910.[2]

most famous piece would confront the growth of John D. Rockefeller's oil empire, the Standard Oil Company, with her inspiration for taking down the monopoly dating back to her childhood, as she remembered how agreements between the oil industry and the railroads had forced out smaller oil producers, such as her father. "There was born in me a hatred of privilege, privilege of any sort," she said.

> It was all pretty hazy, to be sure, but it still was well, at 15, to have one definite plan based on things seen and heard, ready for a future platform of social and economic justice if I should ever awake to my need of one.[3]

The Standard Oil Company for Tarbell represented everything wrong that had emerged from the Reconstruction era's industrialization boom. Formed in 1867, Standard Oil grew in the same climate that had alarmed journalists including Lincoln Steffens, Upton Sinclair, and David Graham Phillips, one rife with unregulated business expansion that had a corrosive effect on public institutions. It epitomized monopolies of the era, and Rockefeller, for the muckrakers, symbolized the elite, or the enemy of the people, as his wealth alone exceeded the vast majority of American incomes combined.

Likely relying on her experience as a biographer of Napoleon, Tarbell described Rockefeller in terms that alluded to his military-like tactics. Take for example the following two passages.

> Ida Tarbell, "John D. Rockefeller, A Character Study," *McClure's*, 25, 3 (July 1905): 245.
>
> It takes time to crush men who are pursuing legitimate trade. But one of Mr. Rockefeller's most impressive characteristics is patience. There never was a more patient man, or one who could dare more while he waited. The folly of hurrying, the folly of discouragement, for one who would succeed, went hand and hand. Everything must be ready before he acted, but while you wait, you must prepare, must think, work. You must put in, if you would take out. His instinct for the money opportunity in things was amazing, his perception of the value of seizing this or that particular invention, plant, market, was unerring. He was like a general who, besieging a city surrounded by fortified hills, views form a balloon the whole great field, and sees how, this point taken, that must fall; this hill reached, that fort is commanded. And nothing was too small: the corner grocery in Browntown, the humble refining still on Oil Creek, the shortest private pipeline. Nothing, for little things grow.[4]

> Ida Tarbell, "History of the Standard Oil Company," *McClure's*, 21, 3 (1903): 320.
>
> With Mr. Rockefeller's genius for detail, there went a sense of the big and vital factors in the oil business and a daring in laying hold of them that was very like military genius. He saw strategic points like a Napoleon and he swooped on them with the suddenness of a Napoleon. Mr. Rockefeller's capture of the Cleveland refineries in 1872 was as dazzling an

achievement as it was a hateful one . . . The man saw what was necessary to his purpose and he never hesitated before it. His courage was steady and his faith in his ideas unwavering. He simply knew what was the thing to do, and he went ahead with the serenity of the man who knows.[5]

While raising public consciousness about Rockefeller's business practices, Tarbell's piece also had legal teeth inasmuch as the details published about the growth of the Standard Oil Company provided prosecutors with evidence of predatory practices. Moreover, in 1890, Congress had passed the Sherman Anti-Trust Act, which allowed the government to break up companies that engaged in monopolistic behavior, and indeed one of its most dramatic applications came in the form of a Supreme Court decision about the size and scope of Standard Oil. At the time of the court's decision, Rockefeller's net worth had grown to almost 3 percent of the national economy by 1910, which in contemporary terms would total $250 billion. The court's decision in 1911 to break up Standard Oil into six smaller subsidiaries—Amoco, Chevron, Exxon, Gulf, Mobil, and Texaco—stemmed at least in part from the attention the company had received in Tarbell's groundbreaking piece of journalism.

The role Tarbell's piece played in halting at least temporarily the growth of a corporate giant earned her respect for decades to come. In fact, toward the end of the twentieth century, scholars and journalists compiled a list of "America's Leading Writers" and listed the top 100 works of journalism in the twentieth century. *The History of the Standard Oil Company*, ranked No. 5.[6] She died on January 6, 1944, with a legacy still praised by many journalists.

PUBLIC RELATIONS CHRISTENED BY PARKER AND LEE

Had a press-related enterprise not emerged at about the same time as Rockefeller's legal troubles, the government might have regulated Standard Oil Company into obscurity. Instead—and perhaps ironically—Rockefeller's image and his company's health enjoyed rehabilitation largely because of members of the press who, although not directly related to the muckrakers, existed in part because of them.

Historians often cite Ivy Ledbetter Lee as the father of public relations, as in 1904 he formed a partnership with George Parker that created the first modern public relations agency. Parker, a former campaign manager for Democratic political candidates, brought Lee clients that included the Pennsylvania Railroad, the Red Cross, and none other than the Standard Oil Company. Among their most significant contributions to press history, Parker and Lee set a precedent for a professionalized representation of business clients in the press that holds public relations representatives to the same standards as journalists.

Lee was born in Cedartown, Georgia, on July 16, 1877. He graduated from Princeton with a degree in economics and pursued a career in journalism as a writer for New York newspapers, inducing the *American*, the *Times*, and the *World*. In his jobs as a writer, he built a sense of how transparency could build a healthy public image for the subjects of his stories, and in doing so, he took an interest in helping business clients move beyond the means they traditionally used of handing out biased literature

Image 9.2: "Lee, Ivy L.," Harris & Ewing, photographer, published between 1905 and 1945.[7]

and instead produced materials that emphasized truthful statements. We now recognize these statements as press releases, a collection of reliable facts that allow organizations to drive news narratives.

When Lee formed his partnership with Parker, the two built clientele by transcending the principles of journalism, representing a full-throated defense of one side—their client's interest—more vociferously than all sides, including that of the public, which journalists had traditionally devoted themselves to doing as members of the Fourth Estate. The strategy proved successful in times of crisis, as businesses prior to this time often had to fight for public sympathy in the face of relentless attacks from the press.

Among Parker and Lee's first clients, a group of coal operators hired the firm to represent their interests during a strike at anthracite mines. Lee made sure that newspapers received daily updates in hard-copy form of materials containing all pertinent facts of the strike. Newspapers received these new creations, press releases, with skepticism and hostility at first, seeing them as manipulative ads instead of information.

In response, Lee issued his "Declaration of Principles," which in 1906 he circulated widely to newsrooms.

The Declaration clarified the mission of Parker and Lee in clear and uncontroversial terms. "This is not a secret press bureau," it began. "All our work is done in the open."

> Parker and Lee, "Declaration of Principles," 1906
>
> We aim to supply news. This is not an advertising agency; if you think any of our matter ought properly to go to your business office, do not use it. Our matter is accurate. Further details on any subject treated will be supplied promptly, and any editor will be assisted most cheerfully in verifying directly any statement of fact. Upon inquiry, full information will be given to any editor concerning those on whose behalf an article is sent out. In brief, our plan is, frankly and openly, on behalf of business concerns and public institutions, to supply to the press and public of the United States prompt and accurate information concerning subjects which it is of value and interest to the public to know about. Corporations and public institutions give out much information in which the news point is lost to view. Nevertheless, it is quite as important to the public to have this news as it is to the establishments themselves to give it currency. I send out only matter every detail of which I am willing to assist any editor in verifying for himself. I am always at your service for the purpose of enabling you to obtain more complete information concerning any of the subjects brought forward in my copy.[8]

The emphasis on the "business concerns" of those the firm represented reveals the document's importance as a manifesto of sorts that laid the foundation for public relations.

A NEW PURPOSE FOR THE PRESS

Meanwhile, the success of Ida Tarbell's series on the Standard Oil Company had posed something of a dilemma for John D. Rockefeller: Either he could fight the press, which had done him little good in the years leading to the 1911 Supreme Court case that broke up his company, or he could coopt the press for his own purposes. Rockefeller—in a case of "if you can't beat them, join them"—turned to Parker and Lee for representation at a time when he needed public image control the most.

A crisis had erupted at one of the Rockefeller family's coal mines in Ludlow, Colorado. Workers had demanded from Rockefeller's son, John D. Rockefeller, Jr., who oversaw the mine, better pay and better working conditions, but disaster ensued after they initiated a strike, refusing to work until the Rockefellers met their demands. The Rockefellers pressured the Colorado governor to deploy the National Guard to break up the protests and order the workers to return to work. In an event called the Ludlow Massacre, the Colorado National Guard and security forces for the Rockefeller-owned mining company on April 20, 1914, attacked the 1,200 striking miners, at first firing a machine gun into the camp. Women and children in the miners' camp had dug pits beneath the tents to escape the gunfire, but at dusk, the Guard moved down from the hills with torches, set fire to the tents, and killed women and children, with survivors fleeing into the hills. Many of them were seriously injured, and a number of family members, including twelve children, burned to death. The number of fatalities varied according to different accounts, but at least nineteen miners and their families perished, along with a National Guardsman.

Accounts from the perspectives of the strikers to this day remain scarce, as Rockefeller's public relations machine went to work quickly to repair the damage from public shock at the event. Lee wrote a publicity leaflet for Rockefeller in the wake of the Ludlow Massacre claiming that the deaths were the fault of agitators paid for by the United Mine Workers of America. The leaflet was a piece of crude propaganda put out on behalf of his employer to attempt to lay the blame for the deaths at the feet of the union rather than accept that they had resulted from the battle between the strikers and the Colorado National Guard. The U.S. Commission on Industrial Relations called Lee to testify before the commission, where he claimed that he stuck entirely to his principles of advising his client to tell the full and frank story. He also claimed that the mine managers had misled both Rockefeller and him.

PRIMARY SOURCES AND THE LUDLOW MASSACRE

Among the few primary sources from the perspective of the strikers published after the fact, Colorado miners issued from headquarters a description that read, "Machine guns had been placed in position two days before. Using them like garden hose, the gunmen swept the tent colony, filled with women and children, from one end to the other." Another bulletin referred to the "charred and distorted bodies" in the cave at Ludlow after the battle. Elsewhere there was a list of those "murdered and cremated by the gunmen militia in the Ludlow Massacre."[9]

Later histories of the event have even turned to folk musician Woody Guthrie for an account of what happened, again, because Rockefeller's public relations machine drove the narrative ordinarily supplied by members of the press. Guthrie, who was a journalist turned musician, created the song the "Ludlow Massacre," first recorded in 1946, as an example of the memory that still exists if later generations look hard enough to find it.[10]

Woodie Guthrie, "Ludlow Massacre" (first recorded in 1946), Verses 3–5

We were so afraid you would kill our children,
We dug us a cave that was seven foot deep,
Carried our young ones and pregnant women
Down inside the cave to sleep.

That very night your soldiers waited,
Until all us miners were asleep,
You snuck around our little tent town,
Soaked our tents with your kerosene.

PUBLIC RELATIONS 159

You struck a match and in the blaze that started,
You pulled the triggers of your Gatling guns,
I made a run for the children but the firewall stopped me.
Thirteen children died from your guns.[11]

American historian Howard Zinn, author of the influential *A People's History of the United States*, has stated his interest in writing about the Ludlow Massacre first came from hearing Guthrie's song, as previously published literature paid little or no attention to the tragic event.[12] The rise of public relations during this period—which was riddled with other episodes of worker-related violence—made itself known by leaving relatively fewer accounts from non-business participants to subsequent history.

The difficulty in finding primary sources from newspapers alone has made a history of the press during this era difficult for historians, but it has also provided a case study in the effect of public relations "spin" on the truth, as Image 9.3 depicts. A male newspaper owner and editor dressed as a female prostitute called "The Madam" takes money from a man labelled "Big Advertisers" as staff sit under a sign with the message "Obey the Madam." The inscription on top left reads, "To Engraver, where you see brown instead of black, like fat man's slippers, please roulette." The inscription on bottom right reads, "Title suggestions: O, no, this is a newspaper office. The kept ladies of the press," and the inscription under original mat describes the newspaper as a "House of Prostitution."[13]

Image 9.3: "Freedom of the Press," Art Young, illustrator, published in New York: *The Masses*, December 1912.

In the years following the Ludlow Massacre, Rockefeller, at Lee's suggestion, carried with him wherever he went a supply of dimes. In actions that went a long way toward repairing his public image, he would hand out the dimes, one at a time, with great enthusiasm to people he would meet, especially children, in everyday scenarios. Over the course of the rest of his lifetime, Rockefeller gave out an estimated $35,000 in dimes alone, a significant expense at the time and no doubt a valuable investment, given the difficulties his business faced in previous years. By the end of his life, historians estimate that he gave away $540 million (unadjusted for inflation) to various causes. He died in 1937 at the age of 97.

However, Ivy Lee's legacy did not fare quite as well as his most prominent client. Through the 1920s and into the 1930s, Lee formed partnerships with problematic clients, including heads of business in both the newly formed Soviet Union and Nazi Germany. One of Lee's clients advocated for U.S. recognition of the USSR, a cause that drew fierce criticism from Americans who saw communism as a threat to national interests. Another of Lee's clients promoted sales for I. G. Farben, Germany's largest chemical company, and with the rise of Adolf Hitler, Lee's connections to Germany forced him to testify before Congress and refute charges that he supported the Nazis. While the hearing was still underway, Lee died on November 9, 1934, of a massive brain tumor, and as a result, the committee simply dropped questions about what he did or did not do for Germany. Although the record is not clear, Lee's contributions to public relations and press history may have fallen victim to bad timing in his business decisions.

EDWARD BERNAYS AND *PROPAGANDA*

If Ivy Ledbetter Lee invented public relations, a successor, Edward Bernays, emerged as its institutional visionary. Beyond the effects of individual press releases, Bernays believed media could change consumer habits by changing how the consumer thinks, an idea attributable in part to the psychoanalytical theories of his uncle Sigmund Freud, whose influence appeared recurrently in Bernays' practice. The interplay between messages and behavior propagated by Bernays created an interdependent web between public relations and the mass media, making him in effect a prophet of the consumerism that drove corporations and entire economies throughout the twentieth century.

Bernays was born November 22, 1891, in Vienna, Austria. His uncle's work at the time influenced wide segments of intellectual thought, including media effects, as attempts to understand the effects of the subconscious on behavior played heavily into theories developed by communications experts seeking to create messages that would reach wide audiences. Among the first successful projects undertaken by these theorists occurred in 1917 when U.S. president Woodrow Wilson formed The Committee on Public Information (also known as the CPI, or the Creel Committee), a group composed of business and media advisors, to help him sell the war to the American public. In the years leading up to U.S. involvement in World War I, the American populace generally opposed intervention in the affairs of Europe. Wilson determined that if the United States were to enter the fight, he would have to convince a public otherwise content to let England, Germany, France, and others settle their own disputes. To do so, he tapped, among others, Edward Bernays, Ivy Lee, and journalist Walter Lippmann to put together a campaign that would convince the American public to support U.S. involvement in the war. Chapter 11 of this book, "The Press at War: Propaganda and Persuasion in Print and in Film," includes additional details on the methods the CPI used to successfully sway public opinion.

Bernays' ability to serve as a master of media-driven influence became clear by the 1920s, which led to the head of the TK Tobacco Company contacting him for his services. George Hill, company president, recognized that nearly half of American consumers—women—represented an untapped market for the tobacco companies, as only men at the time smoked. Cultural norms considered smoking a masculine activity, so in order to convince not just women but society as a whole that cigarettes were not a social taboo, a campaign backed by scientific research and the media would need to change social attitudes in order for marketing toward such a substantial demographic to work.

Bernays conceived of an event he helped produce, which he dubbed the "torches of freedom" march. This staged event—a public relations technique that he helped make an industry practice—linked the act of smoking cigarettes to equality between men and women. In doing so, he integrated for starters an implicit visual of the Statue of Liberty, holding a torch in some measure of femininity. Then, tapping his connections to the world of psychoanalysis, he first contacted for advice A. A. Brill, an Austrian who imported Freud's theories to the United States. Brill told Bernays that the "oral fixation" of women made it normal for them to want to smoke and that the emancipation of women—explicitly expressed in the Nineteenth Amendment (1920)—made it possible for them to engage in activities otherwise designated for men. Taking Brill's advice, Bernays concocted a newsworthy event by paying women who would walk in New York City's Easter Sunday Parade to smoke. The event gained support and publicity from feminist Ruth Hale, who called on women to fight taboos by joining in the march. Bernays then contacted friends at *Vogue* magazine for a list of debutantes for the march. According to Bernays, he had his secretary send a personalized telegram to each debutante telling them that smoking on Fifth Avenue Easter Sunday would serve the interests of equality of the sexes.

On March 31, 1929, at the height of Easter Parade, a young woman named Bertha Hunt stepped out into the crowd surrounding Fifth Avenue to light a Lucky Strike cigarette. Other women followed, and the press, as anticipated, provided widespread coverage. Among other newspapers to cover the event, the *New York Times* ran a story April 1, 1929, titled, "Group of Girls Puff at Cigarettes as a Gesture of 'Freedom.'" In days and months following, the press continued to report on the new scandalous trend. Sales of Lucky Strikes and cigarettes in general doubled by the end of the decade, as Bernays had sold consumers on the idea that smoking somehow equaled freedom, or at least women should feel this way when they smoked.

To his credit, Bernays demonstrated a different way of thinking about the world that genuinely benefitted both his client and society as a whole. In one such case, book publishers including Simon & Schuster and Harcourt Brace in the 1930s approached him with a project that engaged both public relations and a shrewd form of social engineering. Book sales had declined during the Great Depression, as many consumers saw books as purely luxury items and, with limited incomes, low on a list of priorities. The publishers sought to change the downward trend in sales and asked Bernays to develop a strategy for them.

In a show of creative genius, Bernays realized no single advertising message could convince Americans in the 1930s to buy more books. So instead, he needed to create a need—not with traditional media, but with architecture. At the time, major home construction companies built houses using somewhat standard layouts. With a philosophy that reasoned, "Where there are bookshelves, there will be books," Bernays arranged meetings with architects, contractors, and decorators to make a rational case for how their business and the morale of the country as a whole would benefit from the installation of additional bookcases in each new house.[14] Having made the case that additional bookshelves would create a benefit for everyone, construction companies in the 1930s built new houses with these bookshelves, and, naturally, when new owners moved into the homes, the empty shelves inspired them to buy books. Bernays plan worked, and he made the book publishers happy clients, as sales throughout the 1930s and into the 1940s showed dramatic improvement.

GOOD PR

In the 1930s, Edward Bernays demonstrated how public relations could further the interests of companies (e.g. Simon & Schuster and Harcourt Brace) and consumers by providing a service of positive social value. In the following decades, public relations evolved into an industry of its own, developing ethical guides that could act in the interest of both business and the public. One of the more dramatic examples in which public relations served social interests took place when McNeil Consumer Products, a subsidiary of Tylenol producer Johnson & Johnson, confronted a public relations crisis in the fall of 1982 after seven people on Chicago's West Side died mysteriously after taking the popular pain reliever. The actions taken by corporate officials in charge of handing the case received widespread praise as a classic "textbook" way of putting people ahead of profits and, in the end, securing the interests of the client company as well.

Authorities determined that each person who died had ingested an Extra-Strength Tylenol capsule laced with cyanide. In order to save the integrity of both their product and their company as a whole, Johnson & Johnson quickly launched a public relations program to quell fear and explain the safety of their product. Following the guideline of protecting people first and property second, McNeil Consumer Products conducted an immediate product recall of thirty-one million Tylenol bottles from across the country at a loss of more than $100 million while simultaneously halting advertisements for the product. Johnson & Johnson then developed a campaign that re-introduced its product and restored consumer confidence. Newly issued Tylenol products included a tamper resistant package, making the product the first to comply with newly formed Food and Drug Administration mandates. Tylenol's makers encouraged consumers to buy the product again by providing a $2.50 discount coupon toward the product, available in newspapers or by calling a toll-free number.

Part of the reason Tylenol could act so quickly in restoring consumer confidence came from language in the company's mission statement, a traditionally essential component of successful public relations practice. The company's credo, written in the mid-1940s by Robert Wood Johnson, stated responsibility to consumers and medical professionals using its products, as well as the employees who produced it, the communities where its people work and live, and its stockholders. By definition, the company itself depended on maintaining the safety of the product. The professional decisions made by Johnson & Johnson's PR teams restored consumer confidence in Tylenol as a trusted product.

At the core of Bernays' practice included his ability to see non-conventional solutions to problems. While Ivy Lee had used the press and traditional methods to promote his clients' interests, Bernays engaged in tactics that went well beyond the scope of newspapers. His ability to do so stemmed from his appreciation for the role desire and the subconscious played in human behavior. He articulated this understanding in a 1928 book titled *Propaganda*, which argued that governments could and should use of persuasive messages to help members of society make beneficial decisions. "The conscious and intelligent manipulation of the organized habits and opinions of the masses is an important element in democratic society," he wrote. "Those who manipulate this unseen mechanism of society constitute an invisible government which is the true ruling power of our country."

> It might be better to have, instead of propaganda and special pleading, committees of wise men who would choose our rulers, dictate our conduct, private and public, and decide upon the best types of clothes for us to wear and the best kinds of food for us to eat. But we have chosen the opposite method, that of open competition. We must find a way to make free competition function with reasonable smoothness. To achieve this society has consented to permit free competition to be organized by leadership and propaganda.[15]

Throughout *Propaganda*, Bernays described the ways media might help to engineer a society that worked in more harmonious ways. However, as we will see in Chapter 11 of this book, "The Press at War: Propaganda and Persuasion in Print and in Film," governments have not always used the media as a source for public good. The experiences of European and American audiences—indeed, of just about anyone who lived in a society that used mass media—beginning with the outbreak of hostilities before World War II revealed Bernays held overly optimistic ideas about the way media can shape behavior. Regardless, the concepts he outlined in *Propaganda* enabled the later development of a "two-way model" of public relations that implemented elements of social science to better formulate public opinion. He justified and even legitimized public relations as a profession by clearly explaining that no individual or group—and in this group, the press—has a monopoly on a true understanding of the world.

RECAPPING THIS CHAPTER

Looking back on this chapter, you should see how the work of Ida Tarbell triggered growth in the public relations industries. The chapter showed how Tarbell's exposé of The Standard Oil Company inspired public relations pioneers, including Ivy Ledbetter Lee and Edward Bernays, to help repair the image of industrialists, and it showed how, as major parts of modern media, public relations affects content in ways sometimes unexpected for consumers.

Using materials from this chapter, you should know the role of Tarbell's work in what would become public relations and why journalist and historians hold it in such high esteem today. You should know how Parker and Lee's "Declaration of Principles" contained language that both initiated public relations as we know it and also set the practice apart from the traditional purpose of reporting by members of the Fourth Estate, and you should be able to explain how public relations does a service to both corporations and consumers.

The following chapter profiles engineers who helped develop broadcast, which later superseded the role of print as a primary form of information delivery. It describes the competition that went into the development of new technologies, and it describes how inventions went from being small gadgets to part of the modern communications network, how point-to-point communication later became broadcasting on a scale of millions of listeners and viewers.

NOTES

1 Ida M. Tarbell, *All in the Day's Work, An Autobiography* (New York: Macmillan, 1939), 230.
2 "Ida Minerva Tarbell," Library of Congress, accessed May 16, 2016, <item/2001704019>.
3 Ida M. Tarbell, *All in the Day's Work, An Autobiography* (New York: Macmillan, 1939), 26.
4 Ida Minerva Tarbell, "John D. Rockefeller, A Character Study," *McClure's Magazine*, 25, 3 (July 1905): 245.
5 Ida Minerva Tarbell, "History of the Standard Oil Company," *McClure's Magazine*, 21, 3 (1903): 320.
6 Felicity Barringer, "Journalism's Greatest Hits: Two Lists of a Century's Top Stories," *New York Times*, March 1, 1999, accessed February 25, 2017, <nytimes.com/1999/03/01/business/media-journalism-s-greatest-hits-two-lists-of-a-century-s-top-stories.html>.
7 "Lee, Ivy L.," Library of Congress, accessed June 7, 2016, <item/hec2009005741>.
8 Ivy Lee, "Declaration of Principles," 1906, in Sherman Morse, "An Awakening in Wall Street," *The American Magazine*, 62 (September 1906), 457–63.
9 "Split in Policy between Rockefellers and their Colorado Operators," *The Survey*, 33 (January 2, 1915): 389.
10 Matthew Blake, "Woody Guthrie: A Dust Bowl Representative in the Communist Party Press," *Journalism History* 35, 4 (Winter 2010): 184–193. Guthrie is widely recognized as a folk singer and songwriter. Less recognized are his contributions to the communist press, such as the *People's World* newspaper.
11 Woody Guthrie, "Ludlow Massacre," 1946; copyright renewed 1958 by Woody Guthrie Publications, accessed May 7, 2018, <woodyguthrie.org/Lyrics/Ludlow_Massacre.htm>.

12 Howard Zinn, *A People's History of the United States* (New York: Routledge, 2013), 355–57.
13 "Freedom of the Press," Library of Congress, accessed June 6, 2016, <item/2009631229>.
14 Larry Tye, *The Father of Spin: Edward L. Bernays and the Birth of Public Relations* (New York: Holt, 1998), 52. The Bernays quote, "Where there are bookshelves, there will be books" comes from secondary sources.
15 Edward L. Bernays and Mark Crispin Miller, *Propaganda* (Brooklyn, NY: Ig Publishing, 1928), 37.

10

EARLY INFOTAINMENT IN BROADCAST AND FILM

This chapter profiles personalities who contributed to the development of broadcast, which later superseded the role of print as the press' primary form of information delivery:

- It describes the competition that fueled the development of new radio and television technologies—how point-to-point (or person-to-person) communication later became content consumed by millions of listeners and viewers;
- and it concludes with a description of the way artistic creations of Orson Welles, a visionary producer, used media—first theater, then radio, then film—to help create a new entertainment-based landscape for the press to navigate.

Using materials from this chapter, students should know how broadcast's technological innovations affected the storytelling techniques of the press:

- They should be able to describe how individual inventors built upon the successes of one another to create the modern radio and television industries;
- and they should recognize the roots of contemporary mass communication—including uses of social media—as extensions of the work produced by these pioneers.

Key words, names, and phrases associated with Chapter 10 and the readings it references include:

- Broadcasting and infotainment;
- Guglielmo Marconi, Lee de Forest, and Howard Armstrong;
- RCA and NBC (David Sarnoff) and CBS (William Paley);
- and Orson Welles, "The War of the Worlds," and *Citizen Kane*.

The press at the turn of the twentieth century went through a number of remarkable transformations in style, content, and purpose. At the same time, a number of technological innovations began to take hold, changing the press on levels even more profoundly. Not only did print media explode to reach unprecedented levels of readership, engineering developments in radio and later television re-defined the press and the functions of the Fourth Estate to include a new style of news delivery that included entertainment, also known as "infotainment."

The concept and development of infotainment has evolved over several decades, and we will see, later in this book, how contemporary media has more fully integrated it into our news and entertainment culture. The early versions of infotainment featured in this chapter began merging news content with entertainment programs on radio and then on television, which in time affected the press as a whole. Engineers who contributed to the development of broadcast media, which over time superseded the role of print as the press' primary form of information delivery, created a new form of media altogether.

No longer relying on hard copies of paper with ink to transmit messages, broadcast began to add both sound and moving visual images to stories once reserved for newspapers. The history of this transformation can unfold through profiles of the combined efforts of several individuals, all of whom contributed to building new platforms for storytelling delivery. This competition among these individuals—perhaps countless numbers of them—fueled the development of new radio and television technologies, turning originally point-to-point (or person-to-person) communication into content that would be consumed by millions of listeners and viewers. In addition to radio and television, film, at nearly the same time, created new levels of meaning for consumers of mass media. The artistic creations of Orson Welles, a visionary producer, epitomized the way he used media—first theater, then radio, then film—to create new landscapes in which the press would navigate. Understanding this transformation can help to see how the roots of contemporary mass communication—including uses of social media—have emerged from the work produced by these pioneers.

EARLY INNOVATORS IN BROADCAST TECHNOLOGY

Although no single person can take credit for the development of modern media, broadcast (and later, by extension, the Internet) would not exist without the contributions of Italian inventor and physicist Guglielmo Marconi, who generally receives credit for inventing radio. Marconi, born on April 25, 1874, in Bologna, Italy, won the

Nobel Prize for having invented "wireless" telegraphy. Having moved to New York City, in 1896, Marconi—implementing the telegraphic code first established in 1844 by Samuel F. B. Morse—took out a patent on his unique system to transmit the dots and dashes of telegraph messages through the air, and in 1899 introduced the Marconi Wireless Telegraph Company to the United States.

Marconi reached a breakthrough when he found that raising the height of antenna could achieve a much greater range in transmission, and borrowing from a technique used in wired telegraphy, he grounded his transmitter and receiver. Ships at sea could send wireless messages ("Marconigrams") to each in coordinating travel, as well as to wireless stations on the East Coast. With additional improvements, the system was capable of transmitting signals several miles, and by the turn of the twentieth century, Marconi had developed a way to transmit signals across the Atlantic, making transatlantic telegraph cables eventually obsolete.

While Marconi received praise from his contemporaries, a more mysterious figure at the time deserves as much—if not more—thanks from subsequent generations for his creative spirit. Nikola Tesla, a Serbian inventor and immigrant to the United States, now holds a legendary status in history as a man with a vision for of the twenty-first century. He was born in 1856 in Smiljan, Croatia, and he immigrated to New York in 1884 to work as an engineer at Thomas Edison's Manhattan headquarters. After a falling out with Edison, Tesla embarked on his own to create an astounding number of technological inventions, many of which he failed to patent simply because wealth and fame did not interest him.

On March 1, 1893, in St. Louis, Missouri, Tesla gave the first public demonstration of radio, having first lectured on wireless transmissions in 1891. Just days before the St. Louis presentation, Tesla addressed the Franklin Institute in Philadelphia, describing in detail the principles of early radio communication, and his descriptions contained all the elements later incorporated into radio systems. He had initially experimented with magnetic receivers, unlike the devices developed by Marconi and other early experimenters. While Marconi at the time received credit for inventing the radio—and to a large extent he still receives credit for it—the U.S. Supreme Court in the 1943 case of *Marconi Wireless Telegraph Company of America vs. the United States* found that Tesla's presentation in St. Louis deserved recognition. If not in popular memory, the court, at least, declared Tesla the rightful inventor of radio, even though Marconi beat him to the patent office.

Many other pioneers contributed to the development of radio, but among them, Lee de Forest, who was born on August 26, 1873, in Council Bluffs, Iowa, invented the "Audion" tube and took the most credit for radio's widespread usage, even at times when he did not deserve to do so. In his work as an engineer, he claimed more than 300 patents, but his detractors claimed that others had already discovered most of the inventions he claimed to have created. In fact, the Audion, a three-element vacuum tube that became the basis of all electronic devices, took an already existing invention and simply made the device more easily used for auditory purposes. He died July 1, 1961, from a heart attack, virtually broke, but to this day, holds a place in broadcast history with his self-proclaimed title of "The Father of Radio."

Image 10.1: "Woman with Radio," published between 1910 and 1935.[1]

One of the primary targets of de Forest's lawsuits, Edwin Howard Armstrong, without a doubt helped to create radio broadcasts of fine quality, inventing "frequency modulation," or FM. Born December 18, 1890, in New York, Armstrong showed an early interest in electrical and mechanical devices. He started his formal education in Columbia's Department of Electrical Engineering in 1909, and in his junior year of college, he significantly improved the sensitivity and quality of radio receivers with his invention of the regenerative circuit. In 1921, Armstrong discovered super-regeneration, which vastly improved the ability of radio listeners to hear broadcasts. Despite the science community's certainty that he was the inventor of the regenerative circuit, Armstrong lost a lawsuit in 1922 against de Forest, who first patented the invention and sold the rights to AT&T. However, De Forest's testimony during the trial indicated he had no actual idea how regeneration worked, leaving the scientific community to conclude that Armstrong alone deserved recognition for his contribution.

Armstrong continued inventing, creating his best-known innovation, what we now know as frequency modulation, or FM radio. FM had a complicated role in the development of the radio industry. While the method of broadcast vastly improved the quality of amplitude modulation, or AM sound, by eliminating static, hardware producers had made AM receivers a standard part of network infrastructure, making it difficult for Armstrong to penetrate the equipment used with his innovation. After losing a legal battle with the FCC over the licensing of FM, Armstrong's life worsened when he became involved in a new patent suit. The new television networks even began using his FM technologies without paying him royalties. The stress from repeated lawsuits took a toll on Armstrong. After an altercation with his wife, he felt that he had lost everything and leaped to his death on January 31, 1954. Although Armstrong did not live to see his inventions flourish, by the 1970s, FM audience size exceeded AM, and the gap has continued to grow ever since. Today, more than 10,000 FM stations broadcast in the United States.

NBC, CBS, AND THE MAKING OF MASS COMMUNICATION

Among the most widely known and celebrated of the early broadcast pioneers, David Sarnoff worked his way up the American corporate ladder, establishing AM radio as part of mass media. He then helped usher in an era of television with innovations still very much part of our contemporary landscape. While many individuals contributed to the development of radio and television technologies, Sarnoff helped establish the network hardware widely purchased and used by consumers in the 1920s and 1930s, which made a switch from radio to television possible, forever changing our reliance on newspapers as a primary source of information.

Sarnoff was born in Russia on February 28, 1891, and immigrated to New York City in 1900 with his family. He sold newspapers as a boy and later started work at the Commercial Cable Company, making his professional home at the American Marconi Company. As he moved up the corporate ladder from office boy to president of the Radio Corporation of America in 1928, Sarnoff learned both the technical and business side of the industry.

The early practitioners of radio generally had understood communication as a point-to-point endeavor, one that sent one message from one person to another person who received it. This method of message delivery had its roots in telegraphic transmission, which generally sent its series of "dots" and "dashes" from Point A, a sender, to Point B, a receiver. Sarnoff, however, was among the few to recognize that the radio, unlike the telegraph, could send a single message from a single sender to potentially millions of receivers, a point-to-mass model.

His foray into this method of communication began to produce results when in 1925 RCA purchased its first radio station (WEAF, New York) and launched the National Broadcasting Company (NBC), the first radio network in America. Through NBC, Sarnoff built and established AM broadcasting as a preeminent radio standard for the majority of the twentieth century. He invested in the hardware and production of AM radios, as well as the content associated with programming. Millions of consumers purchased RCA's radio units, making Sarnoff one of the most important media figures of his time, a success that later allowed him to launch television programing.

Schemes for television had existed well before Sarnoff endeavored to make the invention a common household utility. In 1928, he met with Vladimir Zworykin, a Russian inventor, who helped develop the new technology, and after years of engineering and investment, under an NBC broadcast, Sarnoff made history with a televised announcement on April 20, 1939, outside the RCA Pavilion at the World's Fair in New York: "Now we add sight to sound." RCA initiated regularly scheduled, electronic television in America under the name of their broadcasting division at the time, the National Broadcasting Company (NBC), with the first television broadcast introduced by Sarnoff himself.

For the next decade, television at first struggled to make an impact on the mass market, as production of the equipment took a low priority relative to the U.S. government's efforts in World War II. At the same time, when Armstrong's superior FM

Image 10.2: "A Television Receiver," photography by Keystone View Company, published 1930.[2]

sound technology appeared, Sarnoff worked to suppress it, seeing it as a threat to his already-established network.

In time, a rival network, the Columbia Broadcast System (CBS), under the leadership of William Paley, born September 28, 1901, emerged to challenge Sarnoff's dominance over the broadcast industry. At first a radio network, Paley saw this as an opportunity to steer CBS in a more successful direction than NBC. Paley changed the network's format to a brand that appealed to advertisers with a business model that provided network programming to stations at low cost instead of relying strictly on advertisers for the station's revenue.

Paley's rivalry with Sarnoff drove both men to improve the quality of broadcast programs. Paley had quickly grasped the earnings potential of radio, recognizing that good programming would lead to advertising revenue. Before Paley, radio operations generally treated individual stations as self-contained outlets, distributing content in a way somewhat similar to the publishing decisions made at a local newspaper. By combining advertising with broadcast programming, Paley developed a broader vision that targeted content to a wide range of listeners and viewers.

To a measurable extent, advertisers—not necessarily listeners or viewers—thereby became CBS's chief source of support, a phenomenon similar to newspaper publishing during the penny press era of the 1830s. With increased program distribution, Paley could charge advertisers more than his competitors did for airtime while at the same time giving clients an incentive to pick CBS, as relatively more viewers would see ads. CBS's affiliates benefitted by carrying programs offered by the network for part of the broadcast day and in exchange receiving a portion of the network's advertising revenue. At other times in the day, affiliates offered local programming and sold local advertising time.

Before his death on October 29, 1990, Paley's news setup, along with his lineup of quality programming, cemented the success of CBS as a radio and television network. Part of his legacy recognizes his ability to have harnessed the potential reach of broadcasting, growing CBS from a tiny chain of stations into what was eventually one of the world's dominant communication empires. Five years after Paley's death, Westinghouse Electric Corporation bought CBS in 1995. In 1999, CBS transferred hands to Viacom, which itself was once a subsidiary of CBS, and today, CBS Corporation, which spun off from Viacom in 2006, now heads Paley's empire.

ORSON WELLES AND THE BATTLE OVER MEDIA

Likely, the most famous radio broadcast aired under Paley's leadership—more likely, the most infamous modern media stunt to date—took place on CBS radio, October 30, 1938. A rising star, a genius, and a prodigy, Orson Welles (George Orson Welles, May 6, 1915–October 10, 1985) had set his scope on mastering the media of the day. At a young age, he had already produced leading productions of Shakespeare and then turned to radio as a way to express his talents and flair for theater.

To this day, Welles has a legacy as a genius, having made his mark as an actor, director, writer, and producer who worked in theater, radio, and film. He is remembered for his innovative work in all three forms of media—in theater, most notably *Caesar*

(1937), a Broadway adaptation of William Shakespeare's *Julius Caesar*; in radio, the legendary "The War of the Worlds" (1938) broadcast; and in film, *Citizen Kane* (1941), which consistently ranks as one of the all-time greatest movie productions.

Among the many radio shows Welles produced, one made history on CBS as part of its Mercury Theatre on the Air segment. For this particular show, Welles adapted theatrical tricks for the radio and produced a rendition of the H. G. Wells science fiction classic "The War of the Worlds." At the same time Mercury Theater on the Air programs ran, CBS's rival, NBC, aired more popular programming. As a shrewd and astute media practitioner, Welles knew that audiences would likely miss the opening monologue to his show, which indicated the script from which he would read found inspiration in H. G. Wells' fanciful version of an invasion from outer space. The radio listeners who did tune into CBS, likely during a commercial break on NBC, therefore discovered to their surprise that an apparent landing of alien ships had taken place, accompanied by sound effects and screams, which sounded all too real.

Image 10.3: "Portrait of Orson Welles," Carl Van Vechten, photographer, published March 1, 1937.[3]

Welles would later feign innocence, pretending he had no intention of frightening listeners to levels of hysteria, but in fact, he privately acknowledged his taste for sensationalism as a kind of self-promotion, using "The War of the Worlds" knowingly as a demonstration of his ability to control both broadcast and audiences.

Scholars have since the infamous broadcast studied the reaction of the press and suggested that the intense criticism he received from newspapers had ulterior motives—publishers saw radio as a threat, and in an attempt to discredit him, newspapers likely exaggerated the public's reaction.[4] Regardless, before delivering press conferences and in an attempt to absolve CBS and himself of any wrongdoing, Welles did create an enormous amount of sensationalism. Headlines from the *New York Times* the day following the broadcast described the panic, reading, "Radio Listeners in Panic, Taking War Drama as Fact," and "Many Flee Homes to Escape 'Gas Raid from Mars'—Phone Calls Swamp Police at Broadcast of Welles Fantasy." The text following the headlines summarized the night as "a wave of mass hysteria" that seized listeners, leading thousands to believe that "an interplanetary conflict had started with invading Martians spreading wide death and destruction in New Jersey and New York."[5]

While it is easy in hindsight to chuckle at the reactions of these listeners, it is important to remember that audiences would have had every reason to fear the unknown at the time. On a simple level, tensions had increased simply because the broadcast, as designed, took place right before Halloween. On a much larger level, ominous war clouds hung over Europe at the time, as Hitler's armies had begun their marches of conquest.

The combined influences of culture and current events at the time produced a reaction to "The War of the Worlds" that created a source for study for decades to follow. Indeed, theorists to this day look at the broadcast as a case study in audience reaction, using it as a way to gauge the influence media has on our behaviors.

The drama surrounding Welles' fateful broadcast in context has other layers for press historians to consider. In the days following his radio sensation, newspapers hit back at him, criticizing him perhaps disproportionately for initiating panic. However, part of their motivation for doing so stemmed from the fact that Welles in particular and broadcast in general posed a direct form of competition to the traditional press. With more and more listeners turning to the radio for a source of news and entertainment, newspaper publishers, including the *New York Times*, took the opportunity to blast both Welles and radio as threats to the peace.

Instead of buckling from pressure from the press, Welles, still only in his early 20s, set his sights on Hollywood as the next source of media to conquer. Studio executives in Hollywood had shown an interest in recruiting him for pictures even before his "The War of the Worlds" broadcast, and following it, George J. Schaefer of RKO Pictures lured him to his office. Recognizing Welles' talent for creating a sensation, as well as his genius for self-promotion, Schaefer had the young star sign an unprecedented contract with RKO on August 21, 1939, which stipulated that Welles would act in, direct, produce, and write for the studio. The most controversial and unprecedented aspect of the contract was granting Welles complete artistic control of his productions—RKO executives could not see any footage until Welles chose to show it to them, with no cuts made without Welles' approval.

Taking advantage of such incredible terms, Welles set out to use the film industry as a vehicle for promoting himself as essentially the king of all media, having conquered theater, radio, and, according to plans, film (at the time television had still not penetrated households on a mass level). To make his claim, Welles set his eyes on dethroning the reigning champion of the press, newspaper giant William Randolph Hearst, who had a long-standing reputation as the leading publisher of newspapers in the nation. In order to topple Hearst, Welles knew he had to keep his project secret, as Hearst's agents in Hollywood worked actively to control their boss' image, keeping any negative press on him from public view.

Welles integrated elements of his classical training, including his flair for Shakespearean drama, along with all of the best cinematographic techniques available to him in producing *Citizen Kane*, a masterpiece of modern film. He used the semi-fictional character Charles Foster Kane as a representative of Hearst, capturing the publisher's flaws along with a few virtues with a story that on at least one level is very simple—paraphrased, money can buy many things, but it cannot buy happiness, or love, or make a shallow man whole.

Had Welles not dug deep into Hearst's personal life and found ways to mock the man mercilessly, the movie *Citizen Kane* might have surpassed all expectations; however, the film failed as a commercial endeavor, primarily because Hearst discovered the project and worked to have it suppressed. Of particular offense to Hearst, the word "Rosebud" appears recurrently throughout the film as a mysterious phrase uttered by Kane. The word, it turns out, was Hearst's pet name for his mistress Marion Davies (January 3, 1897–September 22, 1961), an American film star. Welles had worked this bit of gossip into his film, and Hearst, upon hearing about it, offered millions of dollars to film executives to have the movie destroyed. The movie did appear in a handful of theaters, but it quickly became known only as a failure on Welles' part.

Both Welles and Hearst saw their fame and fortune slide in the years following the war over *Citizen Kane*, but critics well after the episode, including those with the American Film Institute, recognize the film as the greatest American movie of all time.[6]

MASS MEDIA AT MID-CENTURY

When combined with the emergence of the film industry as a powerful force in American culture, the concurrent rise in broadcast affected many industries, with print journalism experiencing some of the most dramatic changes of all. At first, broadcast—specifically television—posed little threat, at least in the 1940s, as the distribution of television sets had yet to spread to households nationally. However, television's rapid rise in the 1950s matched a continued rise in the labor and production costs of the newspaper business, causing publishers to close some newspapers, especially small ones, and merge others. The radio industry likewise adjusted to the growth of television by focusing on local and regional advertising sales.

By the mid-1950s, television usage had exploded, with more than thirty-five million sets reaching more than 70 percent of American households. The accompanying growth in the advertising market for television at first caused a serious drop in national radio advertising sales. Although newspapers for the most part continued to succeed, publishers and editors adapted their content to resemble more closely what was found on television, with news stories reflecting the tastes of broadcast users, resulting in less attention to hard news and more on entertainment.

A Radio, Television, and Film Timeline
Select Dates in the Evolution of Modern Media

See also a timeline for the development of radio with corresponding events between 1887 and 1950 at <www.pbs.org/kenburns/empire/timeline>.[7]

1901:	Marconi sends "wireless" signals across the Atlantic Ocean.
1907:	*Scientific American* first uses the word "television."
1919:	Radio Corporation of America (RCA) founded.
1920:	Westinghouse obtains a license for KDKA, Pittsburgh, which first offers continuous, regularly scheduled programs.
1922:	WEAF, New York, sets a precedent by selling airtime to advertisers.
1923:	Vladimir Zworykin invents the iconoscope tube.
1926:	AT&T sells its radio interest; NBC eventually gains control.
1927:	Philo Farnsworth applies for his first patent on the image dissector tube and broadcasts the first television image, a dollar sign.
1927:	The Radio Act of 1927 establishes the Federal Radio Commission (FRC).
1933:	Edwin Armstrong applies for patents for frequency modulation (FM).
1934:	Communications Act includes provisions for the Federal Communications Commission (FCC) to regulate radio, television, and telephone communication.
1936:	Regularly scheduled television begins in Great Britain.
1938:	Orson Welles airs "The War of the Worlds" on CBS radio.
1939:	The first FM station broadcasts in New Jersey.
1939:	RCA demonstrates television at the New York World's Fair.
1941:	*Citizen Kane*, later called the greatest American film, opens.
1943:	NBC sells a network, which becomes ABC.
1944:	Sponsors begin buying television time.
1945:	The FCC supports the development of television, negatively affecting FM radio.
1947:	The House UnAmerican Activities Committee hunts communists in Hollywood, leading to The Hollywood Ten blacklist.
1948:	Radio nets biggest annual earnings (they grow for television in subsequent years).
1951:	Hundreds of radio stations switch to a deejay format to make up for losses as revenues from network programming declines.
1950s:	Movie attendance begins to decline in cities with televisions.

Part of the transformation allowed networks to bring news to a much larger audience than any newspaper could while at the same time changing the way traditional reporters gathered news and reported on it. Broadcast added audio and visual elements to news. Radio and TV became windows to the world for many people. For the first time, people did not have to read the news, and they did not have to visualize the stories told to them either, as they could both hear and see what happened within the immediacy of their living rooms.

"UNCLE WALTER" AND THE CHANGING FACE OF TELEVISION

For an example of the way television news evolved during the middle of the twentieth century, we can look to a news anchor once described as "the most trusted man in America." In the 1960s, in part responding to a call for a softer approach to news, CBS hired Walter Cronkite to head their nightly newscasts. He did so successfully for decades, bringing a calm demeanor to the living rooms of nightly news watchers. His serious, thoughtful approach to the news attracted audience members who adopted him as a virtual family member, earning him the moniker "Uncle Walter."

Cronkite first anchored for CBS-TV on April 16, 1962, with little advanced training, but he shaped television news for subsequent generations until his retirement in 1981. Among remarkable moments during Cronkite's television career, audiences respected his display of raw, unscripted emotion during the breaking news of President John F. Kennedy's assassination. The November 22, 1963, newscast attracted millions of viewers and made Cronkite a mainstay of evening broadcasts.

Image 10.4: "Walter Cronkite on Television during 1st Presidential Debate between Ford and Carter," in Philadelphia by Thomas J. O'Halloran, photographer, published September 23, 1976.[8]

> After Cronkite's retirement, CBS experimented with a return to the news of a bygone era, hiring Dan Rather to anchor the nightly newscasts from 1981 to 2005. Rather's approach to news resembled more closely Murrow's style inasmuch as the two favored hard-hitting questions and commentary with an emphasis on challenging figures of authority. The strategy for a short time kept CBS ahead of its competitors ABC and NBC, but over time, Rather's ratings suffered. In 2004, Rather's approach eventually backfired, as he produced a highly controversial report about then-president George W. Bush's service—or as Rather alleged, his lack of service—in the National Guard during the Vietnam era. Critics questioned the authenticity of Rather's source, an evidently forged document. The incident reportedly contributed to his departure as CBS anchor after having held the position for twenty-four years.
>
> A decade after Rather's retirement, surveys indicated that television remained the most utilized device for news consumption. However, television news producers have also now increasingly turned to social media in order to reach their audience. Unlike the era in which news consumers depended on CBS, NBC, or ABC to provide accounts of daily events, citizens have grown increasingly skeptical of the media and trust sources they can find according to their own preferences. Journalists affiliated with major news networks—whether television, print, radio, or other—have in turn had to develop reporting, interviewing, and storytelling techniques to keep them competitive with a wide range of providers.

The changes were also in part cultural, as in the 1950s and 1960s, a population explosion that occurred after World War II, the "baby boomers," grew into teenagers and young adults. As the largest single generation until that point in American history, the baby boomers had a tremendous effect on popular culture. Starting as early as the 1940s, marketers identified members of this generation as a valuable demographic and targeted products and entertainment geared to their needs and interests. Television was the ultimate purveyor of this mass culture. Before its arrival, audiences had to pay for a theater or concert performance. With television, entertainment came to them free. Millions could tune in and watch the same show—and millions did. Executives at television networks in turn catered not to the consumers, but to the advertisers, which pushed for content that attracted the most viewers, usually entertainment.

RECAPPING THIS CHAPTER

Looking back on this chapter, you should see how it profiled personalities who contributed to the development of broadcast, which later superseded the role of print as a primary form of information delivery. It described the competition that fueled the development of new technologies, and it described how these inventions went from novel devices to parts of the modern communications network—how point-to-point communication later became broadcasts to millions of listeners and viewers.

Using materials from this chapter, you should understand how technological innovations in broadcast affected the press's storytelling techniques. You should be able to describe how individual inventors built upon the successes of one another to create the modern radio and television industries, recognizing the roots of contemporary mass communication—including uses of social media—as extensions of the work produced by engineers.

The following chapter describes the ways the press during wars in the twentieth century sometimes spread political messages to persuade audiences with tools developed by figures associated with the creation of the public relations industry. It provides a cursory overview of how governments have sometimes coopted the press to work in ways that do not meet the requirements of the Fourth Estate, and it shows how the press can do more than inform—it can change public opinion.

NOTES

1 "Woman with Radio," Library of Congress, accessed June 11, 2016, <item/npc2008011521>.
2 "A Television Receiver," Library of Congress, accessed June 7, 2016, <item/2013647232>.
3 "Portrait of Orson Welles," Library of Congress, accessed May 16, 2016, <item/2004663727>.
4 Brad Schwartz, *Broadcast Hysteria: Orson Welles's War of the Worlds and the Art of Fake News* (New York: Hill and Wang, 2015), 8.
5 "Radio Listeners in Panic, Taking War Drama as Fact," *New York Times*, October 31, 1938.
6 "AFI's 100 Greatest Movies of all Time," accessed May 26, 2017, <afi.com/100Years/movies.aspx>.
7 *Empire of the Air,* "Empire Timeline," accessed November 24, 2017, <pbs.org/kenburns/empire/timeline>.
8 "Walter Cronkite," Library of Congress, accessed June 6, 2016, <item/2005684040>.

11

THE PRESS AT WAR
PROPAGANDA IN PRINT AND FILM

This chapter explains the ways the press during wars in the twentieth century sometimes spread political messages to persuade audiences with tools developed by figures associated with the creation of the public relations industry:

- It provides a cursory overview of the ways governments have sometimes coopted the press and media in general to work in ways that do not meet the requirements of the Fourth Estate;
- and it shows how the press can do more than inform—it can change public opinion.

Using materials from this chapter, students should understand how governments—the U.S. and others—have manipulated messages for purposes not intended by the founders:

- They should understand the historic roots of propaganda;
- and they should also recognize the need for a free press to focus on ensuring citizens receive essential information about their government.

Key words, names, and phrases associated with Chapter 11 include:

- The Committee on Public Information (CPI, or the Creel Committee), and World War I;

- *Triumph of the Will*, Leni Riefenstahl, and World War II propaganda;
- "The Spanish Earth," Ernest Hemingway, and the Spanish Civil War;
- and George Orwell, *1984*, and Dwight D. Eisenhower's farewell address.

Using communication models advanced by Edward Bernays during World War I, intellectuals in the 1920s and 1930s adopted a "magic bullet theory" of communication, which described with an easy-to-understand analogy the way media might deliver messages. Also known under similar model names, such as the hypodermic needle, or the hypodermic syringe, the magic bullet theory suggested that the receiver of a media message would fully accept the content and react in a way intended by the sender.

Theorists in time disputed the theory with other ideas about the way media operates. (Agenda setting, a popular academic theory in recent decades, suggests conversely that media do not do a good job of telling consumers how to think, but media can do an effective job in making them think about certain issues.) But through World War II, at least, producers of media messages continued to subscribe to the idea that citizens respond directly to content targeted directly at them. Members of the press, sometimes unwittingly, aligned with the government and used adaptations of the magic bullet theory to target audiences with propaganda in support of fights against various nations and ideologies. And throughout the rest of the twentieth century and into the present one, governments continued to coopt the press in efforts to spread political messages, even well after theoretical ideas about propaganda had changed.

This chapter provides a sample of wartime messages under the title propaganda, a concept first coined popularly (as we have seen in Chapter 9 of this book) by Edward Bernays in his 1928 book *Propaganda*. While Bernays had a consumer-based propaganda in mind, this chapter describes works more in line with the magic bullet theory of media manipulation used during World War I, the Spanish Civil War, and in the years before, during, and after World War II. It concludes with the observations and warnings of both journalists and politicians—namely George Orwell and President Dwight D. Eisenhower—as reminders of the role the press should take in alerting the citizens to government activities.

THE COMMITTEE ON PUBLIC INFORMATION AND THE ENGINEERING OF CONSENT

The United States government launched a massive propaganda campaign—arguably its first formal one—beginning in 1917 with the establishment of the Committee on Public Information (CPI). Sometimes referred to as the Creel Committee after former newspaper reporter George Creel, who headed the group, members organized to rally support for various war efforts at home and abroad, in particular the conflict in Europe, World War I.

Image 11.1: "CPI Delegates to Europe," published by Bain News Service, created between 1915 and 1920, a photograph showing members of the Committee on Public Information (CPI), a U.S. government agency that worked to persuade Americans to support World War I, with public relations expert Edward Bernays second from the right.[1]

Members of the committee included, among others, Edward Bernays and Ivy Lee, who played, as we have seen, a major role in launching the public relations industry (see Chapter 9).

Americans at the time generally opposed foreign intervention, as many felt ties to their European ancestral homelands and sensed the danger of engaging in a war that to them had personal connections. President Wilson had even successfully won re-election in 1916 as an anti-war candidate, campaigning with the slogan "He Kept Us Out of War." Sentiments began to change both with increased hostilities directed toward American interests, as well as the president's desire to democratize Europe, and to rally support for U.S. involvement, Wilson commissioned Creel and his crew.

The committee responded by using all forms of media available at the time—print, spoken word, telegraph, cables, motion pictures, wireless, posters, sign boards, etc.—to communicate America's reasons for entering the war, the meaning of America, the nature of its free institutions, and its noble goals in the war. A highly professional operation emerged. The CPI used photographs from the Signal Corps of War Department, which had photographers charged with documenting history. Enlisting the help of theater experts, the committee distributed films to play at municipal halls and movie theaters alike. Other experienced insiders from the entertainment industry provided orchestral music, scenic accessories, and canvases to add to film quality. Advertising companies donated space and materials to promote the films, with two-week press campaigns preceding their debuts. Posters, window cards, and attendance by high-profile guests generated additional excitement.

Next, the government enlisted the Division of News, as at the time of the committee's creation, military officials distrusted the press and wanted to keep war information from reaching the public. The government only wanted to tell the "good" stories about a war and believed too much concealed information often got into the press, painting an unflattering picture. Thus, the new Division of News attempted to centralize the information and make it easier for reporters to get the stories without having to call multiple sources in multiple departments.

A different unit associated with committee work, the Division of Pictorial Publicity, produced likely one of the most lasting images from the period, one still recognizable

Image 11.2: "I Want You for U.S. Army: Nearest Recruiting Station," James Montgomery Flagg, artist, created 1917, this war poster with the famous phrase "I Want You for U.S. Army" shows Uncle Sam pointing his finger at the viewer in order to recruit soldiers for the American Army during World War I. The printed phrase "Nearest recruiting station" has a blank space below to add the address for enlisting.[2]

as an official call to arms for U.S. military recruiters. Although the personality known as Uncle Sam had existed in American folklore for almost a century, his modern incarnation first took shape with a poster published by the CPI with a portrait designed by member James Montgomery Flagg.

Flagg's representation of Uncle Sam originally appeared on the cover of *Leslie's Weekly* magazine on July 6, 1916, with the words "What are YOU doing for preparedness?" The following year, the government coopted it and added Uncle Sam's vigorous words, "I Want You for U.S. Army!" Sam points his finger. He has a white goatee on a chiseled face, bushy eyebrows over burning eyes, and silver hair flowing out from under a tall top hat decorated with stars—a commonplace image to this day in imagining the figure. However, these attributes, known now to a lesser degree, were first used as a poster that helped recruit legions of young men to fight in World War I and, later, World War II. It proved effective, with more than four million prints in the final year of World War I, according to the Library of Congress.[3]

Even though the head of CPI, George Creel, had extensive experience as an investigative journalist for several newspapers in the years before his work as a propagandist, the efforts of the committee clearly went beyond the boundaries of traditional journalism. Creel later described his work in terms that glorified American interests internationally, as well as defended the role of the press in advancing them, although to this day, the committee's contribution to the history of the press remains at best problematic. "There was no precedent to guide us; the ground was unbroken," Creel explained. "Our effort was educational and informative throughout, for we had such confidence in our case as to feel that no other argument was needed than the simple, straightforward presentation of facts."[4]

George Creel, *How We Advertised America*, New York, London: Harper & Brothers, 1920.

- Everything with which we had to do was new and foreign to the democratic process. There were no standards to measure by, no trails to follow, and, as if these were not difficulties enough, the necessities of the hour commanded instant action (p. 70).
- It was our insistence that the bad should be told with the good, failures admitted along with the announcements of success (p. 73).
- And it was to the heart and mind of the nation that we directed our appeals—and their response was our reward (p. 108).
- A prime importance was to preach the determination and military might of America and the certainty of victory, but it was equally necessary to teach the motives, purposes and ideals of America so that friend, foe and neutral alike might come to see us as a people without selfishness and in love with justice (p. 273).

At the same time, the United States was by no means the only country to engage in propaganda for wartime efforts. Nations throughout Europe used planes and balloons to drop leaflets touting their own war and foreign policy missives. The German government in Berlin spent millions publishing the *Continental Times* with translations in English by American and English sympathizers. The propaganda of the *Times* pushed narratives to American and British prisoners of war about the depravity of their soldiers, painting Americans especially as greedy imperialists.

When World War I finally ended, President Wilson was for a short time celebrated for engineering a way to bring the United States into the conflict and thereby ending hostilities. In 1918, the Committee on Public Information disbanded, and domestic propaganda ended after the warring nations signed the November 11, 1918, armistice. World War I had received popular support internationally as "the war to end all wars," but the peace agreement did not last, as unresolved conflicts from World War I eventually boiled into a much larger catastrophe for nations around the world. In time, propaganda reemerged as a weapon of war.

A POWERFUL AND HORRIFYING PIECE OF PROPAGANDA

In the years between World War I and World War II, propaganda took on a life of its own, spreading from nation to nation and revealing itself in various forms of media. A film released shortly after a 1934 Nazi rally at Nuremburg, Germany, *Triumph of the Will* (1935), represents one of the most stunning examples of propaganda to reach a mass audience, described by *New York Times* film critic Hal Erickson as "possibly the most powerful propaganda film ever made" and with the passage of time "one of the most horrifying."[5]

German film star Leni Riefenstahl produced *Triumph of the Will* to bring to audiences the story behind the rise of Adolf Hitler, creating a documentary that in time persuaded many viewers that Germany needed the leadership of a dictator. She had enjoyed an illustrious career as a leading figure during a golden era, the Weimar Republic period between World War I and World War II. Hitler recognized her success and approached her to help produce essentially a public relations campaign that would help secure the rise of the Nazi Party. The film Hitler proposed would celebrate his rise as German chancellor in the 1930s and persuade weary masses to support him.[6] While Riefenstahl later received condemnatory criticism for agreeing to make the film, she insisted she had no interest in furthering the Nazi agenda.

The film, which took almost two years to edit from 250 miles of raw footage, included innovative techniques, such as moving cameras, telephoto lenses, frequent close-ups of faithful Nazis, and heroic poses of Hitler shot from well below eye level. From a film-history perspective, Riefenstahl's cinematography on one level put German filmmaking at the cutting edge of world cinema. She perfected a technique of filming from a leading car in a processional to show Hitler gallantly coming toward the viewer. This helped project a message about Germany that resonated in the 1930s. The country had suffered immensely after World War I, so when Hitler promised the common people order and stability, they responded with their support. Riefenstahl's movie made the case they could do so, though no one at the time anticipated what the future held. On another level, film critics and media historians later pointed to *Triumph of the Will* as a use of spectacular filmmaking to promote a profoundly unethical system.

Riefenstahl's mastery of the camera influenced generations to follow. In fact, elements of her style can be seen in Orson Welles' masterpiece, *Citizen Kane* (see Chapter 10), which satirized newspaper publisher William Randolph Hearst as a demagogue. Kane even associates with Hitler in an opening scene, and later, when running for political office, he gives a campaign speech that has an uncanny resemblance in its cinematography to the Nuremburg rally. Even Kane's logo at the rally, a "K," bears a resemblance to fascist symbols.

HEMINGWAY AND "THE SPANISH EARTH"

At nearly the same time of Hitler's rise to power in Germany, a civil war in Spain erupted, capturing the world's attention. The complex conflict lasted from 1936–1939 and transfixed attention from nations everywhere, with governments, citizens, and journalists all watching with fear that the chaos in Spain would further destabilize an already shaky European continent.

General Francisco Franco rose to power by leading a Nationalist counter-reaction to a socialist victory at the polls in 1936. Using the military to establish control in favor of landholders and bankers, Franco appealed to a conservative and religious order. He also attracted the attention of Adolf Hitler, who lent German air support in Franco's initial bombings of the resistance. The Americans and British and their allies, although not officially involved in the war, suspected that if Franco succeeded, so would Hitler, and with the rise of dictators elsewhere, including Italy and the Soviet Union, the whole of Europe teetered on a frightening new totalitarian order.

INTERPRETING THE SPANISH CIVIL WAR

To this day, the Spanish Civil War remains a difficult event to interpret, as several factions fought either with each other or against each other. Primary combatants included Spain's Republicans, centrists who supported liberal reforms, capitalism, and democracy, as well as revolutionary anarchists, who sided with the opposition as a means for revolution. The Nationalists, who in the end emerged victorious, meanwhile, feared national fragmentation and were defined in a large measure by their anti-communism. Their leaders had a generally wealthier, more conservative, monarchist, landowning background.

The propaganda used by all sides during the war has made a determination of the outcome of individual battles and casualties nearly impossible, and historians still struggle to arrive at a precise number of casualties. Estimates put deaths at somewhere around 500,000, with about 5,300 foreign soldiers who died while fighting for the Nationalists (4,000 Italians, 300 Germans, 1,000 others), and approximately 4,900 combatants died fighting for the Republicans (2,000 Germans, 1,000 French, 900 Americans, 500 British, and 500 others).

Propaganda came in the form of published news stories that varied according to the publisher—while Republican-siding press featured stories of victory on one day, on the same day, Nationalist-siding newspapers featured victory in the same battle. Radio reports conflicted, leaflets conflicted, pamphlets conflicted, and the thousands and thousands of posters promoting opposing sides conflicted. In fact, a number of historians have since called the Spanish Civil War simply a propaganda war.

THE FIRST CASUALTY OF WAR

An often-cited quote with, ironically, no clear attribution holds: "The first casualty of war is the truth." While several histories describe Republican Senator Hiram Warren Johnson of California as uttering these words of wisdom in opposition to the United States entering World War I, the sentiment certainly held true during the Spanish Civil War, as journalists had an extraordinarily difficult time reporting events that could reach a wide audience in a truthful manner.

Among the journalist and reporters from around the world who covered the Spanish Civil War, Robert Capa (October 22, 1913–May 25, 1954), a Hungarian, took a photo described as one of the all-time greats, but not without controversy. "Falling Soldier" captured a Spanish Republican at the exact moment an enemy bullet sent him reeling backwards to his death. As people looked to photography to document the realities of the war, this single photo from Capa made the war so real that its skeptics have questioned its authenticity. It was said to have been taken on September 5, 1936, but Nationalists in particular have disputed the date and subject, at least in part because of the drama it depicted and the sympathy it engendered.

Regardless, photos later taken by Capa in World War II earned him lasting respect, as he risked his life numerous times, most dramatically as the only photographer landing on Omaha Beach during the D-Day invasion. Capa final photograph in 1954 was equally telling. He died while patrolling with U.S. troops in Vietnam after stepping on a landmine, at nearly the same moment his camera clicked one last time.

Journalists from around the world traveled to Spain to cover the events, not so much as an internal conflict but as one with far-reaching implications. Most famously, Ernest Hemingway brought his journalism and began to refine and develop his style—opting for the clean, clear, and simple in his sentences. Through such writing, he extracted strong subjects and constructed powerful active verbs. To this day, editors point to Hemingway's style as exemplary, as it requires little extraction of extra words and uses phrasing and structure with clear meaning. His Nobel Prize in Literature (1954) reflects his ability to create stories of lasting influence.

His career in journalism began in 1917 when he first wrote for the *Kansas City Star*. He had not planned a career in journalism, but his work as a reporter for the newspaper blossomed. Seeking adventure, he left the United States in 1918 to travel overseas. With World War I exploding, he enlisted in the ambulance corps and left for Italy. His career as an ambulance driver ended on July 8, 1918, when a machine gun bullet in Italy injured him. After his discharge from the Army, Hemingway returned and took a job in Canada at the *Toronto Star* as a freelance and staff writer. He established a reputation as an expert in outdoor activities and sports and then traveled to France in 1921 to write as a foreign correspondent for the *Star*. Deciding to focus on raising a family, Hemingway temporarily resigned from journalism in January 1924.

In 1937, Hemingway returned to his newspaper skills, agreeing to report on the Spanish Civil War for the North American Newspaper Alliance (NANA), a newspaper service that shined in its coverage of the events. He arrived in Spain with Dutch filmmaker Joris Ivens, who was filming *The Spanish Earth* (1937), a documentary on the war from the Republican perspective. Ivens recruited Hemingway as a writer and narrator for the piece. Hemingway's brand of propaganda, as featured in *The Spanish Earth*, illuminated the conflict's potential relevance to Americans by featuring tales of individuals affected by the war. He aimed his commentary at audiences that could not fathom the human stakes in Spain. The film also enlisted Orson Welles, already known as a master of theater and radio, for his talents, and Welles provided his own brand of styled commentary on behalf of the Republicans.

As a reporter, Hemingway embedded himself in the field, and his surroundings at the time could not help but influence him. The resistance fighters had no good weapons, having to make do with whatever arsenal they could muster. Hemingway's reporting directly reflected his surroundings, and no doubt contributed in a lasting way to the minimalistic style—as found in the following excerpts—for which readers recognize him to this day.

A New Kind of War

Madrid, April 14—The window of the hotel is open and, as you lie in bed, you hear the firing in the front line seventeen blocks away. There is a rifle fire all night long. The rifles go "tacrong, carong, craang, tacrong," and then a machine gun opens up. It has a bigger caliber and is much louder—"rong, cararong, rong, rong."

Then there is the incoming boom of a trench mortar shell and a burst of machine-gun fire. You lie and listen to it, and it is a great thing to be in a bed with your feet stretched out gradually warming the cold foot of the bed and not out there in University City or Carabanchel. A man is singing hard-voiced in the street below, and three drunks are arguing when you fall asleep.[7]

Heavy Shell-Fire in Madrid Advance

Madrid, April 9—Since 6 o'clock this morning I have been watching the government attack on a large scale that is designed eventually to link up the forces on the heights of the Coruna road with others advancing from Carabanchel and Casa de Campo, cutting the neck of the salient that Rebel forces have thrust toward University City and thus lifting the Rebel pressure from Madrid. . . .

A high, cold wind blew the dust raised by the shells into your eyes and caked your nose and mouth, and, as you flopped at a close one and heard the fragments sing to you on the rocky, dusty hillside, your mouth was full of dust. Your correspondent is always thirsty, but that attack was the thirstiest I had ever been in. But the thirst was for water.[8]

Hemingway's style proved quite effective. He focused on the stories of individuals dying, some as heroes, others not. He used haunting imagery to relay the impact of war, an approach that affected his own life, too. A sense of the impact of the war on him also emerges in the passage, "Your correspondent is always thirsty, but that attack was the thirstiest I had ever been in. But the thirst was for water." In his later years, overwrought with despair and alcoholism, Hemingway committed suicide.

When the Spanish Civil War ended, Hemingway returned home to write *For Whom the Bell Tolls*, a title borrowed from a poem by John Donne, which describes the belief that no one dies in isolation. Published in 1940, it immediately became a resounding critical and popular success and helped cement Hemingway's reputation as one of America's foremost writers. *For Whom the Bell Tolls* chronicles the experiences of American college professor Robert Jordan, who has volunteered to fight for the Loyalist cause in the Spanish Civil War. The realities of war temper his initial idealism. Yet his courage enables him to remain devoted to the cause even as he faces death. Hemingway's compassionate and authentic portrait of his characters as they struggle to retain their idealistic beliefs has helped earn the novel a reputation as one of his finest.

THE WARNINGS OF ORWELL AND EISENHOWER

The experiences of the Spanish Civil War affected English journalist Eric Blair (known by his pen name, George Orwell) in ways comparable to Hemingway's struggles. Orwell, the celebrated author of the darkly satirical novels *Animal Farm* (1945) and *1984* (1949), made a career as a social critic, writing essays and commentary for the *London Tribune*. In December 1936, Orwell went to Spain, like many volunteers, eager to aid in the resistance to Franco's military machine. He also fought, joining forces with anti-fascist socialists, later documenting battles and the climate of confusion created by the intense propaganda surrounding all sides.

Homage to Catalonia (1938), among the few journalistic accounts of the conflict, describes Orwell's observations of a communication breakdown between would-be allies. The chaos in Spain created by propaganda aimed at like-minded Republicans left Orwell with a profound bitterness when it became clear Franco's forces had won, a bitterness reflected in several passages in *Homage to Catalonia*, including his thoughts on the role of the press.

> The fighting had barely started when the newspapers of the Right and Left dived simultaneously into the same cesspool of abuse. We all remember the *Daily Mail*'s poster: "REDS CRUCIFY NUNS," while to the *Daily Worker*, Franco's Foreign Legion was "composed of murderers, white-slavers, dope-fiends, and the offal of every European country." As late as October 1937, the *New Statesman* was treating us to tales of Fascist barricades made of the bodies of living children (a most unhandy thing to make barricades with), and Mr. Arthur Bryant was declaring that "the sawing-off of a Conservative tradesman's legs" was "a commonplace" in Loyalist Spain. The people who write that kind of stuff never fight; possibly, they believe that to write it is a substitute for fighting. It is the same in all wars; the soldiers do the fighting, the journalists do the shouting, and no true patriot ever gets near a front-line trench, except on the briefest of propaganda-tours.[9]

Orwell concluded that writers must focus on using clear and objective writing as an antidote to the mayhem created by ideological communications. His insistence essentially that "less is more" can be seen in the style of his writing, as well as in Hemingway's, not coincidentally.

Orwell's prescription for clear writing can be found in a famous essay published in 1946 titled "Politics of the English Language," one any aspiring journalist can take to heart. Orwell criticizes the nonsense too often promulgated by writers, both in the academy and certainly by members of the press. Toward the end of his essay, he proposes a half-dozen very simple and practical ways to counteract these messages in order to create a climate of clarity.

  i. Never use a metaphor, simile or other figure of speech which you are used to seeing in print.
  ii. Never use a long word where a short will do.
  iii. If it is possible to cut a word out, always cut it out.
  iv. Never use the passive when you can use the active.
  v. Never use a foreign phrase, a scientific word or a jargon word if you can think of an everyday English equivalent.
  vi. Break any of these rules sooner than say anything outright barbarous.[10]

While students of journalism can master the first five "rules" without too much difficulty, Orwell also reminds us to keep an entirely essential trait in mind—stay human. That is, we cannot adhere to rules only, as this would constitute dogmatism. We also need to know how to break rules, but only after knowing what they are.

Orwell's advice about the need to be both clear and human were spelled out in novel form with two subsequent publications that critics have since called no less than prophetic. His short novel *Animal Farm* (1945), very much a reflection on his experiences in Spain, tells the story of a revolution gone wrong. It features propaganda as nonsense, including the suggestions that "All animals are created equal, but some animals are more equal than others."[11] Even more alarming, Orwell's *1984* warned of a future dominated by totalitarians who controlled the masses through ideology and the media. The main character, Winston Smith, held a job as a media censor in a world of the "future" dominated by television and surveillance in which agents of the totalitarian dictator Big Brother barked orders for obedience to the state—a prediction of the continued significance of propaganda to this day.

At about the same time Orwell published his most famous pieces, the Cold War between the United States and the Soviet Union entered public consciousness. Members of Congress recognized the need for the U.S. government to spend more time focused on gathering intelligence about the USSR's nuclear program than engaging in propaganda directed at American citizens. In 1948, the Smith-Mundt Act passed as legislation designed to bring to a formal close the government's use of propaganda directed toward its own citizens, as it had done in various degrees since World War I, prohibiting the dissemination of state-produced materials domestically. It allowed propaganda to target foreign audiences, however, as a way of combating external threats (both real and perceived) during the Cold War.

We will define more specifically in the following chapter the issues and climate of the Cold War, but for the purposes of this chapter, it should be noted that the

Image 11.3: "President Dwight Eisenhower Giving a Television Speech in the White House about Science and National Security, Next to a Nose Cone of an Experimental Missile which had been into Space and Back," Warren K. Leffler, photographer, published November 7, 1957.[12]

Smith-Mundt Modernization Act of 2012 effectively nullified the original Smith-Mundt Act, enabling U.S. government programming to broadcast directly to domestic audiences for the first time. Programs now produced by the Broadcasting Board of Governors, which shares a budget with the U.S. State Department, has an annual budget of more than $700 million.

In a message as prophetic as Orwell's warnings, Dwight D. Eisenhower, a beloved two-term president and former Supreme Commander of the Allied Expeditionary Forces in Europe, gave a farewell address to the nation in 1961. Eisenhower had a keen sense of world currents and gave an ominous warning, which in time held merit. "In the councils of government," Eisenhower said, "we must guard against the acquisition of unwarranted influence, whether sought or unsought, by the military-industrial complex."

> The potential for the disastrous rise of misplaced power exists and will persist. We must never let the weight of this combination endanger our liberties or democratic processes. We should take nothing for granted. Only an alert and knowledgeable citizenry can compel the proper meshing of the huge industrial and military machinery of defense with our peaceful methods and goals, so that security and liberty may prosper together.[13]

More recently, social critics and critics of the media have revisited Eisenhower's speech and coined a new phrase from it, one that combines the most troublesome parts of modern institutions together. The "military-industrial-media complex," according to this analysis, is a remake of the "military-industrial complex" that adds the media as an essential player in the goals of the government to influence people both at home and abroad.

The organization Fairness and Accuracy in Reporting (FAIR) has subsequently accused participants in this structure of using media resources to promote militarism, which in turn benefits defense companies.[14] For example, General Electric, which has owned as much as 49 percent of NBC, is a subcontractor for the Tomahawk cruise missile and Patriot II missile, both used extensively during the highly publicized Persian Gulf War. While many other examples of media, military, and government interests have intersected, we will save additional discussion of them for chapters later in this book.

RECAPPING THIS CHAPTER

Looking back on this chapter, you should see the ways the press during wars in the twentieth century sometimes spread political messages to persuade audiences with tools developed by figures associated with the creation of the public relations industry. It provided an overview of the way governments have sometimes coopted the press to work in ways that do not meet the requirements of the Fourth Estate, and it showed how the press can do more than inform—it can change public opinion.

Using materials from this chapter, you should understand the historic roots of propaganda, as well as the ways governments have used the press for manipulative purposes not intended by the founders, recognizing the need for a free press to focus on ensuring citizens receive essential information about their government.

The following chapter opens with an analysis of John Hersey's *Hiroshima*, a compilation of stories from survivors of the nuclear attack on the Japanese city of Hiroshima in 1945 that many press historians consider a masterpiece of modern reporting. It then describes the way the press responded to the climate of the Cold War, including the efforts of Edward R. Murrow to confront fears fueled by firebrand Senator Joseph McCarthy. It includes a cross-section of content featured on television in the 1950s, from CBS's entertainment-based *The Ed Sullivan Show* to its news programming, describing how broadcasters balanced programming between the entertainment interests of their audiences with the need to provide news.

NOTES

1 "C.P.I. Delegates to Europe," Library of Congress, accessed May 16, 2016, <item/ggb2005023376>.
2 "I Want You for U.S. Army," Library of Congress, accessed May 16, 2016, <item/96507165>.
3 Yvonne French, "Everybody's Uncle Sam," Library of Congress, accessed May 27, 2017, <loc.gov/loc/lcib/9510/unclesam.html>.
4 George Creel, *How We Advertised America* (New York, London: Harper & Brothers Publishers, 1920), 4, 5, 100.
5 Hal Erickson, review of "Triumph of the Will" (dir. Leni Riefenstahl), Rovi, "Triumph des Willens," Rotten Tomatoes.
6 Leni Riefenstahl, *Leni Riefenstahl* (New York: Macmillan, 1995), 150.

7   Ernest Hemingway, "A New Kind of War," NANA Dispatch
8   Ernest Hemingway, "Heavy Shell-Fire in Madrid Advance," April 10, 1937, accessed May 27, 2017, <nytimes.com/books/99/07/04/specials/hemingway-advance.html>.
9   George Orwell, *Homage to Catalonia/Down and Out in Paris and London* (Boston, New York: Houghton Mifflin, 2010), 70.
10 George Orwell, "Politics and the English Language," in The Collected Essays, Journalism and Letters of George Orwell, eds. Sonia Orwell and Ian Angos, vol. 4, ed. 1 (New York: Harcourt, Brace, Javanovich, 1968), 139.
11 George Orwell, *Animal Farm* (New York: Signet, 1956), 123.
12 "President Dwight Eisenhower Giving a Television Speech," Library of Congress, accessed June 11, 2016, <item/2012649174>.
13 Dwight D. Eisenhower, "Farewell Address," January 17, 1961, accessed May 25, 2017, <eisenhower.archives.gov>.
14 Norman Solomon, "The Military-Industrial-Media Complex," August 1, 2005, accessed May 26, 2017, <fair.org/extra/the-military-industrial-media-complex>.

12

THE PRESS IN THE COLD WAR

MURROW, MCCARTHY, AND SHAKESPEARE

This chapter provides examples of new styles, new media, and new forms of entertainment popularized by the press during the Cold War, an era of intense competition between national superpowers. It opens with an overview of John Hersey's *Hiroshima*, a compilation of stories from survivors of the U.S. nuclear attack on the Japanese city of Hiroshima in 1945 that many press historians consider a masterpiece of modern reporting:

- It then describes the way the press responded to the ensuing climate of fear tied to the nuclear arms race between the United States and the Soviet Union, and the efforts of CBS newsman Edward R. Murrow to confront anti-communist Senator Joseph McCarthy;
- and it includes a cross-section of content featured on television in the 1950s, such as CBS's entertainment-based *The Ed Sullivan Show*, to describe how broadcasters attracted audiences with entertainment.

Using materials from this chapter, students should identify the growth of "infotainment," as noted in previous chapters, and see how news as delivered by print media continued to take a role of secondary importance to entertainment-based media:

- They should explore the ways television executives often found that "fun" sold more effectively than "fear";
- and they should understand how Murrow's concerns about advertising's effect on news content proved prophetic.

Key words, names, and phrases associated with Chapter 12 include:

- *Hiroshima*, John Hersey, and the *New Yorker*;
- Joseph McCarthy, HUAC, and the Hollywood Ten;
- Edward R. Murrow, *See It Now*, and Hank Greenspun;
- and *The Ed Sullivan Show* and Elvis Presley.

The press in the decades following World War II evolved in response to a changing media that changed in an increasingly inter-connected global society. A conflict between the United States and the Soviet Union (USSR) to some degree replaced the individual conflicts of nation-states preceding the Cold War, which tested each superpower's resolve to develop superiority in their stockpiles of nuclear arms. The American press responded by clarifying to some extent the stakes of the conflict but also by assuaging the fears of a public weary of war.

One of the most remarkable examples of this role for the press has since taken its place as a classic piece of journalism. John Hersey's *Hiroshima*, a compilation of stories from survivors of the nuclear attack on Japan at the end of World War II, provided a segue to the Cold War, an era that in the 1950s more commonly featured escapism in shows such as CBS's *The Ed Sullivan Show*. Combined with news-based shows, such as *See It Now*, CBS and other networks developed marketing formulas that both secured a place for television as a popular form of media and a place for "infotainment," or the now common blend of news and entertainment. The political intrigue of the era, along with the dramatic elements of popular programming, contained at least a few elements found in a Shakespearean play, and indeed individual news figures actually incorporated lines from his plays into their narratives for national audiences.

This era also sets the stage for material found in the remaining chapters of this book, which describe the way broadcast networks and media in general evolved in corporate structures. Continuing a trend that began in Chapter 10, this chapter shows how print media increasingly took secondary importance to the content of broadcast and television entertainment. While this trend continues through today with social media providing a primary source of information, students will see how concerns expressed by Edward R. Murrow in particular have proven prophetic.

HERSEY'S *HIROSHIMA*

News consumers saw the beginning of a new media landscape begin to evolve at the conclusion of World War II, and the way journalists wrote about this world contributed to the way readers saw events transpire. The reconfiguration of post-war national and cultural identities coincided with the launching of television as a major new form of media, leading both consumers and producers of news to no longer understand content in the form of individual mediums but instead as a collection of resources that transcended the boundaries of particular locations.

One of the foundational pieces of journalism from this time that anticipated these changes combined both hard news and feature-style storytelling techniques in a form later dubbed "new journalism," and it has since earned a spot as one of the top pieces of reporting for all time.[1] John Hersey's *Hiroshima*, a piece that appeared in a single 1946 issue of the *New Yorker* magazine, resonated with readers through its use of fictional devices, such as the building of a suspenseful moment with one character and then switching to another.[2] The presentation of these moments with journalistic techniques led to further use by subsequent writers who helped to solidify the style of journalism in following decades.

Image 12.1: "Nagasaki, Japan, under Atomic Bomb Attack," United States Army Air Forces, photographer, created August 9, 1945, photograph shows atomic bomb mushroom cloud over Nagasaki.[3]

Hersey, a Pulitzer Prize-winning novelist, had an unprecedented assignment—to write about the devastation wrought by the atomic bombing of Hiroshima, Japan. On August 6, 1945, the American army had decimated the city, killing an estimated 100,000 people, with a bomb of enormous power. Days later, the United States dropped another atomic bomb on the city of Nagasaki, killing an estimated 80,000 civilians and hastening the end to the war with Japan.

While Americans celebrated the end of the war and the sparing of soldiers' lives that would have inevitably taken place if the war continued, few of them had any actual idea of the destruction this new and mysterious weapon had inflicted. A year after the bombings, Hersey recognized that the overwhelming nature of the nuclear attack made new approaches to storytelling necessary, and for this reason, he used a style that departed from traditional journalistic conventions. His resulting compilation of tales from survivors of the atomic consisted of interviews with people directly affected by the bombing, and in the compilation of the story, he captured the imagery of the event without involving himself directly in the event.

The original presentation of Hersey's narrative came in four chapters—"A Noiseless Flash," "The Fire," "Details Are Being Investigated," and "Panic Grass and Feverfew"—with each one weaving the stories of six survivors into a composite form. The survivors profiled included two doctors, two women, and two religious men, and their stories spanned from the moment of the bomb's detonation to a few months later.

- Dr. Masakazu Fujii, a physician: When the bomb struck, his entire clinic toppled into the water. He died after being in a coma for eleven years with his family in discord.
- Dr. Terufumi Sasaki, a 25-year-old surgeon at the Red Cross Hospital: He worked selflessly in the aftermath of the bombing, and Hersey described how Sasaki risked penalties by treating sick patients in the suburbs without a permit.
- Father Wilhelm Kleinsorge, a German Jesuit priest living in Hiroshima: The only non-Japanese character profiled in the narrative, Kleinsorge fell ill from radiation sickness after comforting the dying and wounded.
- Mrs. Hatsuyo Nakamura, a tailor's widow raising three young children: She and her children survived the explosion without any external physical harm, but she and her daughter, Myeko, suffered from radiation sickness for years.
- Reverend Mr. Kiyoshi Tanimoto, a thoughtful Methodist pastor: He worked to bring the dying and wounded to safety, and although he was unhurt by the bomb, he felt ashamed to be healthy while surrounded by so much human misery.
- Toshiko Sasaki, a 20-year-old clerk: She worked hard to take care of her family and represented the many nameless survivors of the bomb who suffered mostly in isolation.

In 1985, Hersey reissued *Hiroshima* with a postscript, "The Aftermath," which added a fifth chapter to his original piece by reexamining the lives he profiled forty years after the bombing.

From a historical standpoint, critics have agreed that Hersey's story epitomized the ability of the press to communicate a truthful story with an adherence to facts and an effective style. Accordingly, toward the end of the twentieth century, a poll of journalists and scholars from the journalism department at New York University (NYU) and elsewhere compiled a list of the top 100 works of journalism in the preceding century, and Hersey's "Hiroshima" took the No. 1 position for its overall quality, impact, and contribution to the field. His "spare, uninflected, factual account," a respondent noted, "brought home to America the experience of nuclear war by telling the stories of some of its victims."[4]

NOTES ON "NEW JOURNALISM"

Although different movements in the development of journalism history had their own innovative traits, a group of writers in the 1960s and 1970s combined news writing and journalism with literary techniques that represented for readers a unique storytelling approach. Historians sometimes point to John Hersey's *Hiroshima* as setting a precedent for this style, but Hersey himself rejected the label, insisting his writing spoke for itself as non-fiction. Regardless, a group of writers followed Hersey's lead by producing long-form non-fiction that emphasized "truth" over "facts." To do this, they engaged in intensive reportage by immersing themselves in their stories as reporters and participants. Tom Wolfe, one of the practitioners, coined the phrase associated with the movement with a collection of articles he published as *The New Journalism* (Harper & Row, 1973), which included works by himself and, among others, Hunter S. Thompson, Truman Capote, Norman Mailer, Joan Didion, and Gay Talese. Articles published by these "new" journalists generally appeared in magazines such as the *Atlantic Monthly*, *Harper's*, *Esquire*, the *New Yorker*, and *Rolling Stone*.

"Hiroshima" also inspired a generation of new writers to engage in innovative storytelling techniques, and practitioners of this long-form of storytelling continued using it and tuning its features into the 1970s, as we will see in Chapter 13. Later innovators in the style of new journalism emphasized the use of the subjective perspective, a literary style reminiscent of long-form non-fiction and that emphasized experience over fact, which came from intensive immersion in surroundings, an approach that contrasted with traditional journalism, which objectified news narratives.

BRIDGING MEDIA: PRINT, RADIO, TELEVISION, AND FILM

Another reporter whose career launched during World War II epitomized a different kind of storytelling transition—not one of style, but one of media. Edward R. Murrow, who covered the war in Europe for CBS radio, made a reputation for himself as a fearless reporter with reports on the German bombing raids of London in 1940. It had become customary among Londoners at the time, realizing they might not necessarily see each other the next morning, to close conversations with "good night, and good luck," and Murrow, who broadcast famously during actual raids, likewise began ending his radio segment—and later television segments—with "good night, and good luck."

After the war, Murrow returned to the United States and, in 1946, became vice president of CBS and director of news and public affairs. Along with other journalists and GIs who had traveled to Europe in the 1940s and witnessed the horrors of war, Murrow joined forces in speaking out against the kinds of politically driven forms of demagoguery he had seen ravish nations abroad. His new roles at CBS had him crossover from radio to television during a period in broadcast history when the practice occurred regularly.

Former radio network rivals CBS and NBC had branched into television and competed for viewers by sometimes raiding each other's pools of talent, beginning with the personalities on already established radio programs. At times, CBS television would adapt NBC's popular radio programs, and vice versa, and while radio would evolve into a provider of news, talk, and music, television focused on entertainment. Murrow represented this crossover from radio to television in terms of his abilities as a newscaster, but the most recognizable radio stars to join him in the new medium included popular entertainers such as Jack Benny, Red Skelton, and Bob Hope. And while television sets sprouted in the homes of viewers across the nation and brought a tremendous change in broadcast journalism, to be sure, print saw the effects, too, as newspaper publishers reacted to content changes perhaps too slowly.

At the same time, the federal government had intensified its investigation into alleged connections between entertainment industries—especially Hollywood—and the new perceived threat of communist infiltration into areas of American society. The House Un-American Activities Committee (HUAC) headed these investigations during the early years of the Cold War, and committee members quickly settled their gaze on Hollywood studios, which had a reputation as hotbeds of communist activity. Prior to World War II, affiliation with communist organizations posed no formal threat to the interests of the U.S. government, and in the 1930s, struggling actors and studio workers joined leftist groups in the dire economic conditions of the Great Depression. However, in the late 1940s, anti-communist legislators grew concerned that the movie industry could provide a source of subversive propaganda on behalf of the Soviets, who, they alleged, would use their nuclear powers for world domination.

Although popular Hollywood films of the 1930s and 1940s offered little evidence of an overriding communist agenda, the investigations launched with movie figures among their first targets. In October 1947, more than forty people with connections to the movie industry received orders to appear before HUAC on suspicion of holding communist loyalties or being involved in subversive activities. In October, a particular group of ten motion-picture producers, directors, and screenwriters known as the Hollywood Ten publicly denounced the committee's tactics by refusing to answer their possible communist affiliations. The group included Alvah Bessie, Herbert Biberman, Lester Cole, Edward Dmytryk, Ring Lardner, Jr., John Howard Lawson, Albert Maltz, Samuel Ornitz, Adrian Scott, and Dalton Trumbo. Convicted in federal court the following year, they received sentences of six months to one year in prison. The film industry subsequently blacklisted the group, barring them from employment, although some continued their involvement in screenwriting anonymously.

At the same time, the HUAC hearings had supporters in Hollywood, among them, renowned director Elia Kazan, who in 1952 offered testimony that ended the careers of colleagues. Disney creator Walt Disney and President Ronald Reagan (1981–1989), at the time president of the Screen Actors Guild, also provided testimony that implicated leftists in the movie industry. While, according to Disney, the threat of communists in the film industry was a serious one, Reagan testified that a small clique within his union used communist tactics to steer union policy. Kazan's testimony, likely the most damaging of all, resulted in nearly a half-century of controversy and created a problematic legacy for the undoubtedly talented filmmaker.

The paranoia triggered by the HUAC hearings set the stage for the spread of fear into other areas of society, as American citizens began to take the threat of communist infiltration seriously. In this climate, Wisconsin senator Joseph McCarthy grew a career based on manipulation of the press to build his role as a powerful anti-communist crusader. In an era known as the Red Scare, which took place in the early 1950s, the press at first played willing accomplices, as McCarthy's allegations of communist

Image 12.2: "Senator Joseph McCarthy Standing at Microphone with Two other Men, Probably Discussing the Senate Select Committee to Study Censure Charges (Watkins Committee) Chaired by Senator Arthur V. Watkins," Thomas J. O'Halloran, photographer, published June 1954.[5]

infiltration at first provided sensational fodder for publishers who were intent on selling newspapers.

One of the more spectacular events to launch this chapter in press history took place on February 9, 1950, in Wheeling, West Virginia, when McCarthy gave a press conference in which he claimed to hold a list of 205 members of the communist party who worked in the U.S. State Department. The piece of paper he held, which he claimed listed the names, did no such thing, but newspaper writers at the event had no indication to the contrary.

The problems associated with the Red Scare that ensued, however, stemmed at least in part from the unwillingness or inability of the reporters to do appropriate follow-up work, and instead of verifying McCarthy's claims, a number of reporters simply accepted the accusations and printed them without proof. Furthermore, careless headline writers made McCarthy's allegations appear confirmed, and editors who adhered to narrow definitions of "objectivity" provided little context for interpreting his remarks. In efforts to find fresh scoops on the competition, newspapers rarely did follow-up stories on the allegations and often buried rebuttals to the most specious accusations. Among the few to respond to McCarthy's tactics and point to the press's failings, Herbert Block, a cartoonist for the *Washington Post*, helped coin the phrase "McCarthyism" as a pejorative for the style of demagoguery on display. The senator later embraced the term as a rallying cry for his supporters.

THE PRESS REACTS TO THE RED SCARE

While John Hersey had introduced a new style of storytelling to document the end of World War II, veterans from the war joined newspapers to bring a revitalized sense of democracy to readers, a sense sometimes fueled by their own experiences. Murrow had certainly kept in mind his experiences in Europe, which on April 16, 1945, included a famous broadcast describing the liberation of prisoners from the Buchenwald concentration camp. His exposure to the realities of total government control under the Nazi regime influenced broadcasts for the rest of his career, now on television.

Likewise, Herman "Hank" Milton Greenspun, who enlisted in the U.S. Army in 1941, witnessed the ravages of total war and later published his account in his autobiography *Where I Stand: The Record of a Reckless Man*. Born in Brooklyn, August 27, 1909, the Jewish, trained lawyer would rise to the rank of major after advancing under Gen. George Patton through Germany and France, earning the French Croix de Guerre for his courage in the Battle of Falaise Gap.[6]

Greenspun moved to Las Vegas in 1946 with his wife Barbara, and in part because of his experiences during the war and having seen the horrific treatment of Jews in Europe, he supported the establishment of Israel as a homeland for the Jewish people. The state of Israel could not succeed without arms, and Greenspun described in his autobiography how he helped engineer a critical delivery of weapons to the struggling state. Federal officials charged him with violation of the Neutrality Act, and in 1950, he pleaded guilty. U.S. District Judge Peirson Hall refused to send Greenspun to prison, citing the noble motives behind the actions, and instead fined him $10,000 and deprived him of civil rights, including the right to vote. In 1961, President John F. Kennedy pardoned Greenspun.

In 1950, Greenspun bought a small newspaper that he transformed into the *Las Vegas Sun*. Shortly thereafter, his feud with McCarthy erupted. In 1952, the senator visited Las Vegas on behalf of Nevada senator George Malone, who was campaigning for reelection. Greenspun attended the event, and the account of their initial confrontation published in the *Sun* contained descriptions of a drama that unfolded for a national audience. In front of the attending crowd, McCarthy had called Greenspun "an ex-convict," a "communist," and the publisher of "*The Las Vegas Daily Worker*," a slur for a communist propaganda publication. Greenspun challenged McCarthy directly, charging the stage to denounce the false allegations, but McCarthy left the building. "It reminded one of Marc Anthony after he had finished speaking over Caesar's corpse," the *Sun* suggested, and in the newspaper's allusion to William Shakespeare's *Julius Caesar*, it paraphrased Mark Antony's call to war, "Now let mischief do its worst."[7]

The "mischief" the *Sun* cited foreshadowed both the drama that would unfold between McCarthy and Greenspun, and McCarthy and the media as a whole. As McCarthy attempted to quell the bad publicity the *Sun* had given him, Greenspun continued for several years with relentless, sometimes ruthless attacks that ultimately led quite literally to a federal case. As *Time Magazine* reported in 1955, the intensity of their fight required a jury's decision to determine the rights of the press in the matter. "In the columns of the *Sun*," *Time* reported, Greenspun had called McCarthy "a secret Communist" and a "disreputable pervert."

> Reluctant to sue, and thus give currency to Greenspun's charges, but goaded to do something, McCarthy's office last year asked the Post Office Department whether the *Sun* should lose its second-class mailing privileges (*Time*, April 19, 1954). A federal grand jury indicted Greenspun on charges that he violated postal laws by mailing newspapers carrying a column "tending to incite murder or assassination" of McCarthy. Sample lines from the Greenspun column offered in evidence: "Senator Joe McCarthy has to come to a violent end . . . The chances are that McCarthy will be laid to rest at the hands of some poor, innocent slob whose reputation and life he has destroyed through his smear technique." Last week, after a five-day trial, a jury deliberated only two hours and 45 minutes, found Greenspun not guilty. Jurors said later that the Government failed to prove that the Greenspun column actually incited anyone to try to kill McCarthy.[8]

McCarthy had won re-election in 1952 and became chair of the Senate's Committee on Government Operations, where he occupied the spotlight for two years with his anti-communist investigations and questioning of suspected officials. McCarthy's charges led to testimony before the Senate Committee on Foreign Relations, but he was unable to substantiate any of his claims against a single member of any government department. Regardless, his popularity rose, as many in the voting public had grown uneasy with communist activity in China and Eastern Europe. His detractors claimed he abused his power to trample on civil liberties.

Regardless, McCarthy's charges of communism and anti-American activity affected more people at all levels of government, even President Dwight D. Eisenhower, who the senator claimed had stalled his investigations or simply interfered with them, which allegedly by innuendo made the president suspiciously weak on communism.

While Greenspun's attacks had initiated a reaction against McCarthy's most outrageous claims, a different journalist altogether brought such tactics to a halt. Shortly after Greenspun and McCarthy's confrontation in Las Vegas, the case of an Air Force reservist caught the attention of Edward R. Murrow. Milo Radulovich had received a discharge from the Reserve after—in the climate of intense scrutiny and fear brought about by the Red Scare—it was discovered that his father, an immigrant from Serbia, subscribed to several Serbian newspapers, one of which the government identified as a communist publication. Murrow perceived the fundamental unfairness of what had happened to Radulovich, and on October 20, 1953, he dedicated an episode of *See It Now* to exposing McCarthy's tactics. After broadcast of interviews with Radulovich and his family aired on the episode, thousands of letters poured into CBS in support of Murrow's bravery in addressing the Red Scare.

The success of the program led Murrow to host several more episodes on the subject of McCarthyism, culminating in a famous March 9, 1954, broadcast, which media critics often describe as one of the finest moments in television history. In opening the broadcast, Murrow played a clip of McCarthy in which the senator, insinuating that the press had grown in hubris by attacking him, quoted Shakespeare: "Upon what meat doth this our Caesar feed, That he is grown so great?"[9] Murrow responded by playing recordings of McCarthy while he interrogated witnesses. The clips revealed what viewers could easily interpret as a threat to democracy—not in the form of suspected communists, but in McCarthy's demagoguery. Murrow closed the segment by paraphrasing another line from Shakespeare in response to McCarthy, imploring viewers to take responsibility for the climate of fear in which they lived and to do something about it:

> Why, man, he doth bestride the narrow world like a colossus, and we petty men walk under his huge legs, and peep about to find ourselves dishonorable graves, men at some time are masters of their fates, the fault, dear Brutus, is not in our stars, but in ourselves, that we are underlings.[10]

The broadcast provoked tens of thousands of letters, telegrams, and phone calls to CBS headquarters, running 15 to 1 in favor of Murrow.

In part because of the public response to the broadcast, McCarthy's effectiveness as a politician waned. In time, he himself—in an ironic role reversal—had to testify in the Senate about the very tactics he had used in the Senate in previous years. In a nationally televised, thirty-six-day hearing that illustrated clearly to the nation that McCarthy had overstepped his authority, the Senate committee investigating his charges of subversion in the State Department later found the accusations fraudulent, and it censured him in December 1954. With his authority stripped from him, McCarthy's remaining career in politics weakened, and at the age of 48, May 2, 1957, he died a broken man, reportedly from alcoholism.

While Murrow enjoyed a measure of fame for his role in bringing an end to McCarthy's tactics, his career also came to a troublesome close. His insistence on reporting hard news with what some perceived as a heavy hand caused friction with CBS head Bill Paley. Murrow and Paley clearly had different ideas about the value of certain kinds of content on the air, and while Murrow favored the informational value of news, Paley simply had bills to pay. In the summer of 1958, the two clashed in Paley's office over programming decisions. Murrow had complained to Paley he could not continue doing "See It Now" if the network repeatedly provided (without consulting Murrow) equal time to subjects who felt wronged by the program. Paley reportedly responded to Murrow by saying he did not want a constant stomachache every time "See It Now" covered a controversial subject, and as a result, Paley in effect cancelled the show, which aired for a final episode on July 7, 1958, hastening Murrow's retirement from CBS.

Having devoted decades to broadcast, Murrow grew bitter with Paley's decision. He took an opportunity to speak before the Radio and Television News Directors Association in Chicago on October 15, 1958, to blast television's emphasis on entertainment and commercialism at the expense of public interest.

His address opened with the lines, "It is my desire, if not my duty, to try to talk to you journeymen with some candor about what is happening to radio and television," and he followed the remark with a scathing critique of the state of broadcast.

> We are to a large extent an imitative society. If one or two or three corporations would undertake to devote just a small traction of their advertising appropriation along the lines that I have suggested, the procedure would grow by contagion; the economic burden would be bearable, and there might ensue a most exciting adventure—exposure to ideas and the bringing of reality into the homes of the nation. . . . This instrument can teach, it can illuminate; yes, and it can even inspire. But it can do so only to the extent that humans are determined to use it to those ends. Otherwise, it is merely wires and lights in a box. There is a great and perhaps decisive battle to be fought against ignorance, intolerance, and indifference. This weapon of television could be useful.[11]

Although Murrow made a compelling case for the need to keep news an important parts of television broadcasts, he encountered resistance not just from the heads of networks, who had economic interests in mind. His suggestion, just as importantly, received indirect pushback from a new generation of viewers with tastes that broke with the generation that preceded them.

FUN OVER FEAR

With the bloody conflicts of World War II behind them, viewers looked for a softer side of life. They found it in increasing measure on television, as both the content and style of broadcast would match their expectations. While both NBC and CBS experimented with programming techniques that would attract advertisers to sustain operations, the falling out between Bill Paley and Edward R. Murrow at CBS demonstrated perhaps most dramatically that the bottom line determined content. Advertisements in the 1950s (as we have seen in Chapter 10), often came from major producers of commodities, as well as automobiles, tobacco, and daily necessities.

Consumers meanwhile demonstrated a demand for entertainment shows, and on CBS, the leading source of variety, *The Ed Sullivan Show*, consistently attracted viewers and in turn advertisers. From June 20, 1948, to June 6, 1971, airing every Sunday night, Sullivan himself drew viewers who identified with his everydayness, as he had on on-screen presence that by today's standards looked relatively less polished. He spoke with a peculiar diction and used awkward hand gestures that reminded his audience that although he shared many of their traits, the performers on his shows had extraordinary talents. Along with many other television figures during the era, his career represented a crossover, as he had made his start in media as a newspaper columnist.

Among the many remarkable performances on *The Ed Sullivan Show*, controversial rock and roll star Elvis Presley made a significant impression, contributing to what broadcast historians have described as a watershed moment in the proliferation of television use. Presley's embrace of black music and his overtly sexualized motions on stage had triggered both fierce criticism and a kind of fan support that resembled mass

Image 12.3: "Head-and-shoulders Photograph of Ed Sullivan," published 1954.[12]

hysteria. A generation of parents who preceded Presley's primary audience reacted vehemently against the performer's casualness with traditionally African American music, as parts of the United States at the time still lived in segregated communities. Moreover, his gyrations to music on stage apparently encouraged his audience to break sexual taboos, although Presley himself said his dancing was simply reminiscent of the motions he made growing up in a church with mixed races.

Presley's critics dubbed him "Elvis the Pelvis" and even protested his style of performance through formal channels. After a show in La Crosse, Wisconsin, for example, the head of the local Catholic diocese's newspaper sent a letter to FBI director J. Edgar Hoover warning that Presley was "a definite danger to the security of the United States," and that "actions and motions" had aroused "the sexual passions of teenaged youth." The complaint alleged that after the show, more than 1,000 teenagers tried to storm into Presley's room at the auditorium and cited "indications of the harm Presley did just in La Crosse" included two high school girls "whose abdomen and thigh had Presley's autograph."[13]

Despite initial misgivings, Sullivan booked the singer for three appearances at an unprecedented $50,000 sum for the performer. Approximately 60 million viewers—a record 82.6 percent of the television audience—tuned in for Presley's first show for Sullivan's audience on September 9, 1956. Paley and advertisers on CBS no doubt delighted in the numbers, but with Presley's second appearance on October 28, 1956, his swiveling hips and gyrating body movements had caused a massive stir. For his third and final appearance January 6, 1957, producers sought to avoid public backlash and insisted on aiming cameras above Presley's waist so that views could not see his hips or legs moving. Dubbed the "waist up" show, Presley's performance brought the new rock and roll form of music to a national audience.

In likely the most remarkable aspect to the "waist up" broadcast came at the end of the show in a moment of pivotal importance for solidifying the subsequent role of television. While Sullivan himself had played a role in giving the musical phenomenon a certain level of widespread appeal, at the same time, he made it clear that television as a whole could entertain, perhaps even more than it could inform. He came on the stage at the end of the show and to the national audience gave Presley (and indirectly his fans) his blessing. "I wanted to say to Elvis Presley and the country that this is a real decent, fine boy," Sullivan said. "So now let's have a tremendous hand for a very nice person!"[14]

RECAPPING THIS CHAPTER

Looking back on this chapter, you should see examples of new styles, new media, and new forms of entertainment popularized by the press during the Cold War era. It opened with an analysis of John Hersey's *Hiroshima*, a compilation of stories from survivors of the nuclear attack on the Japanese city of Hiroshima in 1945 that many press historians consider a masterpiece of modern reporting. It then described the way the press responded to the climate of the Cold War, an era of fear tied to the nuclear arms race between the United States and the Soviet Union, and the efforts of Edward R. Murrow to confront anti-communist Senator Joseph McCarthy. It included a cross-section of content featured on television in the 1950s, such as CBS's entertainment-based *The Ed Sullivan Show*, to describe how broadcasters attracted audiences.

Using materials from this chapter, you should be able to identify the growth of "infotainment" and see how news as delivered by print media began to take a role of secondary importance to the entertainment featured on television. You should explore the ways television executives often found that "fun" (entertainment) sold more effectively than "fear" (news), and you should understand how Murrow's concerns about advertising's effect on news content proved prophetic.

The following chapter describes how the press in the 1960s and 1970s popularized protests associated with the Vietnam War and other ideas of the baby boomer generation via the mainstream press and popular magazines. It juxtaposes countercultural journalism, as epitomized by Hunter S. Thompson's style of "gonzo" storytelling, with the relatively traditional reporting at the *Washington Post* that exposed the Watergate scandal.

NOTES

1 Felicity Barringer, "Journalism's Greatest Hits: Two Lists of a Century's Top Stories," March 1, 1999, accessed June 14, 2017, <nytimes.com/1999/03/01/business/media-journalism-s-greatest-hits-two-lists-of-a-century-s-top-stories.html>.
2 John Hersey, "Hiroshima," *The New Yorker*, August 31, 1946.
3 "Nagasaki, Japan, under Atomic Bomb Attack," Library of Congress, accessed June 14, 2017, <item/2002722137>.
4 Mitchel Stevens, "The Top 100 Works of Journalism in the United States in the 20th Century," accessed June 23, 2017, <nyu.edu/classes/stephens/Top 100 page.htm>.
5 "Senator Joseph McCarthy," Library of Congress, accessed June 8, 2016, <item/15647009>.
6 "Hank's Battle Over," July 23, 1989, accessed May 7, 2018, <lasvegassun.com/news/1989/jul/23/hanks-battle-over>.
7 Sun Staff, "McCarthy Loses Face in Verbal Fire, Walks out, Refuses to Debate as Greenspun Answers 'Vicious Lies,'" October 14, 1952, accessed June 23, 2017, <lasvegassun.com/news/1952/oct/14/mccarthy-loses-face-verbal-fire>.
8 "The Press: Greenspun Wins," *Time*, 65, 18 (May 2, 1955), accessed July 6, 2017, available at <content.time.com/time/magazine/article/0,9171,866290,00.html>.
9 William Shakespeare, *Julius Caesar*, Act I, ii, 148.
10 William Shakespeare, *Julius Caesar*, Act I, iii, 140–141; Edward R. Murrow, "A Report on Senator Joseph R. McCarthy," *See it Now* (CBS-TV), March 9, 1954.
11 Edward R. Murrow, RTNDA Convention, Chicago, October 15, 1958, accessed November 6, 2005, <rtnda.org>.
12 "Head-and-shoulders Photograph of Ed Sullivan," Library of Congress, accessed February 13, 2017, <item/99471540>.
13 Catholic diocese of La Crosse, Wisconsin, May 16, 1956, in Thomas Fensch, ed., *The FBI Files on Elvis Presley* (The Woodlands, TX: New Century Books, 2001), 15–17.
14 Elvis Presley on *The Ed Sullivan Show*, September 9, 1956.

13

NEW JOURNALISM AND THE COUNTERCULTURE
WATCHDOGS AND WATERGATE

The following chapter describes how the press in the 1960s and 1970s at times used stylistic techniques in new journalism to popularize the ideas and attitudes of a generation of Americans that expressed both idealism and dissent via mainstream outlets and popular magazines:

- It features legal precedents that affected reporting, as well as a sample of countercultural journalism, as practiced by Hunter S. Thompson's style of "gonzo" storytelling;
- and it juxtaposes new journalism with the relatively traditional yet groundbreaking reporting at the *Washington Post* that exposed the Watergate scandal.

Using materials from this chapter, students should understand how different forms of storytelling serve different purposes:

- They should have an understanding of how cultural and political issues addressed by the press during the 1960s and 1970s produced a lasting effect on subsequent generations;
- and they should be able to explain why press historians to this day cite Woodward and Bernstein as exemplary members of the Forth Estate.

NEW JOURNALISM AND THE COUNTERCULTURE

Key words, names, and phrases associated with Chapter 13 include:

- the Living Room War, My Lai, and "Faces of the American Dead in Vietnam";
- *Times v. Sullivan*, the Pentagon Papers, and the Twenty-Fourth and Twenty-Sixth Amendments;
- *Rolling Stone*, Hunter S. Thompson, and gonzo journalism;
- and Watergate, the *Washington Post*, and Woodward and Bernstein.

A generation of Americans who came of age in the decades following World War II assumed the moniker "baby boomers," as the population explosion that ensued with GIs returning from Europe and Asia to build families gave birth to young men and women who shared particular traits. Members of this group were generally born between the early-to-mid 1940s and the early 1960s, and although they shunned conventional labels, baby boomers were often associated with both a rejection and redefinition of traditional values. In making statements about the status quo, they turned to the press—both popular and alternative publications—to express what they saw as a rejection of old values that promoted conformity and conflict, promoting instead ideals of global harmony. (You can find a precedent for these ideas in writers of the transcendentalist movement featured in Chapter 3).

In a moving speech delivered to demonstrators on the Washington Mall in August 28, 1963, Rev. Martin Luther King, Jr., articulated the hope and idealism celebrated by those promoting a new vision of harmony. "I have a Dream that one day this nation will rise up and live out the true meaning of its creed: 'We hold these truths to be self-evident: that all men are created equal,'" he said in a speech televised for national and international audiences. "I have a dream that one day every valley shall be exalted, and every hill and mountain shall be made low, the rough places will be made plain, and the crooked places will be made straight."

Martin Luther King, Jr., "I Have a Dream," August 28, 1963.

With this faith, we will be able to hew out of the mountain of despair a stone of hope. With this faith, we will be able to transform the jangling discords of our nation into a beautiful symphony of brotherhood. With this faith, we will be able to work together, to pray together, to struggle together, to go to jail together, to stand up for freedom together, knowing that we will be free one day.[1]

While regarded as one of the most important speeches communicated in American history, the dream articulated by Dr. King by the end of the decade for many turned into a bitter recognition of problems very difficult to overcome. Moreover, an unprecedented string of assassinations rocked the nation, starting with the murder of President John F. Kennedy just months after King's march on Washington, D.C.

Image 13.1: "John F. Kennedy Motorcade, Dallas, Texas, November 22, 1963," Victor Hugo King, photographer, shows a close-up view of President and Mrs. Kennedy and Texas Governor John Connally and his wife.[2]

Events surrounding the assassination unfolded in nationally televised broadcasts that shocked an entire generation. Then, the national despair over JFK's death deepened in coming years with the assassinations of civil rights leaders Malcolm X (February 21, 1965) and none other than Dr. King himself (April 4, 1968). Finally, the assassination of the president's brother Robert F. Kennedy (June 5, 1968) made it clear that something profoundly wrong had possessed the national spirit, a mood described by journalist Hunter S. Thompson as one of "fear and loathing."[3] This sense combined with a seemingly endless conflict between U.S. forces and communist powers in Vietnam, costing more than 57,000 American lives, appeared regularly in the news reports of the traditional and alternative press.

THE LIVING ROOM WAR

The sense of loss both in idealism and in life affected more than just the baby boomers, as by the late 1960s, scores of young men died each week fighting in Southeast Asia. While Americans had at first generally supported U.S. efforts in Vietnam under the premise that the fight furthered the West's objectives in the Cold War, public confidence eroded with the growing reality of news that contradicted the government's claims of an impending victory.

The news media played a substantial role in this transformation, as reporters delivered daily news stories for the first time in the history of American warfare almost

NEW JOURNALISM AND THE COUNTERCULTURE   211

Image 13.2: "A Man and a Woman Watching Film Footage of the Vietnam War on a Television in Their Living Room," Warren K. Leffler, photographer, published February 13, 1968.[4]

immediately from sites on the other side of the planet, bringing the war to viewers via their television sets. In time, the Vietnam War received the title "The Living Room War," simply because so many of the happenings unfolded for the eyes of the viewing public in their own homes.

The life-and-death drama of real life events during the war as reported by the press contributed to the reputation of at least a few journalists who played more than an indirect role in storytelling, and although no single news story typified the era, a few have stood out historically as significant for press history. One, for example, uncovered crimes committed by commanding officers and troops in ways readers at first found hard to believe. The events of the story began to unfold March 16, 1968, when a division of American troops entered the village of My Lai and killed approximately 500 unarmed men, women, and children. Eyewitness reports indicated that American troops encountered little hostile fire, found virtually no enemy soldiers in the village, and suffered only one casualty, a self-inflicted wound.

Several days after the event, door gunner Ronald L. Ridenhour and pilot Gilbert Honda flew over the site and observed the destruction. Ridenhour had learned about the massacre after speaking with those directly involved. He became convinced that something so disturbing had occurred that he penned his concerns to Congress, catching the attention of select members who then urged Pentagon officials to conduct an investigation. Pictures of the massacre by Ronald Haeberle, an Army photographer, confirmed reports of the deliberate slaughter.

Independent investigative journalist Seymour Hersh (born April 8, 1937), after extensive interviews with Lieutenant William Calley, who carried out the orders to kill the villagers, broke the My Lai story on November 12, 1969, on the Associated Press wire service. On November 20, *Time*, *Life*, and *Newsweek* magazines all covered the story, and CBS televised an interview with Paul Meadlo, a soldier in Calley's unit. In Cleveland, Ohio, the *Plain Dealer* published explicit photographs of dead villagers killed in the massacre.[5]

The press coverage played a direct role in Congressional investigations of one of the worst war crimes committed by the U.S. military in its history. Because of Hersh's ability to go public with an otherwise concealed story, a six-officer jury found Calley guilty of murder. Although the lieutenant received a life sentence, he served only three and a half years under house arrest.[6] Hersh, regardless, won a Pulitzer Prize for his investigative reporting and gained notoriety as "the toughest reporter in America."[7]

At nearly the same time, and among the more widely read feature stories published, *Life* magazine on June 27, 1969, brought to the public faces of the American dead in Vietnam.[8] In a ten-page cover story titled "The Faces of the American Dead in Vietnam: One Week's Toll," the magazine published photos with the names of 242 young men killed in one week. Prior to this issue, the public had ordinarily received information on casualties via newscasts that often used anonymous body counts to depersonalize the dead and avoid a negative public reaction. But the response to the *Life* portraits turned visceral, with some readers expressing amazement that such a presentation had taken so long for the public to see. While other readers expressed outrage that the magazine apparently supported anti-war demonstrators, many simply felt sorrow.

Image 13.3: "Anti-Vietnam War Protest and Demonstration," published January 19, 1968, a photograph showing anti-war demonstrators carrying signs in front of the White House that read, "No More . . . Stop the War!" and "Stop the Draft."[9]

Historians point to the year 1969 as a tipping point in the change in public support for the war in Vietnam, as press accounts began to sour the optimism of an American victory previously held, at least by the older generation. While critics of the press' war coverage claimed negative reporting turned the American public against the war effort and compounded difficulties faced by the armed services at the time, "The Faces of the American Dead in Vietnam" story epitomized the way the media could shape public opinion in a way quite unlike its coverage of previous wars.

In both print and on television, reporters at the time offered first-hand and immediate representations of what happened at a ground level, often in spite of the government's attempts to control information about its maneuvers. However, in efforts to curtail public reaction to scenes such as My Lai, the U.S. government subsequently took measures to distance the press from any direct role in reporting on conflicts. During the outbreak of military actions in the Persian Gulf War, for example, the Pentagon communicated strategic objectives to the American public by placing restrictions on free press coverage. Only select journalists could visit the scenes of military action, and they had to have the military accompany them. Officials claimed national security as a reason for these new policies. Moreover, military actions after the terrorist attacks of September 11, 2001, have created extraordinary challenges for reporters seeking the truth about U.S. war efforts, as the federal government increased its prosecution of those who obtained or released protected information under the Espionage Act.

THE PRESS AND JUDICIAL CHANGE

The way the press reported on the tumultuous cultural issues of the 1960s and 1970s correlated with developments in the legal framework of the nation, as changes in society affected the law and the press accordingly. For starters, two amendments to the Constitution during the period had ties to heavy press coverage of events both at home and overseas, and both more completely democratized the electorate in line with the egalitarian ideals of civil rights demonstrators and the baby boomers alike.

In 1964, the Twenty-Fourth Amendment opened for African Americans in areas of the South still affected by Jim Crow laws more equitable access to voting.[10] The peaceful demonstrations led by Rev. King had sometimes triggered violent reactions from authorities, but in doing so, viewers understood that the status quo could not continue. The Twenty-Fourth Amendment recognized King's call for change and respected the wishes of the President Kennedy, who before he died had called for its ratification.

Another addition to the Constitution, the Twenty-Sixth Amendment, in 1971 lowered the voting age from 21 to 18, empowering a demographic of 18–20 year olds to help decide the commander in chief.[11] News coverage of the war in Vietnam (*Life* magazine's "The Faces of the American Dead in Vietnam," for example) had made it clear that many of the participants who had died fighting it had—under the existing requirements and because of their ages—no right to pick the leaders who had called for them to sacrifice their lives. The new amendment sought to address this disparity, and it received quick ratification in part because of the public visibility of casualties featured on the evening news and in leading publications.

In the same respective years as the ratification of the amendments, two Supreme Court cases opened corresponding opportunities for the press as well. While both cases appeared at first to open new possibilities for the press, in time, their legacies have created unintended consequences, and First Amendment scholars have since studied the implications of the decisions and of how journalists may practice both professionally and ethically in their wake.

The 1964 Supreme Court case *New York Times v. Sullivan* changed standards for establishing libel. L. B. Sullivan, city commissioner in Montgomery, Alabama, had claimed an advertisement in the *New York Times* libeled him, and he sued. A jury initially granted him $500,000 in damages, but the *Times* appealed to the Supreme Court, which ruled that a public figure in a defamation or libel case must prove that the publisher of the statement in question knew that the statement was false or acted in reckless disregard of its truth or falsity. The unanimous court argued that debate on public issues should be "uninhibited, robust, and wide-open" and that a "public official" may not recover damages for defamatory falsehood unless the statement was made with "actual malice" or with "reckless disregard" of the truth.[12]

On the fiftieth anniversary of the Supreme Court's ruling in the *Times v. Sullivan* case, the *New York Times* published an editorial about the case, laying out the rationale for the Court's decision and reflecting on press freedoms since the ruling. The editorial described the decision as "the clearest and most forceful defense of press freedom in American history."

> "The Uninhibited Press, 50 Years Later"
>
> The ruling was revolutionary, because the court for the first time rejected virtually any attempt to squelch criticism of public officials—even if false—as antithetical to "the central meaning of the First Amendment." Today, our understanding of freedom of the press comes in large part from the Sullivan case. Its core observations and principles remain unchallenged, even as the Internet has turned everyone into a worldwide publisher—capable of calling public officials instantly to account for their actions, and also of ruining reputations with the click of a mouse.[13]

While the *Times v. Sullivan* case still allows members of the press to write freely about public figures, including politicians and celebrities—with little fear of retribution, it has also allowed for abuses by unethical writers seeking to make sensational headlines. No doubt, the Court likely had no intention of encouraging reckless publications, but when it comes to public figures, virtually any kind of allegation could subsequently go into print. As a result, anyone who seeks office puts their reputation at risk, likely keeping otherwise capable members of society from participating in high-profile positions. To make matters worse, contemporary talk show hosts, bloggers, and social media users have since sometimes spread ugly lies about and caused without consequence to themselves media consumers to look on their leaders with unjustified suspicion.

Then in 1971, the Supreme Court made another famous decision that reestablished the limits of government interference in press operations. In *New York Times Co. v. United States*, 403 U.S. 713 (or, the Pentagon Papers case, as it was called), the Court determined the press had a right to publish materials without prior restraint from the government. The material, titled "United States–Vietnam Relations, 1945–1967: A Study Prepared by the Department of Defense," contained sensitive information about U.S. activities in Southeast Asia dating back to the 1940s. More specifically, the papers revealed that the U.S. had secretly enlarged the scale of the Vietnam War with the bombings of nearby Cambodia and Laos, coastal raids on North Vietnam, and Marine Corps attacks, none of which the mainstream media reported.

The battle over publication of the contents of the files began after Pentagon insider Daniel Ellsberg leaked classified information to newspapers. After release of the first installment of these documents in the *New York Times* on June 13, 1971, U.S. Attorney General John Mitchell warned the newspaper against further publication, and on June 15, the federal government won an injunction to stop additional publication of the. On June 30, 1971, U.S. Supreme Court lifted the prior restraints in a 6–3 vote. For his disclosure of the Pentagon Papers, Ellsberg faced charges of conspiracy, espionage, and theft of government property, but prosecutors had the charges dropped when they discovered that the staff members in the Nixon White House had engaged in unlawful efforts to discredit him.

Similar to the *Times v. Sullivan* case, members of the press heralded the Pentagon Papers decision as reestablishing the role of the Fourth Estate in checking the activities of the government on behalf of the public. Indeed—as we will see later in this chapter—the press engaged in investigative reporting soon thereafter with the understanding that the government could impose no "prior restraint" on publication of documents of public interest.

However, the Pentagon Papers case, similar to *Times v. Sullivan*, also opened consequences unanticipated for members of the press. Floyd Abrams, a counselor for the *Times* during the lawsuit, later published his thoughts on the case and recognized the "limited and troubling nature" of the victory. The Court left open the possibility of imposing prior restraints and criminal sanctions in other cases, he wrote, and the possibility of criminal prosecutions after publication had hardly encouraged editors to act in bold ways.[14]

GOING GONZO

While the counterculture movement of the 1960s had a wide-ranging scope that evolved over a decade and did not start with any single event, particular people and publications epitomized to a certain extent its general scope, at least as reflected for a media audience. Among the most widely read magazines among baby boomers who turned on to an alternative lifestyle of rock music, psychedelic drugs, and revolutionary politics, *Rolling Stone*, first published November 5, 1967, celebrated values shunned by the older generation.

Jann Wenner, co-founder and publisher of the magazine, had studied at Berkeley but dropped out after meeting Ralph J. Gleason (March 1, 1917–June 3, 1975), a music critic for the *San Francisco Chronicle*. The two, inspired to tap into a wave of interest in rock and roll music as a legitimate art form, helped found *Rolling Stone*. Wenner borrowed $7,500 from family members and his fiancé Jane Schindelheim to start the magazine.

The debut issue featured a photo of Beatles singer and songwriter John Lennon on the cover, which instantly conveyed to readers that *Rolling Stone* would promote a mix of music, politics, and drugs, with which Lennon had developed a reputation. He made several other appearances on the front of the magazine, notably a nude one with his wife Yoko Ono on the November 23, 1968, issue, which at the time pushed the limits of obscenity laws, as in parts of the country, the image was considered pornographic. By far Lennon's most famous appearance on the cover of *Rolling Stone* was newsworthy in its own right. Having come to symbolize the values of the baby boomers, staff photographer Annie Liebovitz took the photo December 8, 1980, with Ono clothed and Lennon nude, embracing her and apparently kissing her goodbye. Later that very day, a deranged follower shot Lennon dead, triggering mournful demonstrations across the globe. The American Society of Magazine Editors (ASME) later identified Liebovitz's strangely prophetic phot as the top magazine cover from the past forty years.[15]

ANNIE LEIBOVITZ

Annie Leibovitz was born in Waterbury, Connecticut on October 2, 1949, and she found her passion for photography during studies at the San Francisco Art Institute. Her first break in photography came in 1970 when she applied for *Rolling Stone*. An exceptional photo of counterculture writer Allen Ginsberg had impressed editor Jann Wenner and landed her a staff photographer position with the magazine. Her work at *Rolling Stone* had the common characteristics of bold primary colors and surprising poses, and for many in the recording industry, appearing on the cover of the magazine in the form of a Liebovitz portrait held a certain status symbol. In 1983, she joined *Vanity Fair* as the first contributing photographer for the magazine, producing portraits of celebrities including Demi Moore naked and holding her pregnant belly, which after her *Rolling Stone* cover of John Lennon and Yoko Ono was named second best cover from the past forty years. Her portraits have appeared in *Vogue*, the *New York Times Magazine*, and the *New Yorker*. In 2000, the Library of Congress named her a "Living Legend."[16]

While *Rolling Stone* in its early issues reported on issues of interest to the counterculture of the late 1960s, it distanced itself from radical publications and embraced relatively traditional journalistic standards. Wenner had written in the inaugural issue that *Rolling Stone* was "not just about the music, but about the things and attitudes that music embraces." Indeed, the magazine's most celebrated contributors wrote very little about music and instead provided a purely unconventional perspective on the culture and climate of the time. Using a style later dubbed "gonzo," Hunter S. Thompson, perhaps more than any other figure, put *Rolling Stone* on the cultural—or, as it was, the countercultural—map.

As a re-incarnation of the new journalism first launched by John Hersey's *Hiroshima* in 1946, Thompson's style of immersive reporting took first-hand experiences to an extreme. While steeped in the style that made for clear reading and compelling narrative, Thompson rejected many of the standard conventions that had restricted publishing to a formal endeavor. In many of his most widely read pieces—a number of them premiering in *Rolling Stone*—Thompson himself (and not the subject he was supposedly covering) was the story, a radical departure from the kind of third-person objectivity commonly found in the traditional press. While journalists of the era including Tom Wolfe, Lester Bangs, and George Plimpton practiced gonzo style, Thompson perfected it, using drugs and alcohol as a means for breaking down boundaries of perception.

DEFINING "GONZO"

The first identifiable use of term gonzo had come from *Boston Globe* reporter Bill Cardoso, who, after reading Thompson's The Kentucky Derby is Decadent and Depraved (1970) proclaimed, "That is pure Gonzo!"[17] According to Cardoso, gonzo describes the last man standing in a drinking marathon, most commonly used among South Boston's Irish drinkers. Gonzo journalism has since grown in definition to describe a style of reporting that mixes fiction and factual journalism. It uses a highly subjective style that often includes the reporter as part of the story via a first-person narrative and events being exaggerated in order to emphasize the underlying message and is considered to be part of the new journalism movement. Gonzo journalism tends to favor style over accuracy and aims to describe personal experiences or the essence or mood of things rather than facts. It disregards the edited product favored by newspaper media and strives for the gritty factor. Use of quotes, sarcasm, humor, exaggeration, and even profanity is common. The use of gonzo journalism illustrates the concept that journalism can be truthful without striving for objectivity. The style uses an energetic first-person participatory language in which the author is a protagonist and draws power from social critiques and satire. While traditional journalism relies on a detached style of fact-based reporting, gonzo journalism focuses on reports of personal experiences and feeling.

Hunter Stockton Thompson (July 18, 1937–February 20, 2005), a self-taught high school dropout, had already made a name for himself as a daredevil journalist. With varied stints as a reporter for newspapers while in his 20s, he used a typewriter to copy F. Scott Fitzgerald's *The Great Gatsby* and Ernest Hemingway's *A Farewell to Arms* in order to master the style of clean and concise writing. In 1965, Carey McWilliams, editor of *The Nation*, hired Thompson to write a story about the Hells Angels motorcycle club in California, which a *New York Times* reviewer described as an "angry, knowledgeable, fascinating, and excitedly written book."[18]

Thompson first came to the attention of Wenner in the early 1970s when the editor thought *Rolling Stone* would have a place for him with a piece about the Mint 400 motorcycle race in the Las Vegas desert, as Thompson had received an assignment from *Sports Illustrated* to write a 250-word photograph caption on the event. Although the initial assignment had basic instructions, Thompson turned his experiences into a modern classic, delving deep into the zeitgeist of the time to produce a scathing and epic critique of the American Dream.

Sports Illustrated rejected the 2,500-word screed submitted by Thompson, but *Rolling Stone* published it as a two-part series first appearing in November 1971. Published as a book in 1972, *Fear and Loathing in Las Vegas* describes two characters, Raoul Duke and Dr. Gonzo, coming to terms with the failure of the countercultural movement. Using Las Vegas as a backdrop for a search of the myth that hard work leads to material success, Duke and Gonzo find that the "fear and loathing" of the 1960s have destroyed the sense of optimism that had launched the decade.

In a passage from *Fear and Loathing in Las Vegas*, known as "the wave speech" and recognized as one of Thompson's finest pieces of writing, he distilled clearly, concisely, and poignantly the optimism of baby boomers and the eventual collapse of the counterculture movement.

> "The Wave Speech," [excerpt], *Fear and Loathing in Las Vegas* (1972)
>
> There was a fantastic universal sense that whatever we were doing was right, that we were winning. And that, I think, was the handle—that sense of inevitable victory over the forces of Old and Evil. Not in any mean or military sense; we didn't need that. Our energy would simply prevail. There was no point in fighting—on our side or theirs. We had all the momentum; we were riding the crest of a high and beautiful wave. So now, less than five years later, you can go up on a steep hill in Las Vegas and look West, and with the right kind of eyes you can almost see the high-water mark—that place where the wave finally broke and rolled back.[19]

While Thompson continued to produce work for a variety of publications in the years following *Fear and Loathing in Las Vegas*, his later writings rarely tapped the same nerve as his commentary on the state of the national psyche in 1972. He developed a cult following of readers who celebrated his penchant for drug use, but in the end, he apparently succumbed to years of substance abuse and committed suicide at his home in Colorado on February 20, 2005. His contributions to journalism as a writer who used an innovative reporting style rank him, in the words of his son, as "a grand master of the written word and one of the great writers of the twentieth century."[20]

REPORTING THE WATERGATE SCANDAL

Combining the *Times v. Sullivan* and Pentagon Papers cases with the general sense of discontent—or "fear and loathing," as Thompson had put it—the circumstances of the era provided a context ripe for a journalistic breakthrough. In a case of reporting still heralded as one of the great investigative works of the twentieth century, staff at the *Washington Post* uncovered an explosive scandal that rocked the highest levels of government, ultimately leading to the resignation of Richard Nixon, the thirty-seventh president of the United States.

Nixon had won the 1968 presidential election in the midst of the turmoil that had shaped the baby boomers. In 1972, he won re-election in a landslide, carrying every state except Massachusetts. He had promised to bring "peace with honor" in concluding the Vietnam War, and his re-election signaled for many a refutation of the civil unrest that had brought regular reminders of generations within the nation at war with one another.

Shortly after his re-election, however, the *Washington Post* published the first in a series of reports alleging a criminal conspiracy that involved his administration's attempt to cover up covert activities. The initial violations included the bugging of the Democratic National Committee's headquarters at the Watergate Hotel in Washington, D.C. (hence the moniker "Watergate" for the scandal) to obtain information on Democratic candidates in the 1972 elections. By the time the *Post*'s reports on the activities ended, information presented to the public focused on a money trail (see Chapter 7 for classic muckrakers) that led to the Oval Office and suggested Nixon had attempted to cover up a host of illegal activities.

Relying heavily upon anonymous sources, *Post* reporters Bob Woodward and Carl Bernstein uncovered information that the upper reaches of the Justice Department, FBI, CIA, and the White House all had knowledge of the break-in and participated in attempts to cover it up. Chief among the *Post*'s anonymous sources was an individual whom Woodward and Bernstein had nicknamed "Deep Throat"—in 2005, William Mark Felt, Sr., deputy director of the FBI at the time, came forward to reveal his identity as this source. Felt had met secretly with Woodward several times to provide leads while warning him the investigation had enormous implications.

With access to FBI reports on the burglary investigation, Felt could confirm or deny what other sources were telling the *Post* reporters. Woodward had agreed to keep the identity of his source secret, and in doing so, secured several scoops. For starters, the *Post* disclosed that Attorney General John Mitchell controlled a secret fund that financed a campaign to gather information on the Democrats. Moreover, Nixon aides had run a massive campaign of spying and sabotage to help secure his reelection. Woodward and Bernstein also interviewed Nixon's bookkeeper, Judy Hoback Miller, who revealed to them information about the mishandling of funds and the destruction of records.

KEY FIGURES AT THE *WASHINGTON POST* DURING THE WATERGATE SCANDAL

Robert Upshur Woodward: Bob Woodward was born on March 26, 1943, in Geneva, Illinois. In 1972, he first worked with *Washington Post* colleague Carl Bernstein. While Woodward enjoyed a certain amount of fame for his endeavors in the 1970s, he has continued work as a reporter and associate editor at the *Post*, leading a team to a Pulitzer Prize for coverage of the September 11, 2001, terrorist attacks on the United States.

> Carl Bernstein: Born February 14, 1944, Bernstein started his career at the age of 16 as a copy boy for the *Washington Star*. The *Washington Post* hired him in 1966. Bernstein had a reputation for aggressively pursuing the truth. After the reporting of the Watergate scandal, Bernstein continued work in print and broadcast. He makes regular appearances in the media in open forums, reporting to the public.
>
> Benjamin Bradlee: Ben Bradlee (August 26, 1921–October 21, 2014) was executive editor of the *Washington Post* from 1968 to 1991. He became a national figure when he challenged the federal government over the right to publish the Pentagon Papers and oversaw the publication stories documenting the Watergate scandal. In the years preceding his death, he held the title of vice president at-large of the *Post*.
>
> Katharine Meyer Graham: Katherine Graham (June 16, 1917–July 17, 2001) led the *Washington Post* for more than two decades as publisher, overseeing Watergate coverage. Her memoir, *Personal History*, won the Pulitzer Prize in 1998. Her husband Philip Graham, who preceded her as publisher, popularized the notion of journalism as "the first rough draft of history" (see the Introduction to this book).

While polls at the time indicated distrust of the media had risen above 40 percent among the public, Nixon and top officials had discussed using government agencies to retaliate against media organizations they perceived as hostile to the administration.[21] However, press representatives continually pointed to the fact that most of the reporting on the Watergate scandal had turned out to be accurate.

Responding to the regular exposures of illicit activities at virtually all levels of the executive branch, Nixon asked for the resignations of high-ranking aides H. R. Haldeman and John Ehrlichman, who later received prison sentences for their involvement in the cover-up. However, President Nixon himself faced increasing scrutiny for his involvement in the attempts to conceal activities, and on February 6, 1974, the U.S. House approved a resolution that initiated impeachment proceedings. Throughout the summer, the House Judiciary Committee recommended impeachment on charges of obstruction of justice, abuse of power, and contempt of Congress. Nixon denied criminal wrongdoing, but the release of a recording between him and Haldeman on June 23, 1972, dubbed the "smoking gun," forced his hand. The conversation revealed that Nixon had ordered a cover-up of the Watergate break-in and that he ordered the FBI to abandon its investigation of the matter.

In light of his loss of political support and the near-certainty that he faced removal from office, Nixon addressed the nation with a farewell broadcast August 8, 1974, saying he chose to resign because his impasse with Congress and the lack of public support made his role untenable. The president's aides Ehrlichman and Haldeman had tried unsuccessfully to get Nixon to grant them pardons, which he had promised them before their April 1973 resignations, but they later received sentences along with

Image 13.4: "Nixon," Edmund S. Valtman, artist, created 1970, a caricature of President Richard M. Nixon with folded hands, seated before a microphone in front of an American flag and making one of his talks to the American people about the Watergate scandal.[22]

several other conspirators. On August 9, 1974, President Nixon resigned due in many respects to the relentless reporting of Woodward and Bernstein, which Gene Roberts, former managing editor of the *New York Times*, praised as "maybe the single greatest reporting effort of all time."[23] The pair earned a Pulitzer Prize for their work, while their non-fiction account of their reporting, *All the President's Men* (Simon and Schuster, 1974), remains a classic story for aspiring journalists and readers of all kinds.

In the wake of Nixon's resignation, public appreciation for the work of Woodward and Bernstein made itself known with a dramatic increase in enrollment in journalism schools across the nation. Take for example news of this trend in the *Time* magazine article "The Press: The J-School Explosion," published November 11, 1974. "Would-be Woodwards and Bernsteins are queuing up for the nation's 213 undergraduate and graduate journalism programs in unprecedented numbers," the *Time* article begins. "Though overall enrollments are beginning to recede from their baby boomers' peaks, journalism education flourishes as never before."

> One reason for the J-school boom is the press's role in Watergate. Says Buck Harvey, 23, editor of the University of Texas' *Daily Texan*, "Journalism is one of the few professions that require integrity. The pay is small. But that doesn't bother me, because you don't have to put up a facade." Prior to the scandal, the old images of tough muckrakers and dashing foreign correspondents had faded. Now some of the glamour is back. . . . What is happening is that Watergate has persuaded many students that journalism is an exciting, socially valuable occupation.[24]

A revitalized interest in the Fourth Estate triggered a new wave of academic classes, and newly trained professionals focused on reporting techniques that had fallen in some cases to the wayside. To this day, contemporary students in journalism courses—yes, even the students reading this particular book—can thank Woodward and Bernstein for demonstrating the level of professionalism expected of the press, especially when reporting on political matters.

RECAPPING THIS CHAPTER

Looking back on this chapter, you should see how the press in the 1960s and 1970s popularized protests associated with the Vietnam War and other ideas of the baby boomer generation via mainstream outlets and popular magazines. It featured a sample of countercultural journalism, as practiced by Hunter S. Thompson's style of gonzo storytelling. It juxtaposed this new journalism with the groundbreaking—yet at the same time relatively traditional—reporting at the *Washington Post* that exposed the Watergate scandal.

Using materials from this chapter, you should understand how different forms of storytelling serve different purposes. You should have an understanding of how cultural and political issues addressed by the press during the 1960s and 1970s produced a lasting effect on subsequent generations. You should be able to explain why press historians often cite Woodward and Bernstein as exemplary members of the Fourth Estate.

The following chapter describes how media and corporations acted both independently and interdependently to create a kind of storytelling that requires attention to multimedia and advertising constraints.

NOTES

1. Martin Luther King, Jr., "I Have a Dream," Speech, Lincoln Memorial, Washington, DC, August 28, 1963.
2. "John F. Kennedy Motorcade," Library of Congress, accessed June 11, 2016, <item/2004676894>.
3. Hunter S. Thompson, *Proud Highway: Saga of a Desperate Southern Gentleman, 1955–1967* (New York: Balantine), xxi.

4 "A Man and a Woman Watching Film Footage," Library of Congress, accessed May 16, 2016, <item/2011661230>.
5 "Cameraman Saw GIs Slay 100 Villagers," *Cleveland Plain Dealer*, November 20, 1969.
6 "Court Material of William L. Calley, Jr.," *Instructions from the Military Judge to the Court Members in United States vs. First Lieutenant William L. Calley, Jr*, 1971, accessed May 3, 2016, <law2.umkc.edu>.
7 Joe Eszterhas, "The Toughest Reporter in America," *Rolling Stone*, April 24, 1972: 72.
8 "The Faces of the American Dead in Vietnam," *Life Magazine*, June 27, 1969, Library of Congress, accessed May 3, 2016, <time.com>.
9 "Anti-Vietnam War Protest and Demonstration," Library of Congress, accessed May 16, 2016, <item/2010646065>.
10 "The Constitution of the United States," Amendment 24.
11 "The Constitution of the United States," Amendment 26.
12 *New York Times Co. v. Sullivan*, 376 U.S. 254 (1964).
13 "The Uninhibited Press, 50 Years Later," *The New York Times*, March 8, 2014.
14 Floyd Abrams, "The Pentagon Papers a Decade Later," *The New York Times*, June 7, 1981.
15 ASME's Top 40 Magazine Covers of the Last 40 Years, "#1 *Rolling Stone* (January 22, 1981)," accessed July 4, 2017, <magazine.org/asme/magazine-cover-contests/asmes-top-40-magazine-covers-last-40-years>.
16 "Annie Liebovitz—Living Legend," Library of Congress, accessed August 5, 2017, <loc.gov/about/awards-and-honors/living-legends/annie-leibovitz>.
17 Bill Cardoso, quoted in Martin Hirst, *What Is Gonzo? The Etymology of an Urban Legend*, unpublished paper (St. Lucia: The University of Queensland, 2004), 5.
18 Eliot Fremont-Smith, "Motorcycle Misfits—Fiction and Fact," *The New York Times*, February 23, 1967, 33.
19 "Fear and Loathing in Las Vegas," *Rolling Stone*, November 11, 1971, accessed July 16, 2017, <rollingstone.com/politics/news/fear-and-loathing-in-las-vegas-19711111>.
20 Juan F. Thompson, *Stories I Tell Myself* (New York: Knopf, 2016), xii.
21 "Covering Watergate: Success and Backlash," *Time*, 104, 2 (July 8, 1974): 74.
22 "Nixon," Library of Congress, accessed May 16, 2016, <item/2002709653>.
23 Gene Roberts, quoted in Roy J. Harris, *Pulitzer's Gold: Behind the Prize for Public Service Journalism* (Columbia, MO: University of Missouri Press), 233.
24 "The Press: The J-School Explosion," *Time*, 104, 20 (November 11, 1974): 9, 10.

14

THE PRESS AND THE MAKING OF MODERN MEDIA

This chapter shows ways the press and media corporations have acted both independently and interdependently to create a kind of storytelling that requires simultaneous attention to multimedia production values and the constraints of advertising:

- It explains the reasons why contemporary mass media tends to focus on soft news, or "infotainment," more than hard news;
- and it describes the growth of what media analysts describe as a media monopoly, a phenomenon that has created difficulties in both maintaining journalistic standards and regulation of institutional practices.

Using materials from this chapter, students should be able to explain how media have evolved with trends in technology into transnational organizations:

- They should have an understanding of the challenges in reporting stories using traditional techniques in this new climate;
- and they should be able to explain how corporate ownership of news outlets affects the content produced by journalists.

Key words, names, and phrases associated with Chapter 14 include:

- "The Media Monopoly" (Ben Bagdikian) and transnational conglomerates;
- Henry Luce, Clare Boothe Luce, and the rise of Time Warner;
- hard news versus soft news in the contemporary media landscape;
- and the Federal Communications Commission (FCC) and net neutrality.

As we have seen throughout this book, journalistic practices commonly rely on the successes of their predecessors. Likewise, a number of the practices in contemporary media have emerged from eras that preceded the contemporary climate in which the Internet now dominates as a source of information. At the same time, changing economic, technological, and societal demands have required journalists to follow new configurations in a rapidly evolving media landscape. Moreover, the structure of modern media corporations has greatly affected the creation of stories, with the difference on the content production side coming primarily from demands to meet advertising and the features of multimedia packages.

We can identify the emergence of contemporary media with the dissemination of Internet use via increased access to the World Wide Web in the final years of the twentieth century; however, the roots of changes we see in the structure of media production preceded the Web by several decades. Our exposure to constant, breaking news, for example, emerged with the moment-by-moment news cycle introduced by cable news programs in the 1990s. Likewise, the media's emphasis on soft news preceded both the Internet and cable media by decades, as newsmakers have often used it to attract audiences, sales, and ratings.

We can also see that contemporary media for a number of reasons have included visual components to illustrate news stories to a much larger degree than did their print predecessors. Video, pictures, and interactive media have demonstrated their effectiveness in engaging readers and thereby building audiences. In turn, the kind of content that draws audiences to particular outlets generally focuses on entertainment, a formula that has fueled the growth of many of the largest and most successful media companies of our age.

Finally, while we can marvel at the sheer scope of any one of the major media companies that now dominate the production of news and entertainment, the problems entailed by their size now go well beyond the jurisdiction of any domestic governing body. Ida Tarbell (see Chapter 9) might ask, after all, how would the government regulate a company that operates both inside the jurisdiction of U.S. anti-trust laws and on an international scale outside of them?

THE NEW MEDIA LANDSCAPE

A recognition of the size of modern media can start, at least indirectly, with a story rooted very much in hard news. Returning for a moment to the Pentagon Papers case (see Chapter 13), an assistant editor at the *Washington Post* at the time, Ben Bagdikian, emerged from the event as a critic of not only the government's control over information but also, in time, the media's dominance over information that belonged to the public. Bagdikian, who persuaded the *Post* to publish the once-classified papers, left his position and in 1983 wrote *The Media Monopoly*, a now famous exposé of big media. At the time of Bagdikian's initial observations, about fifty companies owned the majority of the media. He claimed that the number of owners, which had decreased dramatically over the course of U.S. press history, would lead to a problem of monopolization, which harmed the interests of the American public and ran contrary to the core principles of the First Amendment.

Image 14.1: "Media Position," Maria La Vigna, photographer, published August 13, 1983, included in the photograph is Carl Fleischhauer at a 1983 Omaha powwow in Macy, Nebraska.[1]

Critics initially dismissed Bagdikian's observations as alarmist, but only a decade after publication of the first edition of *The Media Monopoly*, media ownership had shrunk to half of the first reported numbers. Today, less than a dozen corporations dominate the media industry, with the evolution of this trend placing 90 percent of the media in the hands of a few content providers and the decision makers for these corporations now determining what kinds of information reach consumers on widely distributed channels.[2]

> ### BEN BAGDIKIAN AND *THE MEDIA MONOPOLY*
>
> Among Ben Bagdikian's notable contributions to journalism included his book *The Media Monopoly*. First published in 1983, the book allowed Bagdikian to make the case that contemporary media operates as "an oligopoly, the rule of a few in which any one of those few, acting alone, can alter market conditions" (*The New Media Monopoly*, 2004, 5). Bagdikian first rose to prominence after joining the *Washington Post* in 1970, later serving as its assistant managing editor. In June 1971, he met with Daniel Ellsberg, who supplied the Post with 4,000 pages of the Pentagon Papers (see Chapter 13). Bagdikian argued in favor of publication of the documents, arguing the public had a right to know about government activities. He became the second ombudsman of the *Post* in 1972, but

he left the paper after disputes with Ben Bradlee, executive editor, over internal and external complaints about management. Bagdikian taught journalism ethics courses at the University of California, Berkeley, between 1976 and 1990, and served as dean of the UC Berkeley Graduate School of Journalism from 1985 to 1988, earning an honorary title upon departure. Critics first considered *The Media Monopoly*, published during his UC tenure, as overly alarming, but it has since received support for its analysis of the troublesome nature of journalism when practiced under the control of large, corporate interests. *The New Media Monopoly*—published as the seventh edition of the original—described contemporary corporations and their leaders as having "more communications power than was exercised by any despot or dictatorship in history" (Bagdikian, 2004, 3). Bagdikian died March 11, 2016, in Berkley, California. While controversial for his original analyses, he left a legacy as "probably the most quoted, certainly one of the most acute, commentators on media ownership."[3]

While the number of corporations in control of media-related subsidies changes from time to time based on acquisitions, mergers and splits, the most powerful names associated with ownership (at least through the end of 2017) include Time Warner, Disney, News Corporation, Bertelsmann (Germany), and Viacom (formerly CBS).[4] Among a select group of others media giants, the NBC Television Network and NBC Universal Media, and Thomson Reuters top lists of content providers. Newcomers to this list of media giants include Alphabet, the holding company owning Google; ZenithOptimedia, which owns the media networks of Disney, such as ABC; and Comcast, which owns fifteen national cable networks and Hulu.[5]

Until the beginning of the twenty-first century, owners focused on acquiring traditional media outlets, but recent acquisitions demonstrate the importance of new media (or "social media") companies as well. The effect of acquisitions registers in a number of ways, including the consolidation and elimination of media-related jobs. These expectations in turn have resulted in demands for fewer employees to exercise more skills, sometimes described as multi-tasking, for relatively larger companies—certainly a challenge for new journalists entering the media landscape of the twenty-first century.

The increased growth of each media outlet, often fueled by technological innovations, contributes to these pressures. As companies attempt to exercise control over a wider range of media platforms, they face increasingly tight budgets and competition, which in turn—given the space and time constraints of contemporary media, as well as the demand for a constant supply of breaking news—has produced effects on media as a whole, from online content to broadcast and newspapers.[6] Traditional companies in general focused their efforts on providing specialized services, but larger ones now produce a wide range of services that require employees to demonstrate skills in a number of individual and interrelated skills. A new hire at any number of media organizations might need to show, for example, that they can write, edit, and produce content that includes multimedia features, such as visual elements, links to additional materials on the Web, video, and audio content, all as parts of the same package.

In the end, a single corporation that controls dozens of subsidiaries can play a major role in determining the kinds of stories produced. For example, The Walt Disney Company owns the ABC Television Group, ESPN Inc., and Vice Media. If Disney—for whatever reason—played a role in producing a particular news story about the company on any given day (and given its size and power, a likelihood exists), its subsidiaries would out of self-interest cover Disney in only a positive light. Alternatively, if the news brings attention to problems associated with Disney or any of its affiliates, the heads of these outlets may simply decide not to cover it—the same of course applies to any other large company. Time Warner, which for the moment owns CNN, might likewise exert either direct or indirect pressure on its news outlet to suppress negative news stories about the parent company's activities and instead promote other outlets associated with Time Warner.

While these generic scenarios apply to conglomerates in general, they do have real effects, as examples from the world of "traditional" journalism can demonstrate. Consider for example the role that General Electric (GE) played in the delivery of news after it acquired NBC in the late 1980s. In 1987, NBC broadcast a documentary that promoted nuclear power. GE had an interest in the success of the documentary, as it supplied parts and technology for nuclear power plants. The documentary won a Westinghouse-sponsored prize for science journalism, but Westinghouse Electric Company also builds nuclear power stations. Shortly after the screening of the documentary, nuclear power plants in France had accidents that jeopardized the safety of citizens. NBC did not report the story, although some U.S. newspapers did.[7]

News organizations have had longstanding explicit or implicit codes of conduct for employees—more specifically, journalists—as reporters produce work not only for the public but also for their editors and producers. These codes of conduct ensure a level of professionalism in the production of news, but they also sometimes create pressures that run contrary to the principles of the First Amendment. According to surveys, about 1 in 5 reporters indicated they faced criticism or pressure from their bosses after producing or writing stories seen as damaging to their company's financial interests—a form of censorship that has hindered the press from focusing on news at the expense of their respective audiences.[8]

THE FOURTH ESTATE REVISITED

As members of the Fourth Estate, journalists by definition must seek to produce stories that share facts and do not falsely claim that an opinion or biased version of the truth passes as news. With many individual outlets no longer reporting news but instead quite often presenting it in accordance with their own preferences and prejudices, the most prevalent ethical issues faced by modern journalists are how to continue informing the public while meeting business demands, avoiding plagiarism, and doing diligent research. A well-informed citizenry can expect members of the Fourth Estate to practice fair, balanced, transparent, and inclusive journalism—expectations rooted in the best practices of traditional media but shaped by the ways the economy, technology, and society affect it. The media lacks transparency when major corporations are intentionally omitting stories or having them written in a specific way to deceive the public. For these reasons, aspiring press members should take to heart guidelines established by the American Press Institute, which hold that journalism practiced correctly provides citizens with information necessary for them to make "the best possible decisions about their lives, their communities, their societies, and their governments."[9]

Maintaining a level of ethical journalism also ensures that audiences of all types will receive information based in accuracy and fairness and that the media exercises honest and courageous newsgathering and the reporting and interpreting of fact-based information.[10] Considering the United States as a diverse collection of demographics, views, and beliefs, journalists across an array of platforms cannot please every member of their audience; however, they must still remember that their work extends well beyond national borders and has audiences throughout the world. "The story everywhere is one of an uphill struggle," writes Aidan White, director of the Ethical Journalism Network. "Corruption and cynicism inside newsrooms saps the confidence of media staff leading to crumbling levels of commitment to ethics, a lowering of the status of journalistic work and a pervasive lack of transparency over advertising, ownership, and corporate and political affiliations."[11] These realties entail extraordinary challenges, and only the best practitioners in the industry will succeed.

In another example, the CBS News Division encountered a conflict when CBS Corporate prevented the airing of a 1995 story that detailed a public health risk. Jeffery Wigand, a former executive for the Brown & Williamson tobacco company, had provided information to Lowell Bergman, a producer for the popular *60 Minutes* news program, documenting ways the tobacco industry had systematically hidden the health risks of their cigarettes.[12]

MIKE WALLACE

Television journalist Mike Wallace, born in 1918 in Brookline, Massachusetts, found fame primarily for his work on the CBS program *60 Minutes*. In the 1960s, he became a full-time correspondent for CBS. In 1968, the network asked him to co-host *60 Minutes*, a leading prime-time news show. Wallace's role included the exposure of fraud and corruption, and he mastered a style of reporting described as "ambush journalism" in which he used hidden cameras to approach an interview subject without warning. He developed a reputation for asking challenging

> questions and interviewed world leaders, including Ronald Reagan, John F. Kennedy, Richard Nixon, Vladimir Putin, and Ayatollah Khomeini, using a confrontational style of questioning. The 1999 Touchstone movie *The Insider* portrayed Wallace's role in the fiasco surrounding Brown & Williamson tobacco as leaving him bitter about CBS's management of the news division, but he continued with a role at *60 Minutes* until 2006, making occasional appearances thereafter.[13] He died April 7, 2012.

Bergman began developing a report for *60 Minutes* correspondent Mike Wallace to deliver using the inside information, but he ran into opposition from Don Hewitt, who had originally created the series, along with CBS lawyers, who feared a lawsuit from Brown & Williamson. CBS's financial interests took precedent over the public's right to know, and the company's executives prevented it from airing. The *Wall Street Journal* instead broke Wigand's story, and the incident damaged the reputation of CBS news.[14] As the fiasco surrounding *60 Minutes* and Brown & Williamson demonstrated, big media owe a debt to their stakeholders, as the airing of the tobacco exposé would have jeopardized an intended merger between CBS and Westinghouse, along with the interests of CBS's stockholders and advertisers.

As one of the long-term consequences of such conflicts, journalists and reporters have increasingly turned to the already popular genre of soft or features news to communicate their messages. Researchers have documented how soft news over the past two decades has indeed grown in its prevalence over hard news with a demonstrable rise in sensational content and less time-bound stories of practical value. They note that news stories with no clear connection to policy issues have nearly doubled since 1980, and hard news stories have declined by a corresponding degree on local and national levels. This evidence suggests that soft news and critical journalism have diminished public's interest in politics and affected the very nature of the American electoral system.[15]

MAKING A MEDIA EMPIRE

What we have subsequently read, seen, heard, or understood as news in the current media age has demonstrated the conflicts of individual companies with stakeholders on a much grander scale. Advertising constraints have defined more narrowly the kinds of content journalists can produce, pulling them away from the kinds of hard-hitting news formerly covered by the traditional press.[16] As a result, soft news and entertainment have grown as favorite commodities among major media companies, contributing to what media analysts have described as "infotainment," a form of communication that both informs and entertains.

Large media companies generally promote this content, but for illustrative purposes, we can look at one in particular, Time Warner, as a model for the new media industry. The multimedia giant grew from the establishment of *Time* magazine, an influential news publication first produced by Henry Luce. Born on April 3, 1898, Luce established himself as among the most prominent, prolific, and important figures in the history of journalism. On March 3, 1923, he published with Yale classmate Briton Hadden the first issue of *Time*, which summarized and interpreted weekly news and reached a circulation of 200,000 in its first five years. (In November 2017, the Meredith Corporation, an American media conglomerate, bought *Time* for $2.8 billion).[17]

Upon Hadden's unexpected death in 1929, Luce launched *Fortune* magazine, which explored the area of business. He later acquired *Life*, a picture magazine of politics, culture, and society that dominated American visuals in a period prior to the popularity of television. Among his most notable editorials for *Life* included a February 1941 piece titled "The American Century" that exhorted Americans to recognize their role as leaders in a global economy.[18] After World War II, Luce continued to advocate U.S. global dominance. In the *Time* essay "Struggle for Survival" (1948), he urged Americans to take offense in the Cold War against the Soviet Union.[19] He continued to expand

Image 14.2: "Clare Boothe Luce, U.S. Ambassador to Italy, and Husband, Publisher Henry Luce, Arriving at Idlewild Airport, New York, New York," a *World Telegram & Sun* photo by Phil Stanziola, published 1954.[20]

his publishing empire, and by the 1960s made Time Inc. the most successful publishing empire in the world. He died of a heart attack on February 28, 1967, at the age of 68.

In 1935, Henry Luce married Clare Boothe. Clare Boothe Luce played a major role in the success of the family dynasty. As the daughter of a prominent Connecticut family, she emerged as a leading playwright, editor, and politician, representing Connecticut in the U.S. House from 1943 until 1947. As one of the first American women appointed to major ambassadorial positions, she enjoyed access to exclusive stories. *Life*, for example, obtained coverage of NASA's efforts to send Americans to the moon—a scoop that made the magazine the envy of competitors. In 1981, President Reagan appointed Clare Booth Luce to the President's Foreign Intelligence Advisory Board, and in 1983, she received the Presidential Medal of Freedom. She died October 9, 1987, leaving the majority of her estate to The Henry Luce Foundation, and she was buried next to her husband's remains in South Carolina.

In time, the publishing empire birthed by Henry Luce and Clare Boothe Luce grew into a multimedia empire. By most estimates, Time Warner (originally Time Inc.) has grown over the course of almost a century to rank among the top companies in size and net worth on both domestic and international levels. (In November 2017, the U.S. Justice Department announced plans to block a proposed merger between AT&T and Time Warner, which federal officials claimed would create monopoly conditions.)[21]

From a series of acquisitions and mergers, Time Warner now exercises control over three divisions—Home Box Office, Inc., Turner Broadcasting System, Inc., and Warner Bros.—with holdings well beyond U.S. borders. A sample of HBO's influence, for example, includes the seven 24-hour channels HBO Comedy, HBO Latino, HBO Signature, and HBO Family. An even smaller sample of Turner's assets includes channels such as CNN, HLN, TBS, TNT, Turner Classic Movies, Cartoon Network, Adult Swim, Boomerang, and TruTV. Warner Brothers, while primarily concerned with filmmaking, includes several divisions that extend into other areas of media, from music to comic books.

In building their media empire, the Luces developed a method of cross-promotion, which essentially entailed using one of their assets to advertise on behalf of another one of their assets. This strategy ensured growth in a two-for-one approach (or, later, an "all for one" approach). In a simple way, *Time* magazine, for example, might offer discounts to new subscribers of *Fortune* magazine, or vice versa. On a more sophisticated level, Time Warner's divisions can cross promote through a wide range of inter-related media.

We can see the results of this approach in contemporary advertising strategies. Among the most popular content shared on social media channels now includes sponsored magazine articles, online webisodes, music videos, and short films—the kinds of content users find so entertaining, informative, and engaging that they view and share it of their own volition, all the while passing embedded advertising for the producer to their friends or family. The message marketed may be upfront or almost invisible, but the content producer's strategy simply involves spreading the message to as many consumers as possible. Advertisers have used other subtle ways of reaching potential customers by embedding material discreetly in webpages or at the beginning of videos. These successful strategies have led media companies that depend heavily on revenue

Image 14.3: "Set-up for Press and Convention Parties at the Republican National Convention, September 1–4, 2008, CNN Building next to the Xcel Center, St. Paul, Minnesota," photographer Carol M. Highsmith, published September 3, 2008.[22]

from advertisers to alter their coverage of topics to favor advertising interests. Advertisers have responded with even more sophisticated methods of targeting Web users with content tailored to their individual tastes based on previous Internet searches and trending topics.

GLOBAL CORPORATIONS AND CONTENT

While Time Warner may have led competitors in its cross-promotional efforts, other companies certainly followed this trend, and in putting a priority on the interests of their stakeholders and advertisers alike, corporations now reach consumers in even more innovative ways. Using social media, advertisers now market content identified as "branded," with a rationale that social media allows individual content providers to leapfrog traditional media and forge relationships directly with customers.[23] The formula has contributed to the growth of companies well beyond the scope of American borders, as consumers identify with particular names and products regardless of their geographic origin.

One of the most famous American media moguls, Rupert Murdoch, in fact has roots not in the United States, but in Australia. His empire grew steadily from a start in tabloids and through the art of self-promotion, branching into television, social media, and well-established newspapers. News Corporation, like other transnational media conglomerates, has profited from its various assets by promotion of each one individually to build the company's overall strength.

RUPERT MURDOCH AND NEWS CORPORATION

Rupert Murdoch, executive chair of News Corp. and 21st Century Fox, was born on March 11, 1931, in Melbourne, Australia. He inherited two newspapers owned by his father, the *Sunday Mail* and *The News*. He expanded his operations by purchasing Perth's *Sunday Times* and Sydney's *Mirror*, allowing him the opportunity to create Australia's national daily paper, the *Australian*. Murdoch then branched out to the United Kingdom and United States by first purchasing the English the *News of the World* and *The Sun*. In the 1970s, Murdoch acquired several U.S. newspapers, including San Antonio's *Express* and the *Evening News* and the *New York Post* and *New York Magazine*. He diversified his acquisitions with the purchase of the 20th Century Fox Film Corporation, as well as several independent television stations that would become the Fox television network. Murdoch now heads a multimedia empire with assets around the world. He has an estimated net worth of more than $12 billion.

In December 2017, News Corporation CEO Rupert Murdoch demonstrated an interest in scaling back the size of his media empire while at the same time contributing to the growth of another one. The Walt Disney Company struck a deal to acquire much of Murdoch's 21st Century Fox Corporation, paying more than $52 billion in stock, which analysts anticipate will have major implications for Hollywood film studios. The deal gives Disney access to 21st Century Fox's international holdings, including Star India, Sky, Tata Sky, and Endemol Shine Group.[24]

As daunting as these international business trends may appear to aspiring individual journalists, analysts still have mixed reviews about the future of the press. Thomas Patterson, a professor of government and the press at Harvard University, has issued a warning, writing that the continued embrace of soft news by the contemporary conglomerations will lead to the end of journalism. "To believe otherwise is to assume that people follow news for its entertainment or shock value," he writes. Patterson has observed that a news habit takes years to create and years to diminish, and once diminished, a consumer cannot easily restore it.[25]

Still others indicate the contemporary state of media offers grounds for optimism. Although the ownership of media by large companies has had a generally detrimental effect on production of hard news since the 1980s, consumers at the very least now have both more responsibilities and opportunities when it comes to finding news that matters. Dan Gillmor, director of the Knight Centre for Digital Media Entrepreneurship at Arizona State University, suggests that we can still find more quality information than ever before available. "Increasingly, the trick will be finding it," Gillmor writes.

> At some level, we have to ask a lot more of audiences in this new world. People will have to be more literate about how media work, and more willing to go deeper on their own. Most of all, they'll have to be relentlessly skeptical. They'll need help from trustworthy news organizations and from self-designated editors who point to the good stuff.[27]

THE PRESS AND THE MAKING OF MODERN MEDIA   235

Image 14.4: "Remote Control, 2000," Nebojsa Seric Shoba, artist, a poster showing a remote-control device capable of "life/death" decisions, suggesting the power to manipulate one person's life is often in another person's hands, created in response to the September 11 terrorist attacks on the United States.[26]

A NEW REGULATORY ENVIRONMENT

Since its establishment in 1934, the Federal Communications Commission has played a role in regulating communication via the most popular forms of media, including radio, television, wire, satellite, and cable. Its jurisdiction extends over the fifty United States and the District of Columbia, with a Media Bureau advocating innovation in the media industry as a whole. The Federal Trade Commission (FTC)—a separate entity that predates the FCC—works as an agency of the United States government to promote consumer protection and the elimination and prevention of anti-competitive business practices, such as coercive monopoly. The growth in media corporations has increasingly brought the interests of the FCC and the FTC together, posing problems in some cases beyond the ability of either one or both institutions to solve.

With companies such as Time Warner, News Corporation, Bertelsmann, and several others exercising influence in nations around the world, U.S. regulatory systems have only limited effectiveness in controlling monopolistic practices. Take for example a dispute between European nations and the United States over different conditions each party intended to impose on Google regarding its search practices. In early 2014, antitrust authorities for the European Union signaled interest in curtailing Google's

Image 14.5: "Google Headquarters, Mountain View, California," photographer Carol M. Highsmith, published 2012.[29]

domination over searches for online content. U.S. regulators resisted interference with the interests of the American tech giant, but ultimately, the parties settled a three-year antitrust case that required Google to change the way it displays competitors' results. The concessions had the potential of restoring a level playing field with competitors, said Joaquín Almunia, antitrust commissioner for the EU antitrust commissioner. Just one year prior, the FTC dropped its inquiry into Google, ruling the firm's search practices did not harm consumers, and with Google pledging to change operations related to other business, such as patented technology use.[28]

However, instead of making regulatory initiatives clearer and allowing for international precedents, Google has since entered a new cycle of trouble with orders in 2017 from the EU to pay a $2.7 billion fine for abusing its agreement and promoting its online shopping services.[30]

Part of the reason for the difficulties between interested parties—whether governmental or political—stems from constant changes in technology. Increasingly in our contemporary life, advances in technology occur more rapidly than institutions can adapt to them. The FCC, for example, initially exempted strictly informational services, such as broadband Internet access, from regulation, but in 1996, the Telecommunications Act required the FCC to modify its approach to new technologies. By 2015, the FCC recognized that nearly 55 million Americans did not have access to services requiring broadband technologies, and it reclassified broadband Internet access as a telecommunications service, which made it subject to regulation.

In November 2017, the FCC voted to remove key roadblocks to increased consolidation among media companies, potentially unleashing new deals among television, radio, and newspaper owners seeking to compete with online media.[31] The FCC had first recognized these regulations in the 1970s to ensure inclusion in the media a diversity of opinions, but since then, the rise of blogs, websites, and podcasts has posed a dramatic increase in competition to traditional media, making these rules obsolete. One of the long-standing rules repealed had prevented one company in a given media market from owning both a daily newspaper and a television station. Another removed rule blocked television stations in the same market from merging with each other if the combination would leave fewer than eight independently owned stations.[32]

The FCC's new approach to keeping pace with developing technologies now extends into online communications as well. Legal reclassifications stemming as far back as the 1996 Telecommunications Act now allow the FCC a legal basis for imposing rules on the Internet under a system known as net neutrality. The principle of net neutrality holds that Internet service providers must treat all data on the Internet the same and not discriminate or charge differently by user, content, website, platform, application, type of attached equipment, or method of communication. For instance, under these principles, Internet service providers are unable to intentionally block, slow down, or charge money for specific websites and online content.

In the United States, net neutrality has been an issue of contention among network users and access providers since the 1990s. While no clear legal protections had previously required net neutrality, in 2015, the FCC reclassified broadband technologies as a communication service and listed providers as "common carriers" instead of "information providers." The FCC in a long-awaited and for the most part publicly derided maneuver decided in December 2017 to do away with the protections established under the guides of net neutrality. While the FCC Chairman Ajit Pai has argued that net neutrality has interfered with the ability of Internet content providers to flourish, supporters of First Amendment rights, including the American Civil Liberties Union, have pledged to challenge the legitimacy of the agency's action. The outcome of this decision will take years to unfold, but nearly twenty state attorneys general immediately challenged the FCC's assertion that it could block states from imposing their own net neutrality rules. At the same time, according to the ACLU, state legislators across the country have examined whether they could maintain net neutrality mandates through state legislation. Even towns and counties in Iowa, Washington, and elsewhere have explored options to develop locally based net neutrality principles with Internet service providers.[33]

RECAPPING THIS CHAPTER

Looking back on this chapter, you should see how media corporations have acted both independently and interdependently to create a kind of storytelling that requires simultaneous attention to multimedia production values and the constraints of advertising. It explained the reasons why contemporary media tend to focus on soft news, as larger media organizations have had to adjust content to meet the demands of advertisers and large audiences alike. It described the growth of what media analyst Ben Bagdikian called "The Media Monopoly," a phenomenon that has created difficulties in maintaining journalistic standard.

Using materials from this chapter, you should be able to explain how media has evolved with trends in technology into transnational organizations. You should have an understanding of the challenges in reporting stories using traditional techniques in this new climate, and you should be able to identify how ownership affects the content of news.

The following chapter describes how media jobs in the twenty-first century reflect institutional, economic, and social conditions, and it describes the scope and influence of the traditional press relative to social media. It shows how contemporary professionals practice in a world quite different from their predecessors, as employers expect new hires to perform multiple tasks in a media that no longer rewards specialization only.

NOTES

1 "Media Position," Library of Congress, accessed February 13, 2017, <http://hdl.loc.gov/loc.afc/afcomaha.0032>.
2 Ashley Lutz, "These 6 Corporations Control 90% of the Media in America," *Business Insider*, June 14, 2012, accessed December 2, 2017, <businessinsider.com/these-6-corporations-control-90-of-the-media-in-america-2012–6>.
3 C. Edwin Baker, *Media Concentration and Democracy: Why Ownership Matters* (Cambridge, UK: Cambridge University Press, 2006), 54.
4 Ben Bagdikian, *The New Media Monopoly* (Boston: Beacon Press, 2004), 27–54.
5 Lara O'Riley, "The 30 Biggest Media Companies in the World," *Business Insider*, May 31, 2016, accessed December 2, 2017, <businessinsider.com/the-30-biggest-media-owners-in-the-world-2016–5>.
6 David Bauder, "Journalism Net Effect Defies Expectation," *Associated Press*, March 17, 2008.
7 Martin A. Lee and Norman Solomon, *Unreliable Sources: A Guide to Detecting Bias in News Media* (New York: Carol, 1992), 78, 79.

THE PRESS AND THE MAKING OF MODERN MEDIA   239

8   Andrew Kohut, "Self-Censorship: Counting the Ways," *Columbia Journalism Review*, 39, 1 (May 2000): 42, accessed December 2, 2017, <cjr.org/year/00/2/censorship.asp>.
9   "What Is the Purpose of Journalism?" *The American Press Institute*, accessed December 2, 2017, <americanpressinstitute.org/journalism-essentials/what-is-journalism/purpose-journalism>.
10 Sigma Delta Chi, "Code of Ethics," *Society of Professional Journalists*, September 6, 2014, accessed December 1, 2017, <spj.org/ethicscode.asp>.
11 Aidan White, "Time to Act over the Corruption that Is Killing Ethical Journalism," *Ethical Journalism Network*, March 16, 2015, accessed December 2, 2017, <ethicaljournalismnetwork.org/time-to-act-over-the-corruption-that-is-killing-ethical-journalism>.
12 Bill Carter, "60 Minutes' Ordered to Pull Interview in Tobacco Report," *New York Times*, November 9, 1995, December 2, 2017, <nytimes.com/1995/11/09/us/60-minutes-ordered-to-pull-interview-in-tobacco-report.html>.
13 Tim Weiner, "Mike Wallace, CBS Pioneer of '60 Minutes,' Dies at 93," *New York Times*, April 8, 2012, December 2, 2017, <nytimes.com/2012/04/09/business/media/mike-wallace-cbs-pioneer-of-60-minutes-dead-at-93>.
14 Opinion, "Self-Censorship at CBS," November 12, 1995, December 2, 2017, <nytimes.com/1995/11/12/opinion/self-censorship-at-cbs.html>.
15 Thomas Patterson, "Doing Well and Doing Good: How Soft News and Critical Journalism are Shrinking the News Audience and Weakening Democracy," *The Joan Shorenstein Center for Press, Politics, & Public Policy at Harvard University*, January 1, 2001, accessed December 2, 2017, <shorensteincenter.org/how-soft-news-critical-journalism-are-shrinking-news-audience>.
16 Anup Shah, "Media Conglomerates, Mergers, Concentration of Ownership," *Global Issues*, January 2, 2009, accessed December 2, 2017, <globalissues.org/article/159/media-conglomerates-mergers-concentration-of-ownership>.
17 Associated Press, "Meredith Buying Time Inc. for About $1.8 Billion," *Time Magazine*, accessed December 10, 2017, <time.com/5037679/meredith-time-inc-koch-brothers>.
18 Henry R. Luce, "The American Century," *Life Magazine*, February 17, 1941: 61–65.
19 "National Affairs: Struggle for Survival," *Time Magazine*, March 29, 1948.
20 "Clare Boothe Luce and Husband Publisher Henry Luce," Library of Congress, accessed May 18, 2016, <item/00649867>.
21 Brian Fung and Drew Harwell, "Why AT&T's Merger with Time Warner Is Such a Huge Deal," *Washington Post*, October 21, 2016, accessed November 18, 2017, <washingtonpost.com/news/the-switch/wp/2016/10/21/att-could-soon-own-almost-everything-from-hbo-to-cnn-to-dc-comics/?utm_term=.2dd88ed4e18a>.
22 "Set-up for Press and Convention Parties at the Republican National Convention," Library of Congress, accessed December 9, 2017, <item/2010719269>.
23 Douglas Holt, "Branding in the Age of Social Media," *Harvard Business Review*, March 2016, accessed December 1, 2017, <hbr.org/2016/03/branding-in-the-age-of-social-media>.
24 Andrew Nusca, "Why Disney Spent $52 Billion to Acquire Most of 21st Century Fox," *Fortune*, December 14, 2017, accessed December 23, 2017, <fortune.com/2017/12/14/disney-fox-deal>.
25 Patterson, "Doing Well and Doing Good," accessed December 2, 2017, <shorensteincenter.org/how-soft-news-critical-journalism-are-shrinking-news-audience>.
26 "Remote Control, 2000," Library of Congress, accessed June 12, 2016, <item/2002716830>.
27 Dan Gillmor, "Call Me an Optimist, but the Future of Journalism Isn't Bleak," *The Guardian*, December 27, 2013, accessed December 20, 2017, <theguardian.com/commentisfree/2013/dec/27/journalism-future-not-bleak-advertising>.
28 "U.S. Antitrust Policy," *Council on Foreign Relations*, February 6, 2014, accessed December 2 2017, <cfr.org/backgrounder/us-antitrust-policy>.
29 "Google Headquarters," Library of Congress, accessed December 9, 2017, <item/2013630580>.
30 James Titcomb, "EU Closes in on Google as it Prepares Second Antitrust Fine," *The Telegraph*, November 11, 2017, accessed December 20, 2017, <telegraph.co.uk/technology/2017/11/11/eu-closes-google-prepares-second-antitrust-fine>.

31 David Shepardson, "U.S. Regulator Votes to Loosen Media Ownership Rules," *Reuters*, November 16, 2017, accessed December 10, 2017, <reuters.com/article/us-usa-media-regulation/u-s-regulator-votes-to-loosen-media-ownership-rules>.

32 Brian Fung, "The FCC Just Repealed a 42-year-old Rule Blocking Broadcast Media Mergers," *Washington Post*, November 16, 2017, accessed December 20, 2017, <washingtonpost.com/news/the-switch/wp/2017/11/16/the-fcc-just-repealed-decades-old-rules-blocking-broadcast-media-mergers>.

33 Michael Macleoud-Ball, "Who Can Clean Up the FCC's Net Neutrality Mess?" *ACLU*, December 22, 2017, accessed December 22, 2017, <aclu.org/blog/privacy-technology/internet-privacy/who-can-clean-fccs-net-neutrality-mess>.

CONCLUSION

The Conclusion provides an overview of the expectations of media jobs in the context of twenty-first century institutional, economic, and social conditions:

- It shows how media began taking less specialized forms in the mid-twentieth century;
- and it describes the scope and influence of the traditional press relative to social media.

Using materials from the Conclusion, students should have an understanding of how contemporary professionals practice in a world quite different from their predecessors:

- They should identify how social media has both adopted and rejected certain conventions developed well before the introduction of the Internet;
- and they should familiarize themselves with the expectations held by employers for new hires to perform multiple tasks in a media that no longer rewards specialization only.

Key words, names, and phrases associated with the Conclusion include:

- Convergence and its effect on content;
- the Internet, the World Wide Web, and digital media and social media;
- citizen journalism and user-created content;
- and multi-tasking.

CONCLUSION

Welcome to the conclusion of this book. I hope by now you have developed a holistic understanding of the history of the American press so that you can have a better sense of the role of the press today. The Conclusion provides commentary on the current state of the industry with questions about its future.

The press, as previous chapters reveal, consists of much more than newspapers, just as history consists of much more than names and dates; however, both the practitioners of journalism and history share the unique traits of storytelling. Part of the story of the American press has revolved around the rapidly changing economic, technological, and social conditions. The media as we now know differs vastly from the press you saw described in the opening chapters of this book, but since the birth of the first American newspaper, journalists have consistently had to adapt to change. The most notable recent innovation to influence the press came in the form of the Internet and the World Wide Web, with search engines and social media websites now encouraging audiences to consume news in greater amounts and at faster rates. The transition from traditional media to contemporary media has also directly affected the job expectations of journalists in how they execute their reporting methods and the way in which they deliver the news. Despite these changes, news consumers still expect journalists to maintain the duties of the Fourth Estate and to keep a check on government by exposing questionable activities.

Both contemporary media and the traditional press have relied on audiences for their success. Today, even users of social media need an audience to measure their reach. A noteworthy difference between modern and traditional media, however, is that media organizations now have the ability to break news all the time. Audiences no longer have to wait for the daily paper or the 5 p.m. news to know the events of the day—they can simply access their smartphones to look at social media feeds or a personalized news application.

Convergence has also manifested itself in the growth of soft news, or "infotainment" (see Chapter 14), as merged media tend to produce this kind of information more effectively and efficiently than they do hard news. This climate has created opportunities for members of the media industry, but it also presents challenges as journalists struggle to generate revenue while remaining faithful to their professional values.

THE WORLD OF THE WEB

After its widespread dissemination for public use in the 1990s, the World Wide Web has grown in use as one of the most popular vehicles for facilitating a variety of communication and information-sharing tasks worldwide. As a result, previously established forms of media have had to change the ways in which they reach the public in order to stay up to speed with the now dominant forms of online communication. The prevalence of visual items online, for example, has bled into television, as you will now rarely see a news anchor positioned against a plain background; instead, producers tend to fill the screen with an abundance of additional graphics, providing the appearance of constant news coverage.

A TRUNCATED HISTORY OF THE WORLD WIDE WEB

The initial development of interconnected computers in the United States emerged from the needs and demands during the Cold War. A network named ARPANET (from the Advanced Research Projects Agency, which created it) provided a system of networked information beginning in the late 1960s. Because the U.S. government in particular and its citizens in general feared a nuclear attack from the Soviet Union during the Cold War, federally funded projects invested in technology to ensure domestic safety. At first a function of the U.S. military, ARPANET laid foundations for the present-day Internet. Although vastly different from today's Internet, ARPANET served the purpose of safeguarding sensitive information on individually secured and intra-dependent computer sites, a reason why you might say Internet technologies have roots in the Cold War.

The first electronic message sent over the ARPANET—the word "login"—originated in the laboratory of University of California, Los Angeles, professor Leonard Kleinrock, which in 1969 connected the UCLA computer to one in the Stanford Research Institute. In 1989, British computer scientist Tim Berners-Lee developed research that built upon Internet technologies (as utilized with ARPANET) and helped to launch what we now know as the World Wide Web. The Web as originally designed linked documents into an information system that users could access via the network.

Image 15.1: "Marine Corps. H.Q. Computer Rooms," Warren K. Leffler, photographer, published February 8, 1971.[1]

A TIMELINE OF SELECT DATES IN THE DEVELOPMENT OF THE WEB

- 1972: First use of network email.
- 1973: Global networking becomes a reality as the University College of London (England) and Royal Radar Establishment (Norway) connect to ARPANET, coining the term "Internet."
- 1983: The Domain Name System (DNS) establishes the familiar. edu,. gov,. com,. mil,. org,. net, and. int system for naming websites, replacing more complicated designations for websites, such as 123.456.789.10.
- 1984: William Gibson, author of *Neuromancer*, first uses the term "cyberspace."
- 1990: Tim Berners-Lee develops HyperText Markup Language (HTML).
- 1991: The World Wide Web goes public.
- 1992: Popularization of the phrase "surfing the Internet."
- 1993: The number of websites reaches 600.
- 1994: Microsoft creates a Web browser for Windows 95.
- 1995: Compuserve, America Online, and Prodigy begin to provide Internet access. Amazon.com, Craigslist, and eBay go live.
- 1997: PC makers can remove or hide Microsoft's Internet software on new versions of Windows 95, thanks to a settlement with the Justice Department. Netscape announces that its browser will be free.
- 1998: The Google search engine is born, changing the way users engage with the Internet.
- 2004: Facebook goes online, and the era of social networking begins. Mozilla unveils the Mozilla Firefox browser.
- 2005: YouTube.com launches.
- 2006: Twitter launches.
- 2010: Facebook reaches 400 million active users.

Source: Kim Ann Zimmermann and Jesse Emspak, "Internet History Timeline: ARPANET to the World Wide Web," *Live Science*, June 27, 2017, accessed December 24, 2017, <livescience.com/20727-internet-history.html>.

Since the mid-1990s, Internet and Web-based communications have had revolutionary impacts on culture, commerce, and technology, with the rise of communication by electronic mail, two-way interactive video calls, discussion forums, blogs, and social networking. The online takeover of the global communication landscape has also taken place in a relatively fast manner—only 1 percent of information flowed through two-way telecommunications networks in the year 1993; by 2000, this number rose to 51 percent, and within the next decade, it reached more than 97 percent of the telecommunicated information by 2007.[2] Online communications continue to grow, driven by ever-greater amounts of commerce, entertainment, and social networking.

Over the past several decades and inversely correlating with the growth of digital content, newspapers sales have decreased precipitously, with print advertising revenue—a measure of the overall health of newspapers—falling between 2000 and 2015 from about $60 billion to about $20 billion, wiping out the gains of the previous fifty years.[3] Instead of using traditional forms of media for news, audiences now access it via mobile, desktop, or tablet devices, using a number of sophisticated news-delivery apps. Previously print-oriented media have in turn tried keeping up with trends by switching to digital platforms and targeting their readership.

Before social media apps, news consumers might have gathered information from individual television news channels or local or national newspapers. Now, large media organizations such as CNN or Fox News can use Twitter, Facebook, or other social media outlets to break news stories as they happen. This gives their audience live updates of coverage as stories unfold. Twitter in particular has become a one-stop shop for news consumers—the fast pace in which users share information with others puts media organizations in direct competition with private users for scoops on developing narratives.

As audiences now have greater power than ever before to drive what news organizations prioritize, legacy media organizations have struggled to remain profitable enough to maintain large newsrooms. For example, readers of the *Washington Post* do not have to go directly to the *Post*'s website to read its content. They can instead log on to Facebook and consume content from the *Washington Post*, the *New York Times*, Fox News, Buzzfeed, and countless others.

The institutional changes reflect a gradual evolution in the way Americans as a whole have used news. According to surveys, a high percentage of respondents in the 50-to-65 age range indicate they still receive the majority of their news from television, but 50 percent of news consumers between the ages of 18 and 29, and 45 percent between 30 and 49, report that they now obtain most of their news from online sources.[4] While news consumers in general formerly obtained most content from television broadcast, they have increasingly turned to social media, such as Facebook or Twitter, for sources—survey respondents indicate that 12 percent of them (with all of them presumably relying on traditional media in years past) now obtain most of their news primarily from social media outlets.[5]

BALANCING BUSINESS AND ETHICS

This new media landscape has created a significantly more competitive battlefield for news organizations. In a climate that emphasizes getting it first over getting it right, once storied news organizations have made compromises and sometimes published stories that were in fact wrong.

THE PROBLEM OF "FAKE NEWS"

Fake news can contain elements of yellow journalism (see Chapter 8) or propaganda (see Chapter 11) designed to deliberately misinform media users. It has the purpose of damaging the reputation of an institution or person with the use of sensational content or simply false information. On a practical level, it has come to employ eye-catching headlines or tantalizing half-truths to increase readership, online sharing, and Internet click revenue—a measure of reader engagement that advertisers find valuable. Fake news also undermines serious media coverage, making it more difficult for journalists to cover significant news stories.

Fake news became a global subject during the 2016 U.S. presidential election, in which researchers discovered a rise in the number of misleading stories spread on social media about candidates Hillary Clinton and Donald Trump. However, fake news has roots in the expansion of technology in general. As the *New York Sun's* Moon Hoax (see Chapter 3) illustrated, publishers might take the risk of popularizing a story with false content if it will attract readers and produce advertisers and ratings.

Even with historic antecedents, fake news thrives in the contemporary climate of easy access to online advertisement revenue, increased political polarization, and the popularity of social media. Employing the clickbait strategy, marketers have exploited the interests of social media users by providing just enough "news" to make readers curious, but little or no legitimate well-researched news.

Compromises have also come in the form of cutting corners to meet budget demands. Instead of relying on full-time regular staff, these large, storied institutions have increasingly turned to journalists who do not work for any single employer. Facing widespread layoffs of staff that once filled the newsrooms of major news outlets, newspapers especially and media in general have turned instead to less costly freelance reporters and writers to do the jobs of those who previously had decades of experience and a wealth of networking contacts. This shift has resulted in a general restructuring in the organization of the traditional newsroom. While local papers in particular still supply news beats that focus on areas of interest to area readers, such as entertainment, crime, and business, they also employ specialized freelancers who contribute stories about their own particular areas of specialization.

The need for a more localized approach to newsgathering has the support of media users, with trends showing Americans generally do not trust "the news media" in an abstract sense, but they do trust the news they gather from sources they know on personal levels. Take for example the responses of Americans who say they believe news media practice in a "moral" fashion—only 24 percent of respondents indicated they feel news media in general are "moral," but most (53 percent) say they approve of the media they use specifically. In terms of accuracy, just 17 percent of Americans give the news media in general high marks, but twice as many (34 percent) say they trust the accuracy of the media they use.[7]

This trend coincides with attitudes about media among Americans that should trouble members of the press. Almost half of Americans have indicated in a recent poll that they believe the news media has actively fabricated stories about President Trump. Moreover, almost a third of the respondents indicated that they agree with the

Image 15.2: "City News, a Shop and Newsstand in Downtown Mansfield, Ohio," Highsmith, Carol M. Highsmith, photographer, published October 7, 2016.[6]

president's claim that the press opposes the interests of the people by interfering with government functions. Perhaps most troubling relative to First Amendment freedoms, one in four Americans surveyed in the poll endorse limitations on the press by allowing the government to block news stories perceived as biased or inaccurate.[8]

The growth in the use of social media corresponded with these numbers, reflecting both the public's distrust for traditional news outlets and a fascination with a virtually limitless supply of information on the World Wide Web. As citizens of a nation built on the principles of the First Amendment, which require an informed citizenry to hold elected officials in check, we can applaud this aspect of the information age in which we live. However, this supply of information also has a drawback—no one can possibly process all of it, and its sheer volume requires us to cut corners. A study conducted by the Pew Research Center indicates an increase in the use of social media has correlated with a decrease in content actually read, and an American Press Institute survey indicates that one-third of respondents reported following news throughout the day, but only 4 in 10 looked beyond the story's headlines.[9]

USER-CREATED CONTENT

We certainly live in a world and at a time in which a vast range of opinions can register at the simple push of a button. The digital revolution of recent decades has created opportunities for just about anyone to compete with the older, better-established news outlets of previous eras. According to a 2017 report by the non-partisan Aspen Institute think tank, approximately 70 percent of the world's population currently uses a mobile phone, and in four years, that number will rise to 80 percent.[10] Such technologies present unlimited opportunities for the dissemination of public information and the cultivation of knowledge.

Our contemporary information-based society has transformed the meaning, content, and delivery of news. Individual outlets no longer report news but instead quite often present in accordance with their own preferences and those of their consumers.

Image 15.3: "A Rare Sight in America late in 2012," Carol M. Highsmith, photographer, published 2012. The caption includes the following description: "A working payphone in a rural setting, minus any graffiti. This one stood along U.S. 395 in the tiny settlement of Ravendale, north of Susanville, California."[11]

CONCLUSION 249

As a manifestation of this reality, user-created content has emerged as a form of media in the past decade, growing from the ways users of online communications have shared publicly their thoughts and observations through social media. This content most often appears as material associated with social media websites, and it appears in content ranging from blog posts and videos to comments on the sites of others. The term "user-created content" (or, alternatively, "user-generated content") entered mainstream usage in the mid-2000s, having arisen in web publishing and new media content production circles. In 2006, *Time* magazine designated these content producers as the Person of the Year.[12]

The growth of user-created content demonstrates the democratization of news production inasmuch as it has minimized the use of gatekeepers, which until the 1990s included newspaper editors, publishers, and news show producers who all approved content and information before releasing it for public consumption. However, with the increasing ease of producing media through new technologies in recent decades, large numbers of the public began posting text, digital photos, and digital videos online, with little interference from traditional gatekeepers.

Journalists and publishers have subsequently had to consider the effects of user-created content on news. A 2016 study on the business models of publishers suggests that readers of online news sources value articles written by professional journalists and users alike—provided the users are experts in a field relevant to the content that they create.[13] Online news sites have responded by considering themselves sources for articles and other types of journalism, as well as platforms for user engagement and feedback, a development that has allowed sites to garner revenue for publishers, as access and commenting often require subscriptions.

The digital forms of print media provide an opportunity for readers to access articles in real time, and on the go, from their smartphones, tablets, and computers. However, as a tradeoff for this convenience, journalists have abandoned several traditional practices. One example is nuanced headlines. Such headlines provide the depth and context a complicated piece of writing warrants—and one that traditionally appeared in print newspapers—but they often do not include the keywords that push articles to the top of search engine results pages. The visibility of a story as determined by other features, including hashtags and search engine optimization (SEO), has affected content as well by driving reporters to focus on commonly recurring themes and phrases, sometimes at the expense of less popular stories that otherwise might receive coverage. By engaging sophisticated methods of tagging content, SEO makes it easier for particular content providers to reach audiences otherwise untapped.

Digital publishing has also compressed the timescales for journalists and newspaper production staff, making news reporting very low cost on the web.[14] This reality has made it possible for increasing numbers of Web users to create content of their own, as the skills necessary to produce multimedia stories require less professionalization and training with the passage of time. Beyond the use of text and photos alone, the creative options have expanded to include video for online media.

The influence of social media has shaped the very nature of journalism itself by offering incentives to news organizations for particular types of content, such as live video, and by dictating publisher activities through design standards, which revolve essentially around editorial platforms of user-created content. Unlike traditional news media, modern media forms do not have a set standard for every article to follow. For example, story materials published using social media have no finite page space, which in newspapers determined how much paper and ink a writer might use. While Twitter and Facebook might limit the character length of certain posts, these lengths expand, as users can simply add subsequent posts almost without limit. While users of Instagram and Snapchat might look for videos with content that other social media outlets might not feature. Adjusting to the tastes of online news consumers, organizations such as Buzzfeed now specialize in short articles while delivering smatterings of hard news. These stories typically appear in a list format with about one sentence of text per item and an animated photo under each of those lines. Such articles take minimal time and effort to read, and Buzzfeed and similar sites rarely choose to take on challenging or controversial subjects in this style of news content.

While some news organizations have already turned to automation to generate stories about corporate earnings and sporting results, machines cannot totally replace the role of humans in interpreting complex issues. Indeed, trends already show that the public has tired of clickbait stories, and the marketing ploys that exploded with social media's initial popularity have now left consumers hungry for news in a climate otherwise overwhelmed by the derision of politicians, in which readers fear businesses and uniquely American institutions are assaulted.[15]

Digital media has also advanced the possibility of making news more quickly and easily shared across several different platforms and to a variety of audiences. In some ways, the press is more democratized than ever, and almost anyone can publish based on the tools they have available. Women and men can print openly on topics of politics, sex, religion, conspiracy, opinion, and interest of all types, leading to a conundrum for members of the press: If everyone is a journalist, how do we measure the credibility of professional members of the press?

MILLENNIALS AND THE NEXT GENERATION OF MEDIA

As we have seen, the last two decades of the twentieth century produced enormous changes in both the media and the ways we use it. Perhaps no other generation will experience the direct effect of these changes in ways more dramatic than those who came of age during the period, a generation we now refer to as millennials.

On a basic level, the emergence of social media in the first decade of the new millennium helped users keep in touch with their friends and family, with most items posted consisting of simple happenings in daily lives. In time, the world of social media allowed users to interact with reporters, and it allowed reporters to develop large followings across a number of social media platforms. The exchange created a dynamic in which social media allowed users not only to interact with news providers but also to supply news content and in turn determine it.

In a competitive media market, the freedom for the consumer to choose content based on their personal tastes has increased, and every content producer for every media outlet in turn has taken note of its market share and subsequent audience percentage. Analytic research indicates that millennials, a valuable demographic for their relative levels of disposable income, use a mix of social networks for news at a relatively higher rate, with the average 18- to 21-year-old using more than half of the major social network platforms. Of this group, 70 percent indicated that their social media feeds consist of a relatively even mix of opinions.[16]

Comparatively, according to another survey, 65 percent of the U.S. population in general used one or more social networking sites, and of those who use the Internet, 76 percent of them used social media.[17] Almost 40 percent of all U.S. Internet users also contribute to the creation of news, comment on it, or disseminate news via social media sites like Facebook and Twitter.[18] Moreover, a 2017 Pew Research survey reported two-thirds of U.S. adults get news from social media, and most of them consume most of their news online, while very few now read the hard copy version of newspapers. While online, 73 percent of Facebook users interacted with entertainment-themed content, a top genre, followed by community events, people, and sports.[19]

Keeping readers and viewers engaged means news organizations must now spend more resources on making content more easily digestible and getting people to care enough to stay on a page for more than just a few seconds. This often involves restructuring organizations to create positions that focus only on audience engagement. Younger people are also using video as a primary way to consume their news, forcing media organizations to adapt to this change. In June 2017, MTV News, hoping to maintain the attention of young viewers, abandoned long-form journalism to focus instead on short-form journalism and video content.

Many other organizations have since followed this example with a greater emphasis placed on personalized news. While readers have always had the ability to some extent to choose the source of their news, previous generations had a reasonable expectation that their neighbors, colleagues, or peers had followed at least approximately the same stories on any given day. However, the widespread use of Internet technologies has made it easier for the spread of global media, and social media users can now easily connect with others around the globe, creating audiences that can interact live via video conferences or through comments on news articles and stories shared on their profile pages. As a result, individual users vary in their news consumption, and on any given day, 100 people in the same room may have followed 100 or 1,000 different sets of news stories. This trend only reinforces engagement with social media use, as those who use it—instead of turning to traditional news outlets for news—instead check Twitter when news breaks to find a sea of reaction and commentary, and highly compressed accounts of news from an endless supply of often-anonymous sources.[20]

In somewhat prophetic observations written not long ago, social media researcher Ruth A. Harper described a trend we see well on its way to becoming a reality. "Eyewitnesses will become reporters, but the world will still need 'traditional' journalists to go in and verify the facts," Harper wrote. "Perhaps in the future, professional journalists won't be so much pure information disseminators but truth disseminators."

> If you want to see what people say is happening right now, check Twitter; if you want to see what's actually true and what might be false, check CNN or *The New York Times*. In the end, no matter the direction it moves in or the new shape or form it takes, news organizations will never cease to exist as long as democracy and freedom of speech exists.[21]

For natural reasons, news organizations have attempted to stay on top of these trends, which in part explain why hard news stories now attract less attention than features. Hard news runs the risk of alienating a substantial portion of an audience because, while social media may be a main source of news for many people, their primary reason for logging on is still to stay in touch with their friends and family. With more than half of news consumers now accessing social media as their primary source of information, media organizations have in some cases all but abandoned press practices that have been in place for well over a century.

RECAPPING THE CONCLUSION

Looking back on the Conclusion, you should see how it provided an overview of the expectations of media jobs in the context of twenty-first century institutional, economic, and social conditions. It showed how media began taking less specialized forms in the mid-twentieth century, and it described the scope and influence of the traditional press relative to social media.

Using materials from this chapter, you should have an understanding of how contemporary professionals practice in a world quite different from their predecessors. You should be able to identify how social media has both adopted and rejected certain conventions developed well before the introduction of the Internet, and you should be familiar with the expectations of employers for new hires to perform multiple tasks in a media that no longer rewards specialization only.

The Afterword for this book provides a retrospective on American press history, along with commentary on the current state of the industry with questions about its future. It re-emphasizes the importance of the First Amendment in the history of the Fourth Estate, and it summarizes past and present media trends as a way to describe the first rough draft of history.

NOTES

1 "Marine Corps: H.Q. Computer Rooms," Library of Congress, accessed December 23, 2017, <item/2017 646234>.
2 Martin Hilbert and Priscila López, "The World's Technological Capacity to Store, Communicate, and Compute Information," *Science*, 332, 6025 (2011): 60–65.
3 Derek Thompson, "The Print Apocalypse and How to Survive It," *The Atlantic*, November 3, 2016, accessed December 1, 2017, <theatlantic.com/business/archive/2016/11/the-print-apocalypse-and-how-to-survive-it/506429/>.
4 Shannon Greenwood, Andrew Perrin, and Maeve Duggan, "Social Media Update 2016," *Pew Research Center*, November 11, 2016, accessed November 18, 2017, <pewinternet.org/2016/11/11/social-media-update-2016>.
5 Nic Newman with Richard Fletcher, David A. L. Levy and Rasmus Kleis Nielsen, "Reuters Institute Digital News Report 2016," *University of Oxford*, 2016, accessed December 2, 2017, <reutersinstitute. politics.ox.ac.uk>.
6 "City News, a Shop and Newsstand in Downtown Mansfield, Ohio," Library of Congress, accessed June 15, 2017, <2016632413>.
7 "'My' Media versus 'the' Media: Trust in News Depends on which News Media You Mean," *American Press Institute*, May 24, 2017, accessed December 20, 2017, <americanpressinstitute.org/publications/reports/survey-research/my-media-vs-the-media>.

8 "Poynter Releases New Study Examining Trust in the Media," *The Poynter Institute*, December 4, 2017, accessed December 20, 2017, <poynter.org/news/poynter-releases-new-study-examining-trust-media>.
9 "How Americans Get their News," *American Press Institute*, March 17, 2014, accessed December 10, 2017, <americanpressinstitute.org/publications/reports/survey-research/how-americans-get-news>.
10 "The Future of Journalism," *A Report on the Aspen Institute Dialogue on the Future of Journalism* (Washington, DC: The Aspen Institute, 2017), accessed December 20, 2017, <csreports.aspeninstitute.org/Future-of-Journalism/2016/report>.
11 "A Rare Sight in America Late in 2012," Library of Congress, accessed December 23, 2017, <item/2013631207>.
12 "Person of the Year: You," *Time Magazine*, December 25, 2006.
13 Michael A. Zeng, Bianca Dennstedt, and Hans Koller, "Democratizing Journalism: How User-Generated Content and User Communities Affect Publishers' Business Models," *Creativity and Innovation Management*, 25, 5 (November 6, 2016): 536–51.
14 Martin Belam, "Journalism in the Digital Age: Trends, Tools and Technologies," *The Guardian*, April 4, 2010, accessed December 2, 2017, <theguardian.com/help/insideguardian/2010/apr/14/journalism-trends-tools-technologies>.
15 Toby Abel, "The Future of Journalism is Bright, and Paid," *Hackernoon*, December 21, 2017, accessed December 21, 2017, <hackernoon.com/the-future-of-journalism-is-bright-and-paid>.
16 Shannon Greenwood, Andrew Perrin, and Maeve Duggan, "Social Media Update 2016," *Pew Research Center*, November 11, 2016, accessed November 18, 2017, <pewinternet.org/2016/11/11/social-media-update-2016>.
17 Dave Chaffey, "Global Social Media Research Summary 2017," *Smart Insights*, April 27, 2017, accessed December 2, 2017, <smartinsights.com/social-media-marketing/social-media-strategy/new-global-social-media-research>.
18 M. Stone, ed., *From Traditional to Online Media: Best Practices and Perspectives* (Vienna: OSCE, 2013), 28, accessed December 2, 2017, <docplayer.net/19305476-From-traditional-to-online-media-best-practices-and-perspectives.html>.
19 "Social Media Fact Sheet," *Pew Research Center*, January 12, 2017, accessed December 2, 2017, <pewinternet.org/fact-sheet/social-media>; Shannon Greenwood, Andrew Perrin, and Maeve Duggan, "Social Media Update 2016," *Pew Research Center*, November 11, 2016, accessed December 2, 2017, <pewinternet.org/2016/11/11/social-media-update-2016>.
20 Jake Coyle, "Is Twitter the News Outlet for the 21st Century," *Associated Press*, July 1, 2009, accessed December 1, 2017, <abcnews.go.com/Technology/story?id=7979891>.
21 Ruth A. Harper, "The Social Media Revolution: Exploring the impact of Journalism and News Media Organizations," *Journal of Inquiries*, 2, 3 (2010): 1, accessed December 2, 2017, <inquiriesjournal.com/articles/202/the-social-media-revolution-exploring-the-impact-on-journalism-and-news-media-organizations>.

Afterword

Now that you have exercised your skills in interpreting the past, you can more fully appreciate the status of the contemporary press, and you can see more clearly your own path if you choose a career in media. A defining element of press history includes the ability of journalists to explore existential questions. Among these questions: Under the current institutional constraints of media, can members of the Fourth Estate maintain fair reporting, dispel fake news, and count misinformation, all the while presenting the public with the information necessary to maintain a democratic republic?

The most pressing crisis journalists must face in the news industry starts at the local level. While the press has focused resources on covering the federal government, especially personalities in the White House, few reporters have provided information about rural and suburban areas in the United States—areas filled with Americans not only affected by federal policy but also with those who have the most to say at election time. A healthy electoral system, after all, as first recommended by the founders, thrives when the press represents a diversity of opinion.

Image BM1.1: "The Future," Carol M. Highsmith, August 7, 2009, photograph of a statue outside the National Archives in Washington, D.C. Architect John Russel Pope placed four monumental statues around the National Archives—this one, "The Future," was designed by Robert I. Aitken and carved by the Piccirilli Brothers Company from 1933–1935 with a statement that reads "What's Past is Prologue."[1]

Members of the press cannot ignore these trends among news consumers if they intend to remain relevant. If journalism is to thrive, it must produce trustworthy news by giving voice to the voiceless. In other words, there will always be a need for the press as long as humans take interest in other humans. Again, the press consists of more than newspapers, just as history consists of more than names and dates—they are both very human endeavors. At least part of what we can do to create an environment in which the press thrives is study its past to understand how reliable accounts of what has happened have created the press we now know. Having read about the history of the press, you should now have a sense of those who witnessed events and created stories about what they saw and experienced. Learning from their examples, you can begin to do so as well.

NOTE

1 "The Future," Library of Congress, accessed December 23, 2017, <item 2010630511>.

Glossary

Agenda Setting—Agenda-setting theory describes the ability of the news media to influence the relative importance of topics on the public agenda. It suggests media have the ability to tell the public what issues they should find important based on an interrelationship between policy makers and identified priorities among consumers of the news.

American Dream—The American Dream consists of a set of ideals in which freedom includes the opportunity for prosperity and success achieved through hard work in a society with few barriers. The Dream has roots in the Declaration of Independence, which proclaims, "all men are created equal" with the right to "life, liberty and the pursuit of happiness."

Amplitude Modulation (AM)—Amplitude modulation (AM) transmits information via a radio carrier wave. AM was the earliest modulation method used to transmit voice by radio.

Anarchism—Anarchists follow a political philosophy that advocates self-governed societies based on voluntary institutions. Anarchism suggests that the conventional organization of the state is undesirable, unnecessary, and harmful.

Antebellum Era—Historians generally consider the antebellum period of American history as spanning between the War of 1812 and the Civil War. During this same time, the country's economy began shifting in the North to manufacturing as the Industrial Revolution began, while in the South, a cotton boom made plantations the center of the economy.

Articles of Confederation—The Articles of Confederation was an agreement among the original thirteen states of the United States of America that served as its first constitution. A guiding principle of the Articles was to preserve the independence and sovereignty of the states. The federal government received only those powers that the colonies had recognized as belonging to king and parliament.

Atomic (Nuclear) Bomb—A nuclear weapon is an explosive device that derives its destructive force from nuclear reactions. A nuclear device no larger than traditional bombs can devastate an entire city by blast, fire, and radiation. Nuclear weapons are weapons of mass destruction, and their use and control have been a major focus of international relations policy since their debut. A nuclear bomb can use two types of reactions: One depends on fission (an atomic bomb), and the other depends on fusion (a hydrogen bomb).

Audion—The Audion was an electronic amplifying vacuum tube invented by American electrical engineer Lee de Forest. It consisted of a partially evacuated glass tube containing three electrodes, a heated filament, a grid, and a plate. It is important in the history of technology because it was the first widely used electrical device that amplified sound.

P. T. Barnum—Phineas Taylor "P. T." Barnum (July 5, 1810–April 7, 1891) was an American politician, showman, and business entrepreneur remembered for promoting celebrated hoaxes and for founding the Barnum & Bailey Circus. Barnum was also an author, publisher, philanthropist, and for some time a politician.

Bowery—The Bowery is an area in the southern portion of New York City bordered by Chatham Square at Park Row, Worth Street, and Mott Street in the south to Cooper Square at

Fourth Street in the north, while the neighborhood's boundaries are roughly East Fourth Street and the East Village to the north; Canal Street and Chinatown to the south; Allen Street and the Lower East Side to the east; and Little Italy to the west.

Branded Content—Branded content (also known as branded entertainment) is a form of advertising that uses content to promote the brand funding it, with the content typically presenting itself as something other than traditional advertising but also carrying a "sponsored" label with it. This content uses online media, film, music, and video games, among other media, as a vehicle for reaching potential consumers.

Buchenwald Concentration Camp—Buchenwald concentration camp was one of the several Nazi concentration camps and one of the first and the largest of them on German soil. Prisoners in the camp came from all over Europe and the Soviet Union to work primarily as forced labor in local armaments factories. The prisoners at Buchenwald, as at other Nazi camps, included Jews, Poles and other Slavs, the mentally ill and physically disabled from birth defects, religious and political prisoners, homosexuals, ethnic minorities, criminals, and prisoners of war.

Byline—The byline on a newspaper or magazine article gives the date, as well as the name of the writer of the article. Bylines commonly appear between the headline and the text of the article.

California Gold Rush—The California Gold Rush (1848–1855) began on January 24, 1848, when gold was found at Sutter's Mill in California. The news of gold brought some 300,000 fortune seekers to California from the rest of the United States and abroad. The sudden influx of immigration and gold into the money supply reinvigorated the American economy, and California became one of the few American states to go directly to statehood, in the Compromise of 1850. By the time it ended, California had gone from a thinly populated ex-Mexican territory to the home state of the first nominee for the Republican Party.

Chain Ownership—Stores in retail chains are retail outlets that share a brand and central management and usually have standardized business methods and practices. In retail, dining, and many service categories, chain businesses have come to dominate the market in many parts of the world.

Chilling Effect—A chilling effect is the inhibition or discouragement of the legitimate exercise of natural and legal rights by the threat of legal sanction. The right most often described as suppressed by a chilling effect is the right to free speech. A chilling effect may be caused by legal actions such as the passing of a law, the decision of a court, or the threat of a lawsuit.

Cold War—The Cold War described a period after World War II in which the Soviet Union and its allies created tension with the United States and its allies. Historians suggest the tensions emerged in 1947, when President Truman pledged aid to nations threatened by Soviet expansionism, and ended in 1991 when the Soviet Union collapsed. The term "cold" described the lack of large-scale fighting directly, although the major powers were armed in preparation for a possible nuclear world war. In the second half of the war, each side had developed a nuclear strategy that discouraged an attack by the other side with the rationale that such an attack would lead to the total destruction of the attacker. The struggle for dominance was expressed via proxy wars around the globe, psychological warfare, massive propaganda campaigns and espionage, rivalry at sports events, and technological competitions such as the Space Race.

Composing Stick—In printing, a composing stick assembles pieces of metal type into words and lines. Many composing sticks have one adjustable end, allowing the length of the lines and consequent width of the page or column to be set. Early composing sticks had a fixed measure, as did many used in setting type for newspapers fixed to the width of a standard column.

Copyright—Copyright grants the creator of original work exclusive legal rights for its use and distribution. The exclusive rights are not absolute but limited by limitations and exceptions to copyright law, including fair use.

Daguerreotypes—Daguerreotype was the first publicly available photographic process, and for nearly twenty years, it was the one most commonly used. Invented by Louis-Jacques-Mandé Daguerre and introduced worldwide in 1839, new, less expensive processes yielding more readily viewable images superseded use of the daguerreotype by 1860.

Divine Right of Kings—The divine right of kings was a political and religious doctrine of political legitimacy that asserted a monarch is subject to no earthly authority and instead derives the right to rule directly from the will of God, and therefore a king was not subject to the will of the people.

Dwight D. Eisenhower—Dwight David "Ike" Eisenhower (October 14, 1890–March 28, 1969) was an American politician and Army general who served as the thirty-fourth president of the United States from 1953 until 1961. He was a five-star general in the United States Army during World War II and served as Supreme Commander of the Allied Expeditionary Forces in Europe.

Daniel Ellsberg—Daniel Ellsberg (born April 7, 1931) is an American activist and former United States military analyst who, while employed by the RAND Corporation, precipitated a national political controversy in 1971 when he released the Pentagon Papers, a top-secret Pentagon study of U.S. government decision-making in relation to the Vietnam War, to the *New York Times* and other newspapers. Ellsberg was charged under the Espionage Act of 1917 along with other charges of theft and conspiracy, carrying a total maximum sentence of 115 years. He has voiced support for twenty-first century institutions and people who have disclosed sensitive government information, including Wikileaks, Chelsea Manning, and Edward Snowden.

Emancipation Proclamation—The Emancipation Proclamation was a presidential proclamation and executive order issued by President Abraham Lincoln on January 1, 1863. It changed the federal legal status of more than three million enslaved people in the designated areas of the South from slave to free, although it had little immediate effect. Eventually it reached and liberated all the designated slaves. It was issued as a war measure during the American Civil War.

Engineering of Consent—"The Engineering of Consent" by Edward Bernays was first published in 1947 as an essay and later as a book in 1955. Bernays described engineering consent as action based on "thorough knowledge of the situation and on the application of scientific principles and tried practices to the task of getting people to support ideas and programs."

English Civil War—The English Civil War (1642–1651) was a series of conflicts between Parliamentarians and Royalists primarily about the administration of England's government. The war ended with the Parliamentarian victory at the Battle of Worcester on September 3, 1651.

Enlightenment—The Enlightenment was an intellectual and philosophical movement that dominated European intellectual culture during the eighteenth century. Enlightenment ideas put reason at the center of all authority and legitimacy, advancing ideals such as liberty, progress, tolerance, fraternity, constitutional government, and the separation of church and state.

Feminism—Feminism consists of a range of political and social movements and ideologies that share the common goal of establishing rights for women, including educational and professional opportunities that are equal to such opportunities for men.

Francisco Franco—General Francisco Franco (December 4, 1892–November 20, 1975) ruled Spain as a military dictator for 36 years from 1939 until his death. He opposed the abolition of the monarchy and the establishment of a republic in 1931. When in 1936 leftists came to power, Franco followed other generals in a failed coup that precipitated the Spanish Civil War.

Frequency Modulation (FM)—In telecommunications and signal processing, frequency modulation (FM) encodes information in a carrier wave by varying the instantaneous frequency of the wave. In radio transmission, an advantage of frequency modulation is that it has a larger signal-to-noise ratio and therefore rejects radio frequency interference better than an equal power amplitude modulation (AM) signal, and for this reason, most music is broadcast over FM radio.

Sigmund Freud—Psychoanalysis is a set of theories and therapeutic techniques popularized by Austrian neurologist Sigmund Freud related to the study of the unconscious mind, which together form a method of treatment for mental health disorders.

Gatekeepers—A gatekeeper was traditionally a person who controlled access to a location—for example someone who tended a city gate—but in the late twentieth century, the term came into metaphorical use, referring to individuals who decide whether a message will circulate through mass media.

Gilded Age—The Gilded Age occupied a period in U.S. history from the 1870s to about 1900. The term for this period came into use in the 1920s and 1930s from writer Mark Twain's 1873 novel *The Gilded Age: A Tale of Today*, which satirized an era of serious social problems masked by a thin gold gilding.

Graft—As understood in American English, graft is a form of political corruption, being the unscrupulous use of a politician's authority for personal gain. Political graft occurs when funds intended for public projects are intentionally misdirected in order to maximize the benefits to private interests.

Woody Guthrie—Woodrow Wilson "Woody" Guthrie (July 14, 1912–October 3, 1967) was an American singer-songwriter and musician whose musical legacy includes hundreds of political, traditional, and children's songs, along with ballads and improvised works. He frequently performed with the slogan "This machine kills fascists" displayed on his guitar. His best-known song is "This Land Is Your Land."

Halftone—Halftone is the reprographic technique that simulates continuous tone imagery with dots, varying either in size or in spacing, thus generating a gradient-like effect. "Halftone" can also be used to refer specifically to the image that is produced by this process.

Homestead Legislation—Homestead legislative efforts throughout the 1840s and 1850s culminated in the Homestead Act of 1862, which gave an applicant ownership of land, typically called a "homestead," at no cost. In all, 1.6 million homesteaders received more than 270 million acres of public land primarily west of the Mississippi River.

House Un-American Activities Committee (HUAC)—HUAC was an investigative committee of the U.S. House created in 1938 to investigate alleged disloyalty and subversive activities on the part of private citizens, public employees, and those organizations suspected of having communist ties. The committee's anti-communist investigations are often associated with those of Senator Joseph McCarthy, but he actually had no direct involvement with this particular House committee.

Incendiary—Incendiary means "capable of causing fire," and it may refer to an incendiary device, a device designed to cause fires.

Internet—The Internet (not to be confused with the Web) is the global system of interconnected computer networks that consists of private, public, academic, business, and government networks of local to global scope, linked by a broad array of electronic, wireless, and optical networking technologies. The World Wide Web (abbreviated WWW or the Web) is an information space that can be accessed via the Internet.

Inverted Pyramid—The inverted pyramid is a metaphor used by journalists and other writers to describe the prioritization of information while structuring a story. It is a common method for writing hard news stories to communicate the basics about a news report in the initial sentences. It is widely taught to mass communication and journalism students.

Jim Crow Laws—Jim Crow laws were state and local laws that enforced racial segregation in the Southern United States ("Jim Crow" was a pejorative expression meaning "Negro"). Enacted in the late nineteenth century after the Reconstruction period, white Democratic-dominated state governments continued to enforce them until 1965. They mandated racial segregation in public facilities in states formerly part of the Confederate States of America, using the "separate but equal" dogma of the Supreme Court's *Plessy v. Ferguson* decision in 1896.

Martin Luther King—Born Michael King Jr., Martin Luther King Jr. (January 15, 1929–April 4, 1968) was an American Baptist minister and the most visible leader in the Civil Rights Movement of the 1950s and 1960s. He used tactics of nonviolence and civil disobedience based on his Christian beliefs. King helped organize the 1963 March on Washington, where he delivered his famous "I Have a Dream" speech. On October 14, 1964, he received the Nobel Peace Prize for combating racial inequality through nonviolent resistance. In 1968, King had planned a national occupation of Washington, D.C., but James Earl Ray assassinated him on April 4 in Memphis, Tennessee.

Ku Klux Klan—The Ku Klux Klan (KKK), or simply the Klan, is the name of a movement that has advocated white supremacy, white nationalism, anti-immigration, anti-Catholicism, and antisemitism. Historically the KKK has used terrorism, including physical assault and murder, against groups or individuals whom they opposed.

John Lennon—John Winston Lennon (October 9, 1940–December 8, 1980) was an English singer-songwriter and activist who co-founded the Beatles, a tremendously influential pop music band. He formed one of the most successful songwriting duos of all time with bandmate Paul McCartney, producing a record twenty Billboard No. 1 hits. When the Beatles disbanded in 1970, Lennon embarked on a sporadic solo career. He disengaged himself from the music business in 1975 to raise his infant son Sean but re-emerged with Ono in 1980 with the new album *Double Fantasy*. Three weeks after its release, Mark David Chapman, a deranged stalker, murdered him outside his hotel in New York City.

Libel Law—Libel occurs with written or printed defamation. Libel law originated in the seventeenth century in England in part because of the growth of print publications.

Liberal Republican Party—The Liberal Republican Party of the United States was a political party organized in Cincinnati in May 1872 to oppose the reelection of President Ulysses S. Grant and his Radical Republican supporters in the presidential election of 1872. The Liberal Republican Party's candidate was Horace Greeley, publisher of the *New York Tribune*.

Malcolm X—Born Malcolm Little, Malcolm X (May 19, 1925–February 21, 1965) was an African American Muslim minister and human rights activist. To his admirers he was a courageous advocate for the rights of blacks, a man who indicted white America in the harshest terms for its crimes against black Americans, while detractors accused him of preaching racism and violence. He emphasized Pan-Africanism, black self-determination, and black self-defense. In February 1965, three members of the Nation of Islam assassinated him in Manhattan's Audubon Ballroom before an address to the Organization of Afro-American Unity.

Karl Marx—Karl Marx (May 5, 1818–March 14, 1883) was a Prussian-born philosopher, economist, sociologist, journalist, and revolutionary socialist. Marx published various works, including his widely read 1848 pamphlet *The Communist Manifesto*. His work influenced intellectual, economic, and political history.

Media Conglomerate—A media conglomerate (sometimes, a transnational conglomerate or a transnational corporation), is a a media group, institution, or company that owns numerous companies involved in mass media enterprises, such as television, radio, publishing, motion pictures, theme parks, or the Internet.

Mexican-American War—The war with Mexico (or Mexican-American War) was an armed conflict between the United States and Mexico between 1846 and 1848. It followed the 1845 U.S. annexation of Texas, which Mexico considered part of its territory in spite of its de facto secession in the 1836 Texas Revolution.

Millennials—Millennials (also known as the Millennial Generation, or "Generation Y") are the generational demographic cohort following Generation X. Members of this generation are generally defined as having been born between the early 1980s and the mid-1990s to early 2000s. Among the popularly ascribed characteristics of this group include their increased use and familiarity with communications, media, and digital technologies.

Monopoly—A monopoly exists when a specific person or enterprise is the only supplier of a particular commodity or service. Monopolies are thus characterized by a lack of economic competition in the production of a product, which may result in a price well above the seller's marginal cost and lead to a high profit. An oligopoly. by contrast. results when a relatively small number of sellers dominates the production of goods or services.

Nazi Germany—Nazi Germany is the common English name for the period in German history from 1933 to 1945, when Germany was governed by a dictatorship under the control of Adolf Hitler and the Nazi Party (NSDAP). Under Hitler's rule, Germany was transformed into a fascist state in which the Nazi Party took totalitarian control over nearly all aspects of life.

Pamphlet—A pamphlet is an unbound booklet. It may consist of a single sheet of paper printed on both sides and folded in half, in thirds, or in fourths, called a leaflet, or it may consist of a few pages that are folded in half and saddle stapled at the crease to make a simple book.

GLOSSARY

People's History of the United States—*A People's History of the United States* is a 1980 history by American historian and political scientist Howard Zinn, who presented an alternate interpretation of the history of the United States that suggests American history consists largely of the exploitation of the majority by an elite minority.

Pilgrim's Progress—*The Pilgrim's Progress from This World, to That Which Is to Come* is a 1678 Christian allegory written by John Bunyan. It is regarded as one of the most significant works of religious English literature and has been translated into more than 200 languages.

Postmaster—A postmaster is the head of an individual post office. A postmaster responsible for an entire mail-distribution organization (usually sponsored by a national government) has the title of Postmaster General. Responsibilities of a postmaster typically include management of a centralized mail distribution facility, establishment of letter carrier routes, supervision of letter carriers and clerks, and enforcement of the organization's rules and procedures.

Prior Restraint—Prior restraint imposes censorship, usually by a government, on a particular form of expression. Prior restraint can prohibit certain exhibitions by requiring a license from a government authority. It can also take the form of a legal injunction or government order prohibiting the publication of a specific document. The U.S. government cannot constitutionally practice prior restraint.

Progressive Amendments—Reformers known as progressives helped engineer constitutional changes, including ratification of the Sixteenth, Seventeenth, Eighteenth, and Nineteenth Amendments, which respectively made an income tax legal, allowed for the direct election of senators, prohibited alcohol, and recognized women's suffrage.

Radio and Television News Directors Association (RTDNA)—The RTDNA, now known as the Radio Television Digital News Association, is an organization of radio, television, and online news directors, producers, executives, reporters, students, and educators. It functions to maintain journalistic ethics and preserve the free speech rights of broadcast journalists. The RTDNA presents annually The Edward R. Murrow Award for excellence in electronic journalism, as well as the Paul White Award for lifetime achievement.

Reconstruction Amendments—The Reconstruction Amendments are the Thirteenth, Fourteenth, and Fifteenth Amendments to the U.S. Constitution, adopted between 1865 and 1870 in the years following the Civil War. Their proponents saw them as transforming the United States to a nation in which the constitutionally guaranteed "blessings of liberty" would extend to the entire populace, including the former slaves and their descendants.

Reformation—The Reformation was a split between the Roman Catholic Church and followers of Martin Luther and other early Protestant Reformers in sixteenth-century Europe. The publication of the Ninety-Five Theses by Luther in 1517 marks its historical starting point, and the Peace of Westphalia in 1648 (concluding the Thirty Years' War) marks its end.

Regenerative Circuit—A regenerative circuit employs positive feedback, with part of its output used to reinforce its signal and allow an electronic signal to amplify many times by the same active device.

Republicanism—Republicanism proposes that the people of a state hold popular sovereignty. The concept of a republic became a powerful force in Britain's North American colonies, where it led to the American Revolution.

Revolutions of 1848—This series of events throughout Europe remains the most widespread revolutionary wave in European history. The revolutions were essentially democratic in nature with the goal of removing old feudal structures and creating independent national states. Over fifty countries were affected but with no coordination or cooperation between their respective revolutionaries.

RKO Pictures—RKO Pictures, Inc., was an American film production and distribution company, one of the Big Five studios of Hollywood's Golden Age formed after the Keith-Albee-Orpheum vaudeville theatere circuit and Joseph P. Kennedy's Film Booking Offices of America studio merged under the control of the Radio Corporation of America (RCA) in October 1928. RCA chief David Sarnoff engineered the merger to create a market for the company's sound-on-film technology, RCA Photophone.

Robber Barons—"Robber baron" was a derogatory metaphor of social criticism originally applied to certain late nineteenth-century American businesspersons who used unscrupulous methods to get rich.

Search Engine Optimization (SEO)—SEO uses a process to affect the online visibility of a website or a web page in a web search engine's unpaid results, a technique used to boost the frequency a website appears in the search results list and thereby increasing the number of visitors to reach the site.

Second Party System—Historians and political scientists use the phrase Second Party System as a term of periodization to designate the political party system operating in the United States from about 1828 to 1854, after the First Party System ended. Two major parties dominated the political landscape: The Democratic Party led by Andrew Jackson, and the Whig Party, assembled by Henry Clay from the National Republicans and from other opponents of Jackson.

Segregation—Racial segregation is the separation of humans into racial or other ethnic groups in daily life. It may apply to activities such as eating in a restaurant, drinking from a water fountain, using a public toilet, attending school, going to the movies, or riding on a bus.

Senate—The Senate is composed of two senators who represent each state. From 1789 until 1913, senators were appointed by the legislatures of the states they represented; following the ratification of the Seventeenth Amendment in 1913, they are now popularly elected.

Seven Years' War—The Seven Years' War was fought between 1754 and 1763, involving every European great power of the time except the Ottoman Empire and spanning five continents, affecting Europe, the Americas, West Africa, India, and the Philippines. It affected territories in North and South America, and elsewhere.

William Shakespeare—William Shakespeare (April 26, 1564–April 23, 1616), an English poet, playwright, and actor, is recognized as the greatest of all English writers and as a supreme dramatist. His work consists of no less than thirty-eight plays, 154 sonnets, and two long narrative poems, among others. His plays have translations in every major language.

Sherman Anti-Trust Act—The Sherman Antitrust Act is a landmark federal statute in the history of United States antitrust law (or "competition law") passed by Congress in 1890 under the presidency of Benjamin Harrison. It recommended the federal government to investigate and pursue trusts and take legal measures to break up monopolies.

Smith-Mundt Act—The U.S. Information and Educational Exchange Act of 1948 (Public Law 80–402), popularly called the Smith-Mundt Act, is the basic legislative authorization for some of the activities conducted by the U.S. Department of State commonly known as public diplomacy. Congressman Karl E. Mundt (R-SD) first introduced the act in January 1945, and President Harry S. Truman subsequently signed it into law on January 27, 1948.

Social Media—Social media (alternately "new media" or sometimes "citizen journalism") are computer-mediated technologies that facilitate the creation and sharing of information and other forms of expression via online networks. Social media applications generally stem from text posts or comments, digital photos or videos, and data generated from online interactions.

Soviet Union—The Soviet Union was a socialist state that existed from 1922 to 1991 as a union of national republics. Although each republic had its own communist party, the Union was a one-party state, federal in nature and governed by the all-Union party, the Communist Party of the Soviet Union.

Spanish-American War—This conflict between Spain and the United States took place in 1898. Hostilities began in the aftermath of the internal explosion of the USS Maine in Havana harbor in Cuba, leading to United States intervention in the Cuban War of Independence. American acquisition of Spain's Pacific possessions led to its involvement in the Philippine Revolution and ultimately in the Philippine-American War.

The Telecommunications Act of 1996—The Telecommunications Act of 1996 represented a major change in American telecommunication law, as it was the first time that legislators included the Internet in broadcasting and spectrum allotment. The goal of the legislation had focused on deregulation of converging broadcasting and telecommunications markets; however, consumers and legislators alike have since questioned its regulatory policies, which appear to have lessened—not increased—competition.

Transcendentalism—Transcendentalism was a philosophical movement that developed in the late 1820s and 1830s in the eastern United States. It arose as a reaction to or protest against the general state of intellectualism and spirituality at the time.

Uncle Sam—Uncle Sam (initials U.S.) is a common national personification of the American government or the United States in general that, according to legend, came into use during the War of 1812 and was supposedly named for Samuel Wilson. The actual origin is obscure.

Uncle Tom—Uncle Tom is the title character of Harriet Beecher Stowe's 1852 novel *Uncle Tom's Cabin*. Since the publication of the book, the term "Uncle Tom" is more commonly used as a derogatory epithet for an excessively subservient person.

User-created content (or, alternatively, "user-generated content")—User-created content is any form of content created by users of a system or service and made available publicly on that system. This content most often appears as supplements to online platforms, such as social media websites, and may include such content types as blog posts, wikis, videos, comments, or ecommerce.

Vietnam War—Considered a Cold War-era proxy war, the Vietnam War occurred in Vietnam, Laos, and Cambodia from November 1, 1955, to the fall of Saigon on April 30, 1975. It was the second of the Indochina Wars and fought between North Vietnam and the government of South Vietnam. The Soviet Union, China, and other communist allies supported the North

Vietnamese army, and the United States, South Korea, Australia, and Thailand, among others, supported the South Vietnamese army.

Wage Slavery—The phrase "wage slavery" is used pejoratively to draw an analogy between slavery and wage labor by focusing on similarities between owning and renting a person. It usually refers to a situation where a person's livelihood depends on wages or a salary, especially when the dependence is total and immediate.

War for Independence—The American Revolutionary War (1775–1783), also referred to as the American War of Independence and as the Revolutionary War in the United States, was an armed conflict between Great Britain and thirteen of its North American colonies that declared independence as the United States of America after the onset of the war.

Weimar Republic—The Weimar Republic was an unofficial historical designation for Germany between 1919 and 1933. The name derives from the city of Weimar, where its constitutional assembly first took place. In English, the country was simply known as Germany.

H. G. Wells—Herbert George "H. G." Wells (September 21, 1866–August 13, 1946) was an English writer prolific in many genres, including the novel, history, politics, social commentary, and textbooks and rules for war games. Wells is called the "father of science fiction," with his most notable science fiction works including *The Time Machine* (1895), *The Island of Doctor Moreau* (1896), *The Invisible Man* (1897), and *The War of the Worlds* (1898).

Whig Party—The American Whig Party was politically active in the mid-nineteenth century, emerging in the 1830s as the immediate successor to the National Republican Party. Along with the rival Democratic Party, it was central to the Second Party System, originally forming in opposition to the policies of President Andrew Jackson. Whigs supported the supremacy of Congress over the presidency and favored a program of modernization, banking, and economic protectionism to stimulate manufacturing. In the 1850s, the Republican Party replaced the Whigs after the latter's organization collapsed.

Woodrow Wilson—Thomas Woodrow Wilson (December 28, 1856–February 3, 1924) served as U.S. president from 1913 to 1921. His victory in the 1912 presidential election made him a leading force in the Progressive Movement. He also led the United States during World War I, establishing an activist foreign policy known as "Wilsonianism" and championing the proposed League of Nations, but he was unable to obtain Senate approval for U.S. membership.

Woodcuts—Woodcut is a relief printing technique in printmaking. An artist carves an image into the surface of a block of wood, leaving the printing parts level with the surface while removing the non-printing parts. The surface is covered with ink by rolling over the surface with an ink-covered roller, leaving ink upon the flat surface but not in the non-printing areas.

Index

1984 (Nineteen Eighty Four), George Orwell (1949) 181, 189, 190; *see also Animal Farm*; Orwell, George

abolition (or abolitionism, or abolitionists) 29, 55, 61–7, 85–9
Adams, John (founder, president) 8, 19, 21–4, 28, 29, 36–40, 42, 63; *see also* Alien and Sedition Acts
Adams, Samuel 19–22, 24, 26; *see also Boston Gazette*; Colonial press; Stamp Act
ads (advertiser, or advertisers, or advertising) 12, 16, 25, 45–7, 55, 67, 82, 117, 136, 157, 162, 172, 175, 176, 178, 182, 194, 204–6, 225, 229, 230, 232, 233, 245, 246
Advanced Research Projects Agency (ARPANET) 243, 244; *see also* Internet; World Wide Web
Age of Jackson, The 43, 47, 61, 63; *see also* Antebellum press/politics/era; Penny Press
Alger, Horatio 103, 107; *see also* The Gilded Age; The American Dream
Alien and Sedition Acts (1798) 8, 9, 27, 28, 36, 41, 43, 46; *see also* Adams, John; The Dark Ages of American Journalism
American Civil Liberties Union (ACLU) 126, 238; *see also* The Bill of Rights
American Crisis, The, Thomas Paine (1776–83) 25, 27–9, 31–3; *see also Common Sense*; Paine, Thomas; Valley Forge
American Dream, The 103, 107–9, 218; *see also* Alger, Horatio; The Gilded Age
American Press Institute 229, 247
American Revolution 12–25, 28–30, 43, 46; *see also* Revolutionary War
American Telephone & Telegraph (AT&T) 170, 176, 232
AM radio (amplitude modulation) 170, 171; *see also* broadcast; FM radio
Animal Farm, George Orwell (1945) 189, 190; *see also 1984 (Nineteen Eight Four)*; Orwell, George
Antebellum press/politics/era 84, 85–7; *see also* The Age of Jackson; Penny Press
Anti-Federalists (or Jeffersonians, or Republicans) 28, 37–41, 43; *see also* Federalists
"An Apology for Printers," Benjamin Franklin (1731) 13, 16, 17; *see also* Franklin, Benjamin

Armstrong, Edwin Howard 167, 169–71, 176; *see also* broadcast; FM radio
Associated Press (AP) 69–73, 82, 212; *see also* telegraph
atomic bomb 196–8, 273; *see also* Hersey, John; Hiroshima

baby boomers 178, 209, 210, 213–19, 222
Bache, Benjamin Franklin 39–43; *see also Philadelphia Aurora*
Bagdikian, Ben 224–7; *see also The Media Monopoly*
Beecher Stowe, Harriet 84, 86, 88; *see also Uncle Tom's Cabin*
Bennett, James Gordon, Sr. 45, 51–5, 59, 62, 78; *see also New York Herald*; Penny Press
Bernays, Edward 151, 152, 160–4; *see also Propaganda*
Berners-Lee, Tim 243, 244; *see also* Internet; World Wide Web
Bernstein, Carl 129, 208, 209, 219–22; *see also Washington Post*; Watergate; Woodward, Robert
Bertelsmann (Germany) 227, 236; *see also* conglomeration
Bible, The 55, 57, 71, 86
Bill of Rights, The 1, 11, 36; *see also* First Amendment; Jefferson, Thomas
Bly, Nellie (Elizabeth Cochran) 69, 70, 77–83; *see also New York World*; stunt journalism; *Ten Days in a Madhouse*
Boothe Luce, Clare 224, 231, 232; *see also* Luce, Henry; Time Warner
Boston Gazette 12, 13, 19–25; *see also* Adams, Samuel; Boston Massacre
Boston Massacre, The 13, 20–4; *see also* Adams, Samuel; Boston Massacre; Revere, Paul
Bradlee, Benjamin (Ben) 220, 227; *see also Washington Post*
Brady, Mathew 84, 90–6; *see also* photojournalism
broadcast (or broadcasting) 166–78, 191, 192, 194, 195, 198–206, 210, 220
Buchanan, James (president) 76, 85
Buzzfeed 245, 250
byline (or bylines) 19, 88

INDEX

CBS (Columbia Broadcast System) 167, 170, 172–4, 176–8, 194, 195, 198, 199, 203–6, 212, 227–30
chains (or chain ownership, or chain media) 15, 131, 132, 146, 172
Chicago Tribune 78, 98, 113
Citizen Kane, RKO film (1941) 144, 167, 173–6, 185, 186; see also "The War of the Worlds,"; Welles, Orson
Civil War, The (American, U.S.) 39, 55, 58, 62, 64, 74, 77, 84–100, 102, 103, 107–9, 112, 125; see also Lincoln, Abraham
clickbait 246, 250
CNN (Cable News Network) 228, 232, 233, 245, 251
Cockerill, John A. 80, 135; see also *New York World*
Cold War, The 190, 194–206, 210, 231, 243
Colonial press 6, 12–20, 24, 25, 28–30, 48
Committee on Public Information (CPI), or Creel Committee 160, 180–5; see also Creel, George; World War I
Common Sense, Thomas Paine (1775–6) 27–31, 34; see also *The American Crisis*; Paine, Thomas
conglomeration (or media conglomerates) 146–8, 224, 228, 231–4
convergence 241, 242; see also infotainment
Cosmopolitan 116, 117, 126, 131, 146, 147; see also Hearst, William Randolph; Phillips, David Graham; "The Treason of the Senate"
Creel, George 181, 182, 184; see also Committee on Public Information; and propaganda
Cronkite, Walter ("Uncle" Walter) 177, 178

Daguerreotypes (Louis-Jacques-Mandé Daguerre) 85, 90; see also photojournalism
Dark Ages of American Journalism, The 27, 28, 36–43; see also The Partisan Press
Day, Benjamin Henry 45, 47, 48–51; see also moon hoax, *New York Sun*; Penny Press
"Declaration of Principles" (Parker and Lee, 1905) 151, 152, 157; see also Lee, Ivy Ledbetter; Parker, George; public relations
de Forest, Lee 167–70; see also AM radio; broadcast; FM radio
Democratic Party 58, 75, 112, 155, 219; see also Liberal Republican Party; Republican Party; Whig Party
Dial, The (transcendentalist journal) 60, 61; see also Emerson, Ralph Waldo; Fuller, Margaret; Nineteenth Amendment
Douglass, Frederick 46, 63–7, 87, 113; see also Garrison, William Lloyd; *Narrative of the Life of Frederick Douglass an American Slave*

"Ed Sullivan Show" (CBS variety television) 194, 195, 204–6
Eisenhower, Dwight D. (president) 181, 189–92, 202; see also military-industrial complex
Ellsberg, Daniel 215, 226; see also Pentagon Papers
Emancipation Proclamation, The (1862) 58, 89, 113; see also Lincoln, Abraham; "The Prayer of 20 Millions"
Emerson, Ralph Waldo 60–2, 87; see also *The Dial*; Fuller, Margaret
Enlightenment, The (European) 1, 5, 6; see also natural law
Espionage Act (1917) 9, 213; see also Wilson, Woodrow; World War I

Facebook 244, 245, 250, 251; see also social media
"Faces of the American Dead in Vietnam: One Week's Toll," *Life Magazine* (1969) 209, 212, 213; see also *Life* magazine; The Living Room War; Vietnam War
fake news 132, 245, 246, 255; see also moon hoax
FBI (Federal Bureau of Investigation) 206, 219, 220
Fear and Loathing in Las Vegas, Hunter Thompson (1972) 210, 218; see also gonzo journalism; Thompson, Hunter Stockton (S.)
Federal Communications Commission (FCC) 170, 176, 224, 235–8
Federalist Papers, The, Alexander Hamilton, James Madison; and John Jay (1788) 35, 36; see also Federalists; Hamilton, Alexander
Federalists (or Federalist Party, or Hamiltonians) 8, 27, 28, 37, 39–41, 43; see also Anti-Federalists; *The Federalist Papers*
Federal Trade Commission (FTC) 125, 235–7
Fenno, John 27, 37–41; see also Federalists; *The Gazette of the United States*; Hamilton, Alexander
Fifteenth Amendment (1870) 103, 107; see also Reconstruction and the Reconstruction Amendments
First Amendment (1791) 1–3, 5–10, 28, 36, 38, 42, 43, 86, 214, 225, 228, 238, 247; see also Supreme Court
"first rough draft of history" 1, 10, 11, 220; see also Graham, Phillip
Five Points (Manhattan) 117–20, 12; see also Riis, Jacob; Tweed, William Marcy
Flynt, Josiah 115, 120, 121, 125, 128; see also muckraker
FM radio (frequency modulation) 169–71, 176; see also AM radio; Armstrong, Edwin Howard

Fourth Estate, The 36, 46, 128, 139, 151, 156, 167, 180, 215, 222, 228, 229, 242, 255
Fox (or Fox News, or Fox television network, or 20th Century Fox and 21st Century Fox) 234, 244, 245; *see also* News Corporation; Murdoch, Rupert
Frank Leslie's Illustrated Newspaper 85, 89, 91, 98, 106; *see also* *Harper's Weekly*; photojournalism
Franklin, Benjamin 12–19, 29, 36; *see also* "An Apology for Printers"; *Poor Richard's Almanack*; Saunders, Richard; Timothy, Elizabeth
French Revolution 28, 30, 34, 41–3, 46; *see also* the Fourth Estate
Freneau, Philip 28, 37, 39–41; *see also* Anti-Federalists; Jefferson, Thomas; *National Gazette*
Fuller, Margaret 46, 60–62, 66, 134; *see also* *The Dial*; Emerson, Ralph Waldo; Seneca Falls Convention

Garrison, William Lloyd 46, 63–6, 87; *see also* abolition; Douglass, Frederick; *The Liberator*
Gazette of the United States, The 27, 37, 39, 40; *see also* Federalists; Fenno, John; Hamilton, Alexander
General Electric (G.E.) 192, 228; *see also* conglomeration; Westinghouse
Gilded Age, The 102, 103, 107–9; *see also* The American Dream; Twain, Mark
gonzo journalism 208, 209, 215–18; *see also* *Fear and Loathing in Las Vegas*; Thompson, Hunter Stockton (S.)
Google 227, 236, 237, 244; *see also* Internet; net neutrality
Graham, Phillip 10, 11, 220; *see also* "first rough draft of history"; *Washington Post*
Grant, Ulysses S. (president) 58, 103–7; *see also* Reconstruction and the Reconstruction Amendments
"Great Lawsuit, The," Margaret Fuller (1843) 60–2; *see also* *The Dial*; Emerson, Ralph Waldo; Fuller, Margaret; Seneca Falls Convention
Greeley, Horace 45, 55–62, 73, 74, 88, 89, 102, 105–7; *see also* *The New York Tribune*; Penny Press; "The Prayer of the 20 Millions"
Greenspun, Herman (Hank) Milton 195, 201–3; *see also* Red Scare
Gutenberg, Johannes (or Gutenberg Press) 3, 4, 70
Guthrie, Woody 158, 159; *see also* Lee, Ivy Ledbetter; Ludlow Massacre; Rockefeller, John Davidson

Hamilton, Alexander 27, 35–41; *The Federalist Papers*; Federalists; Fenno, John
Hamilton, Andrew 6–8; *see also* Zenger, John Peter (The Trial of John Peter Zenger)
Harper's Weekly 55, 75, 85, 89–96, 105; *see also* *Frank Leslie's Illustrated Newspaper*; photojournalism
Hearst, William Randolph 126, 131–49; *see also* *New York Journal*; yellow journalism
Hemingway, Ernest 181, 186–90, 217; *see also* The Spanish Civil War; "The Spanish Earth"
Hersey, John 194–8, 201, 216; *see also* atomic bomb; *Hiroshima*; World War II
Hiroshima, John Hersey, (1946) 194–8, 201, 216; *see also* atomic bomb; Hersey, John; World War II
History of the Standard Oil Company, The, Ida Tarbell (1904) 151–5; *see also* *McClure's*; Rockefeller, John Davidson; Tarbell, Ida Minerva
Hollywood Ten, The 176, 195, 199, 200; *see also* Cold War; Red Scare (McCarthyism)
Homage to Catalonia, George Orwell (1938) 138, 139; *see also* Hemingway, Ernest; Orwell, George; Spanish Civil War
House Un-American Activities Committee (HUAC) 195, 199, 200; *see also* McCarthy, Joseph; Red Scare
"How the Other Half Lives," Jacob Riis (1890) 115, 118, 119, 139; *see also* muckraker; Riis, Jacob

infotainment 166, 167, 194, 195, 224, 230, 242; *see also* convergence
Internet 4, 77, 148, 167, 214, 225, 233, 237, 238, 241–6, 251; *see also* Advanced Research Projects Agency (ARPANET); World Wide Web
inverted pyramid 70, 73, 88; *see also* telegraph

Jefferson, Thomas (founder, president) 28, 36–43, 63; *see also* Anti-Federalists; Bill of Rights; Freneau, Philip; *National Gazette*
Jewett, Helen (Ellen Jewett) 51, 53, 54; *see also* Bennett, James Gordon, Sr.; *New York Herald*; sensationalism
Julius Caesar, William Shakespeare (1599) 172, 173, 202, 203; *see also* Shakespeare, William
Jungle, The, Upton Sinclair (1906) 116, 124, 125; *see also* muckraker; Pure Food and Drug Act; Sinclair, Upton

Kennedy, John F. (president) 177, 201, 210, 213, 230
Ku Klux Klan (KKK) 103, 111–13; *see also* *A Red Record*; Wells, Ida B.

INDEX

Lee, Ivy Ledbetter 151, 152, 155–61, 163, 182; see also "Declaration of Principles"; Parker and Lee; public relations
libel 7, 8, 42, 214
Liberal Republican Party 55, 58, 102, 105, 134; see also Grant, Ulysses; Greeley, Horace
Liberator, The 46, 63–5, 87; see also abolition; Garrison, William Lloyd
Life magazine 212, 213, 231, 232; see also Boothe Luce, Clare; Luce, Henry
Lincoln, Abraham (president) 58, 59, 74, 85, 87–92, 97, 98, 103, 105, 153; see also Civil War; Emancipation Proclamation
Living Room War, The 209–11; see also Vietnam War
Lovejoy, Rev. Elijah Parish 84–7; see also abolition
Luce, Henry 224, 230–3; see also Boothe Luce, Clare; *Time* magazine; Time Warner
Ludlow Massacre 152, 157–60; see also Guthrie, Woody; Lee, Ivy Ledbetter; Rockefeller, John Davidson
lynching 102, 110, 111–13; see also *A Red Record*; Reconstruction and the Reconstruction Amendments; Wells, Ida B.

Madison, James (founder, president) 1, 8, 9, 10, 35, 36, 38, 40–2, 46, 71; see also First Amendment
"Man with the Muck-rake, The," Theodore Roosevelt speech (1906) 116, 128, 129; see also muckraker; Roosevelt, Theodore; "The Treason of the Senate"
Marconi, Guglielmo (the American Marconi Company, or the Marconi Wireless Telegraph Company) 167–70, 176
McCarthy, Joseph (Senator, Wisconsin) 194–6, 200–3; see also Cold War; Red Scare
McClure, Samuel (S. S. McClure) 121, 152, 153; see also *McClure's Magazine*; muckraker
McClure's Magazine 116, 117, 120–2, 151–5; see also McClure, Samuel; Steffens, Lincoln; Tarbell, Ida Minerva
McKinley, William (president) 144–6; see also The Spanish-American War; yellow journalism
Media Monopoly, The, Ben Bagdikian (first published 1983) 224–7; see also Bagdikian, Ben; conglomeration
Mexican-American War (War with Mexico) 72, 73
military industrial complex, the (or the military-industrial-media complex) 191, 192; see also Eisenhower, Dwight D.
Milton, John 1, 4–6; see also natural law

moon hoax (or "Celestial Discoveries," or "Great Astronomical Discoveries"), *New York Sun* (1835) 48–51, 246; see also fake news; Penny Press; sensationalism
Morse, Samuel F. B. (and Morse code) 71, 77, 168; see also telegraph
muckraker (and muckrakers, or muckraking) 75, 77, 108, 109, 113–29, 132, 133, 145, 146, 151–5, 219, 222; see also "The Man with the Muck-Rake"
Murdoch, Rupert 233, 234; see also Fox; News Corporation
Murrow, Edward R. 178, 194, 195, 198–204; see also Red Scare; "See It Now"
My Lai Massacre 209, 211–13; see also The Living Room War; Vietnam War

Narrative of the Life of Frederick Douglass an American Slave, Frederick Douglass (first published 1845) 46, 65, 66; see also Douglass, Fredrick; Garrison, William Lloyd
Nast, Thomas 75, 105, 108
National Gazette 28, 37, 39–41; see also Anti-Federalists; Freneau, Philip; Jefferson, Thomas
natural law 1, 4, 6, 8, 34, 36; see also The Enlightenment; Milton, John
NBC (National Broadcasting Company) 167, 170–3, 176, 178, 192, 199, 204, 227, 228; see also General Electric; Sarnoff, David
Near v. Minnesota (1931) 9, 10
net neutrality 224, 237, 238; see also Internet; World Wide Web
new journalism 196–8, 208, 209, 216–18; see also gonzo journalism
new media 225–30, 249; see also social media
News Corporation 227, 233, 234, 236; see also Fox; Murdoch, Rupert
Newsweek 10, 212
New York Associated Press (NYAP) 72, 73, 82; see also telegraph
New York Courier and Enquirer 51, 73, 74; see also Raymond, Henry Jarvis
New York Herald 45, 51–5; see also Bennett, James Gordon, Sr.; Penny Press
New York Journal (William Randolph Hearst, publisher) 131–4, 139–46; yellow journalism
New York Sun 45, 48–51, 73, 126, 246; see also Day, Benjamin; moon hoax; Penny Press
New York Times 69, 70, 74, 75, 77, 98, 107, 132, 155, 161, 174, 185, 214–17, 221, 245, 251; see also Raymond, Henry Jarvis
New York Times v. Sullivan (1964) 9, 209, 214, 215, 218

INDEX 271

New York Tribune (the *Daily Tribune* and *Weekly Tribune*) 45, 47, 53, 55–62, 73, 74, 88, 89, 105–7, 117, 134; see also Greeley, Horace; Penny Press; "The Prayer of 20 Millions"
New York Weekly Journal (Zenger Trial) 6–8; see also Hamilton, Andrew; Zenger, John Peter
New York World 77, 80–2, 126, 131, 132, 134–6, 141; see also Pulitzer, Joseph; yellow journalism
Nineteenth Amendment (1920) 62, 113, 147, 161; see also Fuller, Margaret
Nixon, Richard Milhous (president) 129, 215, 218–22, 230; see also Watergate
North Star, The 65, 66; see also abolition; Douglass, Frederick

Orwell, George (Eric Blair) 181, 189–91; see also *Animal Farm*; *Homage to Catalonia*; *1984 (Nineteen Eight Four)*; Spanish Civil War

Paine, Thomas 25, 27–35; see also *The American Crisis*; and *Common Sense*; Valley Forge
Paley, William (Bill) 167, 172, 203, 204, 206; see also CBS; Murrow, Edward R.
pamphlet 5, 13, 30, 106, 113, 186
Parker, George 155–7; see also "Declaration of Principles"; Lee, Ivy Ledbetter; Parker and Lee; public relations
Parker and Lee, public relations agency (1905) 151, 152, 155–7; see also "Declaration of Principles"; Lee, Ivy Ledbetter; Parker, George
Partisan Press, The, or The Partisan Press Era 27, 28, 36–43, 46, 48, 67; see also The Dark Ages of American Journalism
Pennsylvania Gazette 15–18; see also Franklin, Benjamin
Penny Press 45–67, 69, 70, 75, 77, 85, 131, 132, 172; see also Jewett, Helen; sensationalism; Sheppard, Horatio David
Pentagon Papers; Report of the Office of the Secretary of Defense Vietnam Task Force; *New York Times* (1971) 209, 214, 215, 218, 220, 225, 226; see also Ellsberg, Daniel; Vietnam War
Pew Research Center 247, 251
Philadelphia Aurora 39–42; see also Bache, Benjamin Franklin
Phillips, David Graham 116, 126–9, 146–8; see also *Cosmopolitan*; Hearst, William Randolph; muckraker; Seventeenth Amendment; Sixteenth Amendment; "The Treason of the Senate"; yellow journalism
photojournalism 70, 89–100; see also Brady, Mathew; *Frank Leslie's Illustrated Newspaper*; *Harper's Weekly*

Poor Richard's Almanack 15–17; see also Franklin, Benjamin; Saunders, Richard
Post Office Act (1792), postal exchange, or postmaster, or postal service 13, 15, 38, 70, 202
"Prayer of 20 Millions, The," Horace Greeley (1862) 58, 88; see also Greeley, Horace; Lincoln, Abraham; *The New York Tribune*
Presley, Elvis 195, 205, 206; see also baby boomers; "The Ed Sullivan Show"
propaganda (hypodermic needle theory; hypodermic syringe; magic bullet) 5, 22, 29, 35, 126, 158, 180–92, 199, 202
Propaganda, Edward Bernays (1928) 160–4; see also Bernays, Edward; public relations
public relations 151–64, 180, 185; see also Bernays, Edward; "Declaration of Principles"; Lee, Ivy Ledbetter
Pulitzer, Joseph 81, 82, 131–9, 141, 143, 144; see also *New York World*; yellow journalism
Pulitzer Prize 121, 132, 135, 197, 212, 219–21
Pure Food and Drug Act (1906) 124, 125; see also *The Jungle*; muckraking; Roosevelt, Theodore; Sinclair, Upton

Radical Press, The 13, 19–24; see also Adams, Samuel; Colonial press
Raymond, Henry Jarvis (J.) 57, 70, 73–5; see also *New York Times*
RCA (Radio Corporation of America) 167, 170, 171, 176; see also NBC; Sarnoff, David
Reagan, Ronald (president) 200, 230, 232; see also Cold War
Reconstruction and the Reconstruction Amendments 62, 100–13, 127, 154; see also Greeley, Horace; Wells, Ida B.
Red Record, A: Tabulated Statistics and Alleged Causes of Lynching in the United States, Ida B. Wells (1895) 102, 109–13; see also Reconstruction and the Reconstruction Amendments; Wells, Ida B.
Red Scare (McCarthyism) 200–4; see also Greenspun, Hank; McCarthy, Joseph; Murrow, Edward
Republican Party 39, 55, 75, 85, 103, 105, 126, 128, 134; see also Democratic Party; Liberal Republican Party; Whig Party
Revere, Paul 21–4; see also Adams, Samuel; The Boston Massacre; Colonial press
Revolutionary War (American War for Independence) 22, 24, 28, 30, 40; see also American Revolution; Paine, Thomas
Riefenstahl, Leni 181, 185, 186; see also propaganda; "Triumph of the Will,"; World War II

INDEX

Riis, Jacob 115–22; see also "How the Other Half Lives," and muckraker
Robber Barons 108, 109, 135; see also muckraker; Rockefeller, John Davidson
Rockefeller, John Davison (J. D.) 108, 109, 128, 152–60; see also History of the Standard Oil Company; Ludlow Massacre; Parker and Lee; Tarbell, Ida
Rolling Stone 198, 209, 215–18; see also Wenner, Jann
Roosevelt, Theodore (president) 115–17, 121, 124, 125, 128, 129, 142, 143, 145, 146, 153; see also "The Man with the Muck-Rake"

Sarnoff, David 167, 170–2; see also NBC; RCA; television
Saunders, Richard 15, 17; see also Franklin, Benjamin; *Poor Richard's Almanack*
Scripps, Edward Willis (E. W.) (E. W. Scripps Company) 133, 134
"See It Now" (CBS television news) 195, 203, 204; see also McCarthy, Joseph; Murrow, Edward R.
Seneca Falls Convention (1848) 46, 61, 62, 66, 107, 113; see also Douglass, Frederick; Fuller, Margaret
sensationalism 45–51, 53, 55, 70, 75–81, 112, 117, 131–9, 141–6, 174, 201, 214, 230, 246; see also Penny Press; yellow journalism
Seventeenth Amendment (1913) 125, 147; see also Hearst, William Randolph; Phillips, David Graham; "The Treason of the Senate"
Shakespeare, William 29, 172, 173, 175, 194, 195, 202, 203; see also *Julius Caesar*
"Shame of the Cities, The," Lincoln Steffens (1904) 116, 121–3; see also *McClure's*; muckraking; Steffens, Lincoln
Sheppard, Horatio David 47, 48; see also Day, Benjamin; *New York Sun*; Penny Press
Sinclair, Upton 116, 124–6, 129, 154; see also *The Jungle*; muckraking; Pure Food and Drug Act
Sixteenth Amendment (1913) 125, 147; see also Hearst, William Randolph; Phillips, David Graham; "The Treason of the Senate"
Smith-Mundt Modernization Act (2012) 190, 191
social media 166, 167, 178, 195, 214, 227, 232, 233, 241, 242, 245–7, 249–52; see also Facebook; Twitter
Soviet Union (USSR) 122, 123, 160, 186, 190, 194, 195, 199, 231, 243; see also Cold War
Spanish-American War, The 138, 143, 146; see also Hearst, William Randolph; Pulitzer, Joseph
Spanish Civil War, The 181, 186–90; see also Hemingway, Ernest; Orwell, George

"Spanish Earth, The," Joris Ivens, movie (1937) 181, 186–8; see also Hemingway, Ernest; The Spanish Civil War
Stamp Act (1765) 19, 20, 22; see also Adams, Samuel
steam press 70, 71, 82
Steffens, Lincoln 116, 121–3, 129, 154; see also *McClure's*; "Shame of the Cities"
St. Louis Post-Dispatch (St. Louis *Dispatch* and St. Louis *Post*) 134, 135; see also Pulitzer, Joseph
Stowe, Harriet Beecher 84, 86; see also *Uncle Tom's Cabin*
stunt journalism 69, 70, 77–83, 141, 172; see also Bly, Nellie; *New York World*

Tarbell, Ida Minerva 151–5, 157, 225; see also History of the Standard Oil Company, *McClure's*; Rockefeller, John Davidson
Telecommunications Act (1996) 237, 244
telegraph (or telegraphic communication) 51, 53, 69–73, 76, 77, 82, 88, 168, 170, 182
television 4, 166, 167, 170–8, 199–206, 211–13, 227–37; see also CBS; NBC
Ten Days in a Madhouse, Nellie Bly (1887) 80, 81; see also Bly, Nellie; *New York World*
Thirteenth Amendment (1865) 64, 103, 107; see also Reconstruction and the Reconstruction Amendments
Thomas, Isaiah 25, 28; see also Revolutionary War
Thompson, Hunter Stockton (S.) 198, 208–10, 216–18; see also *Fear and Loathing in Las Vegas*; *Rolling Stone*
Time Magazine 202, 230, 232, 249; see also Luce, Henry
Time Warner 224, 227, 228, 230–3, 236; Luce, Henry
Timothy, Elizabeth 13, 17–19; see also Franklin, Benjamin
"Torches of Freedom," Edward Bernays, parade (1929) 152, 161; see also Propaganda; pubic relations
transatlantic (telegraphic) cable 70, 75–7, 82, 168
"Treason of the Senate, The," David Graham Phillips (1906) 116, 126–9, 146, 147; see also *Cosmopolitan*; Hearst, William Randolph; Seventeenth Amendment; Sixteenth Amendment
"Triumph of the Will," Leni Riefenstahl, film (1935) 181, 185, 186; see also propaganda
Twain, Mark (Samuel Clemens) 103, 108; see also Gilded Age; Reconstruction and the Reconstruction Amendments
Tweed, William Marcy ("Boss Tweed") 75, 108, 123; see also Five Points

INDEX

Twenty-Fourth Amendment (1964) 209, 213
Twenty-Sixth Amendment (1971) 209, 213; *see also* The Living Room War; Vietnam War
Twitter 244, 245, 250, 251; *see also* Facebook; social media

unalienable rights 1, 34; *see also* Declaration of Independence; Paine, Thomas
Uncle Sam 183, 184; *see also* Committee on Public Information; Bernays, Edward; Creel, George
Uncle Tom's Cabin, Harriet Beecher Stowe (1852) 86, 87; *see also* abolition; Civil War; Stowe, Harriet Beecher
US Constitution 2, 6, 8, 15, 28, 34–6, 39, 42, 61–3, 66, 87, 103, 126, 129, 147, 213; *see also* First Amendment
US Declaration of Independence 6, 15, 22, 25, 34, 43, 60, 63, 107; *see also* unalienable rights
user-created content (citizen journalism) 241, 247–50; *see also* Facebook; social media; Twitter
USS Maine ("Remember the Maine") 131, 141–6; *see also* Hearst, William Randolph; *New York Journal*; Spanish-American War; yellow journalism
US Supreme Court (First Amendment and media-related cases) 8–10, 43, 168, 214, 215; *see also* First Amendment

Valley Forge 30, 32, 33; *see also American Crisis*; *Common Sense*; Paine, Thomas; Washington, George
Viacom/CBS 172, 227; *see also* CBS; Paley, William
Vietnam War 178, 187, 209–15, 219; *see also* The Living Room War; Twenty-Sixth Amendment
Vogue 161, 216

Wallace, Mike 229, 230; *see also* CBS
Wall Street Journal 17, 230
Walt Disney Company (Walt Disney; and Disney) 200, 227, 228, 234
"War of the Worlds, The," Orson Welles, radio drama (1938) 167, 173, 174, 176; *see also Citizen Kane*; Welles, Orson

Washington, George (founder, president) 29, 30, 32, 36, 38–40; *see also* Paine, Thomas; Valley Forge
Washington Post 10, 201, 208, 209, 218–21, 225, 226, 245; *see also* Bernstein, Carl; Bradlee, Benjamin; Graham, Phillip; Pentagon Papers; Watergate; Woodward, Robert
Watergate 208, 209, 218–22; *see also* Nixon, Richard Milhous; *Washington Post*
Welles, Orson 144, 162, 167, 172–6, 185, 186, 188; *see also Citizen Kane*; "The War of the Worlds"
Wells, Ida B. 102, 109–13, 116, 117; *see also A Red Record*; lynching; Reconstruction and the Reconstruction Amendments
Wenner, Jann 215–18; *see also* baby boomers; *Rolling Stone*
Westinghouse Electric Corporation 172, 176, 228, 230; *see also* conglomeration; General Electric
Whig Party 39, 43, 55, 57–9, 73, 85; *see also* Antebellum press/politics/era
Wilson, Woodrow (president) 9, 125, 160, 182, 185; *see also* Bernays, Edward; propaganda; World War I
Woodward, Robert (Bob) Upshur 129, 208, 209, 219–22; *see also* Bernstein, Carl; *Washington Post*; Watergate
World War I 9, 129, 160, 180–5, 187, 190; *see also* propaganda; Wilson, Woodward
World War II 163, 171, 178, 181, 184, 185–7, 195–9, 201, 204, 209, 231; *see also* Hersey, John; *Hiroshima*
World Wide Web 225, 241–4, 247; *see also* Internet

yellow journalism 77, 115, 116, 131–49, 245; *see also* Hearst, William Randolph; Pulitzer, Joseph; sensationalism
Yellow Kid, The (Mickey Dugan) 131, 136–9; *see also* yellow journalism

Zenger, John Peter (The Trial of John Peter Zenger) 1, 6–8, 13; *see also* First Amendment; Hamilton, Andrew
Zworykin, Vladimir 171, 176; *see also* television